History of the Caribbean

History of the Caribbean

Plantations, Trade, and
War in the Atlantic World

FRANK MOYA PONS

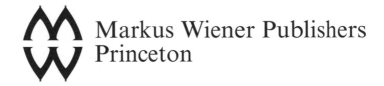

Markus Wiener Publishers
Princeton

For information write to:
Markus Wiener Publishers
231 Nassau Street, Princeton, NJ 08542
www.markuswiener.com

Library of Congress Cataloging-in-Publication Data

Moya Pons, Frank, 1944-
    History of the Caribbean : plantations, trade, and war in the
  Atlantic world / Frank Moya Pons.
    Includes bibliographical references.
    ISBN 978-1-55876-414-9 ((hardcover) : alk. paper)
    ISBN 978-1-55876-415-6 ((paperback) : alk. paper)
    1. Caribbean Region--History. I. Title. F2175.M69 2007
  972.9—dc22
                                        2007019082

Printed in the United States of America on acid-free paper

CONTENTS

PREFACE — ix

Chapter 1. The Spanish Occupation of the Antilles — 1
European Background • The Arawaks •
Early Spanish Rule • Gold and *Encomiendas*

Chapter 2. Sugar and Slaves in the Spanish Antilles — 12
The First Sugar Plantations • African Slaves and Marronage •
Sugar and Ginger Exports • The Portuguese-Brazilian Factor

Chapter 3. Monopoly, Privateers, and Contraband — 26
The Spanish Monopoly • Pirates and Privateers •
Cattle, Hides, and Contraband • English Traders and Corsairs •
The Dutch: Salt and Smuggling • Fighting Contraband: The Devastations

Chapter 4. The Early Tobacco Colonies — 44
Dutch Incursions and War • Tobacco and the English •
The First French Settlements • Filibusters and Buccaneers •
Cromwell's Western Design • The Dutch Expulsion from Brazil

Chapter 5. The Sugar Revolution in the Lesser Antilles — 60
The Dutch and the Sugar Trade • Sugar Beginnings in the Lesser Antilles •
White Indentured Workers and Black Slaves • Sugar Production and
Technology • Mercantilism and the Sugar Trade •
Cuba's Negligible Sugar Production

Chapter 6. Poverty in the Spanish Antilles — 77
Economic Decline and Government Subsidies • The Collapse of Exports •
Epidemics and Demographic Crisis • Social Malaise and Stagnation •
Impoverished Creole Peasants

Chapter 7. The Emergence of Saint-Domingue — 86

From Tortuga to Española • French Settlements in Western Española •
Trading with the Enemy • Fighting for the Land

Chapter 8. Caribbean Sugar Economies
in the Eighteenth Century — 95

From Tobacco to Sugar in the British West Indies •
The Rise of Sugar as a Commodity • Monoculture and Land Concentration •
The French Sugar Business • Financing the Sugar Industry •
Organization of the Slave Trade • Slave Demography and the
Economics of Slavery • Technological Changes: The Jamaican Train

Chapter 9. Caribbean Trade Circuits in the
Eighteenth Century — 110

Navigation Laws and Colonial Trade • Caribbean Molasses and the
North Americans • Spanish Privateering and War • Contraband Trade
with North America • The Spanish Intercolonial Trade •
Cuba's Slow Rise as a Sugar Producer

Chapter 10. Trade and Wars — 126

Expanding the Plantation Economy • The Neutral Ports •
British Naval Dominance • Towards Free Trade • Plantation Development
in the "Ceded Islands" • Consolidation of the Plantation Economy •
The Caribbean during the American Revolution

Chapter 11. The French Revolution in the Antilles — 146

Plantation Economics in Saint-Domingue • Social and Racial Tensions •
Deepening Political Conflicts • Slave Revolt and British Military
Intervention • Toussaint Louverture's Rule • French Military
Catastrophe and the Birth of Haiti • Revolution and Repression
in the French Antilles

Chapter 12. New Peasantries in Haiti
and Santo Domingo — 169

Haiti's Agrarian Policies • Emigration and Decline in Santo Domingo •
The Haitian Invasion of Santo Domingo • The Abolition of Slavery
and the Land Question • Peasants' Resistance to the Rural Code •
Financial Crisis and Economic Difficulties

Chapter 13. Abolitionism and Crisis in the British West Indies — 185

Early Abolitionist Activities • Caribbean Wars during the
Haitian Revolution • Economic Impact of the Haitian Revolution •
The Napoleonic Wars in the Caribbean • The Abolition of the Slave Trade •
Sugar Production: Growth and Decline • Impact of the British-American
Trade War • The "Old" West Indies in Economic Decline •
Towards Amelioration and Emancipation

Chapter 14. Sugar without Slaves in the British and French Antilles — 204

The Apprenticeship Period • Exodus from the Plantations and
Free Villages • Labor Shortages and Imported Indentured Workers •
Mechanization of Sugar Mills • The First French *Centrales* •
End of Slavery in the French Colonies

Chapter 15. The Sugar Revolution in Cuba and Puerto Rico — 220

Cuba's Ascent in the Sugar Market • Impact of the Haitian Revolution •
Slave Labor and Chinese Indentured Workers • Cuba: The World's
Largest Sugar Producer • From Peasant Agriculture to Plantations
in Puerto Rico • The "Cédula de Gracias" • Importing Slaves for
Puerto Rico's Plantations • The Labor Problem and the *Libreta* System •
Puerto Rico: The World's Second Largest Sugar Producer

Chapter 16. Abolitionism in the Spanish Antilles — 237

Proindependence Political Movements • The *Reformista* Movement •
Annexionism and the Slave Trade • Antislavery Revolts and Conspiracies •
Filibuster Expeditions • Santo Domingo's Struggle for Independence •
Liberals and *Reformistas* • The Abolitionist Movement • Rebellion for
Independence • The Ten Years War • Apprenticeship under the
Moret Law • Sugar Production during the Ten Years War •
Patronato and the End of Slavery

Chapter 17. *Centrales* and *Colonos* — 259

Beet Sugar Competition • Central Factories in the French Antilles •
Mechanization of Mills in the British West Indies • Sugar *Centrales*
in Puerto Rico • The Coffee Alternative in Puerto Rico •
Sugar *Centrales* in the Dominican Republic • Sugar *Centrales* in Cuba

Chapter 18. Plantations under American Control — 277

Cuba's War of Independence • Cuba under American Control •
The American Sugar Trust in Cuba • Puerto Rico under American Control •
An American Protectorate in the Dominican Republic •
American Investments in Occupied Haiti

Chapter 19. Migrants, Peasants, and Proletarians — 299

Poverty and Emigration in the West Indies • Peasants and the
Rural Economy in the Spanish Antilles • West Indian Peasants and
Proletarians • Immigration and the Emerging Middle Classes

Chapter 20. Epilogue: Why the Sugar Plantation? — 309

NOTES TO THE CHAPTERS — 313

BIBLIOGRAPHICAL GUIDE — 320

INDEX — 347

PREFACE

The Caribbean is both a sea and an archipelago. The sea is enclosed by the continental land mass of Central America, Colombia, and Venezuela. Most of the archipelago's islands are located between Florida and the mouth of the Orinoco River, but, because of longstanding economic and social connections, some regions, like the Guianas and Belize, are normally considered to have shared their history with the Caribbean.

Initially populated by peoples of Arawak ancestry who had migrated from the tropical forests of northern South America, the Caribbean islands served as the entry way for the first Europeans who penetrated into the New World.

They became the scene of a long-lasting cultural and biological clash that led to the catastrophic decline of the native population and to the gradual occupation of the archipelago by peoples of different European extractions.

These Europeans, in turn, imported millions of Africans, both male and female, to work as slaves on sugar, tobacco, indigo, cotton, coffee, and cacao plantations, whose owners were responding to a growing demand for these products in Europe and elsewhere.

As new markets for colonial goods developed, so did a new economic space, known today as the Atlantic world, and soon the Caribbean was permanently linked to North America, Africa, and Europe as the most important supplier of sucrose, an efficient source of calories which, once tasted, the modern world could not live without.

So important became the Caribbean as a prominent world sugar producer that the European powers vied for possession of the area, initially trying to wrest it from Spain but later confronting one another in several wars fought to control the sugar market, as well as the slave market that provided labor to the plantations.

As the doctrine of balance of power came to prevail in Europe, so it did in the West Indies, and the European powers eventually reached an unstable equilibrium that produced a "fragmented" Caribbean along European political lines. We thus have today cultural zones that can be loosely described as the French, the Spanish, the British, and the Dutch Caribbean.

Behind this fragmentation, the Caribbean colonies preserved a surprising economic uniformity as they became plantation societies built upon plantation economies that depended on the exploitation of African slave labor.

Eventually, a class consisting of free people of color was born out of the mixing of the black and white populations, and also, eventually, a mixed-race free peasantry, neither slave nor proletarian, developed in the larger Spanish colonies (Puerto Rico, Cuba, and Santo Domingo).

When slavery was abolished, a black free peasantry, together with a rural proletariat, emerged in the British and French West Indies, as the emancipated slaves fled from the plantations to reestablish their lives and bring up their families in freedom.

These freedmen were replaced by workers of other nationalities, and thus the Caribbean became a multicultural setting enriched by the presence of indentured East Indians and Chinese, as well as by other groups who immigrated into the region voluntarily or by force.

Despite the region's social diversity, the Caribbean's economic uniformity remained virtually unchanged, as the plantation system not only went unchallenged but evolved into a more powerful organizational system: the sugar *centrales.*

This development was soon followed by the eruption of the United States in the Caribbean political arena. As a result, American corporations ended up displacing European investors in the Spanish Antilles, thereby becoming an indisputable competitor against the French and British interests in the Caribbean sugar market.

The preceding narrative summarizes in essence the contents of this book: the economic and social evolution of the Caribbean as an organic entity, and its functional integration into the Atlantic economy.

This approach, I believe, is useful in counteracting the perception—derived from the enormous mountain of books and scholarly articles published about the Caribbean—of a kaleidoscopic fragmentation of the region's history.

This perception, in my opinion, is misleading, because when one looks closely at the structural continuities of the plantation system, one can understand the Caribbean only as an organic economic system, as a throbbing heart continuously pumping sugar and other commodities to the world market via the Atlantic, while at the same time consuming millions of lives forcefully extracted from Africa and other parts of the world.

Despite the seemingly disparate nature of the colonies, they produced basically the same products for the world market. In the Caribbean, the plantation became such a dominant economic institution that it ended up creating a uniform world around the sugar mills and the slaves who worked there. Examining the ways the Caribbean planters and merchants organized themselves to compete in the world market leads to the unavoidable conclusion that there were more similarities than differences among the colonies.

For all these reasons, this book focuses on the structural economic continuities of the Caribbean societies from that wide perspective that the eminent French historian Fernand Braudel once called the *longue durée*.

This narrative ends in 1930, a year that marked a profound rupture in the history of the West Indies. Beginning in that year, and under the lasting impact of the Great Depression, the plantation system entered into a long crisis, and a new Caribbean began to emerge.

Someday I may write the history of this new, "modern" Caribbean. The older one, investigated in this book, has been the subject of several excellent studies that are quite useful today. Yet, despite the distinction of these books, I wanted to write this one, because I felt we still needed an encompassing narrative that integrated the economic, social, and demographic history of the West Indies in one single volume, that is, in a history that treated the Caribbean as a whole, as a unified region, and not as an area of discrete, unrelated parts, each having its own distinct story.

To accomplish the goal of describing the structural uniformity of the Caribbean, I have had to focus the narrative on some basic variables: production, trade, immigration, demography, and war, leaving aside many other important aspects of the region's social and cultural evolution, for example, the particular history of the slave trade and the lives of slaves above and beyond their functions as economic actors. I have also not been able to dwell on the role of families and women, political events, health and education, and cultural and religious phenomena, among other matters. I hope the reader will accept that had I wished to meaningfully cover all these other questions, I would have had to write a multivolume work, and that was not my purpose with this book.

One task I did undertake was to summarize the massive amount of related scholarly literature produced in the last sixty years. This job was possible only because I had the privilege of teaching at two great research universities with excellent Caribbean collections in their libraries: Columbia University, in New York, where I was a Visiting Professor of Latin American History in 1987-1989, and the University of Florida, in Gainesville, where I taught Caribbean History, also as a Visiting Professor, in 1985 and again in 1989-1991.

I am deeply indebted to Dr. Herbert S. Klein and Dr. Lambros Comitas for inviting me to Columbia, and to Dr. Helen Safa, then Director of the Center for Latin American Studies at the University of Florida, for inviting me to teach there. I wrote some of the early drafts of this book for my lectures at both institutions. I continued working on this book during my stay at the Dominican Studies Institute of the City University of New York, at City College, where I worked as a Visiting Research Professor between 1993 and 1999. I gratefully thank Dr. Silvio Torres-Saillant and Dr. Ramona Hernández for inviting me to do research and write at the Institute. In these three universities I gladly shared my writings with my students, explicating for them the unifying role of the plantation in the economic and social life of the Caribbean.

I also discussed my ideas and hypotheses with my colleagues, and I fondly remember the long conversations with Nicolás Sánchez-Albornoz, then at New York University, who asked me to write this book, a challenge that I gladly accepted without knowing that it would take years to complete. I am particularly grateful to Dr. Herbert S. Klein, then at Columbia University, who inspired me to explore the debates on African slavery in the New World, and who read the final manuscript and offered me indispensable advice on how to improve it.

Prof. Humberto García Muñiz, from the University of Puerto Rico, read one of the earliest drafts and provided me with valuable comments. Later I received useful suggestions from the following friends whom I had asked to read different chapters: Dr. Anne Pérotin-Dumon, then at the University of Virginia; Dr. Muriel McAvoy, then writing her excellent monograph on Manuel Rionda; and Dr. David Geggus, of the University of Florida, who has become one of the world's leading authorities on the Haitian Revolution. More recently, while preparing the manuscript for publication, I was the beneficiary of advice from two new readers, who helped me to improve its clarity and style: Dr. Gerald Murray, of the University of Florida, and Dr. Silvio Torres-Saillant, of Syracuse University.

All these friends have contributed to this book's being more readable, but none of them, of course, can be blamed for any errors contained herein. The same can be said for the three conscientious editors at Markus Wiener Publishers, from whom I received excellent suggestions. Without the help and advice of Richard Burfield, Aaron Wiener, and Janet Stern, the quality of this book would have been diminished.

A special mention of gratitude goes to Dr. Lambros Comitas, Director of the Research Institute for the Study of Man, in New York, and to Mr. Luis Canela, President of the BPD Bank, in New York, both of whom unconditionally supported the publication of this work and contributed two grants to pay for the translation of an early draft, which I later expanded into this book.

In the Spring semester of 2006, I took a leave of absence from my daily occupations in the Dominican Republic and returned to Gainesville to finish the manuscript before sending it to the publisher. Dr. Carmen Diana Deere, the Director of the Center for Latin American and Caribbean Studies at the University of Florida, and her friendly staff led by Margarita Gandía, offered me their academic and administrative support and extended to me again the privileges of a Visiting Professorship. In Gainesville I received such warm hospitality from Dr. Gerald Murray and his wonderful wife, Dr. María Alvarez, that I will never be able to reciprocate it.

Senior librarians Richard Phillips and Paul Losch, assisted by Patricia Prevatt, were most helpful and were always looking for ways to find whatever rare materials I requested. Their efforts on my behalf made me recall the late Rosa Mesa, a former Director of the Latin American Collection at the University of Florida, who in years past was always looking for ways to make my stay there a most productive experience.

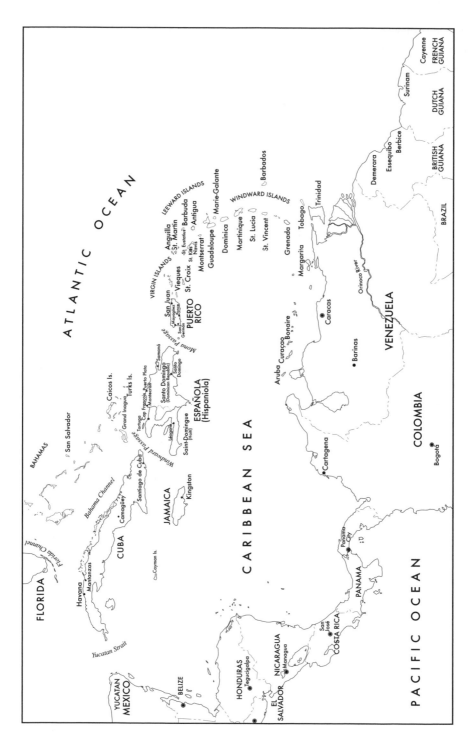

The Caribbean Sea and the West Indies

CHAPTER 1

The Spanish Occupation
of the Antilles

European Background

The arrival of the Europeans in the New World at the end of the fifteenth century was directly connected to the spice trade. Spices and salt were especially important in Europe, for they were used in preserving meat at the beginning of winter when green pastures dwindled and livestock were slaughtered. As meat was a necessary staple for armies, spices were of great strategic value.

Two major spice trade routes connected Europe to Asia and its spice production centers. The Venetians controlled the northern route, which went through Constantinople and the Bosphorus Strait, while the Genoese controlled the southern route, which went through the Suez. When the Turks conquered Constantinople in 1453, they took control of the northern route and forced the Venetians to pay very high taxes on products from the East.

Europeans began to search for new trade routes sailing south into the Atlantic Ocean. The Portuguese searched for gold and spices on the Guinea coast in West Africa, while also trading black slaves there. Later, in 1498, the Portuguese sailed for the first time beyond the Cape of Good Hope, which they had sighted in 1486. Thereafter they reached India, producing an enormous boom in the spice trade.

Equally important to the economy of fifteenth-century Europe was gold. Since gold had largely been used to buy spices in the Orient, the European gold supply was seriously low at a time when the emerging capitalist economies of Europe required an increase in gold coin circulation.

In Spain, gold was particularly scarce due to its depletion during the civil wars preceding the joint reign of King Ferdinand V of Aragon and Queen Isabella of Castile. The need for gold during these wars forced the opposing factions to borrow from Jewish and Italian merchants and bankers with extensive financial networks in large European cities. During their reign, King Ferdinand and Queen Isabella relied heavily on the Genoese and Jewish bankers, even after the expulsion of the Jews from Spain in 1492.

The need for gold and spices led the Genoese sailor Christopher Columbus to propose a commercial enterprise designed to find a shorter route to Asia. Columbus reasoned that, given the roundness of the Earth, it should be possible to sail due west from Europe across the Atlantic to India. After trying to convince kings and princes in several European courts of the viability of his project, Columbus finally found financial support for his plans in Spain.

Having perceived the enormous potential of this commercial venture, Queen Isabella agreed to support Columbus, who demanded a mere eighth of the profits, as he only wanted to invest only an eighth of the capital required to fund the enterprise. Queen Isabella herself obtained a loan from the funds of the Holy Brotherhood, an association of cities administered by a Spanish Jew, Luis Santángel. With this money, the queen financed the bulk of Columbus's first expedition. Columbus contributed his share with the help of a loan from Florentine financiers, as did a wealthy sailor by the name of Martín Yáñez Pinzón, who was also allowed to invest in the expedition and to provide an additional ship.

The Arawaks

Columbus never found India or the desired spices and gold. Between October and December 1492, he encountered various tropical islands in the Atlantic. The inhabitants of these islands went about naked and had no knowledge of black pepper as a spice. Nevertheless, in his letters to his friends in Spain and in his personal accounts to the Spanish monarchs upon his return early in 1493, Columbus created the illusion that he had reached India and referred to the inhabitants of the new lands he found as "Indians."

These Indians "discovered" by Columbus descended from the Arawak peoples of the Orinoco River basin in present-day Venezuela and were culturally related to the indigenous peoples of the Amazonian forests. Earlier groups had begun to migrate from the Orinoco River basin to the Antilles about 3,000 years earlier. The "Indians" Columbus first met called themselves Taínos, meaning "peaceful" or "friendly," a name used to distinguish themselves from a more aggressive group, the Caribs, who since the ninth century had advanced through the Lesser Antilles from South America, gradually expelling the Taínos from various islands.

Since both were of Arawak origin, the Caribs and the Taínos shared many cultural characteristics. They were farmers, fishermen, and hunters. They ate fish, shellfish, iguanas, snakes, and birds, as well as various native rodents, and they cultivated plants of South American origin such as yuca, maize, tobacco, potatoes, pineapples, peppers, and peanuts, all of which were later widely used by the Europeans and Africans who settled in the Caribbean. Yet they differed in some respects. Carib weaponry was superior to that of the Taínos. The Caribs poisoned their arrows, painted their bodies in red and black, and let their hair grow long to look more fearsome.

During Columbus's first voyage, he heard terrifying accounts by the Taíno inhabitants of Cuba and the Bahamas of the ferocity of the Caribs and their practice of cannibalism. Columbus heard the name *caniba*, which he transcribed in his letters and in his diary variously as *caniba* and *cariba*. Thus the terms "carib" and "cannibal" arose and came to be synonymous with fierce, warriorlike, and man-eating. On later voyages, when he made direct contact with the Caribs, Columbus discovered that they were good sailors and well trained in the use of the bow and arrow, as well as ritual eaters of human flesh, a fact also mentioned by later chroniclers.

On their long migration from South America, the Caribs displaced or assimilated with the Taíno inhabitants of the islands of Trinidad and the Lesser Antilles. By 1492, the Caribs occupied the Lesser Antilles, and from there they raided the Taíno population of Puerto Rico and the eastern part of the island of Hispaniola, which Columbus named Española.

During his first voyage, Columbus's knowledge of these peoples was very fragmented, but the news he transmitted to King Ferdinand and Queen Isabella was so extraordinary that the Spanish Court sprang into action. Although they were short of cash, Ferdinand and Isabella managed to finance a second expedition of seventeen ships and 1,500 men.

Early Spanish Rule

Hoping to exploit the resources of the new lands for commercial gain, they planned to imitate the Portuguese *factoría* scheme, which Columbus had seen in Africa. A *factoría* was a fortified trading post attended by salaried workers. Columbus and the Spanish Crown would be the sole owners of the enterprise, and they would share the profits produced by men subjected to a rigid wage labor regime.

Leading his second expedition, Columbus arrived at the northern coast of the most populated island, which he had christened Española the year before. There he chose the site of the *factoría* and called this first European settlement in the New World La Isabela. Columbus and his companions encountered enormous difficulties at La Isabela due to lack of food and medicine. Poor adaptation to the new environment resulted in illnesses, and the eruption of an epidemic quickly killed more than a third of the workforce. The labor shortage and the lack of pack animals forced Columbus to distribute the work equally among all of his companions regardless of social rank. As the workforce dwindled, the tasks became more and more strenuous.

The rigid discipline of the *factoría* irritated Columbus's Spanish companions. Columbus did not seem to understand how alien the model of the Portuguese *factoría* and its obligatory manual labor was to the Spaniards. After several centuries of war against the Arabs, the Castilians felt entitled to have their land worked by Moorish servants, and they rejected manual labor as contrary to their military ethic. As a result, Columbus faced serious problems. He was a foreigner, Genoese by birth and Portuguese by training, whose strict disciplinary style only served to inflame feelings of xenophobia among the Spaniards. A conspiracy soon arose, which Columbus was able to repress by hanging one of its leaders.

Between 1494 and 1495, Columbus launched three long military campaigns to subdue the native population. In the course of these campaigns, he discovered that he could save money by offering enslaved Indians to his workers in exchange for their salaries. To escape Spanish violence, Indians from the interior took refuge in the mountains. The Indians of La Isabela also abandoned the area and stopped supplying food to the Spaniards, thus aggravating the food shortage in the *factoría*.

In the midst of these conflicts, Columbus sailed to Spain in March 1496 to report to the king and queen on the status of the trading post and his recent discoveries of other islands near Española: Cuba, Jamaica, and San Juan (present-day Puerto Rico). By the time he set sail, more than half of his men had died on Española, and those who remained were frustrated, hungry, and plagued with illness.

Back in Spain, Columbus attempted to obtain support from the monarchs to organize a new expedition to replenish the Spanish population with laborers, miners, and soldiers —the workers of La Isabela. But thinking that Columbus had deserted them, the workers of La Isabela rebelled against Columbus's brothers, Bartolomé and Diego, the provisional administrators of the *factoría*. The rebels accused Columbus of poor leadership and claimed that he had abandoned them to their fate in a hostile and unknown world.

With this uprising—headed by one of Columbus's servants, Francisco Roldán— the Spanish laborers freed themselves from a work regime that had denied them access to the benefits of the *factoría*. The Spanish split into two bands led, respectively, by Bartolomé Columbus and Francisco Roldán, and each moved to areas where indigenous communities could provide them with women and food. As a result, La Isabela became completely depopulated. Bartolomé took his few followers to the southern coast of Española, and there he founded a new city on the banks of the Ozama River, which soon came to be known as the city of Santo Domingo. Roldán and the rebels moved to the western part of the island.

When Columbus returned from Spain in August 1498, he was obliged to give in to the rebels' demands for land to be cultivated by Indian slaves. The Spanish monarchs had already authorized Columbus to distribute land the previous year, and he was able to pacify the rebels by offering them the best land of the island and large numbers of Indian slaves. In making these concessions, Columbus offered the rebels the opportunity to dominate an emerging colonial society composed of about 500 working-class Spaniards from Extremadura and Andalucía. These were all that remained of the 1,500 Spaniards who had arrived with Columbus at the end of 1493. By 1502, their number had dwindled to 360.

The rebellion suggested to Ferdinand and Isabella that Columbus, although a fine explorer, did not know how to administer an enterprise intended to satisfy the need for gold and spices in Spain. They demoted Columbus from his position as governor and administrator of the *factoría* and in his place provisionally appointed Francisco de Bobadilla, commander of the Military Order of Calatrava, a soldier accustomed to governing men and land on the Spanish frontier.

Bobadilla was familiar with the Castilian *encomienda,* a system that consisted of giving conquered lands to Christians while permitting them to use Moors as serfs. When he reached Española in July 1500, Bobadilla stripped Columbus entirely of his power and sent him back to Spain as a prisoner. Then he continued the distribution of land and Indians initiated by Columbus and, in alliance with the rebels, established a new government on Española.

Bobadilla's successor was Nicolás de Ovando, another frontier commander chosen by the Spanish Crown in September 1501. Ovando reached Española in July 1502 accompanied by 2,500 colonists. His first task was to subject to his authority the 360 Spaniards living on the island who now owned the best lands and had the largest allotments of Indians. He began by sending Roldán and his main supporters back to Spain with Bobadilla. Shortly after their departure, their boats capsized during a storm and they all drowned.

In order to break the stronghold of those who remained on the island, Ovando ordered the Spanish men to marry the Indian women whom they had taken as concubines. Next, he stripped them of their ownership of Indian servants by claiming that they had assumed the same inferior social status as the natives and thus were not worthy of their previous authority to own them.

It took Ovando some time to put this policy into effect, since the colonists who had arrived with him had serious problems adapting to the tropical climate. During the first few weeks after their arrival, more than 1,000 colonists died of disease. The rest fell under the influence of the remaining original colonists, who provided them with some land, Indians, and food in exchange for clothing and other merchandise.

To strengthen his control of the colony, Ovando needed to empower the bureaucratic elite that he had brought with him. Following the pattern established by Columbus some ten years earlier, in 1504 Ovando organized two military campaigns against the natives of the chieftaincies of Higüey and Xaraguá. These campaigns served to provide the new arrivals with land and Indian slaves.

Gold and *Encomiendas*

In the meantime, large gold deposits had been discovered on the island. The lust for gold, which had begun to grow under Columbus and Bobadilla, was now rampant among the colonists. The washing and melting of gold became the main occupation of authorities and colonists alike. Following orders from Ferdinand and Isabella, who needed gold to pay off their debts in Europe, Ovando took charge of turning Española into a gigantic mining camp. Indians were taken from their communities and forced to work fourteen hours a day in the mines and rivers, breaking rocks and washing gold, under the pretext of indoctrinating them in the Catholic faith.

The *encomienda* system in the Caribbean differed very little from slavery. The Spanish forced the Indians to work as domestic servants and as laborers in mines, public works, and agriculture, and fed them very poorly. Very few Indians managed to survive the mines after eight to twelve months of forced labor on a meager diet of cassava bread and water. To escape this inhumane treatment, Indians committed suicide en masse by drinking bitter yuca juice or by hanging themselves, and they also killed their own children. Pregnant Indian women would often undergo abortions to avoid bearing children who would be born into slavery.

The native population was reduced drastically by the enormous number of deaths in the first few years due to physical abuse, starvation, and illnesses brought by the Spanish, such as influenza, measles, and diphtheria. During the first fifteen years of the colonization of Española, more than 300,000 Indians lost their lives. By 1508, only 60,000 Indians remained of the 400,000 who lived on the island when Columbus first arrived in 1492.

The first census of Indians undertaken in 1508 made the Spanish aware of the need to take steps to preserve the labor force in the mines. The solution was to import Indians from other islands. The islands of the Bahamas, then called Lucayas, were the first slave-hunting grounds. The colonists called the Bahamas "the useless islands," since no gold was to be found there. For several years, expeditions of Indian hunters frequently left Santo Domingo heading for the "useless islands" in search of Indians to enslave.

When the Bahamas were completely depopulated, the Indian hunters looked to Cuba and Jamaica. In the Lesser Antilles, the Carib Indians resisted fiercely and attacked the Spanish settlements on the island of San Juan, later called Puerto Rico, which had been colonized by Juan Ponce de León in 1508. As a result of these expeditions, more than 40,000 Indians were taken to Española as slaves between 1508 and 1513, but the native population continued to decline.

Gold deposits were also discovered in Puerto Rico, and the exploitation of the Indians was similar to that on Española. In 1511 the main chieftains of Puerto Rico rebelled and killed the majority of the Spanish colonists. The Taíno rebels fled to the Lesser Antilles, preferring to face the Caribs rather than work as slaves in the mines. The owners of *encomiendas* (*encomenderos*) from Puerto Rico also armed expeditions to hunt down Indians in the Lesser Antilles. The cannibalism of the Caribs was an ideal pretext to justify these expeditions as "just wars" against the infidel enemies of the Catholic monarchs.

The conquest of Cuba was similar to that of Española and Puerto Rico, although in Cuba gold deposits were found much later. When Diego Velázquez arrived in Cuba in 1511 to begin colonization, the native population was considerably reduced due to earlier slave-hunting expeditions and European diseases. When the first gold mines were discovered, the *encomenderos* organized new slave-hunting expeditions to the coasts of Yucatán in order to supply themselves with manual labor. The colonists in Cuba who did not have access to the mines supported themselves by raising cattle.

Jamaica, which had few Indians and no gold, was of very little interest to the Spanish. The colonization of Jamaica began in 1509 by a handful of men under the command of Juan de Esquivel. These individuals saw such little future in Jamaica that thirty of them, headed by Pánfilo de Narváez, went on to Cuba in 1512. In 1515, however, another group, headed by Francisco de Garay, arrived on the island of Jamaica to raise cattle, thus assuring the continuity of a Spanish settlement there.

When Diego, Columbus's son, replaced Nicolás de Ovando as governor of the West Indies in 1509, the Spanish focused all their attention on obtaining Indian slaves to produce gold. Just as Ovando had already taken away Indians from those who opposed his government, giving them to others in his favor, Diego Columbus also used the distribution of Indians as a political weapon. He alienated himself early on from many colonists by attempting to expropriate their Indian workers in order to redistribute them among his relatives and supporters.

Diego quickly lost the favor of King Ferdinand, who discovered that his governor was acting as a private *encomendero* rather than as an official in the service of the Crown. For this reason, King Ferdinand created a court of appeals in 1511, which provided those colonists who had lost Indians with the right to appeal the governor's decisions.

This court of appeals, or Real Audiencia, effectively checked the governor's power because its judges established an alliance with royal officials of Aragonese origin, loyal to King Ferdinand. Together they formed a political faction in opposition to Diego Columbus and his followers. In 1513 the king canceled Diego's right to confiscate and redistribute Indians in the Antilles. This decision, together with the creation of the court of appeals, stripped Diego of what little power he retained and forced him to return to Spain after the king appointed a new governor.

Having eliminated the governor's power, King Ferdinand ordered a redistribution of the Indians whom Diego Columbus had previously parceled out among his followers. By dividing Indians among those who were loyal to the Crown on the islands of Cuba, Española, and Puerto Rico, Ferdinand sought to concentrate economic and political power in the hands of a small, powerful, colonial elite which had begun to flourish under Ovando but had been obstructed by Diego Columbus with his conflictive government. The king also wished to ensure that the remain-

ing indigenous labor force was put to use by those who still had productive mines.

The reallocation of enslaved Indians was carried out in 1513 in Cuba
and Puerto Rico, and at the end of 1514 in Española. The redistribution
on the island of Española had the greatest social and political consequences, as it affected the largest number of Indians and Spaniards. In
Española, 26,334 Indians were resettled among 743 Spanish residents in
fourteen towns dispersed about the island. These Indians came from 402
communities that had been deprived of their political leadership since
the beginning of the Spanish conquest.

More than half of the Indians distributed in 1514 remained in the
hands of a small elite consisting of eighty-two colonial officials and
absentee courtiers who controlled the few remaining productive gold
deposits. This situation provoked resentment and frustration among
colonists who had their Indian slaves taken away from them. Deprived
of the means to get rich, many sold whatever they had and abandoned
Española. Some went to Cuba and Darién, while others returned to
Spain. This emigration caused the Spanish population to decrease substantially. In 1516 there were fewer than 715 Spanish heads of house-
holds, or *vecinos*, on Española.

In addition to the decline of the Taíno population and the emigration
of the Spanish colonists, the colonial authorities on Española had to
face the problem of the depletion of the gold mines. From 1515 on, the
most important *encomenderos* and royal officials presented numerous
proposals to the king with an eye to reorienting the colonial economy
toward the cultivation of crops such as sugarcane.

During the course of these discussions, King Ferdinand died in Spain
in February 1516. Since Queen Isabella had died earlier, in 1504, the
government fell into the hands of a regent, Cardinal Francisco Jiménez
de Cisneros, who was to handle royal affairs until the heir apparent,
Prince Charles, came of age. Impressed by a campaign by the Dominican friars against the injustices of the *encomienda* system, Cisneros
deposed the late king's officials in Española and decided to reorganize
the government of the Indies. To this end, he sent three Hieronymite friars to Santo Domingo as governors, with a mandate to eliminate the
encomienda system in Cuba, Española, and Puerto Rico. The governors
were to resettle the Indians in towns where they could live and hire
themselves out as free people.

Cisneros's plan to "reform the Indies" was a catastrophic failure. In December 1518, when the Indians were being moved to the new towns, a smallpox epidemic broke out, killing two-thirds of the 11,000 remaining Indians on the island of Española. With indigenous labor reduced to less than 4,000 people and in the face of rising protests from former *encomenderos*, the Hieronymite friars stopped the campaign for reform. The few surviving Indians were returned to their former owners in order to keep the Spanish colonists from abandoning the island.

The reform plan was never carried out in Puerto Rico or Cuba, where smallpox also wrought havoc on the indigenous population. In Cuba, the *encomienda* system remained intact, making it possible to continue mining gold in the Caribbean for two more decades. In 1522, Governor Diego Velázquez conducted a further reallocation of Indians in Cuba. The number of Indians involved in this distribution indicates both a decline in the indigenous population and the concentration of labor in the hands of few *encomenderos*.

According to the records of that distribution, Diego Velázquez gave the last 2,781 Indians to only nineteen *encomenderos* established in five towns on the island. The Indians came from the last forty native communities that had managed to survive Spanish rule. Their very low number indicates the extent of the devastation of the Taíno population in Cuba. In Puerto Rico, the demographic catastrophe was similar: a census taken in 1530 registered only 1,148 Indian survivors.

Like their counterparts in Española some years earlier, the *encomenderos* in Cuba responded to the labor crisis by importing Indians from Yucatán, which had no gold mines. In May 1530, however, a new epidemic of smallpox devastated the island of Cuba, reducing the already-decimated native population to one-third of its 1522 level.

The Cuban *encomenderos* were then convinced that they would have to use African slaves if they wanted to continue mining for gold. This solution had already been tried out with success in Española and Puerto Rico, where massive numbers of black slaves were being imported to work in the mines and on the sugarcane plantations. With the help of enslaved blacks and Indians, the Cuban *encomenderos* managed to maintain gold production until the mines were exhausted in 1538. By that time, Española and Puerto Rico had stopped producing gold in large quantities, and the Spanish elites there were now involved in cultivating sugarcane and raising cattle.

CHAPTER 2

Sugar and Slaves
in the Spanish Antilles

The First Sugar Plantations

The Hieronymite friars had only one option if they were to avoid the complete depopulation of Española. They had to accept the demands of the *encomenderos* for the Crown to lend money to those who wanted to plant sugarcane and construct sugar mills. Sugar prices had been rising in Europe since 1510, and producing sugar looked like a promising venture in the tropical lands of Española. On behalf of the Crown, the Hieronymites handed out in 1518 the first loans for the creation of sugar plantations, and granted the borrowers various fiscal privileges, including tax exemptions, designed to protect their businesses. In the years that followed, the Crown authorized a similar policy in Puerto Rico.

The richest *encomenderos* of Santo Domingo were the first to invest in sugar. Their close political ties to well-placed colonial officials made it easy for them to obtain loans to finance the construction of sugar plantations. By the time the Hieronymite priests began to grant loans, some colonists had already experimented with sugar production. The sugarcane used by these colonists in their early experiments descended from the first sugarcane brought by Christopher Columbus from the Canary Islands on his second voyage in 1493.

La Concepción was the most important mining center of Española, and it was there that a colonist named Aguilón used crude instruments to conduct his first experiments toward the production of sugar in 1506. The mayor of La Concepción, Miguel de Ballester, also built a small sugar mill in 1514, which produced the sugar sold in that city. In 1516

Gonzalo de Vellosa built a successful sugar mill in the vicinity of Santo Domingo to supply the local market.

The success of Gonzalo de Vellosa's sugar mill encouraged the *encomenderos* of Española to build their sugar mills close to Santo Domingo, which, in addition to being the administrative and political center of the Spanish Antilles, was the largest city and the main port outfitted for trade with Seville. Santo Domingo was the only city on Española that boasted colonists with the means to invest in the development of sugar plantations.[1]

In 1520 the authorities of Española reported the construction of six new mills, three of which had already begun to produce sugar. These first sugar mills exploited the labor of several hundred black slaves imported since 1518, in addition to the few hundred Indians who still remained in the hands of their owners. The first shipment of sugar to Spain took place in 1521. The following year, approximately 2,000 arrobas of sugar were exported from Santo Domingo, to be sold at two ducats per arroba in Spain, bringing a handsome profit to the colonists.[2]

In 1527 there were already twenty-five sugar plantations operating at full capacity. Their owners raised capital in various ways: by forming companies of several stockholders, by selling property, and by obtaining loans from the Crown and from merchants of Casa Centuriona, a Genoese trading company with experience in the sugar trade in the Mediterranean. Since slaves were an important part of the investment in sugar plantations, the Genoese traders financially backed the importation of slaves to the Antilles. In 1520 Casa Centuriona received a license from Charles V to transport 4,000 enslaved Africans to the Indies.

The Genoese merchants easily supplied the slaves needed by the new planters of Española, and their quota of 4,000 was met long before the eight-year term of their license expired. Charles V also gave new licenses to several courtiers and other members of the colonial elite of Española, allowing each of them the privilege of directly importing up to 400 African slaves, and soon the sugar plantations close to Santo Domingo were worked by large numbers of slaves, who were sold at 90 to 150 pesos each.

The *encomenderos* of Puerto Rico soon followed the steps of their counterparts on Española. Tomás de Castellón, a colonist of Genoese origin, undertook the creation of a sugar plantation in the Añasco region on the western part of Puerto Rico, close to the town of San German. When Castellón died, this sugar plantation was shut down, but in 1530 the colonists of San Juan requested loans from Charles V to develop sugar plantations. The king did not respond immediately to these requests, and in 1538 the town council of San Juan renewed its bid to establish new plantations. The king eventually granted the colonists of San Juan smaller loans than those given to the Española colonists, about 3,000 pesos per sugar plantation, and sometimes only 1,500 pesos. With the help of these loans, four plantations were put into operation in Puerto Rico by 1548.

In Cuba, on the other hand, gold mining was still foremost in the minds of the Spanish, even though the king offered to grant to the colonists a single loan of 7,000 pesos for the purchase of African slaves in 1532. In later years only three colonists, Gonzalo de Guzmán, Hernando de Castro, and Governor Antonio de Chávez, tried to develop sugar plantations in Cuba. Guzmán and Castro were not successful, despite receiving the same incentives as the colonists of Española, including permission to import black slaves. Governor Chávez had better luck, as he had the foresight to bring sugar masters from Española to help him construct a sugar mill in 1547. This was the only significant sugar mill built in Cuba during the first eighty years of the sixteenth century, but it was short-lived.

The sugar industry thrived on the island of Española. Most plantations were close to the city of Santo Domingo, although there were two in the vicinity of Puerto Plata, in the north of Española, and another on the western side of the island, close to the town of La Yaguana. By permission of Charles V, sugar was exported directly to Seville from Puerto Plata and La Yaguana without going through Santo Domingo. In Puerto Rico, plantations were located on the northern coast, close to the city of San Juan. On both islands, the sugar industry helped to stem the emigration of colonists to Mexico and Peru that had begun with the decline of gold mining in the Antilles. In fact, new colonists from the Canary Islands, Italy, and Portugal came to work on the sugar plantations as sugar masters.

From 1520 to 1540, Santo Domingo became a bustling seaport as sugar plantations multiplied and sugar produced in the southern part of the island was shipped to Europe. Merchants linked to Genoese,

Sevillian, German, and Portuguese trading and banking houses exported sugar, hides, *cassia fistula* (drumstick fruit), and dyewoods from the Antilles while reexporting silver and gold from Mexico and Peru to Europe. Black slaves were also reexported from Santo Domingo to Cuba, Puerto Rico, Panama, Honduras, and Peru to work in haciendas, plantations, and public works there. In addition, all sorts of European merchandise passed through Santo Domingo on its way to various parts of the emerging Spanish Empire.

One of the more visible consequences of the growth of the sugar industry was the decentralization of political power in the Antilles. The sugar plantation owners gradually consolidated their influence in the regions where their plantations had been established, eventually controlling the town councils of San Juan and Santo Domingo. Thus the power of the governors and captain-generals was checked. When Bishop Sebastián Ramírez de Fuenleal came to Española in 1528 as governor and president of the Real Audiencia, the plantation owners were already a powerful group of entrepreneurs protected by the Spanish Crown.

In 1529 the Crown issued a royal decree prohibiting the embargo of sugar from plantations that fell into debt. This ruling reinforced the already privileged position of the owners, who were not required to pay import taxes on the copper used to build their boilers or on the tools and machinery needed for the construction of their sugar mills. The sugar plantation owners were also exempt from paying church tithes, which would have been a heavy financial burden, and they exercised the right of *patronato,* which gave them the power to select the priests and govern the churches on their estates.

Another privilege that the Crown granted the plantation owners was the right of primogeniture in passing down land and other property. Thus the sugar plantations had to be passed on undivided from the fathers to their oldest son. Prior to this ruling, the death of the plantation owner sometimes caused the plantation to go into bankruptcy due to disputes among the inheritors, as was the case for the sugar plantation started by Tomás de Castellón in Puerto Rico. One thing that the Crown did not agree to, because Charles V considered it excessive, was a petition from plantation owners in 1538 to grant them political privileges similar to those of the Spanish nobility.

Technically, the industrial model in the Spanish Antilles was nearly the same as that of the Canary Islands and Madeira, copied from the Sicilian model. The main difference between the early Caribbean sugar plantations and those of the Atlantic islands was that the Spanish Caribbean sugar planters used slaves as manual workers, paying salaries only to the few European masters contracted to direct operations and perfect the sugar. Wage-earning laborers, in contrast, worked the Portuguese sugar plantations of the Atlantic islands.

Sugar plantations all used the same technologies and similar cane varieties. In the early years, some mills consisted of a large round stone that ground the cane in a press. Soon this system was replaced by a more efficient mill made up of two horizontal wooden rollers moved by water or by animal force. The extracted juice was then boiled in large copper pots at high temperatures until it reached a point of sufficient evaporation to form molasses.

Upon reaching the optimum boiling point, the molasses was poured into clay molds in the shape of cones, where it would crystallize as excess liquid drained through a small hole in the narrowest part of the mold. The end product was a sugar loaf in the shape of a cone, comprised of several layers of varying concentrations of sucrose. In the early days of the industry, the loaves were ground indiscriminately and poured into boxes of 750 pounds each for export, but later the layers began to be sorted and sold by grade.

The production of sugar required the cultivation and harvesting of vast quantities of sugarcane. One acre of sugarcane was necessary to produce just over one ton of sugar. The largest sugar plantations could produce 125 tons per year, but this quantity was rarely reached, and the export figures indicate a much lower production average.

African Slaves and Marronage

The land of a sugar plantation was divided into four parts: one for the cultivation of sugarcane; another for the cultivation of yuca, plantains, and other foodstuffs for the slaves; forestland for wood for the furnaces; and pastures for draft animals and beef cattle. Black slaves, supervised by Spanish overseers, free mulattos, or slaves who had earned the trust of their master, did all agricultural work. The sugar mills were run by "sugar masters," who earned high salaries, since the quality of the end product was highly dependent on the delicate work of these technicians.

As time went by, slaves also learned the secrets of the art of sugar making and went on to work as masters and specialists. Many male slaves learned to work as carpenters, ironworkers, boilers, woodcutters, sawyers, boxers, carters, mill operators, crushers, and purifiers. Female slaves worked as cooks, laundry women, orchard keepers, and servants in the plantation masters' homes. In Española, very large plantations had as many as 900 black slaves, but in general the captive population on plantations varied between 60 and 500 people.

Española had thirty-five plantations and sugar mills by 1548. Puerto Rico had eleven by 1568. The continual importation of slaves to meet the rising demand of manual labor increased the black population on both islands dramatically. In Puerto Rico, blacks already outnumbered whites in 1530, when Governor Francisco Lando took a population census. He determined that the island had 1,503 persons of African origin, as opposed to 426 Spaniards. Although the sugar industry still had not begun in Puerto Rico, slaves were being heavily used in the gold mines. In 1546 plantation owner Melchor de Castro estimated the black population in Española to be 12,000, while whites numbered approximately 5,000.

Most slaves were bought on credit from Portuguese, German, or Genoese merchants based in Seville. Generally, both male and female slaves were brought in, since the Crown had ordered in 1526 that one-third of each shipment of slaves to the Antilles should consist of women in order to facilitate the natural reproduction of the enslaved population. In Puerto Rico, according to the census of 1530, more than one-fifth of the black population was female.

The number of slaves in Puerto Rico and Española grew rapidly in the mid-sixteenth century. The Spanish observed that the mortality rate among the Africans in the Caribbean was notably lower than that of the Indians. Unlike these, the Africans had already been exposed to European germs and diseases and had developed immunological resistance to them. Furthermore, the Spanish took much better care of the enslaved Africans than of the Indians, as the black slaves were more expensive, usually representing from a third to half of the capital invested in the plantations.

In addition, the continuous importation of slaves more than made up for losses caused by death or escape. The custom of importing more blacks than the royal license allowed took root quickly. This practice resulted in a surplus in the slave population and allowed the plantation owners of Española to continue the slave trade by reexporting Africans to Honduras, Peru, and other parts of Spanish America.

The demographic imbalance created by the importation and growth of the slave population transformed Caribbean life in the mid-sixteenth century. The most immediate consequences were slave rebellions and the formation of communities of runaway slaves. With such a small Spanish population, it was very difficult to maintain strict control of the plantation workers, who were often able to escape. Runaway slaves congregated with those who spoke their own language or were from nearby tribes in Africa. Banding together, they created communities that tried to reconstruct their original African way of life.

Marronage and rebellions of African slaves in the Caribbean have a long history, continuing right through to the second half of the nineteenth century. That story began when a few black slaves, brought by Nicolás de Ovando to Española from Spain in 1502, ran away as soon as they set foot on the island and were never apprehended. Years later, between 1515 and 1518, when the need to import slaves to Española for plantation work was discussed, colonists recommended that they be brought directly from Africa rather than from Spain. The colonists feared the slaves coming from the Iberian Peninsula who already knew Spanish and could thus communicate among themselves to orchestrate rebellions.

The first slaves imported from Africa turned out to be just as prone to insurrection as those brought from Spain because they belonged to a tribe famous for its pride and reluctance to perform heavy manual labor: the Wolof of Senegal. Placed in plantations owned by Diego Columbus and Melchor de Castro, the Wolofs rebelled in December 1522, killing one Spaniard and escaping to the mountains. This uprising was swiftly repressed, but the Spanish response did not prevent additional rebellions in the years to come.

The number of runaway blacks gradually increased. Initially, escaped slaves on Española joined a community of Indian rebels, led by a chief by the name of Enriquillo. These Indian rebels had been at war with the

Spanish since 1519, sneaking into their plantations at night to steal cattle and liberate other enslaved Indians or blacks. For many years,
Enriquillo operated in the southern mountains of Española successfully evading the Spanish military patrols. His Indians were the only survivors of the *encomienda* regime and obviously had no desire to return
to work for the Spanish. His rebellion became so dangerous that in 1523
colonial authorities formally declared war on Enriquillo and imposed
an excise tax on the sale of meat in order to pay the wages of the bounty hunters in charge of tracking down the Indian rebels.

News of Enriquillo's rebellion in Española encouraged the few
Indians remaining as mine workers in Cuba. In 1520 they began to run
away to the mountains and to small nearby islands, from which they
fiercely resisted the patrols sent by colonial authorities to subjugate
them. In 1532 the leader of the Indian rebels of Cuba, Guamá, and several of his followers were killed during an assault by the Spanish bounty hunters. The survivors were imprisoned and returned to their former
owners. Enriquillo continued the struggle until 1533, when he signed a
pact with the Spanish whereby he obtained amnesty and freedom for his
followers in exchange for helping the Spanish track down runaway black
slaves.

On Española, many African slaves escaped and were not caught. In
1542 the archdeacon Alvaro de Castro wrote to the Crown that there
were 2,000 to 3,000 black maroons on the island. The Italian traveler
Girolamo Benzoni, who spent several months in Santo Domingo that
same year, estimated that there were as many as 7,000 runaway black
slaves on the island. As time went by, the Spanish began to fear that
black rebels might conquer the entire island. When the new governor,
Alonso de Cerrato, arrived in Española in 1543, he found the fear
among the Spanish to be such that very few would dare to go out into
the countryside if they were not in groups of fifteen or twenty armed
men. In that same year, the Spanish calculated that in Baoruco,
Enriquillo's old hideout, there were around 300 male and female rebels,
and that in the area surrounding the old mining center of La
Concepción, there was a group of forty to fifty runaway slaves led by a
man named Diego del Campo.

In 1544 in San Juan de la Maguana, runaways led by Diego de
Guzmán attacked and burned part of a sugar mill and killed a Spanish

colonist. Governor Cerrato responded by sending several patrols of bounty hunters to Baoruco. A battle ensued, in which Guzmán and eighteen other maroons lost their lives. The rest of the rebels ran for the mountains, only to be pursued by Spanish troops, both mounted and on foot, with orders not to return without killing them all. Governor Cerrato also launched an offensive against the maroons in La Concepción. The raid was so successful that their leader, Diego del Campo, surrendered, having seen his followers trapped, hanged, shot with arrows, and mutilated by their captors. To save his own life, Diego del Campo offered to hunt down his former companions.

In June 1546 Cerrato wrote to the king that the island of Española had never been better controlled. Two years later the Spanish launched a final raid against Lemba, a most feared runaway slave, who had led a rebellion for more than fifteen years in the region of Higüey, in the eastern part of the island. Lemba died in this campaign, but the survivors of his maroon community managed to escape to the center of the island, where they joined another group of twenty maroons.

In Cuba and San Juan, the slave upheavals did not reach the proportions of the revolts on Española. The runaway Indians in Cuba were not totally subdued; groups of Cuban Indians continued to rebel, attacking mines and haciendas until the promulgation of the "New Laws" for the protection of the Indians in 1542. In later years, slave escapes were generally individual acts aided by Spanish colonists who encouraged slaves to run away by offering them shelter and better treatment in order to attract them to their service. This practice of enticing others' slaves became so widespread that in 1574, the colonial government of Cuba imposed severe punishment on the colonists who stole slaves in this manner, and ordered all runaway slaves under new ownership to be returned to their previous masters.

In Cuba, as in Española, it was necessary to organize a permanent patrol of bounty hunters to track down maroons. The bounty hunters earned a salary paid for by an excise tax on the sale of meat. Such "slave funds" were used in the sixteenth century in Spanish America in areas where enslaved Africans often ran away. The scarcity of slaves in Cuba forced the *cabildo* of Havana to order patrols searching for maroons to try to capture them alive.

Sugar and Ginger Exports

The impact of the slave uprisings on the sugar production of Española and Puerto Rico was not very significant. In spite of the rebellions, planters and merchants continued producing and exporting sugar. Between 1536 and 1565, 803 ships reached Española with European merchandise, and departed with sugar, hides, cassia fistula, dyewood, and guaiacum.

From 1550 to 1584, Caribbean sugar production remained relatively stable, averaging over 600 tons per year. From 1585 to 1587, however, exports dropped markedly and continued to decline until 1607.[3] By then the slaves' uprisings were a thing of the past. In the last fifteen years of the sixteenth century, witnesses consistently noted the decline of the sugar industry and sugarcane's replacement by other crops, among them ginger. These witnesses said that at the end of the sixteenth century, a general crisis dragged most of the plantation owners into ruin.

What happened to the Caribbean sugar industry during the last quarter of the sixteenth century? Why did the planters of Española and Puerto Rico, who had accumulated decades of experience in the cultivation of sugarcane and the management of sugar mills and plantations, eventually fail in the sugar market? Some local factors contributed to the decline of the sugar industry in Española and Puerto Rico, but the most decisive was the competition created by new producers whose sugar entered the international market and ended up displacing Caribbean sugar.

One local factor mentioned by some observers was the manual labor crisis produced by a smallpox epidemic that decimated Española's slave population in 1586 and subsequent years, killing more than half of the island's slaves. The epidemic, however, is not sufficient to explain the decline of the sugar industry, because, in spite of the death toll, there were still close to 10,000 slaves living on the island, and of those, only one-tenth were used for sugar production.

The cultivation of ginger, on the other hand, did contribute to the decline of the sugar industry in the Spanish Antilles at the end of the sixteenth century. Ginger was a plant of Asian origin introduced to Mexico in 1547 and disseminated throughout the Antilles years later. Ginger root was used as a spice as well as a medicine to cure stomach pain. Its growing popularity in Spain in the second half of the sixteenth century rapidly increased its price, and within a few years ginger became Española's second-largest export product.

In Española, ginger was first planted in 1565, but by 1574 the authorities in Santo Domingo were already reporting that some colonists had harvested twenty-five to seventy-five tons of ginger. The authorities at the time expected a large enough harvest in three years to meet the entire Spanish market demand for ginger. From 1576 on, ginger begins to appear in Española export statistics and, from 1583, in Puerto Rican statistics. Cuban production of ginger was always very limited, apparently due to the relative scarcity of slave labor in Cuba as well as the Cuban colonists' preference for cattle ranching.

In Española and Puerto Rico, many sugarcane fields were converted to ginger fields. This stubborn preference for ginger among plantation owners who had already heavily invested in sugar mills and plantations was due to the difference in price between sugar and ginger and the low cost of ginger production. Export statistics from 1581 to 1607 show that while a pound of sugar averaged twenty-five *maravedís* during the last two decades of the sixteenth century, a pound of ginger was worth about forty-five *maravedís* in 1581 and as much as sixty *maravedís* in 1607.

In addition, sugar cost much more to produce than ginger. After cutting the sugarcane and transporting it from the fields to the sugar mill, it had to be ground and turned into sugar via a manufacturing process requiring careful management and an extraordinary consumption of wood and human and animal power. Once the sugar was made, it had to be boxed and taken on barges or carts to the shipping ports, where it faced the risk of spoiling under high humidity and transportation delays.

Ginger, on the other hand, was a small root that, once harvested, retained its properties for a long time and required no packaging for export. Ginger could also be easily hidden in transport, making it very popular as contraband. Due to its ease of production and shipping, ginger, like tobacco in later years, became the favorite crop of the colonists who did not own livestock or large plantations.

On two occasions in 1598, the Spanish Crown, in an effort to oblige the plantation owners not to abandon sugar production, prohibited the planting of ginger and threatened to deny the plantation owners their privileges if they violated these orders. In 1601 the plantation owners of Puerto Rico responded that they preferred to lose their privileges than to abandon ginger cultivation. The planters of Española probably reacted similarly. The 1606 population census shows that only 800 of the 9,608 slaves on the island worked on sugar plantations. Of the others, 6,742 worked on ginger farms, on which ginger was rotated with corn and yuca, while only 88 slaves were used for domestic service.

The 1606 census of Española shows that the majority of the colonists were engaged in the production of ginger. In 1607 Española exported more than 1,870 tons of ginger, as opposed to an average 220 tons exported annually for the last fifteen years of the sixteenth century. As sugar disappeared from the economic map of Española and Puerto Rico, ginger became a mainstay.

The Portuguese-Brazilian Factor

Ginger alone, however, is not sufficient to explain the Caribbean sugar crisis at the end of the sixteenth century. There were other causes, one of the most important being the competition of Brazilian sugar that flooded the European market during the last quarter of the sixteenth century. As in the Antilles, the Brazilian sugar industry followed the technical model of the Mediterranean and the Portuguese Atlantic islands, particularly Madeira, Cape Verde, and São Tomé. These islands, colonized in the fifteenth century, provided the European upper class with sugar, which prior to that time had only been a pharmaceutical or culinary curiosity, honey having been used as a sweetener. When the Spanish Antilles began to export sugar to Seville, Antwerp had already been importing Portuguese sugar for many years. In 1498, for example, Antwerp imported approximately 500 tons of sugar from the Portuguese Atlantic islands.

There were numerous trading networks in Lisbon made up of Portuguese, Flemish, and Dutch merchants who traded wine, wool, fabric, and grain, as well as sugar, from the Portuguese Atlantic islands. Thanks to the Dutch connection, the Portuguese were able to compete with and eventually displace the Genoese and Venetians who had supplied the European market with Mediterranean sugar, produced mainly in Sicily. Madeira, for example, experienced a complete transformation of its agricultural production during the fifteenth and sixteenth centuries as its wheat fields were converted into sugar plantations.[4]

Sugar production in the Azores was always a minor activity, since the climate and soil there did not lead to high sucrose levels. In São Tomé, on the other hand, the story was completely different. This tropical island, located in the Gulf of Guinea, did have an adequate climate for the growth of sugarcane, which, together with the tax exemptions granted by the king of Portugal in 1580, turned the sugar of São Tomé into the cheapest of Portuguese sugars.

In Brazil, King Dom Sebastião also protected the sugar industry by exempting plantation owners from paying taxes on the importation of copper and iron used to build boilers and other farm machinery. Sugar production had begun in Brazil in 1532 when the Governor of São Vicente, Martim Afonso de Sousa, ordered the construction of the first sugar mill and provided financial support to colonists who wanted to grow sugarcane and produce sugar in the vicinity of Rio de Janeiro. These incentives attracted Dutch, Italian, Flemish, and German capital to Brazil, which helped finance the construction of sugar mills in other areas, especially in the coastal strip from Bahía to Paraíba. In those areas, rich soils and an abundance of rivers and sufficient forestland for fuel immediately attracted the attention of the Portuguese.

The importation of African slaves to Brazil was legalized in March 1559 when King Dom Sebastião authorized the governor of São Vicente to permit each plantation owner to import up to 120 slaves from the Congo, and to pay only one-third of the customary taxes. For more than ten years the enslaved Indians and blacks shared the rigors of plantation life. Dom Sebastião's decree of 1570 prohibiting the use of enslaved Indians threatened the Indian labor supply. From then on, the Portuguese planters accelerated their purchase of African slaves.

In 1575 there were only 55 plantations in Brazil, concentrated mostly in the areas of Porto Seguro, Ilheus, Bahía, Sergipe, and Pernambuco. Between 1570 and 1583, seventy new sugar mills were built in Brazil. Another seventy-two additional mills were built between 1584 and 1610, so that by the beginning of the seventeenth century, the Portuguese colony could boast 40 plantations in the south, 50 in the central region, and 140 in the north. Obviously, the demand for slaves increased. Although there are no definitive records, today it is estimated that during the last quarter of the sixteenth century, the Brazilian planters were importing from 10,000 to 15,000 slaves each year, mostly of Angolan origin.

With such large numbers of plantations and slaves, and virtually unlimited land, the Brazilian sugar industry became the largest in the world at the end of the sixteenth century, surpassing the combined production of the Portuguese Atlantic islands and the Spanish Antilles and flooding the European market with more than 25,000 tons of sugar per year. When these figures are compared with the annual production average of 500 tons in the Antilles, or the 2,500 tons in Madeira in the middle of the 16th century, one can see the enormous impact that Brazilian sugar production had on the European market after 1570.[5]

The plantation owners in Española and Puerto Rico were also unable to compete with the Brazilian producers, whose sugar inundated the Spanish market. Instead, they preferred to move to the production of ginger and hides, which yielded higher profits. These, however, were not the only reasons for the collapse of the plantations. The European religious wars in the sixteenth century and the war of independence in the Netherlands, then called the United Provinces, led to an economic conflict that would have hindered any type of industry in the Antilles in the sixteenth century. These factors will be discussed in the following chapters.

CHAPTER 3

Monopoly, Privateers, and Contraband

The Spanish Monopoly

Many years before Columbus crossed the Atlantic Ocean, the Portuguese had been exploring the high seas west of Europe and had occupied the islands of Madeira and the Azores. Their advanced navigation techniques also led them to occupy lands on the western coast of Africa that had not yet been reached by Europeans. With Columbus, the Spanish were able to penetrate areas much farther west than the Azores. Thus the dominion of Portugal over the Atlantic came into dispute. The Portuguese questioned Columbus's discovery, creating a tense diplomatic situation that was resolved by the Treaty of Tordesillas in 1494.

This treaty divided the planet into two hemispheres along the meridian that passed 370 leagues west of the Cape Verde islands. Spain gained full sovereignty over the lands to the west of the dividing line, while Portugal received control over the territories to the east. Both claimed exclusive control over all production in their new lands as well as over all commercial activities associated with them.

In the case of Spain, King Ferdinand and Queen Isabella established a monopoly with a complicated system of taxes, licenses, privileges, and rents, which guaranteed abundant income to the Royal Treasury. To control those activities, the Spanish monarchs created the Casa de Contratación (House of Trade), which started operations in Seville in 1503.

Authorization from the Casa de Contratación was required for all voyages and commercial transactions between Spain and the Indies as well as for voyages between the Spanish colonies in the Americas. In all

New World ports, the Casa de Contratación maintained officials in charge of controlling trade, such as the production and export of gold, pearls, silver, and other colonial products. Among these royal officials were commission agents, inspectors, bookkeepers, and treasurers. These officials administered the Crown's properties, collected taxes, handled the accounting books of the Royal Treasury, and ensured strict compliance with regulations governing the Spanish monopoly in the Indies.

The Casa de Contratación organized many of the early colonizing expeditions. It was the only institution authorized to undertake trading ventures as well as coordinate the purchase of ships, the recruitment of immigrants and colonists, and the purchase of supplies and munitions for the defense of the new possessions. As the colonies became more self-sufficient, however, colonists began to realize that their interests did not always coincide with those of the Spanish Crown.

The policies established in 1503 prohibited direct trade with foreigners and mandated severe punishment for offenders. Spanish ships sailing to the Caribbean had to depart from and return to Seville, although in exceptional cases, with special licenses, some ships were authorized to leave from the ports of Sanlúcar and Cádiz. Thus all of the other ports on the peninsula and in the rest of Europe were shut out from business generated by the Spanish colonies.

The monopoly system created serious conflicts due to the privileged position held by the Sevillian merchants, who set arbitrary prices for products exported to the New World. Although Spanish colonists constantly petitioned Spain to permit them to trade with other Spanish ports or with other European countries, the Crown never gave in to their demands, and a free market system never existed in the Spanish Caribbean.

A further complication to this situation was the fact that in the sixteenth century, Spain was unable to meet the demands of its colonies for either agricultural or manufactured products. The Sevillian merchants found themselves obliged to import products from other countries and to reexport them to the West Indies. Taxes paid on merchandise both in Seville and in the port of destination, along with freight and maritime insurance, increased the price of goods to the point that when they arrived in the Antilles, they often cost six times their original price.

This situation generated a great deal of resentment, both in Spain and in neighboring countries.

In Antwerp, Amsterdam, Le Havre, London, and Geneva, many merchants wanted to participate in the enormous market that Spain was developing in America, which benefited a small oligarchy of Sevillian merchants. Some European commercial houses managed to circumvent this situation by maintaining agents in Seville in charge of investing in companies that did business with the Indies as shipbuilders, importers and exporters, or lenders to Sevillian merchants.[1]

Since native capital was scarce in Spain, Sevillian merchants in need of quick money sought Genoese, Florentine, and Jewish credit to finance their numerous business ventures in the Caribbean. As the sixteenth century advanced, the Sevillian economy became increasingly dependent on foreign financiers and money lenders, who anxiously awaited the return of ships from the New World to collect their profits. The debt incurred by the local merchants and the king himself reached such an extreme that in some years, almost all the gold and silver shipments from Mexico and other regions of the Indies were committed to foreign firms far before they were shipped to Spain.

The Spanish Crown continued to ignore the colonists who demanded freedom to trade with other nations. To permit such trade would have meant a significant decrease in the income received by the Royal Treasury as well as a decrease in the revenue of the Sevillian merchants who controlled the colonial trade.

To defend their monopoly, the Sevillian merchants formed a group called the Consulado in 1543. Since the local merchants were highly in debt, the Consulado ended up dominated by and representing the interests of several powerful groups of Genoese, Florentine, and German and Jewish financiers operating in Seville. Thus the riches extracted from the Spanish Antilles flowed continuously into those countries from which Spain was trying to keep its colonial wealth.

The bullion collected in Spanish America increased the circulation of gold and silver in Europe and stimulated the growth of the European economy. In Spain, however, the rapid circulation of immense quantities of gold and silver while in transit to other countries created tremendous inflation. Prices went up more than 600 percent during the sixteenth century. The loss of precious metals to other European powers prevented the Spanish economy from saving or financing industries that could meet the demand for manufactured goods in the colonies. Despite its control of the New World, Spain remained less developed than its neighbors.

Furthermore, in trying to combat the Protestant princes who came to power during the Reformation, and in seeking to retain control over the Holy Roman Empire, Spain's Charles I (better known as Charles V of Germany) went to war with the most powerful kingdoms of Europe, incurring huge military expenses that ruined the Spanish economy during the second half of the sixteenth century.

Pirates and Privateers

Spain's wars with the rest of Europe and its policy of maintaining a monopoly in the New World led to the proliferation of privateering. It comes as no surprise that the French were the first privateers to move into the Spanish Antilles, if one considers that Charles V was never at war longer with anyone than he was with Francis I, king of France. Francis I was also a Catholic, but that did not stop him from opposing the imperial plans of the king of Spain, and he allowed French privateers to sail toward the Caribbean to attack Spanish colonies and ships.

As early as 1513, French privateers waited near the Canary Islands for ships returning from Española. In 1522 a French privateer, Jean Fleury, attacked a ship loaded with sugar on its way from Santo Domingo to Seville. Fleury stole the entire shipment and brought it back to France, causing great dismay among the Spanish authorities. The French privateers soon discovered Mona, an uninhabited island in the channel separating Española from Puerto Rico, and turned it into their center of operations.

In 1528 the village of San Germán, near the west coast of Puerto Rico, was attacked and burned by French privateers, forcing the villagers to flee to the countryside. Ten years later, in 1538, privateers again burned the rebuilt San Germán. From then on, that village of a mere forty families was repeatedly attacked by French privateers—in 1541, 1543, 1554, 1569, and 1576. The privateers knew that the farmers of San Germán raised livestock and yuca to supply Nombre de Dios (in Panama) and Cartagena (in Colombia), and wanted a share of the foodstuffs produced there.

Española was also besieged by privateers. In 1537 French privateers attacked the village of Azua and the neighboring area of Ocoa on the south coast of Española, stole sugar from several plantations, and then burned them to the ground. In July 1540 English privateers attacked a Spanish ship that had left port in Santo Domingo loaded with sugar and hides. From then on, Española became a constant target of Spain's enemies.

Cuba was equally easy for privateers to assault. Poor coastal settlements where colonists eked out a living raising subsistence crops and livestock quickly became victims of attack. Havana, then a small village, was raided in 1537 by French privateers, who intended to capture five Spanish ships anchored there on their way to Seville. In the same year, other French privateers, after being forced out of the Bay of Santiago de Cuba, went to Havana, where they successfully plundered goods and burned a Spanish ship moored in the port.

As a result of these acts, colonial authorities ordered the immediate construction of fortifications to protect the port of Havana from privateers. The first fort, completed in 1540, was built at the entrance to the Bay of Havana. Similar measures were adopted in Santo Domingo, San Juan, and San Germán. In 1541 Charles V approved a plan to build a wall around Santo Domingo and gave the colonial authorities permission to raise taxes and to put slaves to work on the project. In Puerto Rico, a fort was built at the entrance to the Bay of San Juan. San Germán, on the other hand, remained unprotected and therefore continued to be a favorite target for privateers in the sixteenth century.

The fortifications of the ports did not prevent privateers from capturing ships transporting Caribbean goods. For this reason, in 1537 Charles V arranged for the Spanish cargo ships to be accompanied by an armed flotilla. The order was repeated in 1540 and 1542, and in 1543 a fleet system was established so that ships would not sail alone between Spain and the Caribbean. Merchants on both sides of the Atlantic were ordered to transport their goods in fleets of large ships of at least of 100 tons, accompanied by an armed ship, to ward off attacks from privateers. These fleets were to leave twice a year from Seville, and then return from Veracruz in Mexico and Nombre de Dios in Panama. Havana was selected as the Caribbean meeting and supply point for the fleets before the return voyage to Spain.

From then on, Havana became the most important port in the Caribbean, as Santo Domingo and San Juan were no longer on the main navigational routes. Havana's port, situated at exit of the Gulf of Mexico, was more conveniently located. There, the fleets would supply themselves with water, meat, yuca, plantains, and vegetables for their return voyage.

Under the new system, ships assigned to Santo Domingo, San Juan, or Santiago de Cuba were required to travel to and from Spain with the fleets every six months. Once they got to the Caribbean, however, they had to make their own way alone, without protection. As the international situation worsened, freight and maritime insurance costs increased, causing navigation through the area to become more expensive.

It took more than twenty years for the fleet system to operate regularly, but in 1566 the fleets began service with some new fortified merchant ships of high freightage and great tonnage called galleons.

In the meantime, while the galleon fleet system was being institutionalized, Cuba continued to suffer frequent attacks from French privateers. In 1546 Baracoa, a poor village on the eastern part of the island, was pillaged. The following year, French privateers seized a Spanish caravel in the Bay of Santiago de Cuba. In 1554 Francis Le Clerc, a famous French privateer also known as "Pata de Palo," attacked and occupied Santiago de Cuba for a month and did not leave until he was paid more than 60,000 pesos' worth of gold, silver, and jewels.

In 1555 it was Havana's turn to be attacked, this time by a former deputy of Pata de Palo, Jacques de Sores, who entered the bay, took the village by force, and occupied it for a month, during which time seventy-five colonists and slaves lost their lives. Upon leaving, Sorés and his men burned Havana to the ground, after collecting a mere 2,000 pesos, which shows the destitution of the population at that time. One month later, another French privateer, William Mermoz, appeared in the bay, attacked several haciendas and farms around Havana, and made off with a caravel that had arrived several days earlier.

To prevent these attacks, Spain gave Santo Domingo and Puerto Rico several galleys and other patrol vessels in the early 1550s. Those ships were destroyed almost immediately, some by storms and others by privateers. Only with the signing of the Cateau-Cambrésis Treaty in

1559 did the long dispute between France and Spain end. After this treaty, French privateers only occasionally reappeared in Caribbean waters for the remainder of the sixteenth century.

Cattle, Hides, and Contraband

The relationship between the Spanish colonists and foreign intruders was not always one of confrontation and war, but also of illegal trade and cooperation. As early as 1526, for example, Charles V complained that African slaves were being smuggled into the Antilles in spite of the prohibitions, and called on the Real Audiencia of Santo Domingo to rectify the situation.

These orders were enforced in 1527 when an English ship appeared in the port of Santo Domingo and requested entry so that its crew could rest and stock up on fresh water. The English captain claimed that they were lost en route to North America. Accepting the excuse, the Real Audiencia allowed the ships to drop anchor, but as soon as they entered the port, the crew showed fabric and other manufactured goods to the curious onlookers. This ship had previously stopped in San Juan, and the captain had inquired about the route to Santo Domingo. The Spanish governor scared off the smugglers with cannon shots, arguing that, as foreigners, they were forbidden to engage in trade with the colonists

Only direct trade with foreign suppliers seemed to meet the population's demand for manufactured goods, but the Spanish Crown did not allow such trade. The Spanish colonists needed soap, wine, flour, fabric, perfume, nails, shoes, medicine, paper, dried fruit, grain, cereal, iron, steel, knives, and many other articles, but none of the Caribbean ports authorized to do business with Seville (namely Havana, Santiago de Cuba, Santo Domingo, Puerto Plata, La Yaguana, San Juan, and San Germán) received enough merchandise to satisfy the demand of the local population.

In addition, it was almost impossible to deliver manufactured goods to an island's interior for lack of roads. Worse still, when anyone attempted such a journey, the enormous effort inflated prices beyond everyone's means. The old native paths, well worn in the past, had been abandoned and disappeared under the fast-growing tropical vegetation. Furthermore, the dangers of coastal sailing due to the threat of the privateers made delivery by sea extremely difficult.

Those most affected by the Spanish monopoly and the lack of manufactured goods were the colonists living in the interior of the islands, yet they managed to survive. As the population of the islands dwindled and the Hispanic Caribbean societies became more rural, the colonists adapted to the large open spaces and abundant pastures. Those who were not part of the small colonial bureaucracy or did not work on the plantations became shepherds or ranchers, and many became owners of large haciendas and cattle herds. Livestock, along with sugar, became central to the Hispanic Caribbean economy in the sixteenth century.

Hides held great strategic importance for the European economy. European armies needed hides for the harnesses and saddles for their cavalry, strings for their crossbows and armor, and shoes for their infantry, as well as for wineskins and other containers. Industries required hides in large quantities for belts and all rigging in their factories, as well as for making kegs, which would later hold the Spanish mercury to be sent to the silver mines in Mexico and Peru. The general populace needed hides for their shoes, hats, pants, coats, and many other domestic products. In the houses of the well-to-do, hides were used to cover furniture, doors, books, and even walls and beds, as well as being used on coaches.

European livestock could not supply the quantity of hides needed in Europe in the sixteenth century, so leather was in high demand. Exactly how many hides were sold illegally in the Antilles is difficult to determine. One document from that period states that in Española, 50,000 hides were sold illegally in 1577. An official report from 1588 says that the Dutch bought 60,000 hides over three years from a town called Maxada Blanca in Española. The Dutch exchanged 800,000 pesos' worth of merchandise and 600 black slaves for the hides. Ten years later, in 1598, another official report estimated the annual contraband to be 80,000 hides. Although the exact number of contraband hides at the time is unknown, it is obvious that legal trade with Seville was being displaced by illegal traffic.

Throughout the Caribbean, contraband became a way of life for those living farthest from the major cities. Hides were used as a universal currency and preferred means of exchange for both colonists and traders. In Española in 1577, for example, slaves were worth 50 hides; in Cuba in 1578, they were valued at 200 hides. In 1577 fine fabric was worth two or three hides per yard in the Caribbean, while one hide could be exchanged for four to six yards of cheaper cotton cloth. A keg of wine could be bought for 20 to 25 hides at that time.

Plantation owners also became cattle breeders in order to feed the hundreds of slaves who worked on the plantations. On the plantations, the meat from the livestock was consumed while the hides were exported. In the interior, however, livestock were raised mainly for hides. Meat was so plentiful that it could not all be consumed, and much of it went to waste. Only in areas near important towns did meat have an economic value. There its sale was regulated by town councils, which periodically imposed an excise tax in order to collect revenue to pay for, among other things, the recapture of escaped slaves.

According to the Spanish chronicler Gonzalo Fernández de Oviedo, big landowners in Santo Domingo often had from 7,000 to 30,000 cattle grazing on the savannas and in the woodlands of Española. Rodrigo de Bastidas, the bishop of Venezuela living in Santo Domingo, for example, owned at least 25,000 head of cattle in Española and more on farms in Puerto Rico. María de Arana owned as many as 42,000 head of cattle between the years 1544 and 1546. A very devout woman, she managed to provide enough meat to feed a very large group of Dominican friars during their three-month stopover in Santo Domingo in 1544.

Cattle raising in Cuba developed more slowly because gold mining lasted longer there than in Española. Nonetheless, by 1578 the merchants of Havana were legally exporting around 20,000 hides per year to Seville. The Puerto Rico colonists, on the other hand, exported only around 5,000 hides per year by the end of the sixteenth century, although some people in the city of San Juan owned up to 12,000 head of cattle in 1598. It was easier for the Spanish colonists living in Havana, Santo Domingo, and San Juan to export hides to Seville on a regular basis because their farms were closer to the ports outfitted for trade with Spain. People living in the more remote parts of the islands had to bring their livestock to the major cities on foot or wait for a boat to take their hides to the main ports.

The inhabitants of the interior of the islands confronted great difficulty in moving their livestock across rivers and mountains, as they were sometimes attacked by bands of runaway slaves who stole their animals. In the early days of hide exportation, the people of Puerto Plata and La Yaguana, in Española, and those from Santiago de Cuba, waited for ships to arrive so that they could sell their hides officially by paying the proper taxes in the presence of the authorities. Eventually, however, as the number of ships arriving in port diminished due to the danger of privateers, the Caribbean planters, cattle ranchers, and hunters began dealing with foreign smugglers, who offered them merchandise and slaves, in exchange for their hides and sugar.

The breakdown of the Spanish trade routes in the Antilles was an open secret widely known by French privateers and Portuguese smugglers, who were then the main suppliers of slaves to the Caribbean. The English also tried to do business with the Spanish Antilles, especially after the French abandoned their operations in 1559, in compliance with the Cateau-Cambrésis Treaty.

English Traders and Corsairs

John Hawkins, a sailor and English merchant who was related by marriage to members of the English upper nobility, formed a company with his in-laws and bought three ships to do business with the Canary Islands, Guinea, and the West Indies. In 1562 Hawkins loaded his ships with European merchandise and sailed via the Canary Islands to Africa, where he traded some of the merchandise for slaves. He then proceeded to trade the rest of the merchandise and the slaves for sugar, hides, and brazilwood in the Caribbean. When he stopped in the Canary Islands on his way to the Caribbean, Hawkins sent a letter to the people of Puerto Plata, in the north of Española, informing them of his impending arrival.

When Hawkins arrived in Puerto Plata in April 1563, the local authorities threatened him and ordered him to leave immediately. He then went to the abandoned village of La Isabela, where he landed and waited for the villagers, headed by the priest and the local authorities, to arrive and trade with him. In order to encourage Philip II of Spain to accept trade between the colonists and the English, Hawkins scrupulously paid the full amount of taxes required by the Spanish. Nonetheless, since trade with the English was not officially permitted, in order to save face, the authorities of Puerto Plata decided to take 100 slaves as a fine, after the villagers had bought the other 200 and most of Hawkins's merchandise.

The Hawkins experiment ended with losses for both parties. The Spanish authorities confiscated Hawkins's hides and sugar from the haciendas and plantations of Puerto Plata when his business partner, Thomas Hampton, believing that the Sevillian authorities were going to tolerate their commercial venture, landed in Spain on his way back to England. In Española, meanwhile, as soon as the authorities of Santo Domingo heard of Puerto Plata's illegal dealings with the English, they sent a judge and sixty militia men with instructions to confiscate all the merchandise bought illegally and punish the traders.

Hawkins's first voyage was an economic failure, but it showed the English that the colonists of the Spanish Antilles were willing to go to any length to do business. Hawkins subsequently prepared two other voyages to the Caribbean. The second did not involve Española, and Hawkins and his partners garnered a 60 percent profit on their invested capital. The third trip to Mexico failed, due to a surprise attack by a Spanish flotilla off the coast of San Juan de Ulúa in Mexico that destroyed Hawkins's flotilla with cannon fire. Among the few men who survived was a sailor by the name of Francis Drake.

This incident exacerbated the conflict between King Philip II of Spain and Queen Elizabeth I of England with respect to English navigation in the Spanish Atlantic. Queen Elizabeth, like several of her ministers, was a stockholder in Hawkins's businesses, and refused to accept pressure from the Spanish government to prevent the penetration of English merchant marines into the Caribbean. The relationship between the English and the Spanish deteriorated even further when England decided to support the Dutch in their struggle for independence from Spanish rule in Flanders. Furthermore, in 1585 Philip II ordered the seizure of all English ships in Spanish ports.

Both monarchs knew that sooner or later they would go to war; therefore Elizabeth I did not hesitate to support Francis Drake financially and politically so that he could sail off to "punish the King of

Spain in his Indies," a plan that he put into action in September 1585 when he attacked the port of Vigo in Spain on his way to America.

From Vigo, Drake headed to Santo Domingo, where he expected to find the prosperous and flourishing city about which he had heard so much about. Instead, he found an impoverished place with minimum trade, decaying buildings, and few inhabitants. Drake arrived in Santo Domingo in early 1586. Until then, Santo Domingo had been the only city in the Antilles that had not suffered attacks from the privateers, but the people were well aware of the danger. When they saw the English sails, everyone, including the governor and the colonial authorities, panicked and ran to the countryside, leaving the city open to attack, defended only by thirty men on horseback.

The English took the city with little effort and stayed there for a month, pillaging everything in sight. Drake agreed to abandon the city only after the population managed to hand over 25,000 ducats worth of jewelry, gold, and silver. In addition to this ransom, Drake managed to take with him the bells from the churches, the cannons from the forts, as well as hides, sugar, and cassia fistula fruits that he found in the warehouses. Before leaving the city, Drake and his men burned more than thirty houses and all the government, municipal, and ecclesiastical archives.

From Santo Domingo, Drake went to Cartagena, which he assaulted with his small army of 1,000 men. The English took the city in March 1586. After collecting a ransom of 107,000 ducats there, Drake sailed toward Havana, but did not dare to land because the Spanish were waiting for him with troops recruited from all over the island. Drake considered an attack on Havana too risky and decided to return to England, pillaging the Spanish fort of St. Augustine, in Florida, along the way. This fort had been built years earlier to safeguard the route of the galleon fleets that sailed on the Gulf Stream when leaving Havana for Seville.

Drake's campaign against the main Caribbean ports demonstrated many things to the world. To the English and other enemies of Spain, it showed that the Spanish Empire was vulnerable and that Spain did not have the strength to completely defend its territories in America. Realizing this, the English continued to send hundreds of privateers to the Caribbean, taking advantage of the fact that England was now openly at war with Spain.

Between 1589 and 1594, around 200 English privateer ships sailed through the Caribbean with license to harass Spanish settlements. These privateers generally operated in Cuban waters and waited for ships from Española, Puerto Rico, and Jamaica loaded with sugar, hides, and ginger, or for ships arriving in Havana from Cartagena, Portobelo, and Veracruz, which they then attacked and pillaged.

These were golden years for the English privateers, who were widely financed by merchant syndicates in London that operated with the direct support of the English Crown. Encouraged by the experience of the English, the French again began sending privateers to the Caribbean and continued to do so until 1598, when France finally signed a peace settlement with Spain, the Treaty of Vervins.

Drake's attacks of 1586 showed the Spanish the urgency of reinforcing their main ports in the Caribbean. Despite the disaster of the Spanish Armada, which sank in a storm in 1588 while attempting to invade England, the Spanish government spent substantial resources to establish a defense system to track the movement of privateers and the departure and arrival of the galleon fleets. This system provided effective communication links between Seville and the Caribbean. In addition, the Spanish government began to spend large sums of money on the fortification of Havana, Puerto Rico, Cartagena, Portobelo, Veracruz, and St. Augustine, to protect them from new attacks.

In November 1595, when Drake intended to reenact his pillaging of Santo Domingo by assaulting Puerto Rico, fortifications had been constructed in El Morro. From there, Drake's flotilla was bombarded when it tried to enter the Bay of San Juan. Drake's own ship was hit by a cannonball, which killed his partner, John Hawkins, and almost cost him his own life. Drake then decided to abandon his plan and left the island. His defeat convinced the Spanish that the new fortifications had been the key to their success.

Two and a half years later, however, in 1598, a new English fleet of seventeen ships under the command of George Clifford, count of Cumberland, again attacked San Juan. After an intense battle in which the city was surrounded, the English managed to occupy the town. In August of that year, the Count of Cumberland left, after dysentery had killed 1,500 of the 2,200 men who had landed with him. As Drake had done in Santo Domingo in 1586, before leaving San Juan Clifford and his men took all the sugar, hides, and ginger they found in warehouses and at the port, stole the bells from the churches, and even took the organ from the cathedral.

The Dutch: Salt and Smuggling

The Dutch war of independence from Spanish rule, which had been going on since 1576, added a special ingredient to Spain's conflicts with its European enemies in the Caribbean. By 1594, thanks to the support received from the French and English armies in the land war, the Dutch were able to take the offensive on the seas. Despite almost twenty years of war, neither the Spanish nor the Dutch had been interested in maritime war because neither wanted to damage trade between Spain and the Netherlands, then called the United Provinces. But when Spain seized more than 400 Dutch ships, in 1595 and again in 1598, that were to be loaded with salt in Spanish and Portuguese ports, the Dutch were forced to search for salt elsewhere without the help of Iberian middlemen, and they responded with a maritime war in the Caribbean.

Salt was crucial to the Dutch economy because it was an essential ingredient in the preservation of the herring that the Dutch exported throughout Europe. The Dutch discovered a new source of salt on the Araya Peninsula, close to Cumaná in Venezuela. During their voyages throughout the Caribbean, the Dutch also discovered the great bounty of sugar, hides, tobacco, ginger, cassia fistula, and salt that the Caribbean islands and South America had to offer, as well as the need for slaves and European manufactured goods in these regions. The Dutch decided to supply these markets and soon were caught up in the wave of contraband trade that was sweeping the Caribbean.

In order to prevent retaliation by the Spanish, the Dutch ships sailed in well-armed flotillas. In this way they not only protected themselves from attack, but they could make sure that villagers in coastal towns traded their products for manufactured goods with them and not with the English. During the last five years of the sixteenth century, there were Dutch fleets dedicated exclusively to contraband in the Caribbean. The largest Dutch fleets had up to thirty ships, while the English never had more than five or six ships operating at one time in the Caribbean.

The number of Dutch ships involved gives an idea of the volume of illicit trade that was taking place in the Caribbean and the northern coast of South America at that time. Over a period of six years, 786 Dutch ships brought salt back to Europe from the Araya Peninsula in Venezuela, at an average of 120 ships per year. Furthermore, 20 Dutch 200-ton ships were sent annually from the Netherlands to Cuba and Española, netting 800,000 florins per year, a very large sum for that period. On the way back to the Netherlands, the majority of the ships stopped by Puerto Rico, Mona Island, Española, and the eastern part of Cuba, where they got water and bought hides and other products. The salt industry in Spain, having lost the Dutch as main buyers, went into decline.

Fighting Contraband: The Devastations

During the last twenty years of the sixteenth century, most people living in the Caribbean were involved in contraband. In Havana, the demand for beef jerky was always very high, and normally herds near the city supplied the fleets. Livestock owners in Havana therefore did not have to deal in smuggled goods, but on the rest of the island, the inhabitants of Bayamo, Santiago, Baracoa, Puerto Príncipe, and Trinidad made contraband their way of life.

As the illicit trade grew, the owners of herds in Española and Puerto Rico began to take their animals to regions where most of the smuggling took place. The transfer of cattle was a large enough phenomenon to cause a meat shortage in Santo Domingo in 1598 because the nearest herds had been moved many miles away. The inhabitants of Puerto Plata, Montecristi, Bayajá, La Yaguana, and Azua in the north, west, and south of Española likewise moved their livestock, as did people in San Germán and Añasco and other places on the west coast of Puerto Rico.

Contraband was practiced in accordance with very clear rules. When foreign ships arrived in bays used for trading, they shot two cannons to alert the people living inland who had already left their hides, cassia fistula, and ginger on ranches near the coast. When they heard the cannons, they would transport their products on packhorses to the shores before the waiting ships. Since everyone was involved, from the poorest *vaqueros* to the main authorities, there was no way to correct the situation. Every time the Real Audiencia of Santo Domingo or the governors of Cuba and Puerto Rico sent a judge or official to carry out the law, the smugglers would cover for each other.

Colonial officials during the last decade of the sixteenth century observed that commercial houses that exported legally to Seville from Santo Domingo, San Juan, and Havana suffered because the foreign smugglers paid higher prices than the Spanish merchants linked to the Sevillian monopoly. Several officials pointed out that by losing control of exports, the Spanish Crown was losing annual revenue of up to 200,000 ducats.

Officials also noted that trading with foreigners endangered the Catholic faith of the colonists because the English and Dutch smugglers were Protestants. They believed that regular contact between colonists and these "foreign heretics" was beginning to affect the colonists' loyalty to the Spanish Crown and that Spain risked losing these islands forever. In 1594 priests observed that the people living in the northern part of Española were forgetting their duties as Catholics and as Spanish subjects and were baptizing their children with foreign Protestant godparents and rites.

To investigate the situation, the archbishop of Santo Domingo sent a special envoy through the northern region of Española. Then he reported that his representative had confiscated some three hundred Bibles in annotated Romance language which contained scriptures "according to Luther and other heretics." The archbishop said that these Bibles had been imported by Dutch and English traders, and that the close connections between the traders and the colonists made it much more difficult to put an end to contraband.

By the end of the sixteenth century, the authorities began to consider specific measures against contraband. The archbishop of Santo Domingo thought that the best solution was to permit the inhabitants of the northwestern coastal areas of Española, Cuba, and Puerto Rico to trade directly with Seville. The archbishop's proposal was completely ignored, as were previous similar proposals made by some colonists from these three islands. The Consulado of Seville had used its political influence to persuade King Philip II to reject these proposals, and thus the situation remained unchanged. Another measure discussed in this period was to send an armada to clear the coast of smugglers and pirates. Because of Spain's numerous internal problems, this plan was not implemented, and the proposed armada never left Spanish waters.

More drastic measures were suggested to the Spanish Crown in several briefs written in 1598 and 1603 by a colonial official associated with Sevillian commercial interests. This official, Baltasar López de Castro, proposed the destruction of the villages of northern and western Española and the relocation of the villagers to the area around Santo Domingo. Lacking more effective proposals, King Philip III accepted this proposal without hesitation and ordered its immediate execution, thus drastically changing the course of history in the Caribbean.

Although it was not easy to depopulate the northern and western coasts of Española due to the resistance of the colonists, the plan was carried out as ordered during 1605 and 1606. With the assistance of 150 soldiers sent from the garrison of San Juan, Puerto Rico, the Spanish governor evicted all villagers from their homes, burned all houses and buildings, and forced the colonists to move by land or sea with their belongings, animals, and slaves to an extremely rainy and humid area near Santo Domingo.

The sugarcane plantations of Puerto Plata and La Yaguana were destroyed, and convents were closed and burned. The villages of Montecristi and Bayajá were also demolished, as were all the Spanish settlements in the southwest of Española, where ranchers had regularly traded with the Dutch. In La Yaguana, the entire population rebelled. Some people ran away to the mountains, and seventy were caught and hanged. Despite the resistance, the town was still destroyed. The majority of the colonists of La Yaguana sailed to Santiago de Cuba to escape relocation. Some took refuge on board the Dutch ships anchored in the Bay of Gonaïves.

With the few villagers left from La Yaguana and Bayajá, the Spanish authorities created a new village called Bayaguana. The colonists of Montecristi and Puerto Plata were likewise relocated to a new village called Monte Plata. Both villages were established in the very humid savannas and jungles north of Santo Domingo. The two settlements were quickly destroyed by fire, and the settlers lost all they had, since they were unable to bring with them the livestock and slaves they owned when they were forced to flee.

The destruction of these villages did reduce contraband in the north-ern and western coasts of Española. In western Cuba and Puerto Rico, however, smuggling continued, as the authorities decided not to execute similar measures there when they discovered that the depopulation of the coasts of Española had only served to give the Dutch access to the livestock of the region without middlemen. The devastation of the trad-ing villages in Española marks an important juncture in the history of the Caribbean because large areas of land, already domesticated, were left empty and immediately available to Spain's enemies. Eventually, these areas were populated by French, English, and Dutch adventurers and were finally separated from the Spanish Empire.

CHAPTER 4

The Early Tobacco Colonies

Dutch Incursions and War

The depopulation of western Española took place at a time when the international scene was favoring Spain's interests. In 1598 France had signed the Treaty of Vervins with Spain, which forbade French corsairs to operate in the Caribbean. In 1604 Spain and England had also signed the Treaty of London, which put a similar halt to the flow of English privateers to the Caribbean. Since the Spanish and Portuguese crowns had been united since 1580, the Portuguese had long abandoned their smuggling activities in the Caribbean and had concentrated their attention on their colonies in Africa and Asia, which were constantly threatened by the Dutch.

During the first years of the seventeenth century, the Netherlands was Spain's only enemy operating in the Caribbean. A large number of Dutch ships continued to look for salt in Venezuela and to do business with the Caribbean coastal villages. It was this massive Dutch penetration that had caused King Philip III of Spain to order the villages of northern and western Española to be depopulated. Realizing Spain's inability to face Dutch power, Philip III began in 1606 to seek a truce with the Netherlands. Finally, after lengthy negotiations, a truce was signed in April 1609, thus keeping the Dutch temporarily out of the Caribbean.

When Philip IV ascended to the Spanish throne in 1621, the truce ended, and Spain entered again into a war with the Netherlands. In the preceding twelve years of peace, the Dutch had greatly profited from the Portuguese colonies in Asia and Africa. During this renewed conflict, the Dutch continued their attacks against the Portuguese in Africa and the East Indies, as well as against the Spanish galleon fleets and ports in the Caribbean, and now threatened to extend their influence to Brazil, which played a strategic role in the maintenance of the Spanish/ Portuguese monopoly in the West Indies.

To fight the Spaniards in America, the wealthiest merchants in Amsterdam, Middelburg, Rotterdam, and Groningen invested eight million florins and formed the Dutch West India Company in 1621, a commercial, naval, and military enterprise organized according to the model of the East India Company, which operated in Asia and the Indian Ocean. The purpose of both companies was to promote Dutch trade and to attack Portuguese and Spanish possessions.

At the end of 1621 the Dutch West India Company sent a very strong squadron to the Atlantic. After a few attacks in the Caribbean, the squadron went to the city of Bahía, in Brazil, which the Dutch took in 1624 but had to relinquish the following year to a Spanish fleet. The Dutch also took San Juan, Puerto Rico, in September 1625, but since they could not capture the castle El Morro, they had to evacuate the city. Before doing so, however, they pillaged and burned the city, leaving it in ruins.

The intense war in the West Indies forced the Spanish to reinforce the cities and main ports of the Caribbean. The defense of San Juan from El Morro in 1625 demonstrated the usefulness of strong military fortifications. Money to finance new fortifications and the supply of troops to the forts of Havana, Santo Domingo, San Juan, Cartagena, and Portobelo was sent from the royal coffers in Mexico. In San Juan, the fortification program included the construction of the fort of San Cristóbal, which began in 1630, and the walls of San Juan. Both structures were later integrated into the system for the defense of El Morro. Other impressive forts and walls were built in Cartagena, San Juan de Ulúa, and Veracruz. Almost all these fortifications took nearly a century to complete.

With the exceptions of San Juan, and Bahía, the Dutch did not directly attack major cities. They generally targeted ships and fleets and some marginal possessions of the Spanish Empire. In the summer of 1628, the Dutch managed to capture, in its entirety, the fleet transporting almost all the silver mined during the prior year in Mexico and Guatemala as it sought refuge in the Bay of Matanzas in Cuba. The Dutch took the equivalent of some fifteen million florins, which ended up in the hands of the investors of the Dutch West India Company. As a result, Philip IV was left with virtually no money to finance the war against the Netherlands in Europe.

With that single blow, the company reaped enough profits to pay all shareholders 75 percent of their investment in 1628. As a result, Spain began to concentrate its efforts on protecting its galleons by building warships in new shipyards in Havana and having them sail along with the fleets to make attacks more difficult. The Dutch naval force, however, far surpassed that of Spain. Between 1621 and 1636 the Dutch West India Company sent 806 ships manned by 67,000 sailors and soldiers to the Caribbean. During those fifteen years, the Dutch were able to destroy 62 Spanish ships and capture 547 others, including their cargo. Thus, on average, three Spanish ships were either captured or destroyed every month during the first half of the Thirty Years War (1618–1648).

While the shareholders of the Dutch West India Company reaped the benefits of the Spanish silver seized in Matanzas, the company directors prepared a new war fleet intended to sail to Brazil to attack the sugar center of Pernambuco. In December 1629 the Dutch took Olinda and Recife, the main cities of that region, with little difficulty, and this time neither Spain nor Portugal was capable of ousting them as they had done in Bahía in 1625. From 1629 to 1654 the Dutch controlled Brazil's most productive sugar-producing lands and organized a new major trade route between Pernambuco and Amsterdam, with a stopover in Curaçao, a new Dutch possession in the Caribbean.

When the Dutch took over Curaçao in 1634, only sixty-two Spanish colonists lived on the island. Served by some 400 Indians, the colonists eked out a living by raising livestock. For the Dutch, however, the island was important for the natural salt pits located on the adjacent islands of Aruba and Bonaire, which they also occupied almost immediately. Before occupying Curaçao, the Dutch had occupied the island of Tobago in 1628, but could not hold it for long because of Indian attacks. In 1630 the Dutch took the island of St Martin in the Lesser Antilles, west of Puerto Rico, just when the French were establishing themselves near the island of St. Kitts. Saba and St. Eustatius, two neighboring islands that were also uninhabited, were taken by the Dutch in 1635.

On all these islands, the Dutch were primarily interested in salt.

Having lost control of the salt pits of Punta de Araya in Venezuela during the truce, the Dutch tried to occupy other points in the Caribbean with natural salt pits. This explains why they selected such isolated islands, where even drinking water was scarce. Eventually, some Dutch colonists who started cultivating tobacco converted these islands into trading posts to sell European merchandise and African slaves in the Antilles. Many Dutch Sephardic Jews participated in these ventures.

In the meantime, during the Thirty Years War the Dutch systematically attacked all Spanish ships sighted in Caribbean waters, particularly the fleets carrying silver sailing from Cartagena, Portobelo, and Veracruz toward Havana. Sometimes the Spanish succeeded in defending themselves, as was the case in 1643 when a silver fleet from Cartagena was saved by the bravery of its commander, Don Carlos Ibarra, who engaged the Dutch attackers in battle. The smaller Spanish flotillas and individual ships were more vulnerable than the fleets, but many managed to dodge the Dutch privateers in the Caribbean and the Atlantic. Nonetheless, many Spanish ships were destroyed, and the attacks had a marked impact on the Spanish commercial economy.

Tobacco and the English

During the Thirty Years War, France and England also began to take on active roles in the New World. The long truce created by the peace treaties signed in 1598 and 1604 kept French and English privateers away from the Caribbean, but people who returned to Europe at the end of the sixteenth century stimulated the European imagination with tales about vast lands where tobacco could be cultivated utilizing Indian labor and where those persecuted for their religious or political beliefs could find refuge.

Some adventurers, such as Charles Leigh, Robert Harcourt, Walter Raleigh, and Roger North, made unsuccessful individual attempts to establish colonies of immigrants in the Guianas and the Amazon in the years 1604, 1609, 1617, and 1620, respectively.[1] These English adventurers had gone in search of appropriate ecological niches for the cultivation of tobacco, the use of which was spreading rapidly in Europe.

When it was first discovered, tobacco had been considered a botanical curiosity or a satanic drug associated with Indian rites. Later, black slaves who worked on the early Caribbean plantations learned to smoke it and used it extensively. Runaway slaves and rebel Indians did the same, and for this reason the Spanish authorities deplored its use for many years. Nevertheless, tobacco gained popularity among sailors who used it to treat phlegm and colds and to fight off dampness and chills. Mixed with spurge and pepper to produce purifying sneezes, tobacco entered the European pharmacopoeia, and pharmacists were authorized to purchase it and use it in medicine. This was the only license granted to use tobacco legally, for in November 1586 the Spanish Crown prohibited the cultivation and sale of tobacco to deter contraband.

Despite this prohibition, sailors and traders gradually spread tobacco in the form of snuff throughout the port taverns of Europe. By 1600 tobacco was one of the most coveted products sought by Dutch smugglers roaming the Caribbean. The poorest colonists who could not afford to produce sugar or hides quickly discovered tobacco as a convenient crop, which a single family could harvest on its own after a short planting cycle. In addition, tobacco leaves served as a primitive paper currency that permitted colonists to buy smuggled European merchandise.

Since tobacco was the preferred means of exchange for smugglers, in August 1606 Philip III prohibited its cultivation for a period of ten years in Puerto Rico, Española, Cuba, Margarita, Cumaná, Venezuela, and New Andalucía. At that time Venezuela had become the number one producer of tobacco and was also the main supplier to the Dutch. That year, the Venezuelan region of Barinas produced some 35,000 pounds of the highest quality tobacco available. There were ninety-five colonists in Española who produced tobacco in 1606, but the Dutch preferred the leaves grown in Barinas. Since Española's tobacco was not in great demand, the colonists of this island utilized much of it to appease their slaves on the plantations. The surplus was exported to Spain for medicinal use. In Cuba and in Puerto Rico, tobacco was also cultivated for export in 1607 despite its prohibition.

Contraband of tobacco grew in spite of the controls, and the colonists secretly continued to cultivate it illegally. Realizing the enormous loss of tax revenue incurred by contraband, Philip III changed the Crown's policy and in 1614 ordered that all tobacco not consumed in Venezuela and the Caribbean be exported under official supervision directly to Seville.

The political truce in Europe made it possible for the Spanish Crown to attempt to control the tobacco market. Thus in 1620 Philip III dictated new regulations in an effort to create a Spanish tobacco monopoly. Spain's objective was to become the intermediary for all the Caribbean and Venezuelan tobacco en route to England. In 1616 this was estimated at more than 50,000 pounds.

During the first twenty-five years of the seventeenth century, the consumption of tobacco increased considerably in Europe. The Dutch and the English spread the use of pipes, as the habit of smoking quickly became more popular than snuff. The economic success of Virginia in North America, based on tobacco cultivation since 1613, quickly attracted thousands of English immigrants there. To profit from this trade, the English Crown imposed a monopoly on tobacco in 1625 while prohibiting the cultivation of this plant in England. Tobacco was allowed to be produced only in the English colonies, provided that the product would be sold exclusively in England, and could not be imported from other countries.

In the early 1600s England went through several economic crises, caused by the incapacity of its textile industry to assimilate the excess manual labor generated by population growth and by a series of cereal crop failures that resulted in high prices, unemployment, and starvation. In the south of England, the economic difficulties exacerbated the already tense climate of religious intolerance, which caused thousands of Puritans to emigrate to Scotland, Ireland, and North America. Approximately 60,000 English people crossed the Atlantic between 1605 and 1640 in search of liberty and fortune. The majority established themselves in North America, but several thousand went to the Caribbean.

Some of the first English colonists arriving in the Caribbean came from failed settlements in Guianas and the Amazon. Others arrived as deserters of English war fleets operating in the Caribbean at the beginning of the Thirty Years War or as adventurers attracted by the prospect of cultivating tobacco on uninhabited islands. Almost all had a clear idea that their future was linked to tobacco cultivation, and for this reason the first settlements were organized as tobacco-growing colonies. Tobacco had the advantage of not requiring a large capital investment, as was the case with sugar, and it had a high value relative to its volume and weight. Also, since the crop could be harvested shortly after planting, merchants were willing to help colonists finance their plantations in order to secure a continuous supply of tobacco.

The first colonies the English attempted to establish in the Lesser Antilles failed. Carib Indians killed the colonists after they landed on St. Lucia in 1605 and on Grenada in 1609. Later, the English were luckier. In 1622 a group of survivors of Roger North's 1619 expedition to the Amazon landed on the island of St. Kitts. This group, led by Thomas Warner, was searching for a quiet island far from the Caribbean trade routes commonly used by the Spanish. They decided to settle on St. Kitts, which they found suitable for growing tobacco due to its fertile land, its abundant drinking water, and a native population that was less hostile than on other islands. The following year Warner traveled to England with samples of tobacco harvested on the island and managed to win the support of various businessmen, who gave him cash advances in exchange for future harvests.

Warner returned to St. Kitts at the beginning of 1624, and in March of the following year again sailed to England with 9,500 pounds of tobacco in a ship sent from London for this purpose. This shipment was sold at a great profit, and Warner was able to recruit around 400 workers in London who in 1626 traveled with him to St. Kitts. As the first permanent English settlement in the Caribbean, this island was to become the center of operations for several London firms interested in the tobacco business.

The First French Settlements

Meanwhile, during the fall of 1625 a damaged ship arrived in St. Kitts carrying French privateers who had been attacked by the Spanish near Jamaica. The English welcomed them with open arms, as they needed more hands to help start up the new tobacco plantations and to help protect them from the Indians who were showing increased hostility toward the Europeans. With the help of the new arrivals, the English massacred the native population of St. Kitts. The two European groups then agreed to share the island and drew two divisional lines to mark the English and French jurisdictions. The English retained the central part, which had the most fertile lands, while the French, under the command of their leader, Pierre Belain d'Esnambuc, occupied the land on each end of the island. In both the English and the French zones, the main activity of the colonists was tobacco cultivation.

This agreement remained in effect until 1629, when the Spanish admiral Fradique de Toledo, commander of the Barlovento Armada that escorted the silver fleet from Cartagena, received orders to dislodge the French and English from St. Kitts. This was not a difficult mission because disagreements between the English and the French had weakened the defense of the island. After a violent attack launched by the Spanish, the French and the English capitulated, saving their lives by agreeing to abandon the island while the Spanish burned their tobacco fields.

Many of the French and English went to St. Martin, where they were welcomed by the Dutch; others went to Tortuga, a small island off the coast of Española, which had been abandoned since the devastations of 1606 and where there was a large population of feral livestock. Conditions were so favorable in Tortuga that many never returned to St. Kitts, having found in Tortuga a safe haven where they could cultivate tobacco. Furthermore, the colonists could obtain hides by merely crossing the strait between Tortuga and Española to hunt wild cattle on the latter island.

The French and English who decided to stay on Tortuga were approached by representatives of the Dutch West India Company, who offered to supply them with European merchandise in exchange for hides and tobacco. Thus began a period of prosperity for a community of more than 300 livestock hunters and tobacco planters, whose success later attracted people from the other islands to Tortuga and the north coast of Española.

The rapid growth of this settlement alarmed the Spanish authorities of Santo Domingo and prompted them to launch a surprise attack on Tortuga in 1635 to expel the settlers. The Spanish killed 195 people and took thirty-nine prisoners. Among the prisoners were three women and twelve black slaves. The booty taken by the Spanish troops included six English cannons, which had been supplied by the Providence Company in 1631 in exchange for an annual 5 percent share of the tobacco and hides produced on the island. When the Spanish troops left after the attack, those adventurers who managed to escape by hiding in Española returned to Tortuga and resumed their activities.

In 1636 there were eighty English and 150 black slaves working on Tortuga and the north coast of Española. Their numbers continued to increase until 1638, when the Spanish admiral Don Carlos Ibarra received orders to evict the English and their slaves and to execute anyone who fell into his hands. During this second attack, only those who crossed the strait to the northern coast of Española managed to save themselves. When the danger had passed, the few survivors returned to Tortuga. There they were reinforced the following year by some 300 adventurers from other islands led by an Englishman named Roger Flood.

Flood managed to impose his leadership on everyone, both English and French, and tried without success to create a tobacco monopoly to compete with the Compagnie des Isles des Ameriques founded in France by Cardinal Richelieu in 1635, modeled after the Dutch West India Company. Flood had previously been a Providence Company official, and his effort to control tobacco trade in Tortuga later had serious consequences. The Compagnie des Isles des Ameriques had a contractual agreement with the French colonists of Tortuga and was encouraging French peasants to immigrate to the Caribbean to produce tobacco.

The French coveted two other islands, Guadeloupe and Martinique, both of which the English had avoided for fear of the Carib Indians, who attacked anyone who dared to enter their territories. These islands were the largest and most fertile of the Lesser Antilles. The first French colonists who attempted to colonize Guadeloupe in 1635 under the direction of the Compagnie des Isles des Ameriques found themselves at war with the Indians for more than five years, thus deterring rapid colonization of the island. By the end of 1640, however, the colonists of Guadeloupe managed to expel all the Carib Indians from the island, and as new immigrants arrived, tobacco and cotton production expanded.

The French also occupied Martinique in 1635 under the command of Belain d'Esnambuc, a Norman adventurer with a long history of conquest in the Caribbean who had participated in the initial colonization of St. Kitts. D'Esnambuc became a serious competitor for the new Compagnie des Isles des Ameriques and used every means possible to maintain absolute personal control of Martinique. His objective was to rule the island as his own private tobacco colony, managed locally by his representatives. D'Esnambuc and his nephew, Jacques Dyel du Parquet, stayed in power in Martinique until 1658, recruiting workers from the impoverished masses in France, just as the English had done on other islands.

The Compagnie des Isles des Ameriques repopulated the island of St. Kitts in 1639 and established its center of operations there. The company was overseen by the governor-general of the French Antilles, Phillipe de Lonvilliers de Poincy, who was based in Martinique. Poincy tried to impose his control on all territories with French inhabitants and even forced the Dutch to accept the division of the islands of St. Martin and St. Eustatius in 1648. In Tortuga, Poincy's lust for power in the Antilles led him to demote the English commander Roger Flood in August 1640. Under the pretext that Flood had abused some of his men and captured a ship sent from St. Kitts to look for provisions, Poincy sent a former privateer named Jean Levasseur and forty-nine other men to storm Tortuga and depose Flood.

For more than two years Levasseur maintained absolute control of Tortuga. He was even able to repel a Spanish attack in 1643, having built a fort that turned Tortuga into an unassailable fortress. As the north coast of Tortuga consisted of cliffs and reefs, enemies could approach the island only via the narrow southern channel, which was now dominated by the new fort. While Tortuga was under his control, Levasseur officially worked for the Compagnie des Isles des Ameriques, but in practice he acted as if he owned the island. According to Alexander Olivier de Exquemelin, a Dutchman living in Tortuga at the time, the island, like the northern coast of Española, experienced an increase in population because it came to be known as a safe haven whose inhabitants could defend themselves. People from the neighboring islands went there in droves. Pirates saw the island as an ideal base from which to operate, and Levasseur aided them in their endeavors.

Filibusters and Buccaneers

Two large groups of settlers could be easily distinguished. The freebooters, or "filibusters," who arrived in Tortuga were adventurers of many nationalities who engaged in piracy under the supreme command of Levasseur. They used Tortuga and its superior fortifications as a refuge, setting sail in search of booty from Spanish ships and settlements in the Caribbean and Central America. Their life was the sea, and their safe haven was Tortuga. The "buccaneers," on the other hand, lived on "*la tierra grande*" (Española), where they hunted cattle, which roamed by the thousands on the island's vast and uninhabited savannas. They ate smoked meat seasoned with orange and lemon juice and prepared on grills called *boucans*, from which they got the name buccaneers.

In Española, the buccaneers typically hunted in pairs, accompanied by packs of domesticated dogs that would find the feral livestock. After each hunting expedition, which lasted several months, the buccaneers crossed the strait separating Española from Tortuga, and on the latter island they sold their hides. After buying foodstuffs, clothes, gunpowder, and munitions, they would go to the taverns and spend all the money they had left on rum and food. Then they would return to Española to hunt again for six months to a year. Buccaneers also supplied meat and lard to settlers involved in the cultivation of tobacco.

Levasseur levied a tax in the name of the Compagnie des Isles des Ameriques on all commercial operations on Tortuga. He took part of that revenue for himself, thus offending some adventurers. In 1652, just as Poincy was preparing to fire him, Levasseur was killed by irate taxpayers.

In the following years, Tortuga continued to flourish as the main center of piracy in the Caribbean under Levasseur's successor, Timoleón Hotman de Fontenay, who was much more tolerant, eliminated torture, and allowed the practice of Catholicism by freebooters and buccaneers, which Levasseur, a fanatic Calvinist, had forbidden. Levasseur had even burned a small shrine built by Catholic adventurers and expelled a priest who had attempted to establish himself in Tortuga.

Spanish navigation in the Caribbean was almost completely paralyzed during the last decade of the Thirty Years War, due to attacks by the Dutch and Tortuga's freebooters. Spanish ships traveling unprotected found it extremely difficult to reach their destinations. Even after the Netherlands signed a peace treaty with Spain in 1648, pirates from Tortuga continued to attack the Spanish in the Caribbean. Spain, weakened by the Thirty Years War, lost its ability to ward off naval attacks.

The Spanish colonies, protected by their walls and fortifications, resorted to self-defense. Trade between Seville and the Spanish Main became increasingly expensive and inefficient because it could only be done using the costly system of galleon fleets. By the mid-seventeenth century, it was evident that Spain could no longer defend its monopoly in the Caribbean.

Cromwell's Western Design

Recognizing Spain's weakness, some people in England thought that if an adequate war plan were organized, it might be possible to expel the Spanish completely from the Caribbean. One of the first persons to draw attention to that possibility was Thomas Gage, a former Dominican priest who had become an Anglican. After traveling extensively throughout Central America in 1648, Gage published a book entitled *A New Survey of the West Indies*. In it, he described the advantages that the English could derive from going to war with Spain in order to take away its American possessions. A year earlier, a group of London merchants had come up with a similar plan of conquest, but such plans were abandoned with the signing of the Peace of Westphalia in 1648. Furthermore, the political instability resulting from the overthrow of the English monarchy and the decapitation of King Charles I did not bode well for such large ventures.

When Oliver Cromwell came to power, the idea of conquering the Spanish colonies as recommended by Gage and others found fertile ground. Cromwell, needing money and wanting to assure his power, supported such ideas and resolved to put them into action.

Until then, the English possessions in the Caribbean had consisted only of Barbados, settled in 1627; Providence, a small island near the coast of Honduras, settled in 1629; and Nevis, Montserrat, and Antigua, small islands off St. Kitts, which were settled in 1632. During their early colonization, the main crop on all these islands was tobacco. Some colonists also planted cotton, ginger, and indigo, all annual crops, which permitted quick harvesting and a fast return on money invested.

The first step of Cromwell's "Western Design" was to attack the weakest of the fortified cities in the Spanish Caribbean, namely Santo

Domingo, then to proceed from there to the other strongholds in the Caribbean and eventually to the continent. In the mid-seventeenth century, Santo Domingo was an impoverished town with its sugar industry in ruins. The majority of its population had emigrated, its slave population had disappeared, and it was minimally defended by a garrison of 700 soldiers and an ill-paid and impoverished local militia.

At the beginning of 1655, the English sent an imposing fleet to attack Santo Domingo, made up of thirty-four war ships with 7,000 sailors and 6,000 soldiers, reinforced by almost 3,000 men recruited during a stopover in Barbados in February of that year.

Although England had not declared war on Spain, colonial authorities took the warning of an attack very seriously. Having received reports from the Spanish ambassador to London that a fleet would soon set sail against Santo Domingo, Spanish authorities spent the year prior to the attack reinforcing the defenses of the city, and to this end they recruited all able-bodied men capable of bearing arms.

The fleet landed fifty miles away from Santo Domingo in April 1655, and immediately the English troops marched to the city. Oblivious to the fact that they were being surrounded by Spanish militia, they were surprised by a violent attack by more than 1,300 lancers, who spread panic among the English soldiers and mercenary troops recruited in Barbados. The operation ended in chaos, and the English commanders found themselves forced to order their men back onto the ships and to abandon their plans for conquest.

To console themselves after this defeat, the English attacked the semi-deserted island of Jamaica, where some 1,500 Spanish farmers and cattle ranchers lived scattered in the woods and savannas. In May 1655 Jamaica was taken without difficulty, although a handful of Spaniards remained in the forests with their slaves and fought a guerrilla war against the English for the following five years, aided by the colonial governments of Cuba and Puerto Rico.

One of the immediate consequences of the English occupation of Jamaica was the extermination of approximately 20,000 head of cattle owned by the Spanish colonists. The English killed all the animals, without sparing younger animals for reproduction, and exported the hides. Jamaica was the only prize England obtained from Cromwell's "Western Design." Meanwhile, Cuba, eastern Española, and Puerto Rico remained unharmed, protected by their walls, garrisons, and forts.

The Dutch Expulsion from Brazil

The English occupation of Jamaica occurred at almost the same time as the expulsion of the Dutch from Pernambuco, Brazil, in 1654 after a protracted war with the Portuguese. Far from weakening the Dutch colonies in the Antilles, this defeat served to reinforce the Dutch colonies of Curaçao, St. Martin, St. Eustatius, and Saba, because many Dutch who left Pernambuco relocated to the Caribbean, where they continued their businesses, becoming the great suppliers of European merchandise and slaves for the other European colonies in the Caribbean.

Pirates and immigrants from the Netherlands, France, and England helped change the political and economic map of the Caribbean during the first half of the seventeenth century. From the second half of that century on, Spain would no longer reign alone in the Caribbean, as other European powers gained new possessions in the Lesser Antilles.

As these new possessions were all small islands, it was not possible to raise livestock on the scale seen in Cuba, Española, and Puerto Rico. The economies of the French, English, and Dutch islands therefore came to rely on agriculture and trade. Not all tropical products, however, were in equal demand in Europe. Only the tobacco market assured the economic stability of the first European settlements in the Lesser Antilles. For this reason, the occupation of the smaller Caribbean islands by Spain's enemies went hand in hand with the cultivation of tobacco.

Barbados illustrates this process well. Barbados had been explored in 1625 by Captain John Powell, an English smuggler who operated off the coast of Venezuela on behalf of a English company with Dutch connections. When the owners of the company heard about Thomas Warner's excellent profits from the first tobacco harvest in St. Kitts in 1626, they quickly began to recruit potential tobacco farmers to Barbados. The first two shiploads of 170 colonists arrived on Barbados in February and May 1627. By 1639 the population had grown to 8,707 people over the age of fourteen, all of whom earned their living by growing tobacco and cotton. The latter was beginning to replace tobacco in some areas in the wake of a sudden rise in demand for cotton in England.

Barbados enjoyed an enviable tranquility during the Thirty Years War. Being the easternmost island in the Caribbean, Barbados was situated far from Spanish navigation routes and the traditional Carib Indian war zones. Its geographic position just windward of the Lesser Antilles also made Barbados the first port of arrival for English ships sailing to the Caribbean and a preferred stopover port for Dutch ships traveling between Brazil and the Caribbean. For these reasons, Barbados soon became the most populated of the English colonies, as it drew large numbers of colonists and workers due to the great demand for manual laborers.

The first immigrants divided the entire island among themselves, and, as they had no slaves, they soon found themselves obligated to hire workers from the poor and unemployed masses in England and Ireland. The most sought-after individuals were those willing to go the Caribbean as indentured servants. They were required to work for three to five years, in exchange for their passage, lodging, clothes, food, and a parcel of land at the end of their contract. This pattern of contracting white servant laborers to work in the tobacco and cotton fields became the norm in the English and French Antilles during the first half of the seventeenth century.

Initially, the landowners used African slaves and Indians from the islands and the Guianas in addition to white indentured laborers. The Indians, however, proved to be difficult to control and soon were no longer used as agricultural workers. The demand for manual labor became much greater after 1640, when, due to falling tobacco prices in Europe caused by competition from the North American colonies of Maryland and Virginia, English planters in Barbados began to experiment with sugarcane as an alternative crop.

By 1643 it was clear that the future of the colony was in sugar production. Contacts were made with Dutch merchants who had connections in Pernambuco. These merchants offered financial support, technical advice, shipping, and African slaves in exchange for a portion of the sugar produced in Barbados.

In this period the island received many workers recruited either voluntarily or by force from among the poorest strata of the population of England and Ireland. In 1648 Barbados also took in several thousand people loyal to the English monarchy who had gone into exile after the revolution that established the British Commonwealth and culminated in the beheading of King Charles I.

When Cromwell sent his fleet to conquer Santo Domingo in 1655, Barbados was at the center of a sugar revolution. At that time, Barbados was taking many Dutch planters and middlemen expelled from Brazil. The Dutch transformed the agriculture of the island by encouraging and assisting in the production of sugar. During this period, the English also began to import black slaves in large numbers to work on the sugar plantations. In 1655 the population of Barbados, the most densely populated area in the New World, consisted of 23,000 Europeans and close to 20,000 slaves.

CHAPTER 5

The Sugar Revolution in the Lesser Antilles

The Dutch and the Sugar Trade

When the English cane farmers of Barbados began to produce sugar in the mid-seventeenth century, the sugar industry in the Spanish Antilles had long ceased to be important. Pirate attacks and competition from Brazilian sugar left the Española and Puerto Rico producers unable to survive in the international market. These islands' sugar production was gradually reduced to meet only local demand. The development of the Brazilian sugar industry had another lasting impact on the Caribbean, as it was directly connected to the first sugar revolution in the English and French West Indies.

The long war between the Netherlands and the Spanish-Portuguese alliance did not critically affect the distribution of Portuguese sugar in the Dutch market. Between 1580 and 1640, when Spain and Portugal were united under one crown, sugar flowed without major interruptions from the Bay of Pernambuco, in Brazil, to northern Europe via Antwerp and Amsterdam. In Antwerp, dozens of firms legally distributed Brazilian sugar at fairs in France, England, Denmark, Poland, Sweden, Italy, Austria, Germany, Monrovia, and beyond the Baltic Sea as far as Russia.[1]

The truce signed by France and the Netherlands in 1609 normalized Dutch trade with other Spanish and Portuguese possessions. This peace contributed to a rise in investment in the Brazilian sugar industry, especially after May 1614, when the Spanish/Portuguese Crown officially granted new financial incentives, over a ten-year period, to those who wanted to enter the sugar business in Brazil. As a result of this policy,

116 new sugar plantations were established in the three main Brazilian sugar production centers between 1609 and 1629.[2]

These Brazilian mills were built following a new model imported from Peru by a Spanish priest who showed plantation owners that grinding sugarcane was more efficient and that more sugarcane juice was extracted when the cylinders of the sugar mills were vertical rather than horizontal and when a third cylinder was added. This new three-cylinder wooden sugar mill quickly became the model machine for grinding sugarcane throughout Brazil.

As Brazilian production increased, so did the demand for ships to transport the sugar to Europe. The regions of Pernambuco, Itamaraca, and Paraiba alone required between 130 and 140 ships per year to export their sugar. Due to their long-standing relations with Brazilian sugar producers, the Dutch transported almost two-thirds of the Brazilian sugar in 1621. It is therefore not surprising that Brazil became a major target for the Dutch, when the truce between Spain and the Netherlands ended in 1621.

In 1624 the Dutch West India Company sent its ships to attack the city of Bahía, but the assault ended in failure. Later, in 1629, the Dutch successfully attacked and occupied Olinda and Recife, the two main cities of Pernambuco. In 1635 the Dutch managed to expel the Portuguese from the sugarcane fields and reinforced their military positions there. Once the Dutch were firmly established in northern Brazil, sugar production entered a new phase of growth as new firms and immigrants from the Netherlands settled there attracted by the profits of the sugar business. Dutch Brazil was now called New Holland.

Many of these new immigrants and investors were Calvinists, Sephardic Jews, and "New Christians," that is, forced converts from Judaism.[3] The Dutch took advantage of the situation by buying up sugar mills and plantations from planters eager to emigrate to Portuguese Brazil. At first, these new plantation owners did not know how to make sugar, but they were given special support by the new governor, John Maurits, Count of Nassau. In 1637 he made a concerted effort to attract Portuguese planters from other parts of Brazil who were familiar with the technology of sugar production, some of whom had emigrated to Portuguese Brazil during the war. As a result, production began to recuperate, and by 1645 Pernambuco sugar production had returned to the levels that existed prior to the Dutch occupation.

The success of the sugar industry in New Holland was also due to other factors. Dutch merchants were provided with a new investment opportunity when the Dutch West India Company attacked and took over Portuguese possessions in West Africa. The slave market in Elmina and Guinea then became open to all venture capitalists who wished to invest. Furthermore, the Count of Nassau was able to convince the Dutch West India Company to permit the free trade of all sugar produced in Dutch Brazil. Both the increase in supply of manual labor and the increase in demand for sugar led to higher sugar production. Since the sugar plantations of Portuguese Brazil were not affected by the war, their owners also increased production to compensate for the loss of Pernambuco. The result was even more Brazilian sugar destined for the European market.

Although many plantations in New Holland changed ownership during Maurits's seven-year term in office, his stable government allowed the planters to buy slaves directly from the Dutch West India Company. These middlemen resold their slaves on credit to plantation owners who were willing to pay high interest rates to ensure a steady supply of manual labor. As a result of these profitable financial deals many Dutch investors who had begun as mere financiers and transporters of Brazilian sugar were then able to buy their own plantations, thus acquiring firsthand knowledge of every aspect of sugar production.

The Dutch occupation of Brazil did not go uncontested. In 1645 the Portuguese colonists and Brazilian Creoles of Bahía and Pernambuco initiated a long guerrilla war against the occupiers. This war was waged in spite of opposition from João IV, the new king of Portugal who came to power when Portugal separated from Spain in 1640. During the Thirty Years War, Portugal had suffered great losses in Asia, Africa, and America to the Dutch West India Company, and João IV did not want to continue fighting the Dutch in Brazil.

Nonetheless, the Brazilian sugarcane farmers went to war. In 1649 a Dutch attack on Bahía destroyed twenty-three plantations, and the Dutch made off with more than 500 tons of sugar.[4] To retaliate, the rebellious Brazilian guerrillas burned the Dutch plantations and mills to the ground and continued the war, despite continued demands for peace by King João IV. In 1652, when Holland went to war with England, the

Dutch position in Brazil began to deteriorate, and the situation changed in favor of Portugal. Finally, in January 1654 the Dutch capitulated and left Pernambuco in the hands of the Portuguese, after having occupied it for a quarter century.

When they lost their grip on Pernambuco, the Dutch Jews dispersed all over the world. Very few opted to stay in Brazil. Some returned to Holland; others went to France or New Amsterdam, on the island of Manhattan in North America. Many established themselves in the Lesser Antilles, particularly on Curaçao, Martinique, Guadeloupe, St. Martin, St. Eustatius, Saba, and Barbados. On several of these islands, the Dutch provided capital, experience, and business connections to help develop a new sugar industry. The case of Barbados is illustrative.

Sugar Beginnings in the Lesser Antilles

Long before they left Pernambuco in 1654, the Dutch had maintained commercial and financial relations with the English cane farmers of Barbados. The first sugarcane planted on Barbados was imported from Brazil by a Dutchman named Peeter Brower in 1636. Later, in 1644, two Dutchmen, James Drax and James Holdip, aided an Englishman who wanted to produce sugar and who had contracted white indentured workers, but these first efforts to produce sugar in Barbados were not very successful. The English knew little about growing sugarcane. They did not know when to cut it, how to extract the sugar, or how to build sugar mills.

This situation began to change between 1647 and 1650, when several English sugarcane farmers from Barbados traveled to Pernambuco to learn the art of making sugar. With help from some Dutchmen visiting Barbados during that time, the English colonists began to perfect their sugar mills and techniques, and by 1650 they were beginning to produce sugar for export. The quality of this sugar was still inferior to Brazilian sugar, but it had enough potential to persuade some Dutch merchants to offer loans for the construction of new sugar mills and the purchase of slaves.

This story was to repeat itself later in Martinique and Guadeloupe. On these islands, the first efforts to produce sugar were beset with difficulties. In 1639 the French-owned Compagnie des Isles des Ameriques signed a contract with a Dutchman named Daniel Tretzel for the construction of a sugar mill in Martinique and two others in Guadeloupe. The contract stipulated that he invest his own capital and provide the necessary laborers. In exchange, he was to receive 3,000 acres of land and a monopoly on sugar production on the French islands for a period of six years. Due to insufficient manpower, however, Tretzel could not hold up his part of the contract, despite subsequently receiving an exemption from export taxes on the sugar that he produced over the next fifteen years. In 1643 he had not finished building his mill.

In light of Tretzel's failure, the governor of Guadeloupe, Charles Hoüel, decided to help with the construction of a sugar mill for the Compagnie des Isles des Ameriques in exchange for 10 percent of the profits. In 1644 Hoüel, along with Daniel Tretzel's son, began to plant sugarcane, and finally, in 1647, one sugar mill was functioning in Guadeloupe. From that point on, other colonists tried their hand as well. Because of Hoüel's efforts to monopolize the local sugar industry and to compel them to supply their cane to his mill exclusively, these colonists met with little success, and only ten sugar mills functioned in Guadeloupe in 1656. As a result, the sugar industry on the French islands lagged behind that of Barbados.

In 1654 more than 600 Dutch and Flemish refugees arrived in Guadeloupe after having been expelled from Brazil by the Portuguese who accused them of being heretics and Jews. They brought with them 300 Brazilians, both freemen and slaves. Governor Hoüel received them in Guadeloupe and offered them land, draft animals, and carts to facilitate the construction of their own sugar mills. In exchange, Hoüel demanded not only that they pay one-fifth of their sugar, but also that they share their knowledge of sugar production technology.

The governor of Martinique, Phillipe de Lonvilliers de Poincy, offered similar incentives to Jewish and Dutch immigrants. One of them, Benjamin da Costa, established himself in Martinique and built the island's first sugar mill. Others soon followed. By 1671 Martinique already had twelve mills producing sugar, although the sugar produced was inferior to that of Brazil. Encouraged by the collaboration of the Jews and New Christian converts, in May 1671 King Charles IX of France decreed that all Jews and New Christians who cultivated sugarcane and produced sugar in the French Antilles would from then on enjoy the same rights and privileges as Catholics.

In this manner, the Dutch and Jews who had been expelled from Brazil came to play a critical role in the development of the sugar industry on the French islands. No other nation's traders enjoyed the economic advantages of the Dutch: Dutch ships transported goods at a lower cost than English and French ships; their merchants, shipbuilders, and captains had more capital than their English and French counterparts; and they could offer longer-term loans with lower interest rates than their European competitors. Familiar with the sugar business, the Dutch were willing to take more risks than the French and English, especially when it came to supplying slaves. Their astute management of capital and transportation networks, as well as their dominant position in the slave trade, allowed them to play an important role in the transformation of the Lesser Antilles from a tobacco economy to a sugar economy.

Jamaica, occupied by the English in 1655, also received an influx of capital and training from the Dutch and Jewish refugees from Brazil. When they arrived in Jamaica, many of these immigrants requested citizenship, which was immediately granted by authorities eager to populate the island and promote sugar production. The early governors of Jamaica believed that Dutch refugees would be loyal to the English Crown, in view of their pronounced aversion to the French and Spanish. As sugarcane planters, merchants and financiers, and slave dealers, the Dutch and Jewish settlers helped the English improve the sugar industry in Jamaica, which by 1675 had increased to about seventy plantations.

Despite their importance to the sugar industry, the Dutch and Jewish refugees were never very numerous on the French and English islands, and in later years they were expelled from them entirely. Without them, however, the rapid transition (1650–1670) to a sugar-based economy would not have occurred in the Lesser Antilles. The Dutch were also responsible for the establishment of the first sugar colonies in Surinam (Dutch Guiana). After 1644 many Jewish and Dutch planters had moved with their slaves from Brazil to Surinam, where they founded sugar plantations. In 1658 new contingents of Dutch refugees arrived from Brazil, and although the English and French later attacked the set-

tlements of Essequibo and Cayena, from then on the planters of Dutch
Guiana also produced sugar for the European market.

White Indentured Workers and Black Slaves

When tobacco was the foundation of the economy of the Lesser
Antilles, land was usually cultivated by white indentured laborers, generally contracted to serve a master from three to five years in exchange
for clothes, lodging, and food, as well as a plot of land and 300 pounds
of tobacco at the conclusion of the contract. Under this system, the
English and French succeeded in recruiting thousands of workers to
populate the early tobacco colonies and clear forests to make way for
the first plantations.

As sugarcane overtook tobacco as the leading export of the Lesser
Antilles, African slaves began to replace white workers, but the latter did
not disappear entirely from the plantations. In 1680, for example, plantation owners in Barbados still employed 2,317 white indentured servants, compared to 38,782 black slaves. In similar fashion, white
European laborers were replaced with enslaved Africans on the French
islands. However, the use of European indentured labor in the Lesser
Antilles did not disappear until well into the eighteenth century.

During the transition from tobacco to sugar, a good deal of land
changed hands. The land that had initially been divided among the early
tobacco farmers had to be continually parceled out among the white
workers upon completion of their contracts, thus decreasing the size of
the lots and increasing the number of landowners. In Barbados, for
example, in 1635, 85,000 acres of arable land was divided among 764
landowners; by 1680 the number of landowners had reached 3,044,
although a group of 175 planters was responsible for the bulk of sugar
production in that year. Many of those who began as landowners managed how to hold on to their property, but others lost their land, sold it,
or subdivided it among their heirs and indentured laborers.

The other islands of the Lesser Antilles -Nevis, Monserrat, Antigua,
and St. Kitts- followed the same pattern as Barbados. They began to
produce sugar after 1655 with the aid and financing of the Dutch,
although on St. Kitts, the Dutch had helped produce sugar several years

earlier. In the beginning, the planters of these islands, known as the Leeward Islands, used white indentured servants to cultivate sugarcane and produce sugar, but shortly thereafter African slave labor became more prevalent. In Nevis, for example, around 500 white laborers worked together with 3,849 black slaves in 1678.

The main difference between Barbados and the Leeward Islands at that time was the speed with which African slave labor was adopted. As the Leeward Islands were smaller, drier, and poorer than Barbados, their cane farmers found it more difficult to afford slaves. For this reason, in 1678 the white population was still larger than the black population (10,408 whites to 8,449 blacks). Nevertheless, the rapid development of the sugar industry during the last quarter of the seventeenth century transformed the demographic profile of the Leeward Islands to such a degree that thirty years later, blacks were three times as numerous as whites. In 1708 the Leeward Islands had a population of 23,500 blacks as compared to 7,311 whites.

Jamaica likewise followed the same demographic evolution. By 1673 the enslaved black population surpassed the white population, with 9,504 black slaves to 7,768 whites. Half a century later, in 1722, the slave population of Jamaica was over 80,000, while the white population remained nearly unchanged at around 7,100. In an effort to remedy this racial imbalance, the planters of Jamaica continued to contract white manual labor until the mid-eighteenth century, although in decreasing numbers.

The development of the sugar industry required a steady supply of slave labor. Early on, the French and English tried to exploit the native population of the Lesser Antilles, but they quickly found that the Carib Indians often escaped from the plantations and were difficult to keep in captivity. The French and English had continual problems with the Caribs, who attacked European intruders occupying their lands. In contrast to other neighboring islands, in St. Kitts the Carib Indians were wiped out early on in quick campaigns organized by the French and the English in 1626 and 1627.

The Caribs were similarly hunted and killed on other islands in the following years, and thirty years later only pockets of the indigenous populations, remained in Trinidad, Tobago, Grenada, St. Lucia, Martinique, Dominica, and Guadeloupe. In 1654 the Caribs attacked and destroyed the French colonial villages in St. Lucia and Grenada. In retaliation, the French attacked the Carib population of St. Vincent, and a war ensued between the French and the Caribs throughout the Lesser Antilles. This war ended in 1658 with the expulsion of the Caribs from Guadeloupe and Martinique and their virtual elimination from St. Vincent, Dominica, St. Lucia, and Grenada. Left without indigenous manual labor and lacking the necessary workforce to sustain the growth of the sugar industry, the French and English planters resorted to buying African slaves from the Dutch.

At first the English preferred to hire indentured white workers, but the favorable loans offered by the Dutch as well as the harsh economic realities of the plantation business quickly convinced the English to make use of slave labor. The average cost of a white indentured worker in 1640 was about 12 pounds sterling, while a slave cost about 25 pounds sterling. But in addition to the initial price of an indentured servant, the planter had to add the costs of feeding, housing, and clothing the white workers, not to mention the payment in tobacco and land required at the end of their three- or five-year contract. When the price of slaves fell to 15 pounds sterling in 1670 and to 12.5 pounds sterling in 1683, the Caribbean planters came to view African slave labor as their best economic option. Slaves had the additional advantage of being permanent property and were less expensive to feed, dress, and shelter than white workers.

African slaves compared favorably to white workers in various other ways. First, they were adapted to tropical climates and enjoyed some immunity to such tropical ailments as malaria and yellow fever, which wrought havoc among the Europeans. Second, many slaves were from regions in Africa with an agricultural tradition, which made them particularly suited to the type of work done on plantations. Third, uprooted forever from their native lands and with nowhere to go, most slaves initially confronted servitude with more fatalism than did the white workers, who expected to become independent farmers someday and were often disobedient and rebellious, obliging their masters to punish them severely. Furthermore, white workers were Christians, on whom many planters considered it inappropriate to impose the same drastic sanctions that they applied to African slaves. For all these reasons, the English and French planters soon became accustomed to black slaves as the labor solution of choice. As a result, West Indian colonial societies underwent a demographic transformation in the second half of the seventeenth century.

An examination of the number of slaves imported to the French and English Antilles between 1640 and 1700 makes their demographic impact during the sugar revolution immediately clear. According to modern estimates, during those sixty years the English imported 54,654 African slaves to Barbados, 37,988 to Jamaica, and 14,695 to the Leeward Islands, for a total of 107,337. In the French Antilles during the same period, fewer slaves were imported due to the slower development of the sugar industry. Nevertheless, between 1651 and 1700 the French imported as many as 52,000 slaves from Africa. By 1700, however, the same demographic imbalance experienced in the English colonies was now evident on the French islands. Guadeloupe had a population of 6,097 black slaves and 4,018 whites at the time, while Martinique had 14,566 black slaves and 6,597 whites. Saint-Domingue, in western Española, had barely begun to develop its sugar industry, but by 1700 it already had more than 10,000 slaves.

The massive importation of slaves was carried out through several channels. Between 1640 and 1672, Dutch and English private brokers dominated the slave trade. Between 1673 and 1688, the English colonies in the Caribbean were mainly supplied by the recently established Royal African Company, while the French islands received their slaves from the Compagnie du Senegal. These two companies operated under royal licenses. After 1689 Dutch, English, and French smugglers invaded the market, supplying slaves directly from the African coasts. The smugglers were so successful that the licensed companies were forced to leave the slave trade in private hands.

The Spanish Antilles, on the other hand, depended on the few slaves supplied by the Sevillian merchants who were granted a monopoly on the slave trade by the Spanish government. Even at the end of the seventeenth century, King Charles II of Spain was determined to maintain control over the slave market by using a special contract system, called *asiento*. In this system, a merchant bought from the Crown the monopoly rights for trading a certain number of African slaves over a certain number of years. Yet the Spanish contractors were never able to adequately supply the Spanish colonies, and therefore the smuggling of slaves continued to flourish in the Spanish Main.

The large imbalance between black and white populations on the islands soon engendered numerous tensions, most notably the rebellion and flight of the slaves from the plantations. There were as many as seven major rebellions in the English Antilles between 1640 and 1713. These rebellions were put down by hanging or beheading the leaders and amputating the limbs of or otherwise mutilating those who were implicated. In addition to the rebellions, six conspiracies were discovered before they could turn into full-scale revolts. Throughout the islands, slaves tried to escape to the hills. Runaway slaves were not successful in Barbados due to the small size and flat topography of the island, but in Martinique, Guadeloupe, Jamaica, and Saint-Domingue, runaway slaves and maroons were a constant problem for plantation and sugar mill owners.

The planters' colonial assemblies on the English islands adopted numerous "slave laws" that attempted to regulate the conduct of their plantation workers as had been done previously in the Spanish Antilles. The colonial assembly of Barbados passed the first slave laws in the English Caribbean in 1661. The Jamaican assembly copied them in 1664, and they were ratified by subsequent assemblies on both islands. Similar laws were enacted in Antigua and the Leeward Islands in the final decades of the seventeenth century. As for the French islands, the Code Noir of 1685, promulgated by Louis XIV for all French colonies in the Caribbean, regulated the conduct of slaves and their treatment by their owners.

The purpose of such laws and codes was to secure a disciplined mass of slaves in order to guarantee the continuity of sugar production. Once the cane harvest began, no tasks could be interrupted until the last grain of sugar was stored. The plantation owners had learned that sugarcane began to lose sucrose as soon as it was cut and had to be taken to the sugar mill as quickly as possible to be ground. For this reason, the mill owners also soon learned to plant sugarcane sequentially in contiguous fields to extend the harvest period from November through May.

Sugar Production and Technology

The manufacturing process was simple but exhausting. The cane juice extracted by the sugar mills was channeled into the boiler house. There it was emptied into a cauldron and boiled to begin the process of evaporation. The foam produced in this first boiling was removed using a skimmer, a large colander at the end of a pole. The purified, denser juice was decanted into a second and then a third boiler, where it continued boiling and evaporating until it became molasses. The molasses was then poured into a last boiler, called the sugar pan, heated with a very hot fire, where the molasses cooked until it was ready to be poured into clay molds in which it became sugar. These molds had a conical shape with an orifice at the narrow end through which the excess water of the molasses was drained.

In the mold, the molasses began to crystallize and dry. The end result was a cone-shaped "sugar loaf" made up of various strata with different proportions of sucrose. These loaves were crushed to make the product uniform and prepare it for export and then placed into wooden boxes of 625 to 750 pounds each. Due to the molasses residue, the sugar had a dark color and was called *azúcar prieta* (black sugar) in the Spanish Caribbean, *sucre brut* (crude sugar) on the French islands, and raw sugar, or *muscovado* sugar, in the English West Indies.

Manufacturing sugar was a continuous process that consumed an enormous amount of energy. Usually, the sugar mill was at rest only during the early morning, in anticipation of the arrival of the cane carts. The sugar mill workers and furnace operators had shifts of twelve to sixteen hours daily. The furnace's fire had to remain constant because part of the secret of sugar production was maintaining a consistent boiling temperature. The slaves considered the work in the boiler house to be the most exhausting and dangerous because both the sugar masters who processed the juice and molasses and the furnace operators worked in an extreme, suffocating heat and suffered frequent burns.

The sugarcane cutters who worked in the fields also had shifts of more than twelve hours per day and were supervised by overseers equipped with whips, dogs, and guns. Other slaves cut wood. Still others transported the sugarcane and wood to the sugar mill and the boiler house. Wood was generally cut and stacked throughout the year, especially during the so-called dead season in the summer months. At that time the slaves cleared weeds from the fields, planted new sugar-cane, cut and transported wood, and repaired the sugar mill. On Sundays the slaves worked in the plantation gardens, raising food for their families and for those living on the plantation, including the owner and his family.

The technology of the established sugar mills in the Antilles during the second half of the seventeenth century was fairly uniform. The mills all used three vertical cylinders to crush the cane and between four and five boilers to boil the juice and evaporate the water from the molasses. Wood and dried sugarcane bagasse were used to feed the furnaces, and the cane was transported to the mill in carts or by pack animals.

The sugar mills of Barbados, however, were quite distinct from those established on other islands. Thanks to its location and flat topography, Barbados enjoyed constant, strong trade winds that were used to power windmills, thus saving the plantation owners both manpower and horse-power. The windmill owners generally also had a second mill run by animal power in case the wind stopped blowing. Windmills became so common in Barbados that 409 out of 485 of the sugar mills operating in 1709 were powered by wind.

Windmills were less common on the other islands because the wind patterns were less regular. However, the planters on the Leeward Islands used windmills almost to the same extent as those powered by animals. In the French Antilles, windmills were rare because the hilly topography of Martinique and Guadeloupe blocked the flow of wind currents. As a result, the French opted for sugar mills powered by water or draft animals. The French islands had more streams and rivers available for waterpower than did the English islands, which were generally flatter and drier. On the Spanish islands, all the mills were moved by animal force. Regardless of the type of power the mills used, the end products were molasses and sugar of varying dark color that required subsequent refinement before sale and consumption in Europe.

Mercantilism and the Sugar Trade

As soon as Caribbean sugar began to arrive in London and Le Havre, the governments of England and France decided to exclude the Dutch from this trade. In 1651 the English government enacted several customs duty laws addressing navigation and trade. These "Navigation Laws" required that sugar, tobacco, and other colonial products bound for England be transported exclusively by English ships. In following years, the English Parliament required that merchandise imported by the colonies be of purely English origin and that it be transported to the islands on English ships. In exchange, colonial products were protected from foreign competition in England by customs duties that guaranteed a secure market for the sugar mill and plantation owners in the Caribbean and North America. According to mercantilist principles, the colonies existed for the benefit of their home country. For that reason, the supply of slaves was also placed under a monopoly handled by the Royal African Company, to which the British government had given the exclusive right to sell slaves in its colonies.

Monopolistic mercantilism also took root in the French colonies. Between 1664 and 1667, France established trade controls with its colonies at the suggestion of Jean Baptiste Colbert, the minister of finance. This new system, known as "L'Exclusif," ensured that the French navy, not the Dutch, was to transport all products, including slaves, to and from the French colonies. Colbert also dictated that all products consumed in the colonies be produced in France, thus supporting the development of French industry. In 1665 France imposed a special customs duty to protect the French sugar industry from foreign competition and to assure the exclusivity of the French market for its Caribbean producers.

The Navigation Laws and L'Exclusif helped England and France, respectively, eliminate Dutch intermediaries from the slave market in the colonies. This was not easily accomplished, because the Dutch had for decades defended the doctrine of free trade and immediately rejected these new monopolies, just as they had previously rejected the Spanish monopoly many years earlier. In 1652, just a few months after the promulgation of the first Navigation Laws, the Dutch protested, but to no avail. Realizing that their objections were not being heeded, the Dutch had no other recourse than to go to war against the English. The First Anglo-Dutch War (1652–1654) was a true colonial war. It weakened the Netherlands and contributed to the Dutch loss of Pernambuco.

When they lost the war, the Dutch had to adhere to the English Navigation Laws, but since their colonial interests were so important, they again went to war with England between 1665 and 1667 and again between 1672 and 1674. The English also went to war with France for similar reasons on two occasions in the second half of the seventeenth century. The first of these wars took place between 1672 and 1678. The second, between 1688 and 1697, in which Spain was also involved, was known as the War of the League of Augsburg. This last great colonial war of the seventeenth century ended up greatly changing the political map of the Caribbean.

These conflicts did not ruin Holland, but its power and influence were curtailed as the Dutch were forced to withdraw to their own colonies in the Caribbean. During these wars, almost all the Dutch colonists were expelled from the English and French Antilles, leaving the sugar business in the hands of the English and French colonists. From 1697 on, the Dutch were reduced to selling only sugar from their own colonies in Europe. That did not stop them, however, from continuing to supply manufactured products to almost all of the West Indies as contraband. The reason was simple: the rigid monopoly systems made it impossible for metropolitan merchants of France, England, and Spain to adequately supply their Caribbean colonies.

Cuba's Negligible Sugar Production

Cuba was a secondary actor during the seventeenth-century sugar revolution, even though the Cuban colonists entered the sugar industry a century earlier than the English and French colonists of the Lesser Antilles. The first shipments of sugar produced in Cuba were sent out in 1580. The quantities exported between 1580 and 1593 were always small, never surpassing 7.5 tons annually. The Cuban colonists tried to take advantage of the decline in sugar production in Española and Puerto Rico and asked the king of Spain to give them subsidies similar to those given to colonists on the other Caribbean islands. In 1600, after a long battle of petitions and demands, King Philip III agreed to lend 40,000 ducats to the Cuban colonists, whose primitive sugar plantations were still small and had very few slaves.

When the loans were granted in 1602, only sixteen colonists qualified to receive them because they were the only ones who had been producing sugar. The impact of these loans, however, was significant. By 1607 sugar exports climbed to more than 113 tons, indicating a clear increase in the production capacity of the Cuban planters.

In subsequent years, other colonists ventured into the sugar-making business, taking advantage of the fact that the Spanish colonial government had begun to exploit the copper mines in Bayamo, in the eastern part of the island. The copper extracted from these mines was sold at a reduced price to sugar plantation owners. Copper was one of the more expensive items needed on sugar plantations. Cane juice boilers were made exclusively of copper, and it deteriorated rapidly and had to be repaired or replaced frequently. The existence of copper in Cuba helps explain why Cuban colonists would dare to invest in the sugar industry despite the crises on the other Spanish islands produced by Brazilian competition.

In 1617 there were already eleven small sugar plantations in Bayamo and seventeen in Santiago. These were small plantations, each capable of producing up to ten tons per year, but were built around the new model of sugar mill consisting of three vertical cylinders moved by horsepower. According to a report sent from Cuba to the Council of the Indies in July 1617, the three-roller sugar mill was invented in the eastern part of Cuba by colonists who did not have enough slaves to run their mills.[5]

During the Thirty Years War, Santiago and Bayamo were attacked and razed on several occasions, and their sugar was lost to pirates, who also burned some of the sugar plantations. To avoid this danger, some plantation owners concentrated their mills in the vicinity of Havana, but some of the first sugar mills had to be demolished later when it was discovered that their proximity to the coast attracted pirates and privateers. The newer sugar plantations of Havana were founded on former cattle ranches to the south of the city that were gradually converted into cane fields by authorization of the *cabildo* of Havana. Although King Philip IV did not lend any more money for the construction of sugar plantations, despite numerous requests between 1630 and 1667, the *cabildo* of Havana granted at least eighty-one land concessions to establish cane fields and set up sugar plantations.

Even with this support, the sugar industry did not develop as quickly in Cuba as it did in the English and French Antilles, since the Cuban colonists lacked money to purchase slaves. The sixteen colonists who were granted loans at the beginning of the seventeenth century had an average of only thirteen slaves on their plantations. None had more than twenty-three slaves, and several had only between two and nine slaves. Over time, the typical Cuban sugar plantation came to have about twenty slaves with an average annual production of less than seven tons of sugar, which indicates the small scale of the Cuban sugar industry in the seventeenth century.

For these reasons, several decades later, in 1670, the Cuban planters were experiencing problems similar to the ones faced by planters in Española and Puerto Rico at the end of the previous century. This time, however, competition originated not only in Brazil but also in Barbados and the Lesser Antilles. The lack of a regular navigation system compounded the problems. After 1650 Spanish galleon fleets no longer made annual stopovers at the port of Havana. Sugar prices in the world market dropped after 1670, when new English and French sugar entered the market. This discouraged the Cuban planters and on several occasions they requested that the Spanish government prohibit the importation of sugar from Brazil as well as from the French and English Caribbean, but they were not successful.

In 1690, according to the *cabildo* of Havana, many sugar producers abandoned their plantations rather than face the impossible task of competing with sugar from Brazil entering Spain via Portugal. By 1690 one-third of the Cuban sugar plantations had been abandoned by their owners, reducing their number to only seventy. After a powerful hurricane destroyed part of Havana in September 1692, there were only thirty plantations left. From then on, sugar production was severely diminished in Cuba, while livestock, tobacco, and contraband continued to provide the main sources of income for its colonists, as was the case on the other Spanish islands.

CHAPTER 6

Poverty in the Spanish Antilles

Economic Decline and Government Subsidies

With few or no slaves and a precarious sugar industry, most colonists of Cuba, Española, and Puerto Rico remained in poverty, dedicated mainly to raising livestock and subsistence farming. Ginger and tobacco, the two main cash crops, had been reduced to almost insignificant quantities, which did not allow for the sustenance of these colonies. Therefore, Spain had to send a special subsidy to Santo Domingo and San Juan each year to defray the expenses of the two colonial governments.

Española exported an average of 163 tons of sugar annually at the beginning of the seventeenth century, but this quantity declined as time went by. Between 1612 and 1614, the average was 125 tons; from 1639 to 1641 it had declined to around 88 tons; and from 1646 to 1649 it was only 15 tons. In Puerto Rico, the decline in sugar production was even worse. The seven sugar plantations left on the island in 1650 exported less than 10 tons of sugar between 1650 and 1655, averaging less than 2 tons per year. Between 1681 and 1685, only 1.3 tons was exported from the port of San Juan. From then on, the six sugar plantations remaining on the island at the end of the century were not able to supply even the island population, and the Puerto Rican colonists were forced to import sugar for their own consumption. During the last fifteen years of the seventeenth century, the port of San Juan received 282 tons of imported sugar.

Throughout the seventeenth century, the authorities and colonists continually complained about the lack of merchant ships making the voyage to Española and Puerto Rico. As the years went by, it became very dangerous for small ships to venture alone through Caribbean seas.

To supply the colonists of Santo Domingo and San Juan during the Thirty Years War, a ship had to be outfitted once a year in early spring so that it could arrive there by Holy Week. This "Lenten ship" sailed from either Veracruz or Cartagena, accompanied by another well-armed ship that carried the yearly subsidy, or *situado*, to pay the salaries of the royal officials, the clergy, and the soldiers of the garrisons.

Very few other ships visited the harbors of Santo Domingo and San Juan with any regularity. When these rare merchant ships arrived, they typically encountered a scarcity of hides and declining amounts of sugar. As a result, Española and Puerto Rico were practically abandoned to their fate, and their sugar industry fell into ruin. In Cuba, the *situado* also arrived sporadically. The funds were used to pay the garrisons of Havana and Santiago and to finance military construction and fortification.

Due to the need for defense during the Thirty Years War, the Spanish Antilles remained under the control of the commanders of the garrisons of San Juan, Santo Domingo, and Havana. In these cities, an elite military class developed, led by captains general and sergeants major who over time came to exercise almost absolute power. In 1647 the garrison of San Juan had 400 soldiers and Santo Domingo had 300, most of whom were Portuguese soldiers recruited before the separation of Spain and Portugal in 1640. Although small, these garrisons greatly affected the lives of the dwindling colonial populations of the islands.

According to the 1646 census, the city of San Juan had about 1,000 white inhabitants, while Santo Domingo had around 4,000. Due to the low populations of the islands, the presence of the military had a strong impact on local life, especially as the fortification of San Juan and the construction of the walls in Santo Domingo progressed. The once-powerful plantation owners who had controlled the *cabildos* and local life during the sixteenth century were replaced by a powerful elite of military and town merchants. Most of the *situado* money that arrived from Cartagena and Veracruz to pay the soldiers, the civilian bureaucracy, and the clergy soon ended up in the merchants' pockets to repay debts incurred over the course of the year, thus allowing them to buy on credit again.

The dates when Española, Puerto Rico, and Cuba began to depend on the *situado* define the point when internal production was no longer capable of sustaining the small bureaucracies of these colonies. The Spanish Antilles, previously generators of wealth, were transformed into subsidized territories whose value was more geopolitical than economic. Puerto Rico began to receive the *situado* from Cartagena in 1586, while Española started in 1609, immediately after the devastating depopulation of the northwestern territories. The Cuba *situado* was sent as early as 1563 to pay for the construction of some fortifications in Havana. The *situado* for both Española and Cuba was sent from the Royal Treasury of Mexico. This subsidy was barely sufficient to support the civilian bureaucracy, the military, and the clergy, and was certainly not enough to generate wealth.

The Collapse of Exports

Documents from the seventeenth century are full of reports of poverty in the Spanish Caribbean. On Española and Puerto Rico, numerous documents provide evidence of a decline not only in the sugar industry but also in ginger sales. In 1627 Española was still producing 600 tons of ginger per year, but by midcentury ginger was no longer cultivated in large quantities. Puerto Rico still produced 700 tons of ginger in 1641, but by 1651 exports had dropped to around 225 tons. Many cultivators opted to abandon their crops due to the drop in prices, along with loss of market share to Brazilian ginger and the unavailability of ships to export the product during the war. Between 1646 and 1649, only 442 tons of ginger were exported from Española, averaging a mere 110 tons per year.

As ginger production declined, the colonists of Puerto Rico and Española began to experiment with planting cacao, intending to export it to Mexico and Spain to meet the high demand in those years. In 1639 the first 675 pounds of this seed were exported from Santo Domingo to Seville. Ten years later, in 1649, exports had risen to 13,150 pounds and to almost 20,000 by 1652. Yet there were not enough cacao cultivators to meet demand. According to one traveler's description of Santo Domingo, only fifty families were cultivating it in 1650. The main cacao plantations in Española were located in the vicinity of Santo Domingo and near the towns of El Seibo and Higüey in the eastern part of the island. In Santo Domingo, some farmers had plantations of almost 30,000 trees, although 3,000 seems to have been the average.

The number of people raising this plant in Puerto Rico is still unknown, but witnesses estimated that the cacao harvest for 1650 would load several vessels. Some reports say that the planters of Bayamo had planted up to 14,700 cacao trees by 1657. In San Germán, Luquillo, and Humacao, plantations were smaller, ranging from 1,500 to 2,000 trees. Well-to-do colonists noted the potential of cacao, and those with suffi-cient land and capital imported new slaves, since the majority of the existing slaves had died during the smallpox epidemic of 1651, which devastated the Spanish Antilles.

For some time it seemed that cacao would be the salvation of Puerto Rico and Española. On both islands, it was evident that cacao had replaced ginger. The colonial authorities sent different petitions to the Spanish government requesting licenses to import slaves for the cacao plantations. But the few Africans workers the planters managed to import did not survive a new epidemic of smallpox in 1666. Worse still for the planters, that same year a plague attacked the cacao plantations in the Antilles, killing all the trees and thus putting an end to this new agricultural experiment in Española and Puerto Rico. In 1670 and 1671 a similar plague struck and killed the cacao trees that the English had planted in southern Jamaica, but did not affect the ones planted on the north coast. Thus Jamaica was able to continue to export cacao for sev-eral more years.

New seeds were imported from Venezuela, but cacao was never again exported from Santo Domingo or Puerto Rico during the following 150 years. There it was produced only for local consumption. The few trees remaining on Española in 1672 were destroyed by a hurricane, which also leveled the garden plots of yuca and plantain. The following year, another plague killed off the remaining cacao trees of Puerto Rico.

Epidemics and Demographic Crisis

Española and Puerto Rico were also affected by epidemics that stifled population growth and even led to demographic decline on both islands. In 1647 the white population of San Juan fell to 880 individuals after a smallpox epidemic, which became chronic over the next four years. After another epidemic, there were only 343 white survivors in 1659, along with a few surviving black slaves and free mulattoes. When the epidemic was finally over, the city's population recuperated slowly. In 1673 it reached only 792 whites, 304 mulattoes, and 667 black slaves— that is, a total of 1,763 people over the age of ten. As the population of San Juan was almost equivalent to that of the island's interior, it can be estimated that there were about 3,500 adults in Puerto Rico in 1673.

Another epidemic in 1673 killed more than 1,500 people in Española, reducing the island's population to 6,000 people. In 1686 and 1689 two more smallpox epidemics devastated the populations of both islands. The epidemic of 1689 killed at least 918 people in Puerto Rico, as it reached all the towns on the island, significantly reducing the populations in each one. These events explain why Puerto Rico barely reached a total of 2,900 inhabitants in 1691.

Epidemics, low production, the delays of the *situado*, limited trade with Spain, and the lack of contact with the outer world, especially with Spain, caused profound pessimism among the colonists of Española and Puerto Rico. People began to move to the countryside to raise pigs or other livestock and to live off subsistence farming. Due to this migration, the old Spanish diet almost completely disappeared. Because it was almost impossible to import flour, cassava substituted for bread. Wine was consumed only during mass, and often even mass could not be celebrated until the Lenten ship arrived with a small wine shipment. Plantains replaced rice, although some families were able to cultivate rice in small quantities in Puerto Rico. Chicken and eggs became very scarce and were replaced by pork, beef, or fish in coastal regions. The preferred fruits were citrus fruits, coconuts, and pineapple.

Life in the countryside allowed those who opted to stay away from the cities to at least feed themselves with fruit and meat, while in San Juan and Santo Domingo people who were not merchants or government-paid employees had barely enough to live on. Numerous accounts describe people leaving the cities so as not to be embarrassed by their shabby clothes. Those residing in the countryside hunted, farmed, and lived in straw huts isolated from the urban population and with minimal commercial contact with the outside world, except for the times when they went to town to trade their cow hides for other goods.[1]

The trading of hides remained the main source of income for house-holds in Cuba, Puerto Rico, and Española over the course of the seven-teenth century. Española continued to produce about 20,000 hides annually during the first half of the century, but in the second half regular exports through the port of Santo Domingo declined to around 7,000 hides per year. In the meantime, the quantity exported from San Juan was only about 3,000 hides per year. Almost as many other hides went unreported, as contraband dominated the economic life of the isolated regions of both islands.

Social Malaise and Stagnation

As poverty increased, people changed their habits. Churches in Santo Domingo and San Juan altered the schedules of their masses to enable people to attend church at night or before dawn so that their threadbare clothing would not be so evident. Retail trade in Santo Domingo was reduced to eleven small stores, while in San Juan there were only six such stores. In these shops, the limited amount of cloth and merchandise that arrived from Spain in the registered ships that brought the *situado* from Mexico was sold at very high prices. Shop inventories that still exist show the general destitution of both cities, neither of which had the merchandise necessary to meet people's basic needs.

Sometimes three or four years would go by before a well-supplied merchant ship would stop in San Juan or Santo Domingo, and the local population lacked clothes and shoes. Occasionally, the islands were able to procure merchandise from Venezuela, Margarita, Portobelo, Veracruz, Trinidad, or the Canary Islands in exchange for a few hides and limited quantities of the lard, cassava, corn, tobacco, cotton, sugar, or ginger still produced in Puerto Rico and Española, but this merchandise did not meet the needs of the population. Between 1664 and 1700, only eight registered ships and twenty-seven unregistered ships landed in Puerto Rico, less than one ship per year.

Like Puerto Rico and Española, Cuba was also subject to controls of the Sevillean monopoly, and its colonists likewise lived in need of clothes and European merchandise. The extensive reports of contraband and the numerous documents from the period highlight the impossibility of legally exporting tropical produce through the established ports. At the same time, the Lesser Antilles and Jamaica were being populated by the English, French, and Dutch, whose home countries had not yet developed a regular system for supplying their new colonies. Illegal trade with foreigners was common. Given the small size of the new sugar islands and the fact that they had no cattle or horses, the French, English, and Dutch colonists did not lose any time establishing contact with their neighboring Spanish islands, with offers to trade European-manufactured goods for salted meat, livestock, hides, ginger, and tobacco.

Contraband, which diminished considerably during the Thirty Years War, once again became a universal practice. Most governors, top officials, civilians, military personnel, priests, and bishops of the Spanish Antilles became involved, not to mention the common people who were eager to offer their products to foreigners. In contrast to the more discreet illegal trade of the sixteenth century, contraband in the second half of the seventeenth century also occurred in the main ports of the Spanish islands, where the authorities made frequent exceptions to the monopoly by allowing the entrance of foreign ships to cope with the scarcity of manufactured merchandise, particularly in times of drought or after hurricanes. Since the authorities regulated and controlled such preferential treatment, most colonists preferred to trade with smugglers in inlets and beaches far from the main cities. In such places, illegal trade prospered: hides, tobacco, ginger, and livestock were freely exchanged for European merchandise arriving on foreign ships.

Contraband increased after 1670, when Spain and England signed a peace treaty that allowed ships from one nation to seek refuge and provisions in the domain of the other when there was a justifiable cause. Although this treaty clearly prohibited ships from unloading or selling their merchandise in the ports that gave them refuge, very soon the Spanish and English authorities allowed the exceptions that officially sanctioned contraband in the ports of Havana, Santiago, Santo Domingo, and San Juan.

Impoverished Creole Peasants

Contraband was the key to economic survival in the Spanish Antilles. Due to their meager production, the islanders would not have been able to get by otherwise. Contraband trade provided clothes, shoes, flour, salt, preserved food, spices, and slaves. It also allowed cattle ranchers in the Spanish Antilles to survive, since the demand for hides and meat continued until the end of the following century. Finally, contraband lent a special stimulus to the peasant economy in the Spanish Antilles, as it linked their production to the plantation economies on the French and English islands.

The production of tobacco supported an early class of independent Creole peasants in the Spanish Antilles who clearly differed from the planter class and the white indentured colonists on the English, French, and Dutch islands, not to mention the slaves. In Cuba, in particular, where sugar and ginger were not produced in large quantities, tobacco was the favorite crop of the colonists, especially after King Philip III legalized its cultivation in 1614. Many poor Cuban colonists became tobacco planters, exporting as much as 260 tons to Seville in 1699. In Puerto Rico, tobacco had little significance as an export crop in the seventeenth century, although small quantities appeared as exports in the registers of ships that went to Seville. After the cacao fields were destroyed, however, some Puerto Rican colonists turned to tobacco.

In Española, tobacco cultivation increased after its legalization in 1614. Tobacco export figures from Santo Domingo show a significant rise from 29 tons in 1617 to 73 tons in 1620, leveling off to 74 tons in 1639. Foreign competition and the lack of transportation eventually obstructed the sale of tobacco in Seville, and legal exports dropped to 41.5 tons in 1640, 26 tons in 1648, 8.5 tons in 1649, and just 5 tons in 1650. During the following thirty years, exports dropped to a minimum due to various crises in the colony, but began recuperating little by little as the colonists developed commercial relations with the French colonists on Tortuga and on the western half of Española.

Neither tobacco nor cacao cultivation was capable of rescuing the Spanish colonists from poverty. As the English and French colonies on the neighboring islands increased their population, the number of people in the Spanish Antilles declined. While the English and French islands prospered as tobacco colonies and, later, as sugar economies, the Spanish colonies struggled for survival, with limited results. The most visible contrast between Spanish and French colonization schemes could be seen in Española, the oldest Spanish colony. There, in the western territories abandoned after the devastation of 1605–1606, a thriving French colony bloomed in the second half of the seventeenth century, forever changing the political and economic landscape of the Caribbean region, which was no longer called the Spanish Main.

CHAPTER 7

The Emergence
of Saint-Domingue

From Tortuga to Española

In 1654, the year before Oliver Cromwell's expedition invaded Santo
Domingo, the Spanish military attacked the pirate haven of Tortuga,
expelling the French and ravaging the island but abandoning it soon
afterward, as they had done several times previously. For decades, the
Spanish sent expeditions and military patrols, by sea and by land, to
take over the French establishments, both on Española and Tortuga,
but the French had always managed to return, each time better
equipped and with more reinforcements. The preparations to resist
Cromwell's invasion forced the Spanish authorities to concentrate their
attention on the city of Santo Domingo.

Despite defeating the English here, in April 1655, the Spanish did not
dare to divert resources by sending troops to Tortuga again. This permitted a group of Frenchmen who had taken refuge in western
Española to travel to Tortuga on a barge and resettle there in December
1655. They immediately set to planting tobacco and rebuilding the old
fortifications. The following year, in December 1656, a French adventurer named Jérémie Deschamps was appointed by Louis XIV as
"Governor and Lieutenant General of Tortuga Island and other
Dependencies." Deschamps took two years to prepare for his trip to the
colonies that he was to control. He finally left in 1659, after recruiting
more than 500 buccaneers in Port-a-Margot. With these reinforcements,
Deschamps assaulted Tortuga just as Levasseur had done in 1640, sub-
jecting the settlers to his authority. As royal governor of Tortuga,
Deschamps ruled over the buccaneers and tobacco growers until

November 15, 1664, when he was compelled to sell his property rights to the French Company of the West Indies.

The company assigned a longtime employee, Bertrand d'Ogeron, to govern Tortuga. D'Ogeron arrived in June 1665 and took his place as governor, replacing a nephew of Deschamps who had managed the colony while his uncle negotiated the sale. At the time there were between 250 and 300 buccaneers and 800 other Frenchmen living on the north coast of Española who hunted livestock and grew tobacco. D'Ogeron thought that if these men abandoned Española and settled on Tortuga, it would be easier for him to prepare a military force to attack and take over the city of Santo Domingo.

In a trial maneuver carried out in 1667, d'Ogeron marched with a strong contingent of buccaneers against the second-largest city of Española, Santiago de los Caballeros, located in the center of the island. Santiago was pillaged and burned, but D'Ogeron did not dare to cross the mountains that separated it from Santo Domingo. During this attack, the buccaneers discovered just how uninhabited the Spanish colony was and how much feral livestock it contained. Having learned this, in the following months they began to fan out throughout the savannas of the eastern part of the island, creating the first French settlements on the flatlands of Cul-de-Sac and La Yaguana, soon to be known as Léogane. By then, the lands occupied by the French in Española were known as Saint-Domingue.

With their indiscriminate hunting, the buccaneers killed off the feral livestock in most of western Española. The rapid depletion of cattle in the French-dominated lands encouraged D'Ogeron to conquer new territories on the eastern part of Española. These ambitious plans required the backing of the company and also that of Louis XIV, and with this in mind, d'Ogeron left for France in 1668. He remained there until the middle of the following year, attempting to obtain the support needed for the complete occupation of Española as well as the establishment of a new French colony in Florida.

While D'Ogeron was gone, the French colonists rebelled violently against the French Company of the West Indies; they objected to its taxes and other monopolistic restrictions on tobacco and hide production that kept them in economic stagnation. Similar to the rebellions that had occurred in Martinique between 1665 and 1667, these first "white revolts" were the precursors of numerous later tensions between the colonists and France over L'Exclusif's commercial monopoly. The company received annual benefits of close to 80,000 pounds *tournois*, while the majority of the French colonists remained in dire poverty. In the entire colony, there were only fifteen relatively rich inhabitants.

Returning in August 1670, d'Ogeron almost lost his life when he was attacked while trying to pacify a group of colonists protesting their inability to trade with Dutch ships. D'Ogeron managed to subdue the rebels with the help of a French squadron, but the following year he was unable to control the buccaneer inhabitants of Cul-de-Sac, which had become the main French tobacco-growing center.

Discouraged by the rebellions, d'Ogeron concentrated his efforts on his projects in Florida and two pirating exploits against Curaçao and Puerto Rico between 1672 and 1674. These expeditions failed spectacularly when the Puerto Rican authorities imprisoned him and many of his filibusters in March 1673. With great difficulty, d'Ogeron managed to escape, but the other prisoners were never rescued, and the French colony lost more than 400 inhabitants.

French Settlements in Western Española

At that time, the French colony needed more field hands for the tobacco harvest. Some manual laborers employed by the French tobacco growers were the so-called *engagés*, white indentured workers contracted in France to serve for a fixed period in exchange for clothes, food, and land at the end of their contracts. D'Ogeron traveled to France again in 1674 to recruit workers and to obtain new resources from the company so as to eventually begin the conquest of Spanish Española.

At the same time that d'Ogeron was departing for France, the French minister of finance, Jean Baptiste Colbert, ordered the dissolution of the French Company of the West Indies. By then he was convinced that the French king should exercise strict control over his new colonial territories. Colbert placed the governments of Tortuga, Saint-Domingue, Martinique, and Guadeloupe in the hands of governors who would answer directly to the French Crown. Before leaving, d'Ogeron left the government of Tortuga in the hands of his nephew, Jacques de Pouancey, who officially became governor following the death of d'Ogeron in January 1676.

During his seven-year rule, de Pouancey imposed new colonial order in Saint-Domingue, while his colleagues did the same in Martinique and Guadeloupe. De Pouancey made an effort to control piracy by forcing the filibusters to restrict their activities and operate in accordance with his political directives. He fortified the most important settlements to avoid their being recaptured by the Spanish, and he encouraged even more tobacco cultivation by forcing pirates to abandon their maritime adventures and become farmers. In 1677 tobacco production in Saint-Domingue reached 1,000 tons, a quantity that made the production of Santo Domingo, Cuba, and Puerto Rico look insignificant.

All this occurred at a time when France was at war with Holland, Spain, and England, as these nations attempted to defend themselves from the invading armies of Louis XIV. The French, expecting the Spanish to attack Saint-Domingue at any moment, accelerated their fortification process, and by 1677 there were eleven fortified settlements on Saint-Domingue. These areas included Samaná, Cap François, Port de Paix, Cul-de-Sac, Léogane, Petit Goave, Nippe, Le Rouchelot, La Grande Anse, L'Ile à Vache, and La Tortuga, with a total population of about 4,000 people, mostly men, who made their living as free farmers, buccaneers, filibusters, and *engagés*. There were also some black slaves. With the exception of Samaná, all of the fortified areas later became important towns of the French colony of Saint-Domingue.

In 1681, when de Pouancey took a first census in the eleven fortified towns, the population had increased to 6,648 people, among whom were 1,421 white men, 435 white women, 438 white children, 477 free servants, 1,565 *engagés* or indentured workers, 1,063 black male slaves, 725 black female slaves, 314 black boys and girls, and 210 mestizos, mulattoes, and Indians. When reporting the results of this census, de Pouancey declared that almost the entire population of the colony grew tobacco. For the French governor, that was a bad sign because that same year the French market was saturated with tobacco from the other tobacco-growing islands in the Antilles, and prices fell quickly. According to De Pouancey, many tobacco growers became disillusioned and began to think of raising livestock or switching to other crops like sugarcane, cotton, cacao, or indigo.

In 1682 the French planters agreed not to produce more than twelve rolls of tobacco per person per harvest. At the same time, many began to cultivate indigo and cotton, while others planted cacao. Still others followed the example of the Spanish and started raising cattle, sheep, and goats. "These activites are the main concerns of today's inhabitants, and these are the ways that they make a living," de Pouancey wrote to Colbert in 1682. The only problem the French colony had at the time, the governor said, were the constant complaints of the Spanish authorities about livestock trading.

Trading with the Enemy

Trade between the French and the Spanish on the island of Española had begun in early 1679, immediately after the colonists learned that France and Spain had signed the Nijmegen Peace Treaty to put an end to the war. Both de Pouancey and the governor of the Spanish colony, Francisco de Segura Sandoval y Castilla, received instructions from their governments to suspend the hostilities they had maintained for years, partly as a reflection of the wars in Europe. Both governors immediately communicated with each other to end the conflict. The Spanish governor, however, wanted to prohibit the French from hunting feral livestock in the western part of the island and argued that the French presence there was illegal. De Pouancey responded that the French would not under any circumstances abandon the island because they had acquired the land more than forty years earlier by "right of conquest."

This exchange was followed by discussions regarding the possibility of establishing trade relations and a boundary between the colonies. The Spanish and French colonists were legally prohibited from doing business with nationals of other countries, but the basic needs of both groups took precedence over politics. From 1681 on, active trading of horses, corn, salted meat, cattle hides, and European merchandise began to occur. For the French, this trade was necessary to supply meat to their colony, as the buccaneers had almost completely exterminated the wild cattle population without replacing it with domesticated herds for the future food supply.

Once again, just as a century earlier, people living in poverty in areas far from Santo Domingo entered into commercial deals with foreigners despite existing prohibitions. Such were the economic connections between the two colonies when de Pouancey died in the summer of 1683. De Pouancey was replaced by Tarin de Cussy, a new governor who tried to improve French relations with the Spanish in order to expand the livestock trade.

In the meantime, the fall in tobacco prices forced the French colonists to diversify their crops. In 1685 the tobacco crop was reduced to a minimum, but indigo production was beginning to increase, and in some areas efforts were made to harvest cotton. Everywhere the ex-buccaneers, now converted into farmers and planters, were trying to start indigo and cotton plantations with the help of white indentured workers and black slaves. Since the French did not produce sugar, they needed relatively few slaves and imported only 200 Africans per year. They still preferred white indentured servants over slaves because the former could be easily recruited from the lower classes in France and required a smaller initial investment. Most of the French colonists of Saint-Domingue were still very poor and did not have enough money or credit to buy large numbers of slaves.

During the years when the French were experimenting with indigo and cotton, they kept an uneasy relationship with the neighboring Spanish islands. In August 1687 a Spanish brigantine, apparently from Cuba, attacked the village of Petite Goave, compelling its inhabitants to flee to Ile-à-Vache. Another incident occurred in May 1688 when a ship from Santo Domingo captured two French ships and took them back to Santo Domingo, where the Spanish governor had the French sailors imprisoned, refusing to return them to the neighboring French colony.

Fighting for the Land

The Spanish attacks on French territory and capture of French prisoners damaged the relationship between the colonial governments and resulted in further attacks and skirmishes in border areas. The French interpreted such clashes as a preparation for war, particularly after receiving news that Spain, England, and Holland were going to war against France in Europe. In the spring of 1690, Governor Tarin de Cussy decided to respond to Spanish attacks on Saint-Domingue by reinvading the inland city of Santiago de los Caballeros, and on July 6, 1690, he entered the city with some 1,400 men, looting and destroying 160 of the city's 200 houses.

Several months later, on January 21, 1691, the Spanish counterattacked, defeating the French in a large battle in Sabana del Guarico, close to Cap François. Governor de Cussy lost his life in the battle, along with 400 other Frenchmen, while the Spanish troops suffered only forty-seven deaths. The following day, the Spanish advanced and took the city of Cap François and pillaged and burned it completely. The French survivors ran westward to take refuge in the village of Port de Paix. There they were safe because Spanish commanders did not want to send their exhausted troops into the swamp, preferring to return immediately to Santiago to search for food and medicine for the wounded. In their retreat, just as during their advance, the Spanish pillaged all the French settlements they found, leaving the northern part of the French colony completely devastated.

Between 1689 and 1697, during the years of the War of the League of Augsburg, the authorities of both colonies made preparations to take over the entire island. The new French governor, Jean Ducasse, reorganized the devastated regions and created several militia companies to defend the French against the Spaniards. Ducasse also helped arm privateers so that they could raid and pillage English colonies in the Caribbean, whose new sugar plantations lured attackers.

Jamaica, the primary English possession, was the main target of the remaining French privateers in the Caribbean during the final years of the seventeenth century. Ducasse and his privateers continued harassing Jamaica, attacking coastal towns, stealing the English colonists' slaves, and burning their sugar fields and sugar mills. As the war continued, the rumor spread that the English and Spanish would jointly attack the French colony. In an attempt to preempt his enemies, Ducasse launched a powerful and devastating attack against Jamaica in 1694. More than 100 English colonists were killed and wounded, fifty sugar mills were burned, 200 houses were destroyed, and 1,600 slaves were stolen.

Retaliation was organized on a large scale. At the beginning of 1695, the Jamaican authorities asked the Spanish governor of Santo

Domingo to give land support to a naval attack that the English were planning against the French settlements in the northern part of Española. Following this attack, plans were made to sack the rest of the French colony, particularly Léogane and Petit Goave, which privateers and pirates had used as ports of departure for their attacks on Jamaica. When the English fleet arrived in May 1695, approximately 1,500 Spaniards joined them in a new attack against Cap François, whose terrified inhabitants fled while the English flotilla bombarded the village and the Spanish troops leveled and burned the surrounding French settlements.

The English pillaged the village before the Spanish arrived. They did the same with the town of Port de Paix, about thirty miles to the west, and left very little war booty for the tired Spaniards, who had arrived on foot after walking from the eastern part of the island. Annoyed and discouraged, the Spanish abandoned the campaign and returned home, refusing to march to the south to attack the villages of Petit Goave and Léogane, which were the main English targets. Lacking the Spanish land support, the English had to give up their plan, and they withdrew to Jamaica.

Ducasse was not discouraged by the attacks. He ordered the colonists of the northern area who were taking refuge in the forests to come to Cap François, which they then rebuilt and which continued to function as the capital of the colony. Ducasse had to abandon his plan to attack Santo Domingo because the French government had ordered him to organize an attack against the rich city of Cartagena de Indias. Under Ducasse, the French successfully executed the attack in the middle of 1697, pillaging the city entirely. This was the privateers' last attack against Spanish possessions in the seventeenth century, because in September 1697 the warring European nations signed the Treaty of Ryswick, thus putting an end to the War of the League of Augsburg.

Ducasse later invested the spoils obtained from Cartagena in the establishment of various sugar plantations in the north of Saint-Domingue. These sugar plantations were the first constructed in the French colony. For labor, Ducasse used the slaves stolen from the English in Jamaica in 1694. In 1698 the first three sugar plantations went into operation, thus beginning the transformation of Saint-Domingue into a sugar economy.

The change in the use of the land was immediately noticeable. As the cane fields in the north of the colony grew, the French began to kill off or move the herds they had raised there since 1685 to supply meat for the colony. Unlike the other sugar colonies in the Lesser Antilles, where the plantations were established on uninhabited land, the sugar plantation owners of Saint-Domingue had to compete with cattle ranchers, who refused to move their herds unless they were given similar land on other parts of the island. To encourage the first sugar plantations, Ducasse annulled the original concessions of rangeland and reappropriated fertile land on the northern plains for the first sugar companies. The cattle ranchers were given new land to the east, closer to the Spanish possessions.

The concession of new rangeland stimulated beef cattle farming. Little by little the herds multiplied and spread toward the east, to the point that in 1712, there were 10,000 head of cattle in the eastern region of the French colony. By 1714 the number had risen to 14,000. This increase in French livestock would have been sufficient to satisfy the meat demand of the sugar plantations of the northern plains of Saint-Domingue had the population of these plantations not continued to grow so rapidly. In September 1701 thirty-five sugar mills were working to full capacity in the French colony. By the end of the year, twenty additional mills were almost operational, and another ninety were under construction.

Despite their flourishing herds of livestock, the French continued to buy Spanish cattle to supply their meat markets and to provide bulls for the transportation of sugarcane to the mills. In 1702 the Spanish exports of livestock, horses, and hides to the French colony increased to 50,000 *escudos* annually. This trade defined the relationship between the two colonies for the next ninety years and helped foster the sugar revolution in Saint-Domingue in the eighteenth century.

CHAPTER 8

Caribbean Sugar Economies in the Eighteenth Century

From Tobacco to Sugar in the British West Indies

One of the consequences of the establishment of new agricultural colonies on the Caribbean islands was the gradual replacement of natural vegetation with domesticated crops. Former jungle and savannas were converted into sugarcane fields or pastures, while in drier areas, tobacco fields alternated with cotton. The seventeenth century was a period of experimentation with new plants and agricultural technology. Some crops, such as cacao, vulnerable to production-slowing diseases, took many years to produce a profit. Ginger, on the other hand, quickly became profitable. It lost its competitiveness, however, when Brazilian ginger saturated the market. Though cotton always had a market, it was never the dominant crop. Instead, it was marginally cultivated in the driest regions of the islands. Likewise, the demand for medicinal plants like drumstick tree fruit and sarsaparilla was always minimal.

Market dynamics and experimentation brought sugarcane to the fore as the most profitable product, but it was also the crop that demanded the heaviest investment. Therefore the transition from tobacco to sugarcane in the Antilles took several decades, since the earliest cane farmers had little initial capital to invest. Moreover, not all landowners wanted to convert from tobacco to cane. Thus sugarcane and tobacco coexisted as the main export crops until the price of tobacco plummeted between 1670 and 1680. From this decade on, the shift to sugarcane proved irreversible.

These transition years were characterized by three important events. The first was the virtual elimination of the ruined tobacco farmers, forced now to sell their lands to sugar plantation owners. The second was the conversion of Barbados into a monocrop sugar economy. The third was the abandonment of cacao cultivation in Jamaica and the conversion of cacao fields into sugarcane fields.

The emergence of sugar as the dominant product in the Caribbean was accompanied by a change in the labor force from white indentured workers to African slaves. In 1680 Barbados had a population of 38,782 slaves and 2,317 white indentured servants. Four years later the number of slaves had increased to 46,000, while the number of indentured workers remained about the same.

By then Barbados had an elite class of 175 sugarcane planters who owned more than half of the island's slaves. This group represented less than 7 percent of Barbados's 2,311 sugarcane planters. Jamaica and the Leeward Islands also fell quickly under the domination of large plantation owners. In 1670 Jamaica had 724 landowners, among whom 102 owned holdings as large as the elite plantations on Barbados. In sharp contrast, Nevis, St. Kitts, Montserrat, and Antigua together could boast only twenty large plantations.

The concentration of property in Barbados and the loss of fertility of the land forced many tobacco cultivators and white indentured workers who had finished their contracts to immigrate to Jamaica and to the Carolinas in North America. In 1664, when Thomas Modyford, one of the large planters of Barbados, was appointed governor of Jamaica, a group of immigrants left with him. Many more emigrated from Barbados during the final decades of the seventeenth century.

Fearful that others would come to Jamaica to establish themselves as competitors in the sugar market, some Jamaican landowners quickly bought up the best land in an effort to block the creation of new plantations. Although they owned the largest holdings in all the English Antilles, the Jamaican planters could not equal the sugar production of their counterparts on Barbados until 1720. During these years, Jamaica had a scarce population of white manual laborers and even fewer major English investors. For this reason, during the first sixty years of its history as the largest British colony in the Caribbean, Jamaica ranked second in sugar production. Knowing that the likelihood of obtaining land was poor, very few white workers were willing to emigrate from Great Britain to Jamaica.

Another factor that delayed Jamaica's economic growth during the second half of the seventeenth century was the domineering presence of pirates in Port Royal. These unruly freebooters made the colony undesirable for agricultural colonization. The War of the League of Augsburg (1688–1697) and the War of Spanish Succession (1701–1715) turned Jamaica into a militarized zone. During the latter conflict, French and Spanish attacks on English trading ships in the Caribbean put Jamaica under the constant threat of enemy invasion. The Jamaican economy was also affected by frequent uprisings of organized runaway slaves, which terrified sugar plantation owners and destabilized life on the plantations.

Despite these difficulties, the planters gradually increased their sugar production to meet the European demand.[1] Sugar consumption in Europe grew rapidly, and the English became the main consumers and reexporters of sugar at the beginning of the eighteenth century.

The Rise of Sugar as a Commodity

By then sugar slowly but surely had ceased to be merely a medicine and a culinary curiosity for the rich. It had turned into a popular item in the diet of the middle class and the poor. At the beginning of the eighteenth century, it was already clear that this was an irreversible change. The caloric value of sugar was more efficient than that of flour and animal fat. Everyone, rich and poor alike, consumed sugar in tea, coffee, chocolate, syrups, jams, and marmalades. When tea eventually surpassed beer as the most common drink in England, the importance of sugar increased as a major ingredient in the English diet.

The extraordinary rise in the demand for sugar in Europe spurred the rapid expansion of sugar production in the Antilles. As sugar became more abundant, however, prices fell 70 percent. The reduction in the price of sugar between 1645 and 1680 led to an increase in sugar consumption in Europe. Between 1660 and 1700, sugar consumption quadrupled. This excess demand brought about a surge in the world sugar supply, particularly in the Caribbean, where production also quadrupled during this period.

The War of the League of Augsburg broke the cycle in which increases in production were followed by drops in the price of sugar. The war destabilized navigation in the Caribbean and caused sugar prices to double, until they reached their highest point of the century on the London market.[2] Wildly fluctuating prices stimulated production for almost a quarter of a century, that is, from 1689 up until the end of the War of Spanish Succession in 1715. These fluctuations encouraged speculation and attracted new producers, including the new French investors in Saint-Domingue.

Despite large oscillations, the price of sugar consistently fell during the first three decades of the eighteenth century. As a result, demand continued to grow, with consumption tripling between 1700 and 1740. Planters responded by increasing production, which in turn kept prices low, motivating Europeans to consume even more sugar. When prices began to rise again in 1734, sugar consumption was already well established in Europe, and consumers were no longer willing to do without sugar, regardless of price increases.[3]

Monoculture and Land Concentration

This increase in European sugar consumption in the eighteenth century led to the proliferation of the sugar monoculture and land concentration in the Caribbean. Barbados was the first among the sugar-producing islands to feel the effects of monoculture. By 1680 the islanders already had to import their food, lumber, and draft animals. In Barbados, as in the rest of the English Antilles, the development of a sugar monoculture coincided with the consolidation of the landowning elite. In 1712 Barbados had 1,309 sugar plantations and 485 sugar mills, but by 1750 the number of sugar plantations had declined to 536 and the number of sugar mills to 356, without a decline in sugar production or acreage cultivated.

The concentration of land in the hands of a small sugar-producing minority is one of the best-documented phenomena in the history of the British West Indies in the eighteenth century. The Leeward Islands were also turned into sugar plantations, with little land used for the production of food or other commercial crops. In St. Kitts, the conversion of land to sugarcane plantations became more intense after 1713, when

France ceded its rights to the island to Great Britain under the Treaty of Utrecht. From then on, land on St. Kitts previously occupied by the French was distributed among the British planters. By 1784 almost all the cultivable land of St. Kitts was planted with sugarcane under the ownership of only 120 planters. Between 1713 and 1784, sugar exports from St. Kitts increased sixfold and continued to rise during the last years of the eighteenth century.

Nevis, Montserrat, and Antigua, three Leeward Islands that had abandoned tobacco farming, also saw a decline in the number of sugar plantations, accompanied by a rise in their average size, in the eighteenth century. In Nevis, there were close to 100 sugar plantations in 1719, but by the end of the century the concentration of land and the emergence of larger plantations had reduced their number to fewer than 50. In Montserrat after 1729, sugarcane occupied 98.6 percent of the available land—a dramatic indicator of the extent of the monoculture on this island. In 1729, when a census of population and property was taken, it was discovered that only 30 plantations occupied almost 90 percent of the land planted with sugarcane and accounted for 75 percent of all sugar mills. Montserrat also continued to increase its sugar production from some 1,800 tons in 1729 to 2,750 tons in 1764.

In Antigua, the administrative capital of the Leeward Islands, the concentration of land into the hands of a landowning elite was less marked due to a land distribution policy enacted by the first plantation owners. In addition, unlike certain other islands of the British West Indies, Antigua had always maintained a low proportion of absentee cane farmers. For several generations, a small group of twelve families maintained control of the best sugar-producing lands. Antigua, however, was the only British island in the Leeward Islands where the number of plantations grew in the eighteenth century, rising from 150 in 1706 to more than 300 in 1764. Nevertheless, as was true on other islands, sugarcane monoculture in Antigua resulted in the gradual decrease of the white population and the accompanying growth of the slave population.[4]

Jamaica manifested the same characteristics of a monocultural sugar colony: a declining white labor force and an increasing number of black slaves, as well as an expanding sugar economy. To reduce the danger of slave revolts, the colonial authorities tried to increase the white population of Jamaica. With this purpose in mind, they enacted the so-called deficiency laws, which obliged the large landowners to maintain a minimum number of white workers on their plantations.

These laws were numerous. The first ones were approved at the beginning of the eighteenth century in response to the failed efforts to compel landowners to sell part of their lands to new cane farmers in order to broaden sugar production. Thanks to these laws and to the pressure from British consumers, the colonial government of Jamaica permitted poor cane farmers to immigrate from the Leeward Islands and Barbados, and offered them marginal land in the north and east of the island.

The deficiency laws helped Jamaica's white population grow throughout the eighteenth century, but always in a smaller proportion than the black population. In 1673, at the beginning of the sugar revolution, Jamaica had some 7,800 whites; one century later, in 1774, its white population had slightly more than doubled, reaching approximately 18,000. During the same period, the number of enslaved blacks in Jamaica grew almost twentyfold, from 10,000 to more than 193,000.

The number of plantations and the volume of sugar production increased steadily during the eighteenth century, but the Jamaican planters always agreed to control the quantity of land used for sugar to prevent prices from dropping. Therefore, when sugar prices began to rise after 1734, consumers and merchants in England supported new legislation submitted to the British Parliament that would require the Jamaican planters to sell or rent their uncultivated land to new cane farmers.

The major Jamaican absentee landowners, who were organized into a powerful parliamentary group in London, resisted these pressures and managed to keep their large estates intact for the rest of the century, only gradually increasing their production. Due to its landmass, Jamaica could have been the leading sugar colony in the Caribbean in the first half of the eighteenth century, but that title belonged to the French colony of Saint-Domingue.

The French Sugar Business

The success and continuous expansion of the French sugar industry in the Caribbean in the eighteenth century was partially due to the French government's policy of allowing the production of semirefined sugar in the Antilles (known as *sucre blanc* by the French and clayed sugar by the English). This product was somewhat more expensive than the *muscovado* sugar, but many consumers preferred it because it cost less than refined sugar and was of better quality than *muscovado*.

Other factors also explain France's rise in the sugar market. While England dominated the world sugar market in the second half of the seventeenth century, West Indian *muscovado* sugar competed directly with Brazilian sugar in Europe. As long as sugar production in Barbados and the West Indies exceeded Great Britain's internal demand, English merchants were able to reexport the surplus. When the War of Spanish Succession ended in 1714, the rise in internal demand forced the British to cut sugar exports. The European market was then quickly captured by the French, who consumed less sugar per capita and offered a better product at lower prices than the British. The wars between France and Great Britain in the eighteenth century created fluctuations in the volume of sugar reexported to the rest of Europe, but the French tended to dominate the market because they sold semirefined sugar at low prices.[5]

Even from a mercantilist perspective, the French government's policy was much more logical than that of the English. In April 1717 the French government rejected the demands of the sugar refiners in France who wanted to limit the colonies to the production of *muscovado* sugar, as was the case in the English colonies. Instead, the French government eliminated the colonial trade monopoly held by a few companies since the seventeenth century and opened up the colonial market to merchants and traders of the thirteen largest ports in France, giving them exclusive rights to trade with the French colonies.

The Letters Patent of April 1717 restricted colonial trade to French nationals only and prohibited foreigners from selling or buying in the colonies. At the same time, import taxes on West Indian sugar were fixed at 2.5 pounds *tournois* per hundredweight of *muscovado* sugar, and 8.0 pounds *tournois* per hundredweight of refined sugar. These taxes were far lower than those paid by English importers, who were charged as much as 7.5 pounds sterling per hundredweight of *muscovado* sugar and 15 pounds sterling per hundredweight of semirefined sugar. The French government also reduced the export taxes on this latter product to a mere 3 percent.

This fiscal policy led to a gigantic increase in French production in the following decades. Martinique, for instance, quadrupled its production from 5,192 tons in 1721 to more than 20,000 tons in 1750. In the meantime, Saint-Domingue increased its production from 9,700 tons in 1720 to 36,959 tons in 1767. This made it possible for France to reexport far more sugar as well. While France was reexporting between 15,000 and 17,000 tons of sugar in 1730, by 1790 it was able to reexport as much as 62,000 tons.[6]

Financing the Sugar Industry

An enormous investment was required to produce such large amounts of sugar. When the West Indian sugar industry was in its early stages, Dutch merchants provided the capital. After the Navigation Laws and L'Exclusif were enacted, English and French merchants began to finance sugar production, mostly after their governments expelled the Dutch from their colonies in the second half of the seventeenth century. In London, Liverpool, and Bristol, and in Le Havre, Nantes, Bordeaux, and Marseille, merchants who were interested in controlling the sugar supply for their refineries formed numerous companies that loaned money to West Indian sugar producers. These merchants served both as moneylenders to the sugar producers and as direct buyers of their sugar.

The initial financing of the Caribbean sugar industry was achieved with European commercial capital. Since money was scarce in the West Indies in the seventeenth and eighteenth centuries, the merchants demanded payment from the planters in the form of sugar and other colonial products. The planters considered such a system beneficial because their sugar had a guaranteed buyer, and they were assured of constant credit, which allowed them to invest in the expansion of their plantations, if needed. The merchants liked the system because with it they secured the supply of sugar and could thus speculate on future prices. In those cases when the planters incurred debts with the merchants, those debts were guaranteed by future deliveries of sugar.

In spite of the reciprocal advantages of this system, the planters complained that they were constantly indebted to the merchants and had no control over the price of their product. Therefore the planters wanted to emancipate themselves from their original creditors. To do this, many West Indian planters abandoned their plantations and returned to Europe. Planters also marketed sugar on their own through commission agents, who put the product on the market and placed the planters' revenues in special accounts.

The two systems coexisted for many years, but eventually the system of commission agents prevailed. Large sugar-marketing houses run by commission agents received the sugar from the West Indies and placed it on the European market at prices fixed in London, Amsterdam, or Nantes, not in the West Indies. The planters never succeeded in freeing themselves from the need for commercial credit, but the mobility with which they operated in the European financial sector permitted them to seek other sources of financing. Alternative credit sources became so numerous in the eighteenth century that the financing and distribution mechanisms of colonial profits became extremely complex.

Organization of the Slave Trade

Over time, all the economic sectors of Great Britain and France ended up either directly or indirectly involved in colonial commerce and the slave trade. Initially, European governments were closely associated with the merchants who organized the first slave-trading companies. In England, the first such company was the short-lived Royal Adventurers into Africa, founded in 1660, followed by the Royal African Company in 1672. The latter had a monopoly on the slave trade until the company was abolished in 1698 due to the complaints of the Caribbean planters about the high prices of the company's slaves.

In 1689 the planters protested that the Royal African Company had raised the price of slaves up to twenty pounds sterling per slave from an average price of twelve to fourteen pounds sterling in Barbados and

Jamaica. The company argued that the maintenance costs of their out-posts on the African coasts made it difficult to reduce the price of slaves. The company also imposed strict repayment conditions for slaves bought on credit. This quickly led to an increase in smuggled slaves, who could be bought in exchange for sugar.

Given the scarcity of slaves in the colonies, many merchants and absentee planters formed their own companies to participate in the slave trade. The struggle between the West Indian planters and the Royal African Company ended in 1698, when the British Parliament author-ized the free flow of slaves to the New World. From then on, individual traffickers had to buy a license from the company and pay a fee equiva-lent to 10 percent of the value of each slave transported. Between 1680 and 1708, the Royal African Company brought 64,156 slaves into the British colonies, while during the first ten years of the so-called 10 per-cent system, independent traffickers are estimated to have sold almost 90,000 slaves in Jamaica, Barbados, and Antigua.

The 10 percent system was abolished in 1712, when the British gov-ernment eliminated the monopoly held by the Royal African Company and allowed all merchants to procure slaves in Africa and transport them to the West Indies. From then on, there was an abundant supply of slave labor for the English sugar colonies. Most of the English slave traders were concentrated in Liverpool, London, and Bristol and, to a lesser extent, in Lancaster and Manchester.

In France, the slave trade evolved in a similar manner, and monopo-listic companies also had to give way to individual traders. The first company that dealt in the trade was the Compagnie des Indes Occiden-tales. This company enjoyed a monopoly until it was supplanted in 1685 by two other companies, the Compagnie du Sénégal, founded in 1672, and the Compagnie de la Guinée, founded in 1685. These companies controlled the slave market in the French Antilles for many years, direct-ed by various groups of businessmen in Paris and Rouen who were closely connected to Louis XIV.

These French consortia were never able to meet the colonies' demand for slaves. For this reason, the price of slaves went up more than the sug-arcane planters were willing to tolerate. This situation provoked protests and revolts in Martinique, Guadeloupe, and Saint-Domingue. Pressure from merchants in the main ports of France and the threat of smugglers convinced the French government of the need to eliminate the monopoly. In January 1716 King Louis XV issued the first Letters Patent in relation to the slave trade, allowing merchants in the ports of Nantes, Rouen, Bordeaux, La Rochelle, and St. Malo to put together expeditions to traffic slaves between France, Africa, and the Antilles, paying a tax of 20 pounds *tournois* per slave imported to the colonies. This tax was utilized for the construction and maintenance of French outposts on the African coast. Later on, other ports, such as Le Havre, Honfleur, Lorient, and Marseille, were also authorized to trade slaves. After the Letters Patent were issued, the French slave market became highly dynamic and was able to supply sufficient manual labor precisely when the sugar industry of Saint-Domingue was rapidly expanding.

Although some companies engaged in the slave trade retained exclusive rights in certain zones of Africa, many independent traders preferred to operate in these areas, even if they had to pay for their licenses. In this manner, they avoided the dangers of the British, Portuguese, and Dutch domains.

At the beginning of the eighteenth century, slave traders used a triangular trading circuit. After trading manufactured goods for slaves on the African coasts, ship captains would transport the slave cargoes to the West Indies and sell them to planters in exchange for sugar. The ships would return to England and France with the sugar, and the cycle would begin again.

In the mid-eighteenth century, the slave trade began to lose its triangular character, as shipbuilders learned to design special ships called West Indiamen that were exclusively dedicated to travel back and forth between the European ports and the West Indies. These carriers were larger than the typical slave ships and had a different deck layout. Slave ships, which the French called *négriers*, now traveled directly from Africa to the West Indies without needing to return to England or France fully loaded with sugar. Sugar transportation was gradually separated from slave transportation, as many *négriers* returned to Europe in ballast or with very little cargo to start the cycle again. Slaves were paid for in Africa principally with Asian fabrics but also with manufactured goods produced in the main industrial cities of England and France. The most important of these articles were clothes and textiles, gunpowder and munitions, iron and copper bars, knives and other metal utensils, brandy, wine and rum, glass, tobacco, pipes, ornaments, and even toys.

At each stage of the cycle, the entrepreneurs stood to gain: the industrialists whose goods were traded in Africa and the West Indies, the merchants who sold slaves to the planters in exchange for sugar, and the refiners and sugar traders who sold sugar to European consumers. In many cases, the entire process was handled by a single firm, whose trade was dictated by the availability of European manufactured goods, African slaves, and West Indian sugar.

The financing of colonial development, which began with an infusion of European capital to develop the first sugar plantations, ended up reversing itself, with the colonies financing their own economic growth as well as contributing to the development of commercial and industrial capitalism in Great Britain and France.

The accumulation of capital in Europe contrasted greatly with the lack of investment in infrastructure on the Caribbean islands. Absentee planters were hardly interested in public works, and little was maintained beyond the plantations. The roads were primitive, the cities had no significant public buildings, schools were almost nonexistent, and hospitals were scarce. The plantation owners put all of their efforts into developing and preserving the sugar plantations, as they became the center of colonial life in the British and French Antilles. Travelers who visited the West Indies in the eighteenth century agreed that life there revolved around the plantations and that production was sustained only by the incessant labor of the slaves.

Credit existed in different forms and served to maintain the diversity of the planters' capital resources. Capital was invested almost equally in three areas: slaves, land, and means of production, including machinery, tools, buildings, and supplies. Land and buildings constituted fixed capital, but slaves, machinery, tools, and supplies had to be constantly replaced. Therefore, the financing of the slave trade became the main axis of the colonial economy.

Slave Demography and the Economics of Slavery

As the life expectancy of slaves was relatively short, plantation owners had to continuously replace them in order to maintain sufficient levels of manual labor to meet production. High mortality rates and low birth rates caused an annual decline in the black population on the plantations, estimated between 2.5 and 5.0 percent. In other words, if a plantation stopped periodically replacing its slaves, they could all disappear within twenty years. Female slaves were therefore valued from early on, since they could contribute to the reproduction of the slave population.

Illness, abortions, and excessive work kept slave women's fertility at a very low level, and the West Indian planters discovered that the natural reproduction of slaves was not a reliable source of labor. Nonetheless, planters continued to import African female slaves because many worked well as cane cutters, having come from societies where women were in charge of agricultural tasks. They were also used as domestic servants.

About 35 percent of the slaves imported to the British Antilles in the eighteenth century were women, 51 percent were men, and the rest were boys and girls. In the French Antilles, the proportions were similar. In total, the French imported more than 1.3 million slaves to the Antilles between 1701 and 1790, while the British imported close to 1.1 million during the same period. The price of slaves varied constantly over the course of the eighteenth century but always tended to rise. Thus the cost of the average slave in the British West Indies was fourteen pounds sterling in 1707, thirty-four pounds sterling in 1775, and forty-seven pounds sterling in 1791.

Some modern studies question the profitability of the slave trade, but there is abundant evidence indicating that the profits increasingly attracted new merchants over time. Between 1738 and 1744, the French bought slaves in Africa for 300 pounds *tournois* on average, and could sell them in the Antilles for almost 615 pounds *tournois*. Half a century later, between 1783 and 1789, the average cost of acquiring a slave in Africa was about 750 pounds *tournois*, but that individual could then be sold in the French Antilles for 1,325 pounds *tournois*. Still, these were gross profits, and to determine the real profitability of the slave trade one needs to take into account other factors, such as the mortality of the Africans crossing the Atlantic, the expense of the expeditions, and other financial costs, such as interest payments.

Recent studies show that mortality on ships declined consistently from 20 percent at the end of the seventeenth century to 5 percent at the end of the eighteenth century. Some calculations suggest that a mortality rate between 10 and 15 percent on a shipment of 300 slaves would have reduced the profits of the expedition by 20 to 30 percent. Nevertheless, even with higher mortality rates, the slave trade must have been profitable; otherwise, it would not have attracted so much capital investment over such a long period of time.

The most serious problem investors faced was not selling slaves or colonial products, but recuperating credit given to merchants, shipbuilders, and planters, many of whom had a tendency to accumulate debts. As the eighteenth century advanced, planter and merchant debts to European financiers increased steadily. This caused many European investors to complain about the dubious commercial practices of their West Indian debtors.

Investor complaints led the British Parliament to enact the famous Credit Act of 1732. The Credit Act established that land, sugar plantations, and slaves owned by West Indian planters could be used to repay loans. The act simply repeated a common practice in England that permitted the use of land to repay debts. This law broadened the collateral base for loans to planters and English merchants, allowing capital to flow more easily.

Due to low, stable interest rates (around 5 percent during the eighteenth century), large amounts of capital were available for investment in colonial ventures. The permanent availability of capital stimulated the continuous growth of the West Indian sugar plantations, particularly in Jamaica and Saint-Domingue. The number of sugar plantations in Jamaica rose from 124 in 1701 to 651 in 1768,[7] and in Saint-Domingue it rose from 170 in 1716 to 793 in 1785.[8]

Technological Changes: The Jamaican Train

The eighteenth century witnessed an increase not only in the number of the plantations but also in their size and productivity. While the average sugar plantation in the English Antilles in 1670 produced 11.8 tons of sugar per year, a century later production had quintupled to 56.6 tons.

The sugar plantations' increase in productivity was due to a technological innovation called the "Jamaican train." The sugar mills that employed this system heated their boilers on a train of furnaces designed with an innovative variable heat firing system. Boiling of the cane juice started at lower furnace temperature. As the water content of the juice evaporated, it passed to other boilers sequentially heated at higher furnace temperatures until the semifinal product, molasses, was obtained. In this manner, the removal of impurities from the cane juice was regulated more efficiently than with the traditional system, which used a separate oven for each boiler fed by separate fires and required more labor. Sugar was made by decanting and crystallizing the molasses later.

The Jamaican train helped extract more sucrose from the cane juice. The origin of the Jamaican train is still debated. From its name, it is conventionally assumed that it originated in Jamaica, although some scholars believe it came from Saint-Domingue, where it was also called the "French train." Others claim that this innovation began in Barbados. No matter where it first originated, the Jamaican train was the model for the majority of the sugar mills built in the West Indies in the eighteenth century.

Thanks to the Jamaican train, the technology for making sugar became standardized, allowing today's scholars to conduct comparative analysis across plantations and colonies. Sugarcane planted in the Antilles (*Saccharum officinarum*) stayed the same until the last decade of the eighteenth century, when new varieties were introduced from Asia and the Pacific Islands, particularly Tahiti. The cultivation methods, transportation systems, and management of slave labor also remained constant. There was no significant variation from island to island with regard to the techniques for sedimentation, crystallization, or the drying and packing of sugar for export to European ports.

Interisland technological similarities led to substantial homogeneity in plantation work as well. When an island changed hands due to wars, the sugar plantations continued to function without changes in the manufacturing process or in the quality of the sugar. One of the reasons sugar became a "commodity" was its relative physical uniformity. Even if there were visible differences in quality between the *muscovado* and semirefined sugars, these differences disappeared following the refining process in Europe. The final result was the same: a more or less brownish grainy substance with the same taste and sucrose content.

CHAPTER 9

Caribbean Trade Circuits in the Eighteenth Century

Navigation Laws and Colonial Trade

In addition to sugar, the Caribbean islands also produced molasses and rum. These products were an important part of colonial trade and were almost as instrumental as sugar in linking the West Indian plantations to the British colonies of North America and integrating the Caribbean into the Atlantic economy. As the world sugar market emerged, the Caribbean was likewise connected to the European economy as a regular supplier of a basic commodity.

The integration of the Caribbean into the world market and the commercial relationship between the Caribbean islands and the North American colonies were always affected by the rigid European monopoly systems that provoked long and costly wars. English and French colonies established in the seventeenth century were developed under mercantilist principles, which led to the promulgation of laws of navigation and trade enacted to keep the colonies under the exclusive control of their ruling country.

In England, the first such laws were passed in 1651 and declared that exports and imports from the English Antilles had to be transported exclusively on English ships. Nine years later, in 1660, the English government decreed that sugar, tobacco, cotton, indigo, ginger, and dyewood had to be taken to England before being resold in other parts of Europe. From then on, these products were known as "enumerated articles" and were given special treatment by British customs. In 1661 tariffs were enacted for *muscovado* sugar from the English Caribbean colonies that were one-third as high as those for similar foreign sugar.

In order to protect English refiners and discourage the installation of refineries in the West Indies, however, the English government taxed refined sugar coming from its colonies almost as highly as foreign sugar.

Another English law enacted in 1663 declared that the colonies could import only English products, with a few exceptions. For example, wine and salt could be imported from the Mediterranean, as could horses and grains from Ireland and Scotland. Later, in 1671, it was decreed that West Indian sugar first had to go through English ports before being imported into Ireland. In 1673, the English government prohibited Scottish trade with the Caribbean islands and placed a high tax on intercolonial commerce to prevent North American colonists from reexporting Caribbean sugar to Europe.

Until 1673 the English Caribbean and the North American colonies had enjoyed free trade that benefited both regions. Although initially the two regions produced some of the same products, such as tobacco and cotton, over time the North American colonies concentrated on exporting hides, grain, flour, salted fish, lumber, iron products, ships, nautical supplies, tobacco, cotton, rice, horses, and mules. The English Antilles, on the other hand, exported sugar, molasses, rum, and other tropical products. A commercial trade circuit between the English Caribbean and the North American colonies gradually began to form.

With this trade, the two regions could exchange surpluses and were connected to the broader trade circuits of the Atlantic economy, including the Europe-Africa commercial axis. The integration of the colonies into the Atlantic economy was a slow but continuous process, unforeseen in the seventeenth century when the Navigation Laws were enacted, but more evident as early as the beginning of the eighteenth century during the consolidation of the French sugar industry in the Caribbean.

Caribbean Molasses and the North Americans

Caribbean molasses played a central role in the development of the new Atlantic economy. Molasses was needed to produce rum and spirits, which were then traded for slaves on the African coast. The demand for molasses rose continuously as sugar production increased. But since the molasses production of the English Antilles was not sufficient to supply the North American and British demand, the merchants of Jamaica, Barbados, and the Leeward Islands soon discovered that they could reexport smuggled molasses from the French islands to England and North America as if it had been produced in the British West Indies.

In the French Antilles, there was always an abundance of molasses. While England tried to protect its sugar refiners by prohibiting sugar from being refined in its colonies, France attempted to protect its wine, brandy, and liquor industries by preventing its colonies from exporting molasses to France to be converted into rum and spirits. Brandy and poor-quality wines were among the products used to buy slaves in Africa, and for that reason French wine and brandy producers did not want competition from West Indian molasses being converted into rum in France. At the beginning of the sugar revolution, molasses was underutilized, with only a very small quantity being distilled and converted into rum for residents of the plantations.

As time went by, rum became an important colonial export. In addition to its use in the slave trade, rum was widely exchanged for furs from the North American Indians. The demand for West Indian molasses grew quickly in Massachusetts, Rhode Island, Connecticut, New York, New Jersey, and Pennsylvania. Distillers from North America, England, and Ireland were in constant competition for Caribbean molasses, and English distillers took great pains to block the export of molasses from the Antilles to their competitors.

For some time, the English colonists in the West Indies were the main providers of French molasses to the North American colonies and Ireland. But by the beginning of the eighteenth century, the North American and Irish colonists were avoiding the middlemen and buying molasses, sugar, and rum directly from the French.

At the end of the War of Spanish Succession in 1715, the French Antilles directly bought more products from North America than from the British West Indies. During the war, the British Antilles constantly faced shortages of lumber, flour, salted fish, horses, and mules. Among other things, this problem could be traced to the fact that merchants from Rhode Island, New York, Pennsylvania, and the Carolinas were sending their ships directly to Curaçao and St. Thomas, where Dutch merchants would buy their cargo in order to resell it as contraband in the Spanish Antilles.

The English colonists in the Antilles thought that it was unfair to allow the Dutch to supply the Spanish islands with North American merchandise. Jamaican colonists had previously done most of the smuggling to the Spanish Antilles and had been paid in Spanish silver coins. To convince the British government that it should protect them more effectively, the Jamaican merchants argued that Dutch competition would make it impossible for Jamaica to afford imported goods from England, thereby affecting the English economy adversely.

The English colonial authorities tried to stop smuggling through attempts to enforce the old Navigation Laws, but the North American colonists continued to trade with the French and Dutch Antilles. Unwilling to be left out of the market, many Jamaican merchants joined in the smuggling of sugar, molasses, and rum to North America. This practice violated a 1686 treaty between France and England that prohibited this type of intercolonial trade. Nevertheless, between 1715 and 1730 the majority of the distilleries of New York, Rhode Island, and Massachusetts were almost exclusively processing molasses from Martinique, Guadeloupe, and Saint-Domingue. In Rhode Island, for instance, of an average 14,000 barrels of imported molasses each year, 11,500 came from the French Antilles.

In the early 1700s the trade of French molasses and sugar with North America grew considerably, creating serious worries for the British authorities. Since some of the sugar went to Great Britain as if it had been produced in the British West Indies, full tariffs were not paid on it. The absentee planters living in England tried to get the British government to eliminate this trade, but they had no success because many English colonists from Barbados, Jamaica, and the Leeward Islands served as middlemen between the French and Dutch smugglers and the North Americans. The colonial assemblies of Barbados, Jamaica, and Antigua failed when they tried in 1715, 1716, and 1721 to prohibit intercolonial trade.

The situation continued until 1730, when the absentee planters began a propaganda campaign in London to convince the British public and Parliament that Barbados's declining economy was due to competition with the North American colonies. This argument had been presented to the colonial assembly of Barbados at the end of 1729, and in following years it was repeated numerous times to the British Parliament by the absentee planters, who continually proposed laws to restrict inter-colonial trade.

In May 1733 the pressure on the British Parliament culminated in the approval of the famous Molasses Law, which required that all sugar, molasses, and rum from foreign territories be declared. Import taxes on foreign produce were fixed higher than those on British West Indian sugar products, at four shillings per hundredweight of sugar, nine cents per gallon of rum, and six cents per gallon of molasses. Later, the tax on sugar was increased to five shillings per hundredweight.

The North American colonists immediately protested and argued that if they were prevented from doing business with the French and Dutch Antilles, their colonies would be ruined. They said that the British Antilles' demand for North American lumber, provisions, and horses was too low, and that the quantity of molasses that the islands could supply was also too small to satisfy the growing demand of the North American distilleries. Given that rum was a key article of exchange for fur pelts, fish, and slaves, the North American colonists claimed that if their supply of molasses from the Caribbean was suppressed or obstructed, the British economy would also suffer because the North Americans would not have as much income with which to purchase British goods.

The Molasses Law constituted the first important parliamentary victory for the absentee planters in London, giving them a previously unknown influence. This law, however, by no means stopped the smuggling of sugar, rum, and molasses to North America. Despite the law, the following thirty years were a golden period for smugglers from all areas, especially North America. Jamaica became an important center of clandestine trade thanks to the negligence of its customs authorities and its proximity to the French colony of Saint-Domingue. The Jamaican traffickers bought and reexported cheap French sugar and molasses to England and North America, claiming that these goods were produced in the British West Indies.

Spanish Privateering and War

Trading with the Spanish Antilles, on the other hand, was highly dangerous for English and North American colonists. During the War of Spanish Succession, the risk was even greater due to the constant surveillance of Creole Spanish privateers, officially called the *guardacostas* (coast guard). The *guardacostas* were organized to help Spain militarily, but they soon occupied themselves by supplying merchandise stolen from British traders to the poverty-stricken Spanish colonial towns.

After the War of Spanish Succession, the Spanish continued to send out their privateers to attack all the ships they could find in the Caribbean. Between 1715 and 1720, the French authorities of Saint-Domingue, the English colonists of Jamaica, and merchants from Boston, Salem, Providence, Newport, New York, and Philadelphia made frequent reports to their respective governments concerning attacks and pillaging carried out by the privateers of Santo Domingo and Puerto Rico under the protection of the Spanish authorities. These attacks led to a breakdown in diplomatic relations between Spain and England in 1718, but the rupture only served to intensify the activity of the Spanish privateers. The raids against the French ceased in 1721, but those against the English continued throughout the following decade. They became more intense after 1727, when war was again declared between Spain and England, instigated by Spain's attempt to recover the Gibraltar Peninsula, which had been taken over by the British in 1704.

For some years, privateering was the main activity of the colonists of Santo Domingo, San Juan, San Germán, Havana, Santiago de Cuba, Baracoa, and Trinidad. Both the authorities and the colonists participated, as investors, expedition organizers, and sailors. Privateers, such as Miguel Henríquez and Pedro de la Torre of Puerto Rico and José Domingo Cortázar, Bartolomé Valadón, and Bartolomé López of Cuba, became famous and amassed fortunes, which they later invested in ships, land, and urban properties. These privateers sold their captured booty in Havana, Santo Domingo, and San Juan, and sometimes even in St. Thomas and Curaçao. The Puerto Rican privateers normally operated between Mona Island and the Leeward Islands, while the Dominicans patrolled between Saona Island and Jamaica. The Cuban privateers operated south of Cuba and in Jamaican waters, and some would go as far as New York and Rhode Island.

For more than twenty years, British diplomats protested the attacks of the *guardacostas* before the Spanish king in Madrid, but Spain made little effort to the stop its privateers' plundering in the Caribbean. The Spanish government continued to claim that its *guardacostas* were necessary to defend Spanish trade in the Caribbean. Spain protected its colonial possessions just as France and England did, and fought against foreign ships in waters under Spanish jurisdiction, especially English wood traffickers operating in Belize, Honduras, and Campeche, on the Yucatán Peninsula. On more than one occasion, these lumber traders were captured and expelled from the area, despite protests by the British.

Guardacostas privateering was finally brought before the British Parliament in 1738. At that time, both merchants and members of Parliament demanded that Spain be penalized for allowing its privateers to prey on British trade and navigation. By advocating the notion that war stimulates commerce, an idea then in vogue, these groups mobilized public opinion in Great Britain in favor of declaring war on Spain.

The merchants and British parliamentary opposition also stirred up British public opinion by citing the alleged Spanish attack on an English captain, Robert Jenkins, who claimed to have lost an ear when his ship was attacked by Spanish *guardacostas*. As proof, having preserved his "evidence" in a small box, he presented the ear dramatically to the British Parliament. Although there were members of Parliament who did not believe Captain Jenkins's story, England declared war on Spain in October 1739. France entered the conflict the following year as a Spanish ally for reasons linked to the succession of the Austrian throne. For the first time, the cause of a European war could be traced directly to a conflict in the Caribbean.

Early in the conflict, the English tried to gain territory and launched a series of attacks against the main Spanish fortified cities in the Caribbean. The English took the city of Portobelo and razed it, but failed in their attempts to do the same to Cartagena and Santiago de Cuba. Another expedition against Guantanamo Bay in 1741 also failed, despite the participation of 600 North American colonists from Massachusetts, New York, Pennsylvania, and Virginia who wanted to settle in Cuba.

The capture of Portobelo and the activities of the British war ships in the Caribbean showed the Spanish system of galleon fleets to be obsolete; in fact, during the war, only one fleet was able to complete its journey between Spain and the colonies. Deprived of Spanish merchandise, the Spanish colonies saw the flourishing of contraband as never before. As the war proceeded, the Spanish privateers kept trying to do as much damage as possible to British trade in the Caribbean. In Havana and Santiago de Cuba alone, the authorities issued more than 130 privateering permits between 1743 and 1745.

In those two years, privateers captured 80 British and North American ships but also stirred up a violent reaction from the North Americans, who decided to organize pirate expeditions against Spanish and French ships. In 1744, 113 North American ships were already operating around Cuba. The French, on the other hand, sent privateering expeditions out from Guadeloupe, Martinique, and Saint-Domingue to fight the British, who were blocking their ports and attacking their merchant ships.

Because the war disrupted the flow of sugar from the French colonies to Europe, the price of sugar began to rise, giving British merchants a wide margin for speculation. Since the British were unable to reach their objective of capturing new territories, they concentrated their efforts on preventing French sugar from reaching Europe.

During the last years of the war, the French position gravely deteriorated because the British navy kept Martinique, Guadeloupe, and Saint-Domingue under blockade. The French could not retaliate because British warships continually escorted merchant ships with sugar and molasses to Great Britain. Once the war was over in 1748, sugar prices began to normalize. A peace treaty was signed in which none of the countries at war were formally granted any new territory. It was also clear that neither England nor France was interested in expanding its colonial possessions.

One incident in particular shows why France and England were reluctant to take new colonies during that period. In 1741, when preliminary negotiations to end the war had begun, diplomats discussed the possibility of Spain ceding its portion of the island of Santo Domingo to France. In exchange, France would cede other Caribbean possessions like Guadeloupe to Great Britain, and Britain would compensate Spain by returning Gibraltar. The French colonists opposed this agreement by arguing that if the fertile plains of Santo Domingo were used for sugar production, the market would be glutted, sugar prices would plummet, and the existing sugar producers in the Antilles would be ruined.

One important consequence of the so-called War of Jenkins's Ear was the clarification of the status of various sparsely populated islands in the Lesser Antilles whose sovereignty was in constant dispute in the courts of London and Paris. When the Treaty of Aix-la-Chapelle was signed in 1748, the parties agreed that the islands of Dominica, St. Lucia, St. Vincent, and Tobago should be evacuated by the few French and English colonists living there and be considered neutral territories under the dominion of the Carib Indians, who had taken refuge there after being expelled from neighboring islands in the previous century. The status of Belize, however, was not resolved at this time and would later spark new conflicts between Spain and Great Britain.

During the War of Jenkins's Ear, much of the smuggling was done from the so-called neutral ports, that is, from the Dutch possessions of Curaçao, St. Eustatius, and St. Martin and the Danish colonies of St. Thomas and St. Croix. The merchants from these islands regularly traded with the Spanish and French colonies and kept their markets open to ships from all nations. In 1740 it was reported that Great Britain was annually importing several thousand tons of French sugar acquired in neutral ports and introduced to the market as if it had been produced in the British West Indies.

Furthermore, despite the efforts of the British navy to block trade with the French Antilles, the French colonies likewise used the neutral islands for their own benefit, trading French colonial products for English and North American merchandise. The neutral ports became gigantic warehouses of North American flour, lumber, horses, salted fish, cereals, cheese, bread, cakes, beer, cider, tools, iron items, and nautical supplies, and numerous types of European manufactured goods imported by the Dutch and Danish, such as textiles, wine, candles, soap, iron products, jewelry, medicine, shoes, and sausages and other foodstuffs, as well as slaves from Africa.

Contraband Trade with North America

At the end of the war, the colonists of Massachusetts, Rhode Island, and New York played an important role in furthering French colonial trade. Many North American colonists did not bother to hide their operations by using the neutral islands and sent their ships directly to Cap François, Léogane, and other ports of Saint-Domingue, as well as Fort-de-France in Martinique and Basse-Terre in Guadeloupe. The colonists of the Leeward Islands followed the example of the North American and Jamaican traffickers, buying sugar from the French in St. Eustatius and then reexporting it to Great Britain. St. Eustatius, in fact, became one of the main commercial centers of the Antilles during the war.

The Spanish colonists also successfully resisted the eradication of smuggling. Since Spain could not adequately supply its colonies, they were forced to seek supplies elsewhere. Contraband on the Spanish islands came from several sources. One was direct contact with Holland and Denmark, the two nations that dominated the clandestine trade, periodically bringing European manufactured goods to the rivers and coasts of Cuba, Santo Domingo, and Puerto Rico in exchange for hides, ginger, cacao, and coffee.

With fluctuations in the political situation in Europe and in the level of tolerance of Spanish military governments, Dutch and Danish ships were often legally allowed to enter the main ports of the Spanish Antilles to trade openly. Puerto Rican and Dominican sloops and schooners loaded with hides, ginger, cattle, and foodstuffs traveled to St. Thomas, St. Croix, St. Eustatius, and St. Martin to exchange their goods for European merchandise. The strong Dutch presence in the Spanish Caribbean is clearly represented in the records of legal entries and exits of ships into and out of the ports of Havana, Santo Domingo, and San Juan between 1700 and 1800.

The Spanish Intercolonial Trade

The merchants of the Spanish Antilles constantly traded among themselves and with those of the continental ports of La Guaira

Maracaibo, Coro, Cumaná, Margarita, Cartagena, Santa Marta, Portobelo, and Veracruz. Sloops typically transported the trade goods,
although schooners and brigantines were also utilized. The shipments
were generally small, but the contents varied. They included unpro-
cessed hides and leather, sugar, cacao, ginger, salt, corn, cassava, drumstick fruit, tar and pitch, horses and mules, dry beans, onions and garlic, oil and vinegar, and tobacco. Goods were sent from one area to
another to satisfy temporary deficiencies in local production.

Despite the variety of products traded, the volume of this trade was
very small in comparison with the large volume of contraband occurring on the non-Spanish Antilles. Even so, Spanish intercolonial trade
was crucial to the survival of the impoverished haciendas of Cuba,
Santo Domingo, and Puerto Rico, which relied on it for food and provisions. Official documents of the time usually mention trade between
the principal island ports, but several North American products, such as
flour, cheese, butter, ham, and salted meat and fish, are mentioned as
well, in addition to other products from Spain and the Canary Islands,
such as wine, oil, vinegar, and dried fruit.

The French and Spanish colonists also conducted extensive trade in
the eighteenth century along the border between their respective
colonies on the island of Española. The Spanish authorities condemned
this trade for many years, until the French began to establish sugar mills
and plantations on land previously utilized to raise livestock. Since the
few cattle that grazed in the French area were quickly consumed, the
French relied heavily on their Spanish neighbors for livestock.

In Santo Domingo, at the beginning of the French sugar industry, the
French would pay up to 25 pesos for one cow and her calf. A mule
imported from the Spanish side of the island cost up to forty pesos. In
1702 the French authorities estimated that about 50,000 pesos worth of
cattle, horses, and mules were purchased annually from the Spanish. For
this reason, in the first fifteen years of the eighteenth century, the
French made a serious attempt to breed their own cattle to reduce
dependency on the Spanish. The French herds, however, barely reached
14,000 head of cattle by 1714. Soon thereafter, cattle almost disappeared, as sugar plantations gradually took over their rangeland. In
1716 more than 100 sugar mills were operating in the French colony.
Workers at these mills required meat, and the mills themselves needed

horses, mules, and bulls as draft animals.

The Spanish authorities tried to take advantage of the livestock trade and charged taxes and commissions from the Spanish ranchers and Frenchmen visiting the Spanish side of the island to buy livestock. In so doing, the Spanish authorities obstructed the flow of livestock across the border, caused numerous arguments between the French and Spanish colonial governments, and even brought about a popular uprising against Spanish rule in 1721. This uprising, led by several military officers who owned ranches themselves, took place in Santiago de los Caballeros, in the center of the island.[1]

After the uprising of 1721, the Spanish authorities agreed to facilitate and stabilize trade with the French. Finally, in 1731 the authorities of both colonies signed their first pact regulating the flow of livestock and merchandise from one side of the island to the other and defining the boundary line between the two colonies. By then it had become quite clear that livestock from the Spanish side of the island was a cheaper source of protein for the slaves on the French plantations than Cuban livestock, North American dried meat, or imported salted fish.

Trade along the border with Saint-Domingue, together with privateering, helped Santo Domingo recover economically. Large numbers of its colonists raised livestock, an activity that soon became the foundation of the colony's economy. All efforts to find other productive sources of income fell short of the success of raising and hunting livestock and exporting hides and live animals. In addition to the large number of live cattle that crossed the border, the Spanish colonists legally exported 159,000 hides through the port of Santo Domingo between 1700 and 1746, an annual average of almost 3,500. Illegal exports were estimated to constitute an equivalent number.

In Puerto Rico as well, illegal trade with foreigners enabled the population to survive without importing merchandise from Spain. Although smuggling stimulated agriculture and cattle raising in Puerto Rico, it was never able to provide enough income to bring the majority of the population out of poverty. Even though the island was more populated than Santo Domingo or Cuba, land was always available. Town councils would give unclaimed land to anyone who requested it, including laborers and soldiers. Gradually, the Puerto Rican population dispersed throughout the island, raising livestock and produce that were sold to the Danish sugar plantations of St. Thomas and St. Croix and the Dutch islands of St. Eustatius, Saba, St. Martin, and Curaçao.

St. Croix and St. Thomas, where 30,000 slaves worked on sugar plantations, were the most important of these markets. Due to the monoculture of sugarcane, the planters on St. Croix, as on the other sugar islands, were forced to import draft animals, livestock, food, and other necessities from North America and the neighboring islands. Puerto Rican colonists supplied St. Croix directly and indirectly through St. Thomas. Sometimes the Puerto Rican colonists used their own schooners, but they normally waited for British, Dutch, and Danish brigantines to come to preassigned smuggling sites. This trade was fairly specialized: the British generally bought logwood and guaiacum, the Dutch bought tobacco, and the Danish bought food and coffee. All of them tried to buy as many head of cattle, horses, and mules as possible to satisfy the constant demand for these animals on the West Indian plantations.

Reduced mortality from epidemics contributed to the growth of the population of the Spanish Antilles in the eighteenth century. In Puerto Rico, the population grew from 6,000 in 1700 to 44,883 in 1765, including 5,037 slaves. Santo Domingo also recuperated from its demographic stagnation, as its population grew from 18,410 in 1718 to 30,058 in 1739 and 70,629 in 1769. This last figure included 8,900 slaves. The Cuban population grew similarly from 50,000 in 1700 to 172,620 in 1774, including slaves and free blacks. In 1763 there were 43,000 slaves and 30,000 free blacks living in Cuba.

Cuba's Slow Rise as a Sugar Producer

Between 1717 and 1739, when the South Sea Company controlled the procurement of slaves, the British legally imported 5,784 slaves to Havana, averaging 262 slaves per year. Compared with the figures for the British and French West Indies, these numbers seem insignificant, but they do show that the Cuban planters were also connected to and familiar with the routes used in the slave trade.

Nonetheless, during the first third of the eighteenth century, Cuba continued to have a largely livestock- and service-based economy, serving the fleets that periodically visited Havana. Most people on the island were concentrated in Havana and produced salted and smoked meat, pork, cassava, and other food to supply the fleets, as well as tobacco. In eastern and southern Cuba, livestock smuggling continued because the livestock prices set in Havana were so low that they did not even cover the cost of transportation from the interior of the island to the city. Occasionally, the French colonists of Saint-Domingue would buy livestock from the ranchers of eastern Cuba, but their main source of meat was Santo Domingo.

The main limitation to Cuba's development at the beginning of the eighteenth century was the Spanish commercial policy that allowed French sugar to enter Cadiz duty-free while Cuban sugar was burdened with high taxes. In 1696 and 1713 King Philip V of Spain had established customs duties that made Cuban sugar less competitive than French sugar. The importation of slaves to Cuba was also highly taxed. Under these circumstances, very few people wanted to invest in the creation of Cuban sugar plantations, and many planters abandoned the business completely. In 1717, for instance, the councilmen of Havana pointed out that only twenty-eight sugar plantations were left of the many that had been built in the seventeenth century. The others had been converted to rangeland and tobacco fields.

King Philip V continually stated that he approved of the development of the sugar industry in Cuba, but his economic policy did not reflect this. Additional taxes levied in 1720 on the importation of Cuban sugar to Spain and the increase in the tax on transportation on royal ships caused Cuban sugar prices to soar by more than 75 percent in Spain.

After protesting the policies of the Spanish government for years, the Cuban colonists eventually convinced King Philip V that if he wanted to encourage sugar production, he had to reduce taxes. In 1730 he lowered the tax on the import and sale of sugar in Spain to 5 percent and also reduced the transportation tax by a third. The Spanish government argued that with these measures, Cuban sugar could compete with French sugar, which was subject to a 7 percent tax. The Cuban planters, however, quickly pointed out that the French product was superior in quality and that the French could easily bribe customs officials in Cadiz.

Havana landowners continued to press for more protection for Cuban sugar, and some gambled their future on the sugar industry. With great effort, the planters of Havana managed to build twelve sugar plantations between 1717 and 1740. By 1740 there were forty-three plantations in the area around Havana. Compared to the other Caribbean islands, this growth was very meager. In a 1723 rural census, the Cuban colonial authorities counted 118 sugar mills in the central part of the island. These, however, were very small mills that employed few slaves, used little land, and largely produced molasses and *muscovado* sugar for the local market.

The situation gradually began to change after 1740, with the creation of the Real Compañía de Comercio de la Habana. This company, organized and protected by the Spanish government, monopolized the sugar and tobacco trade and assured the supply of tobacco to the Real Fábrica de Tabacos of Seville. When the company was just commencing operations, its directors concluded that to encourage the sugar business, high taxes had to be repealed and slaves needed to be imported to Cuba. In response to pressure from the company, on December 18, 1740, Philip V issued a royal decree that eliminated customs duties on Cuban sugar in Cadiz and Seville. The Real Compañía de Comercio de la Habana then proceeded to encourage the establishment of new sugar plantations by offering loans to colonists, increasing the market price of sugar, and introducing black slaves.

By 1757 the results of this new policy were already visible. In that year there were eighty-eight sugar plantations in the area around Havana and 253 small sugar mills on the rest of the island. The average annual production of these smaller mills barely reached 10 tons. The sugar mills around Havana were larger; their average production in 1751 was 37.5 tons. By 1763 the average production of the ninety-six *ingenios* around Havana had increased to 43 tons. Nonetheless, compared to the sugar mills of the French and British West Indies, the Cuban mills were still small. In 1759 the total Cuban sugar production was 5,662 tons, 4,250 tons of which was exported to Spain. This volume constituted only 12 percent of Jamaica's sugar exports to Great Britain that year.

Despite its small size, the Cuban sugar industry took an important leap forward during the twenty years (1740–1760) in which the Cuban economy was controlled by the Real Compañía de Comercio de la

Habana. The company contributed the necessary credit to finance the construction of new sugar plantations and the importation of several thousand slaves. At the time, it was estimated that 4,986 slaves were legally imported between 1740 and 1760, but recent studies suggest that the number was twice as large, somewhere between 8,000 and 11,000.

During the eighteenth century, the Caribbean became a fairly integrated and fluid regional market. France, Spain, and Great Britain tried to control the market through their rigid monopoly systems, but they failed. Once the European governments recognized that an open market functioned better than a monopoly, they gradually accepted free trade on the neutral islands and later, in the second half of the eighteenth century, in specially designated Caribbean and European ports. But to reach that stage, two major wars had to be fought, a series of intermittent hurricanes and droughts had to create a critical chain of regional food crises, and some important political and market changes had to occur in both the Caribbean and in North America.

CHAPTER 10

Trade and Wars

Expanding the Plantation Economy

Despite wars and blockades, the Caribbean economies continued to produce sugar, import slaves, and trade with the North American colonies. But three new conflicts contributed to the transformation of the economic, political, and social map of the Caribbean in the second half of the eighteenth century. The first was the Seven Years War, from 1756 to 1763, which took place in Europe, Africa, North America, and the West Indies. The second was the American Revolution between 1775 and 1783, which exerted a strong impact on the Caribbean colonial world that lasted for at least four decades. The Haitian Revolution (1791-1804) was the most important conflict of all. In each of these events, the Caribbean served as the theater for diverse military operations and experienced powerful economic effects.

After 1748 the West Indies experienced their fastest growth. Although production in Barbados and the Leeward Islands increased slowly, the economies of Jamaica and Saint-Domingue expanded considerably, as did those of St. Croix and Demerara, two new colonies developed respectively by the Danish and Dutch. In 1746 the Dutch began to produce sugar in Demerara with the help of planters from Barbados, as had happened in Essequibo, which had been producing sugar since 1664. In the mid-eighteenth century, Essequibo and Demerara together had almost 100 sugar plantations worked by nearly 5,000 slaves. Their entire production was exported to Amsterdam.

St. Croix, on the other hand, was bought by the Danish Company of the West Indies from France in 1733, after remaining uninhabited for almost half a century, except for serving as a pirate refuge. Between 1735 and 1755, Danish surveyors measured the island and sold the land in lots of about 150 acres to colonists from other Caribbean islands who wanted to move there. Within a few years, St. Croix experienced an agricultural revolution: by 1742 there were already 264 plantations, of which 120 produced sugarcane and 122, cotton. In the following years, the larger planters began to consolidate their land holdings to the extent that by 1750 only fifty-three sugar plantations remained. Nevertheless, sugar production continued to increase. In 1750 St. Croix had a population of about 6,000 slaves and nearly 700 free laborers, mostly employed for the cultivation of sugar.

The sugar economy of St. Croix experienced a growth spurt during the Seven Years War, due to a disruption in the world sugar trade caused by the British blockade of the French Antilles. Since France reexported most of its production to northern Europe, the delay in its shipments created a vacuum, which was quickly filled by the Danish and Dutch. Also, in 1754 the king of Denmark revoked the monopolistic rights that he had previously granted the Danish Company of the West Indies and declared a policy of open trade similar to the one that existed in St. Thomas and St. John, Denmark's other possessions in the Virgin Islands.

In the wake of these changed policies, the planters of St. Croix managed to increase their sugar exports in the twenty years that followed. In 1753 St. Croix produced only 320 tons of sugar, but by 1773 its production had multiplied twenty-five times to 8,200 tons. The slave population of St. Croix almost quadrupled, growing quickly from 1,906 in 1742 to 7,566 in 1753.

With their consistent policy of neutrality, the Danish were able to maintain control of St. Thomas after 1672 and St. John after 1718. They traded freely in the Caribbean, unaffected by the conflicts between England, France, and Spain. In 1727 St. Thomas had 177 plantations of sugarcane, cotton, and other products. St. John, a smaller island still fairly unexploited in 1728, had only had 87 plantations, but by 1733 that number had already increased to 109. Along with the rise in sugar production, the population of St. Croix increased from 11,200 in 1760 to 22,244 in 1773.

In St. Thomas and St. John, just as in St. Croix, the growth of the sugar industry accelerated markedly during the War of Jenkins's Ear and the Seven Years War. These islands were open to immigration, especially by colonists from other Caribbean islands. They therefore received numerous immigrants from St. Kitts, Nevis, Tortola, and Virgin Gorda, producing a curious phenomenon: the majority of the European population on the Danish Islands was of British origin, with Danish and Dutch colonists in the minority.

The Neutral Ports

Even though the economies of St. Thomas, St. John, and St. Croix were based on their plantations, these islands continued to function as commercial ports, joining St. Eustatius and Curaçao as the main centers of neutral trade. This became evident during the Seven Years War, when the British government again tried to force the North American colonies to suspend trade with the French Antilles by embargoing and confiscating ships from Martinique, Guadeloupe, and Saint-Domingue.

North American merchants were then moved to seek an indirect route to continue to supply themselves with French sugar, rum, and molasses, namely smuggling through the Danish and Dutch islands. During the war, St. Eustatius became extremely important as the main center of commercial exchange in the Lesser Antilles. The French would send their products to St. Eustatius or to Curaçao, where they would be picked up by North American or Irish ships in exchange for North American products. As the war caused all prices to rise to exorbitant levels, contraband flourished as never before.

As a result, new neutral ports began to emerge in long-forgotten places. For several years, one of the most important ports was Montecristi, on the northwestern border of the Spanish colony of Santo Domingo. Discovered by merchants from Rhode Island at the very beginning of the Seven Years War, by 1757 Montecristi had become a meeting point for ships from New England and French schooners and barges from nearby Saint-Domingue. The Spanish authorities turned a blind eye to the ships from Massachusetts, Rhode Island, New York, Philadelphia, and even Ireland, which would drop anchor in Montecristi with shipments consigned to Spanish merchants. In turn, these merchants would trade them sugar and molasses, supposedly produced in the Spanish colony, although in fact these goods had been sent over in barges and vessels from the neighboring towns of Fort Dauphin and Cap François.

In 1759 more than 200 North American ships visited Montecristi, many of which arrived with very little merchandise but with sufficient money to buy sugar, molasses, and rum. Upon returning to North America, the captains would show papers that pointed out the "neutral" origin of their shipments, thus earning the suspicion but ultimate approval of North American customs authorities who knew that the economy of the northern colonies depended on trade with the Caribbean.

The British authorities, however, were not fooled by North American contraband in the so-called neutral ports and decided to eliminate trading in Montecristi and St. Eustatius by blocking the departure of ships and seizing them on the open sea. After the English naval squadrons seized the ships, they took them to Jamaica. There the military courts condemned the owners and captains for trading with the enemy and confiscated their shipments.

In August 1760 the British government again ordered its colonial governors to inform it about contraband trade and to punish the contraband dealers severely. But with new connections in Montecristi and St. Eustatius and the large volumes of English and North American merchandise that were exchanged, it was easy for the colonial North American authorities to ignore the orders of the British government.

The colonial assemblies and merchants of Pennsylvania, New York, Connecticut, Rhode Island, and Massachusetts defended their trade in "neutral" ports, saying that it was necessary for the North American colonies and, ultimately, for British industry. Ignoring these arguments, the British navy, upholding the Molasses Law of 1733, continued its campaign against the clandestine trade and managed to reduce it significantly during the three last years of the Seven Years War.

British Naval Dominance

One of the factors that helped cut down North American contraband trade with the French islands was the seizure of Guadeloupe by the English in May 1759. After that, the entire production of the island was sold directly to the British market. Furthermore, when the British took the strategic island of Gorée, off Dakar in Senegal, they directly controlled France's former main slave supply center. Guadeloupe, which until then lagged behind the other French Antilles in sugar production, was immediately supplied with slaves by English merchants, and its sugar industry received an extraordinary boost.

British Prime Minister William Pitt's goal at this point was the construction of a great colonial empire, in which the Antilles and North America would form the main productive axis. Although the British had previously been content to thwart French trade, their seizure of Guadeloupe in 1759 exemplified their new strategy of conquering enemy territories. In 1758 the English navy captured Louisbourg and Cape Breton, in Canada, after keeping the French at bay for more than two years, blocking their ports on the Atlantic and impeding their navigation through the English Channel. The British continued to advance in Canada and won important victories at Fort Niagara and Quebec, taking the latter in September 1759. In 1760 the English finally took Montreal, definitively ending French control of Canada.

After more than a year without significant military operations in the Antilles, the English took Dominica in June 1761. French losses continued to mount as a British squadron commanded by Rear Admiral George Rodney conquered Martinique in January 1762. In the following months, the islands of St. Lucia, St. Vincent, Granada, and Tobago also succumbed to the British navy. In an attempt to reinforce its position, the French government dragged Spain into the war in 1761 with the signing of a new Family Pact, which committed Spain to launch an offensive against the English by May of the following year.

To confront the Spanish, the English government sent a new war fleet to the Caribbean in March 1762. This fleet arrived in Cuba at the beginning of June with 15,000 soldiers, commanded by George Keppel, Earl of Albemarle. After two months of operations, the British conquered the city of Havana on August 7, 1767.

The conquest of all these territories exposed one of the great contradictions of English colonial politics, as sugar, rum, and molasses from the conquered islands quickly began to flow to the British market. After the seizure of Guadeloupe, the abundance of sugar on the London market provoked a dramatic drop in the price of sugar from forty-five shillings nine cents per hundredweight in 1759 to thirty-six shillings six cents per hundredweight in 1761, creating consternation among the British Antillean planters. The seizure of Havana in 1762 caused prices to drop even more, until they reached an average of thirty-two shillings six cents per hundredweight in 1763.

Due to the fall in sugar prices, when peace negotiations began at the end of 1762, the British Parliament debated whether to keep or return the conquered territories. During the debate, the West Indian planters and their representatives lobbied for Great Britain to return the colonies to France and Spain, so that sugar prices could rise to their previous levels. On November 3, 1762, France and Great Britain signed a preliminary agreement that was ratified by the Treaty of Paris in September 1763.

Thus, despite the wishes of the British sugar refiners and consumers who wanted to retain the French islands to keep prices low, France recovered Martinique and Guadeloupe and also obtained recognition of its sovereignty over St. Lucia. The Senegalese island of Gorée was also returned to France. In exchange, the former French territories of Canada and the Mississippi Valley were given to Great Britain, as were the once neutral islands of Dominica, St. Vincent, the Grenadines, Granada, and Tobago, which were from then on known as "the Ceded Islands." Great Britain also received Florida, taken by Spain during the war, in exchange for Havana, which was returned to the Spanish after the withdrawal of British troops. France was forced to give Louisiana to Spain to compensate for the loss of Florida.

In 1764 the French and the Spanish tried to reverse the new order imposed by the Treaty of Paris the previous year. The French sent a new naval squadron to the Antilles commanded by Charles Hector, Count of Estaing, who took the Turks Islands and fourteen British ships that were loading salt there. The British, however, forced the French to return the Turks Islands and to pay reparations. The Spanish, meanwhile, threatened to expel the British loggers who had settled in Belize and on the Yucatán Peninsula. However, when a new English naval squadron was sent to Belize to protect the loggers, Spain decided against using force in Central America. The Treaty of Paris of 1763 left England triumphant and dominant in the West Indies and North America.

Towards Free Trade

The Seven Years War significantly affected the attitude of the French officials toward trade with North American and British West Indian colonists. After four years of British occupation in Guadeloupe, the French authorities could do very little to eliminate contraband. The French government therefore decreed the creation of several "free ports" in Martinique, Guadeloupe, and Saint-Domingue. The decree, enacted on April 18, 1763, was proclaimed in the colonies on August 18 of that year. Its provisions were already being applied by November 1, with certain limits, however, so as to protect French navigation and industry. From then on, importation of lumber, food, and horses from the North American colonies was freely permitted, provided that the traffickers of these products received sugar, molasses, and rum as payment.[1]

The Danish government followed the French example and declared St. Croix and St. Thomas "free ports" in 1764. From then on, European merchandise imported by the colonists of these islands was taxed at only 2 percent of its value, but the merchandise had to be transported in Danish ships with appropriate documentation. Furthermore, products from North American colonies could be freely imported in ships from any nation. Foreigners paid only minimal taxes and were authorized to load and freely export any merchandise they wanted from the islands, except for sugar destined for the Danish market.

The Spanish government also developed its own policies of "free trade," following numerous suggestions made by the liberal thinkers of the court of Charles III. On October 16, 1765, Spain granted the islands of Cuba, Santo Domingo, Puerto Rico, Trinidad, and Margarita the right to trade freely with the Spanish ports of Barcelona, Cartagena, Alicante, Málaga, Cádiz, Seville, Santander, La Coruña, and Gijón. From then on, ships traveling between the above-mentioned islands and Spanish ports were required only to register their route and shipment and pay the corresponding customs duties. These duties were reduced substantially, numerous bureaucratic procedures were eliminated, and direct trade between the islands of the Spanish Caribbean was opened up.

The following year, on November 1, 1766, Great Britain created several "free ports" in Jamaica. As with their French and Spanish counterparts, the free ports in the British West Indies still had many limitations. For example, the Jamaican ports of Kingston, Savannah la Mar, Santa Lucia, and Montego Bay were authorized to import livestock from other colonies freely, but were not permitted to import foreign manufactured goods or sugar, molasses, tobacco, coffee, or ginger. The ports of Rouseau and Prince Rupert's Bay, in Dominica, could import anything from the other colonies except tobacco, provided that the foreign ships that transported the cargo were small, with only one deck.

Both Dominica and Jamaica were permitted freely to reexport the slaves who arrived on British ships, together with a variety of British merchandise, including North American products in demand in the West Indies. The British government created new taxes to be paid for each slave, either imported or reexported, in addition to taxes on other merchandise. Since Dominica was close to the French islands of Martinique and Guadeloupe, its exports to Great Britain and North America were treated as if they were of foreign origin and were subject to taxation.

On July 29, 1767, the French government opened two additional "free ports" for trade with the North Americans, one in Carenage, in St. Lucia, and another in Môle St. Nicholas, in the northwest of Saint-Domingue. In these ports, North American merchants were authorized to exchange their lumber, horses, resins, cereals, and other products for molasses, rum, and French merchandise, paying only 1 percent in taxes. All other merchandise traded in these ports had to be of French origin and transported in French ships.

However, the "free ports" established in the Antilles between 1763 and 1767 did not eliminate the mercantilist system, which supported the colonial monopolies. The liberties granted were valid only in the domain of the home country, with the exception of the Danish and French islands. Nonetheless, the establishment of "free ports" was the beginning of the legal dismantling of the European trade monopoly in the West Indies. From then on, the notion that free trade was more convenient for all gradually spread, even though the main stockholders of the monopolistic companies fought hard to keep their privileges intact. This concept of free trade was promoted by an otherwise conflicting set of actors, which included the European liberal philosophers of the Enlightenment, the colonial governors who were constantly struggling to keep their colonists well supplied, and the colonists themselves, whether or not they were involved in contraband.

In the following years, Spain continued to create new "free ports": Louisiana in 1768; Yucatán and Campeche in 1770; and Santa Marta and Río de la Hacha, in New Granada, in 1776. Santa Cruz de Tenerife, Palma de Mallorca, and El Ferrol were also declared free ports. In 1778 the Spanish government passed the "Customs Duty Bylaws for Free Trade in Spain and the Indies," which authorized free trade between twelve European ports and twenty-five colonial ports in Spanish America and the Antilles, excluding Venezuela and New Spain. These two regions had to wait until 1789, when the infamous monopolistic companies of Guipuzcoana and Caracas were finally integrated into the free trade system.

Plantation Development in the "Ceded Islands"

Another important consequence of the Seven Years War was the British colonization of the so-called Ceded Islands. Previously, these islands were semideveloped, settled only by some independent French, English, and Dutch colonists growing sugarcane, coffee, cacao, cotton, and indigo. These pioneers lived precariously, trading among themselves and avoiding conflict with the Carib Indians. Gradually, the most fertile lands on these islands were cultivated. By 1763 the islands were clearly showing their potential for large-scale colonization.

The Ceded Islands differed very much from one another. In 1763 Grenada was the most developed, with eighty-one sugar plantations and 208 coffee, cacao, and livestock farms. Sugarcane had not yet been planted on any of the other Ceded Islands, but there were plantations of cacao, coffee, cotton, and indigo. In 1763 Dominica had 1,400 white colonists and more than 5,000 slaves. St. Vincent was a "maroon" island, populated by a handful of Frenchmen and approximately 2,000 "black Caribs," descendants from a group of African slaves who had been shipwrecked on the island and had interbred with the Carib Indians. The inhabitants of St. Vincent produced enough cacao, coffee, and cotton to trade for European manufactured goods. The Grenadines were almost uninhabited, as was Tobago, which had no permanent settlement despite being claimed at different times by Spain, Holland, and France.

In spite of opposition from the West Indian planters and their representatives in London, the British government decided to promote the colonization of the Ceded Islands, fostering the production of sugar and other tropical products there. The Ceded Islands thus came to be the new Caribbean frontier, where one could acquire cheap land. However, the immigration policy had only limited success during its first ten years, when Grenada received only 166 immigrants and some of the other islands received even fewer. Nonetheless, considerable capital was brought into the Ceded Islands to support their colonization. By 1772 Grenada had 334 plantations with 26,211 slaves; 69 percent of the land cultivated that year was used for sugarcane, on 106 plantations that supplied 107 sugar mills. The colonists of Grenada took advantage of its topography and rivers and built ninety-five water-powered mills and twelve windmills.

On the other islands, the development was similar. In Dominica, the British colonists acquired more than 95,000 acres of land during the first ten years of their occupation by the British. By 1773 there were already 103 new plantations, 41 of which were devoted to sugarcane. Mill technology was diversified; of the fifty existing mills, twenty-nine were driven by animals, fifteen by wind, and six by water.

Tobago developed later. In 1770 the colonists of Tobago made their first sugar shipment. In that year, Tobago had 238 white inhabitants and 3,164 slaves, and there was a total of only seventy-eight cacao, cotton, ginger, clove, cinnamon, and nutmeg plantations. Nutmeg began to be exported in 1768, sometime after the first forty plantations were established. In the following five years, Tobago's economic growth accelerated; in 1775 there were 391 white colonists, 8,643 slaves, and more than a hundred plantations. The rapid importation of slaves resulted in rebellions in 1770, 1771, and 1774, which were harshly put down by the colonists.

St. Vincent's plantation development also lagged somewhat due to the black Caribs' resistance to the distribution of the land on the island in 1769. The black Caribs were harshly repressed in 1772, leading to several clashes with troops sent from North America and other parts of the British West Indies. In February 1773 this rebellion ended when the

British government signed a treaty with the black Caribs, allowing them to live peacefully on one side of the island in exchange for their acceptance of British sovereignty over St. Vincent. By then, immigration had already begun, with more than 20,000 acres of land auctioned off to new colonists from other islands. The white population of St. Vincent, about 695 in 1763, grew slowly until it reached 1,475 in 1787. A 1779 census listed sixty-one sugar plantations in addition to several others where coffee, tobacco, cotton, cacao, and indigo were grown.

The Ceded Islands prospered quickly. Cacao exports from Grenada increased from 54 tons in 1763 to 252 tons in 1771. Coffee exports went from 700 tons in 1764 to 1,200 tons in 1775. In St. Vincent, cacao exports increased from 15 tons in 1764 to 60 tons in 1775.

Sugar production experienced similar growth in Grenada, increasing from 3,284 tons in 1764 to 9,496 tons in 1775. In St. Vincent, sugar exports grew from 35 tons in 1765 to 2,582 tons in 1775. Tobago's sugar industry had developed later; nonetheless, production rose from 84 tons in 1770 to 2,500 tons in 1775. The sugar exports from Dominica were not registered because the island was declared a free port in 1766, shortly after it had been returned to England.

All the Ceded Islands went through their own "sugar revolutions" between the end of the Seven Years War in 1763 and the beginning of the American Revolution in 1775. The Ceded Islands exported 16,630 tons of sugar to Great Britain in 1775. This was equal to 61 percent of the amount exported from the Leeward Islands that same year, yet it was still four times more than the average amount exported from Barbados in the previous five years. In spite of their relatively small collective landmass of 674 square miles, only 15 percent of the size of Jamaica, by 1775 the Ceded Islands were producing the equivalent of one-third of Jamaica's sugar production.

As on the older sugar-producing islands, this economic revolution resulted in the development of a plantation system with large contingents of African slaves and a separate class of white planters who dominated the land, business, and local politics. These planters also became allied with a powerful group of absentee colonists in Great Britain known as the West Indian Committee.

The Ceded Islands began to be developed at a time when the older sugar colonies of Barbados and the Leeward Islands were showing signs of stagnation. Sugar production in Barbados decreased from an annual average of 9,000 tons between 1761 and 1765 to 4,350 tons between 1771 and 1775. With great effort, the Leeward Islands managed to maintain stable production at a little less than 25,000 tons per year between 1761 and 1775. Due to the low productivity of the land and the high cost of fertilizer, the production costs of sugar and molasses were much higher in Barbados and the Leeward Islands than on the other Caribbean colonies. Furthermore, sugar exported from these British islands had been burdened for more than a century with an export tax of 4.5 percent, which had diminished its competitiveness on the world market.

The North Americans looked to the French Antilles for their supply of sugar and molasses simply because prices were lower there. For that reason, British occupation of Guadeloupe during the last four years of the Seven Years War was resented by the colonists of the British West Indies. During the occupation, the colonists of Guadeloupe, Basse-Terre, and Marie-Galante imported a collective total of 18,871 slaves and increased sugar production. By 1767 Guadeloupe and its neighboring islands were producing almost 8,000 tons of sugar. In 1769, 405 sugar plantations were counted. Of the mills, 22 were powered by wind, 143 by water, and 240 by animals. St. Lucia, which remained in French hands after the war, was also developing at that time. By 1776 there were forty-four sugar plantations and 800 other plantations on St. Lucia growing cacao, cotton, and coffee.

Consolidation of the Plantation Economy

These numbers indicate that between the Seven Years War and the American Revolution, the Caribbean islands were beginning a new era of agricultural development based on diversification of production. The plantation system remained intact, and manual labor continued to be supplied by slaves, but now cacao, cotton, tobacco, ginger, and indigo were supplementing sugar as products for export. Sugar continued to be the staple of the economy, but as the years went by, coffee, a new crop first introduced to the Caribbean in Martinique in 1723, began gaining ground and gradually became a predominant export product.

Coffee had an advantage in that it did not compete with sugar for land because coffee plants grow best at elevations between 1,000 and 5,000 feet. Thus it was possible to make use of the mountainous land on the islands. Furthermore, unlike sugar, coffee did not require a high initial investment because it could be planted as a marginal crop following routine logging operations that removed only selected trees. Because coffee trees thrive in the shade, the land did not have to be cleared completely.

Jamaica and Saint-Domingue were the leaders in coffee production in the Caribbean in the eighteenth century. Among the sugar-producing islands, they had the most land suitable for coffee production, and their colonists had always maintained a tradition of crop diversification. Saint-Domingue had an enormous output as compared to the other West Indian colonies; by 1783 its coffee production was more than 20,000 tons annually, almost fourteen times more than all the British colonies combined, which in 1785 produced only 1,850 tons a year. Saint-Domingue also surpassed the British colonies in all other products with the exception of cotton. Its production costs were lower, its lands were more productive, its slaves were cheaper, and, as a result, prices for goods were much more competitive.

Cotton began to be cultivated in larger quantities in the Caribbean after 1760, when the invention of the mechanical carder arrived as part of the Industrial Revolution in England. The Caribbean islands responded quickly to the growing demand for cotton in Manchester, Glasgow, Liverpool, London, and other English industrial cities. The elasticity of the cotton supply can be explained by the geography and ecology of the islands, where mountains divided the land into rainy and dry areas, thus mapping out the most cultivable lands.

Since cotton was grown in zones where the rainfall was not sufficient for the cultivation of sugarcane, it did not compete with sugarcane. Cotton exports from the British West Indies grew impressively from 1,000 tons in 1780 to 6,600 tons in 1790. The French islands displayed a similar trend. Saint-Domingue exported only 2,250 tons in 1783, but by 1789 export production had increased to 3,500 tons.

By the end of the eighteenth century, the Caribbean colonial world functioned as a diversified raw material production center for the European and North American markets. The Caribbean colonists were always attentive to signals from those markets in order to meet their demands quickly. By 1775 the flow of investment capital had been restored after an interruption in credit during the English financial crisis of 1772. Furthermore, the floating of interest rates authorized by the British government in 1774 caused some of the islands, previously stagnant, to show signs of recuperation as their planters could obtain new loans to venture into buying slaves to create new sugar plantations.

The Caribbean during the American Revolution

Nevertheless, the persistent political crisis that began with the Sugar Act of 1764 was exacerbated by the promulgation of other tax laws over the next few years. These crises provoked thirteen of the North American colonies to be in a constant state of rebellion against Great Britain and eventually to declare independence in 1776.

After their defeat in 1763, the French and Spanish governments began to prepare themselves to recover their lost territories. France rebuilt its navy and reinforced the defense of its colonial possessions. The Spanish government likewise reinforced its territories in the Caribbean, particularly Puerto Rico and Cuba. Spain invested enormous sums to enlarge the impressive fortifications of El Morro and San Cristóbal in San Juan and La Fuerza in Havana.

When France signed the treaties of alliance, friendship, trade, recognition, and defense with the United States on February 6, 1778, the French military was already prepared to support the American Revolution and go to war against Great Britain. In April 1778 France sent a large fleet across the Atlantic, and military and naval operations began almost immediately in the Caribbean.

In September 1778 French troops commanded by the governor of Martinique invaded Dominica, forcing the capitulation of the British garrison there. More than 1,500 French soldiers were left in charge of defending this island, briefly leaving Guadeloupe, Dominica, Martinique, and St. Lucia under the control of France. In December 1778, however, the British conquered the island of St. Lucia, and the French could not dislodge them. Several months later, in June 1779, St. Vincent fell to the French, and in July Grenada also capitulated to an attack by the French navy.

Encouraged by France, Spain joined the war against Great Britain in June 1779, immediately besieging Gibraltar and shortly thereafter opening the port of New Orleans to French and American warships. Throughout the following year there were frequent naval maneuvers and movements of troops in the Caribbean. Spanish and French colonial authorities received instructions to aid each other and to support American merchants and privateers in the war against Great Britain. Spanish fleets transported merchandise, provisions, and soldiers to the French Antilles, while French warships guarded the Spanish colonies.

The war became even more complicated after July 1780, when a British squadron attacked and captured several American merchants and privateers on the Dutch island of St. Martin. On December 20, 1780, Great Britain declared war on Holland in protest of a secret treaty signed by Holland and the United States in September 1778, stipulating that the Dutch would commit themselves to support the independence of the North American colonies. The war between Holland and Great Britain had important implications. What the British resented most was not that the Dutch had agreed to back the independence of North America but that in the previous few years St. Eustatius had been converted into the main Caribbean supply center for the Americans.

Prior to the war between Great Britain and Holland, St. Eustatius had been a neutral port exporting French molasses, sugar, and rum, which the French colonists could not sell directly to the Americans. The French likewise stocked up on North American products there, to the dismay of the British, since the British West Indies greatly lacked North American supplies. Some daring smugglers from the British West Indies also went to St. Eustatius to trade, leading the authorities to believe that their shipments were from St. Kitts.[2]

Among the most active American traders during those months were the Baltimore merchants, whose ships brought 4,900 tons of merchandise to the Dutch Antilles in 1780. In that year, Spain also permitted the Americans to trade directly with its colonies in the Antilles, and suddenly the port of Havana began to receive ships from Baltimore, Philadelphia, and elsewhere along the Chesapeake Bay. These ships were loaded with flour and other merchandise that, until then, had been difficult to import directly from North America. Consequently, trade between Havana and Baltimore increased from 100 tons in 1780 to more than

1,600 tons in 1782. In Havana, sugar and molasses were exchanged for all kinds of merchandise produced in North America. Trade between Baltimore and the Antilles grew from about 4,500 tons in 1780 to more than 15,000 tons in 1782.

The trade that most worried the British, and which was considered the most pernicious, was that of St. Eustatius. Therefore, on December 20, 1780, the same day that Great Britain declared war on Holland, the British government sent orders to its commanders in the Caribbean to attack St. Eustatius and the other Dutch possessions. Admiral Rodney received these orders at the end of January 1781, while his fleet was anchored off Barbados. At the beginning of February 1881, the British forces led by Admiral Rodney attacked St. Eustatius, taking it with little effort and forcing the Dutch garrisons of Saba, St. Martin, and St. Barthélemy to capitulate.

The spoils taken from St. Eustatius are an indication of the volume of trade that took place on that little island. More than 160 merchant ships from different nations were captured, including 50 from North America. These ships were loaded with tobacco, arms, European merchandise, sugar, molasses, rum, and other cargo. A contemporary estimate calculated the value of the booty confiscated in St. Eustatius at more than three million pounds sterling. Rodney took almost all the spoils to Jamaica, where they were immediately auctioned off. After that, St. Eustatius lost its importance. The British had to evacuate the island at the end of November 1781, and St. Eustatius was never again the bustling seaport it had once been.

After the fall of St. Eustatius, and in the last three years of the American War of Independence, the ports of Cap François, Môle St. Nicholas, and Port-au-Prince in Saint-Domingue and Fort-Royal and St. Pierre in Martinique became the main centers of trade with the Americans. From the beginning of the war, Môle St. Nicholas had served as a meeting point for American ships, where they would stock up on gunpowder, munitions, military uniforms, and other war provisions brought from Europe by the French. Saint-Domingue became the main base of operations for the French fleet in the war against the British in the Caribbean. The need for war provisions stimulated production in order to meet American demand and feed the French troops garrisoned for many months in different ports of the colonies. The economic impact of these operations was felt even in the Spanish colony of Santo Domingo. During the war, the Spanish had to increase the livestock quota for export to the French colony from 15,000 to 23,000 head annually.

After the British took St. Eustatius, naval operations continued elsewhere. The British and French squadrons alternated their Caribbean operations with battles in North America and return voyages to Europe. The Caribbean islands therefore witnessed active military encounters followed by periods of relative calm. At the end of February 1781, the British captured the Dutch colonies of Demerara and Essequibo. In May of that year the French attacked Tobago and took it at the beginning of June, after destroying some of its sugar mills. Six months later the French launched a surprise attack and took St. Eustatius, St. Maarten, Saba, and St. Barthélemy. In January 1782 the French struck again, this time capturing St. Kitts, Monserrat, and Nevis, in whose waters they fought one of the biggest naval battles of the war. By the end of January, the Leeward Islands, with the exception of Antigua, had fallen into the hands of the French.

Jamaica could have met the same fate had it not been for the defeat of Admiral Count François de Grasse's fleet in the naval battle off the islands of Les Saintes, south of Guadeloupe, on April 12, 1782. Despite winning this battle, the British were unable to repel the Spanish forces that took New Providence, in the Bahamas, on May 8, 1782, although they did manage to expel the Spanish from New Providence one year later. Early in 1783, the French occupied the Turks Islands, but they had to return them almost immediately, as peace negotiations were underway. In November 1782 the British and the Americans had signed a preliminary agreement to put an end to the war, followed by another agreement in January 1783 signed by France and Spain as well.

The final pact that put an end to the American Revolution was the Treaty of Versailles, signed by France, Spain, Great Britain, and the United States in September 1783. As before, some territories were returned to their previous colonizers, while others were retained as spoils of war, as was the case with Tobago, which became a French colony. The British returned the island of St. Lucia to France. In exchange, France returned to Great Britain its old possessions of Grenada, the Grenadines, St. Vincent, Dominica, Montserrat, Nevis, and St. Kitts, while Spain regained Florida. The Bahamas and Belize remained British possessions. After squandering large amounts of resources, the Caribbean islands were again under the same dominion as before the war. The only territories that changed hands were Tobago and Florida.

The formation of the United States of America was a powerful blow to the economy of the British West Indies. From 1783 on, the Americans were free to trade with all of the Caribbean islands, and they almost completely abandoned their trade with the British West Indies, preferring to deal predominantly with the French and Danish colonies.

The interruption of trade with North America was accompanied by numerous calamities that decisively affected the economy of the British islands. In the first two years of the war, the British West Indies were supplied by Ireland and the French and Spanish Antilles, but the entrance of France and Spain into the war meant that the Spanish Antilles no longer served as supply centers.

The scarcity of lumber affected the maintenance and repair of sugar mills as well as the construction of boxes and barrels; the lack of horses and mules reduced productivity; and the difficulties of importing fabric to make clothing for the slaves generated discontent among the slave population. The war also hampered the food supply of the British West Indies. Some Jamaican landowners planted their fields with plantain, yuca, potatoes, and yams to feed their slaves, but on the other islands where there was less surplus land, the slaves suffered long periods of hunger, and many died of starvation. In 1778 more than 1,000 slaves starved to death in Antigua, along with 1,200 in Montserrat and close to 400 in Nevis.

The American Revolution produced an increase in prices, particularly of imported food. The disruption of navigation, the French occupation of the majority of the British West Indies, and the activities of privateers from all nations led the price of sugar to almost triple in the London market between 1776 and 1782. These factors also caused an increase in the prices of British manufactured goods destined for the West Indies, including flour, dried meat, and salted fish. After the war, prices did not decrease substantially.

To make things worse, in 1781 two powerful hurricanes ruined vast areas of Jamaica and Barbados, leaving 3,000 dead in Barbados, as the capital, Bridgetown, was almost completely destroyed. In 1784, 1785, and 1786 three more hurricanes pounded the Caribbean, hitting Jamaica severely. According to contemporary estimates, by 1783 the number of slaves in Barbados had declined by more than 11,000 people, due to the hurricanes and other causes as well. In 1785 a committee calculated that more than 1,500 slaves had died in Jamaica in the previous few years.

As slave prices rose dramatically (the average price per slave rose from thirty-four to forty-seven pounds sterling between 1772 and 1778), it became extremely costly for the Jamaican planters to replace them. The 1785 hurricane also devastated the Leeward Islands, which were left without sufficient supplies for many months. After the hurricanes, a series of droughts and plagues hit the sugarcane plantations of the Leeward Islands and put many plantation owners on the brink of ruin.

The crisis extended to the other British West Indies. With the American ports now closed off to British trade, prices in the Leeward Islands rose 50 percent above wartime prices. In 1787 the majority of the planters of Antigua, St. Kitts, Montserrat, and Nevis found themselves in debt to London, Liverpool, and Bristol merchants. In Anguilla, the few inhabitants who had previously sold salt to the Americans now had no market for their product. In 1788 it was calculated that the price of lumber in the British West Indies was 37 percent higher, the price of meat 22.5 percent higher, and the price of smoked herring 66 percent higher than in previous years.

On all the Leeward Islands and Barbados, large quantities of rum remained unsold after the war. The colonists of Dominica, St. Vincent, and Grenada could not obtain loans and were still in debt to the British government for land they had bought when the islands were yielded to Great Britain twenty years earlier. In Dominica, many colonists opted to abandon their plantations; in 1790 only fifty out of eighty plantations were in operation.

In contrast to the dire situation in the British West Indies, the French and Spanish Antilles enjoyed a period of previously unknown prosperity. Immediately after the war, the French government opened additional Caribbean ports for trade with the United States. On August 30, 1784, France authorized the merchants of Carenage, in St. Lucia; St. Pierre, in Martinique; Point-à-Pitre, in Guadeloupe; Scarborough, in Tobago;

and Cap François, Port-au-Prince, and Les Cayes, in Saint-Domingue, to sell their molasses and rum openly. Consequently, the ports were filled with American merchant ships as maritime traffic increased dramatically.

The French government tried to maintain its monopoly, but free trade had already taken deep root and eroded the government's control. Therefore contraband in the French Antilles flourished as never before. The French colonists resented France's colonial monopoly and did not accept the fiscal obstacles imposed by their home country. This defiant attitude on the part of plantation owners and colonists bred a wave of discontent, leading to the outbreak of several "white revolts" in Saint-Domingue, Martinique, and Guadeloupe, and to a slave revolution in Saint-Domingue.

CHAPTER 11

The French Revolution in the Antilles

Plantation Economics in Saint-Domingue

When Jean Ducasse, the French governor of Saint-Domingue, started the construction of the first sugar mills at the end of the seventeenth century, the colony was still an impoverished territory. Fewer than 1,500 French colonists struggled to cultivate the land with almost 1,000 black slaves and around 2,000 *engagés* (white indentured workers). These white workers had been employed to cultivate tobacco and indigo, but the experiences of other colonies indicated that the *engagés* would not be a reliable source of cheap manual labor on sugar plantations.

The increase in the number of sugar plantations in Saint-Domingue led to the importation of larger contingents of slaves, and in a very short time the African population outnumbered the *engagés* on the plantations. In 1713, there were 24,146 slaves in Saint-Domingue. This number increased to 117,400 in 1734, distributed over more than 300 sugar plantations, to 172,000 in 1754, and to 206,000 in 1764. Twenty-five years later, in 1789, the number of slaves had more than doubled to 452,000, while the white population was only 38,000. By this time sugar, coffee, indigo, cotton, and cacao plantations were importing more than 30,000 slaves per year, requiring several hundred ships to transport them from Africa.

Companies created by the French government in the seventeenth century initially supplied the slaves. Later, when these companies were abolished, the slave trade fell into the hands of the merchants who had previously helped the colonists finance the acquisition of white indentured workers. The merchants of Bordeaux, Nantes, La Rochelle, Marseille, and Le Havre procured slaves on the African coasts in exchange for firearms, iron bars, fabric, rum, and wine. They also exported large quantities of manufactured goods and food directly to Saint-Domingue, Martinique, and Guadeloupe.

Many of the industries that developed in France between 1700 and 1789 were linked, directly or indirectly, to the slave trade. Companies that made bottles, fabric, salted meat, shoes, brandy, and other articles built their factories near the most active ports in France and England to take advantage of the market created by the slave trade.

Sugar refineries proliferated in the French ports and were soon among the most profitable European businesses of the eighteenth century. There were sixteen sugar refineries in Bordeaux alone, while Nantes had not only refineries but also textile mills that processed cotton imported from the colonies. The fabric produced there was then traded for slaves on the African coast. Shoes, flour, biscuits, wine, butter, jam, vegetables, cheese, and dried meat were also exchanged for slaves.

Even before the American Revolution concluded, Saint-Domingue benefited from the increasing trade with the rebellious North American colonies. After 1783 the trade in sugar, molasses, and rum with the United States greatly increased, as its commercial ties with the British West Indies became permanently severed. Between 1783 and 1789, the merchants of Bordeaux provided 100 million pounds *tournois* in credit to the colonists of Saint-Domingue to finance colonial production. Thus, despite the huge volume of exports, the economy of Saint-Domingue was burdened by debt.

In 1760, before the American Revolution, it was estimated that the merchants and planters of Saint-Dominque owed European moneylenders more than 10 million pounds, and few thought that those debts could ever be collected. By 1780 the total debt had risen to 100 million pounds. The metropolitan merchants, however, continued to provide credit and loans to Saint-Domingue because it surpassed all other French colonies in production and consumption. At the end of the eighteenth century, Saint-Domingue consumed almost two-thirds of the products France exported to its colonies.

Despite growing trade with the Americans, the French Antilles remained subjected to a maritime monopoly that forced merchants to ship their products on French ships and to buy only manufactured goods shipped out of French ports. This monopoly irritated the colonists, who demanded the right to trade freely with France's allies. In 1784 the French government finally gave in to these demands and opened eight ports to foreign trade in the French Antilles, thus legalizing trade with the United States. Export production quickly doubled, and the slave trade reached unprecedented levels.

Social and Racial Tensions

In spite of these changes, the large plantation owners felt uncomfortable with the French colonial system. These "*grands blancs*" wanted more autonomy and resented the fact that they were denied access to political representation, given the fact that the French West Indian colonists had not been permitted to create local colonial assemblies. The tensions that had always existed between the colonists and their metropolitan government became serious at times, as many planters opted to default on their loans and return to France rather than continue working abroad to pay back the European moneylenders. Some absentee planters formed the famous Club Massiac in Paris in 1789, taking steps to achieve the political autonomy of Saint-Domingue. Some actually advocated independence, in the spirit of the American Revolution.

The free mulattoes (*gens de couleur*) constituted another sector with economic interests similar to those of the white planters, but with different political views, as they were even more dissatisfied with the French colonial system. The *gens de couleur*, who in 1789 numbered 28,000 individuals, were a powerful group who claimed to control one-third of the land in the colony. Mulattoes were shunned by white colonists, who could not accept the fact that the descendants of slaves had reached such a prominent place in the colonial economy. The mulattoes, however, considered themselves more entitled than the white Europeans to control the colony, having been born and raised on the island.

As the economic power of the mulatto sector grew, the white Europeans took steps to thwart their social mobility by enacting numerous discriminatory laws designed to convert them into second-class citizens. Almost all of these laws violated the Code Noir,[1] because they did not allow mulattoes and their descendants their full freedom, as guaranteed under the Code. One law passed in 1758, for instance, prohibited mulattoes from carrying arms, while another, enacted in 1767, forbade the sale of arms and munitions to them. Moreover, in 1768, another law was passed prohibiting mulatto women to marry white men in France. In 1771 the colonial government declared mulattoes unfit to hold high-ranking positions in the militia or appointments in the court. Furthermore, this law denied them work as druggists, pharmacists, or physicians because the white colonists feared that the mulattoes would use their medical knowledge to kill them and inherit their property. As time passed, more restrictions were imposed: mulattoes bore the stigma of wearing poorly cut suits of inferior fabric as a sign of their condition as second-class citizens; they were forbidden to assemble in public meetings after nine o'clock in the evening; it was made illegal to address them as "monsieur" or "madame"; and they were also forbidden to adopt the name of their fathers or former masters.

In order to defend their rights, some rich mulattoes living in France organized the Société des Colons Americains (Society of American Colonists) in September 1789, and obtained the support of the Société des Amis des Noirs (Society of Friends of the Blacks), organized by a group of French abolitionists in February 1788. The Société des Colons Americains attained the acceptance of the more liberal bourgeois groups in France that were fighting for recognition of their own rights. At this time, the French nobility kept the bourgeoisie and the rest of the population in a state of subordination, allowing them little or no participation in government. When the French Revolution erupted in 1789, some connections already existed between some important revolutionary leaders and the representatives of the wealthy mulattoes living in Paris who attended the meetings of the Société des Amis des Noirs.

This society maintained contact with British abolitionist societies that were struggling to put an end to the slave trade. Although these rich mulattoes were slave owners, the fact that their British allies were abolitionists did not seem to trouble them at first. In 1789 the mulattoes lobbied the French National Assembly to enact a law that would force the white planters and colonial authorities to recognize their full rights as citizens. To advance their cause, once the French Revolution started, the wealthy mulattoes in Paris offered six million pounds *tournois* to help the new French government pay off the accumulated public debt, an issue that had helped spark the Revolution.

This offer did not immediately impress the French bourgeoisie, however, since many bourgeois had made a fortune in the slave trade. The revolutionaries hesitated before recognizing the mulattoes as equals, because this would set a precedent for granting similar rights and freedom to slaves who, sooner or later, would likewise take up the claim from the Declaration of the Rights of Man and of the Citizen that "men are born and remain free and equal in rights." Many thought that the abolition of slavery would mean the ruin of the colonies and would bankrupt the French maritime bourgeoisie, whose wealth and power directly derived from colonial domination.

To counteract the activism of the mulattoes and the Société des Amis des Noirs, the Club Massiac, supported by powerful merchants from France's slave ports, incessantly lobbied at the National Assembly against both abolition and the concession of full-citizen rights to the mulattoes. Caught between the fierce debates between the leaders of the Amis des Noirs and the Club Massiac, the French National Assembly postponed its decisions on the colonial question.

The wavering of the National Assembly encouraged the whites of Saint-Domingue to lobby for the right to govern themselves through colonial assemblies, similar to those existing in the British West Indies. The *grands blancs* hoped that such colonial assemblies would help them achieve political and commercial autonomy. After a series of violent uprisings in Martinique, Guadeloupe, and Saint-Domingue, the French government accepted the formation of colonial assemblies in the French Antilles on March 8, 1790. Three weeks later, however, the government stipulated that only taxpayers could be elected to those assemblies.

Deepening Political Conflicts

The agitation for the creation of colonial assemblies had started before the beginning of the French Revolution, and among its protagonists were the poorer whites of Saint-Domingue. These *"petits blancs"* were a numerically important group on the French islands. They made a living as artisans, shopkeepers, farmers, and soldiers, as well as small traders and professionals. As a consequence of the French Revolution, the majority of the *petits blancs* adopted radical revolutionary ideas and entered into conflict with the *grands blancs*, thus complicating the political panorama in the French Antilles. These revolutionary *petits blancs* wanted to overthrow the colonial bureaucratic regime and replace it with one that would grant them full representation in colonial assemblies. Thus *petits blancs* became the most radical agitators, particularly in the port cities of Guadeloupe, Martinique, and Saint-Domingue.

When the first assemblies were organized in November 1789, mulattoes were not represented. This created another source of violent confrontation in the colonies. Since their political situation did not change with the formation of the colonial assemblies, the Société des Colons Americains sent one of their members to England, and then to the United States, to seek support from the abolitionist organizations of these countries in their struggle against white domination. Vincent Ogé, the society's envoy, arrived in Saint-Domingue in October 1790 and tried to organize an armed movement, along with his brother and the brothers Marc and Jean Baptiste Chavannes.

Vincent Ogé managed to gather a small army of 700 mulattoes in the north of Saint-Domingue, while a similar group was being organized in the south, near the city of Les Cayes. The military force of the colonial authorities was superior to that of Ogé and his followers, however, and the mulattoes were forced to retreat to the Spanish part of the island. In accordance with an agreement signed in 1777 for the restitution of runaway slaves, the authorities of Santo Domingo denied them asylum and returned them to the French authorities despite the fact that they were free people. Once captured, and after having their bones crushed, Ogé and his followers were hanged in March 1791.

After the executions of Ogé, Jean Baptiste Chavannes, and twenty of their companions, the enraged mulattoes began to organize themselves for an armed struggle against the French authorities and the white colonists. At this point, the deteriorating relations between the two groups led to other incidents of violence. As the news from revolutionary France reached the islands, the power of the colonial authorities vanished. Confrontations occurred between soldiers and officers, *petits blancs* and *grands blancs*, and mulattoes and the white groups. The colonial power structure of the *ancien régime* rapidly collapsed.

To pacify the colonies, the National Assembly issued a decree on May 15, 1791, declaring all land-holding mulattoes and free blacks born of free parents (*gens de couleur*) to be free and to have full citizenship. Believing that this decree covered all mulattoes, including slaves, the *grands blancs* owners felt betrayed by the French revolutionary government. Though they had formerly opposed the monarchy, this decree, in the context of the overwhelming revolutionary power of the *petits blancs*, moved them to join the royalist camp while planning their separation from France. To this end, they sent a delegation to Jamaica to solicit British protection for the colony of Saint-Domingue.

The French government tried to avoid civil war by sending a civil commission to Saint-Domingue, consisting of three members, along with 600 soldiers. As soon as the soldiers landed in March 1791, they were harassed by the wealthier white colonists, who saw them as French revolutionary propaganda agents. In response, the French soldiers allied themselves with the poor whites of the colony, while many high-ranking officers supported the grands blancs.

By then, the colonial assemblies had experienced two years of revolutionary fervor in which all groups spoke of the liberties of the French Revolution and of the justice of its causes. "Men are born and remain free and equal in rights" was repeated constantly, as each group attempted to assert its interests. The *grands blancs* were trying to achieve political autonomy and, likewise, eventual independence. The *gens de couleur* were striving for equality with whites and, eventually, independence. The *petits blancs* were seeking full political participation and the same rights enjoyed by the *grands blancs*. No one seemed to notice, however, that the slaves were also listening to this talk about liberty and equal rights promised to the French people by the Revolution.

Slave Revolt and British Military Intervention

Every day, the slaves became more and more conscious of their condition, and they began to organize with the utmost secrecy. Thus, with no warning, on the night of August 22, 1791, the slaves from the plantations in the north of Saint-Domingue revolted. With the French

troops politically divided, there was very little that the colonial authorities could do to confront the rebelling slaves decisively. Faced with this
new threat, whites and mulattoes put aside their quarrels and formed a
common front to combat the rebel slaves. But this alliance did not last
long, and whites and mulattoes soon engaged each other openly in a
civil war while simultaneously attempting to put down the rebellion.

The *grands blancs* sought military help from Jamaica, and the governor of that island immediately sent arms and munitions. The mulatto
leaders, on the other hand, enjoyed the support of the French troops in
fighting the *grands blancs*.

During this war, while both sides destroyed and pillaged each other's
property, the representatives of the sugar traders and refiners in London
took notice: they stood to profit from the revolt in Saint-Domingue, as
it would disrupt sugar production in this French colony and, therefore,
prices would rise. The uprisings helped them make a case against the
abolitionists' radical discourse. Realizing that this black and mulatto
rebellion could spread to Jamaica and other English colonies, the
British abolitionists softened the tone of their campaign and allowed
Parliament to support the *grands blancs* of Saint-Domingue.

The *grands blancs* openly opposed the revolutionary government and
received military support from the British government. Political quarrels continued among the French soldiers and aggravated the situation:
some of the high-ranking military officials supported the *grands blancs*
and opposed the mulattoes, while the rank and file supported the *petits
blancs* and the radical Jacobin revolutionary party in France. In turn,
the *petits blancs* supported the Revolution and the civil commission that
represented France's National Assembly.

There was little hope of reaching a consensus that would resolve the
crisis in the colony. The mulattoes refused to abandon their struggle
because the decree of equality had not been enforced. In Paris, more
and more influential voices rose in the National Assembly, claiming that
the decree of equality of May 15, 1791, was a mistake that should be
revoked. This in fact was what happened on September 23, 1791. When
news of this revocation reached the French Antilles the following
month, the *gens de couleur* became even more embittered.

The black slaves, on the other hand, soon found their own foreign
ally: Spain. Throughout 1792, the rebel slave leaders, Georges Biassou

and Jean François, established contact with the Spanish authorities of Santo Domingo and received arms and provisions in exchange for help in expelling the French. The Spanish saw the rebellion as a great opportunity to regain the western part of the island, which they had lost almost two centuries earlier. If Spain managed to exploit the situation, it could capture the richest colony in the world. The black rebels were more numerous every day and operated on every front with Spanish logistical support.

To establish order in Saint-Domingue, in March 1792 the French National Assembly nominated a second civil commission, given that the first one had failed. This commission arrived in Saint-Domingue at the end of September of that year accompanied by 7,000 soldiers. Again the colonial governor and certain military leaders of the French garrisons, as well as the *grands blancs*, opposed the commissioners, but the head of the commission acted quickly and deported the disobedient royalist officers. The commission also tried to appease the *grands blancs* by declaring that slavery would be preserved, and at the same time sought the support of the *gens de couleur* by asserting that France would recognize only two classes of people, independent of their color: free people and slaves.

Meanwhile, important political changes were occurring in France. The Girondist bourgeois government was overthrown by the Jacobins, who on September 22, 1792, immediately proclaimed the Republic. On February 1, 1793, France declared war on England and Holland, and a month later on Spain. As a result, France was at war with most of Europe, having already declared war on Austria, Prussia, and Sardinia four months earlier.

The English exploited the situation and responded to the *grands blancs'* call for help in 1793 by sending well-armed, disciplined troops from Jamaica to Saint-Domingue. In a short time the British occupied the southern and the western parts of the French colony. On their side, the Spanish of Santo Domingo established a military cordon along the border with Saint-Domingue. With the support of the black militia of Biassou and Jean François, the Spanish military penetrated the northeastern part of the Saint-Domingue and occupied this territory in a quick and successful military campaign.

The Spanish and British would have defeated the French had it not been for a shrewd decision by Commissioner Léger Félicité Sonthonax. He invited the blacks to join his side, asking for their military support in exchange for the abolition of slavery. On August 29, 1793, the second civil commission enacted a law confirming this decision.

The political impact of the abolition of slavery was considerable. Rebel blacks were divided because some of their main leaders chose not to respond to the call of the civil commissioners and preferred to continue fighting as "auxiliaries" of the Spanish. Nevertheless, one of the leaders, François-Dominique Toussaint Louverture, whose influence had grown rapidly during this period, accepted the call and joined the French commission with about 4,000 men. The *gens de couleur*, on the other hand, were also divided. Some supported the French Republic, although they were dissatisfied with the abolition law, while the wealthier ones supported the *grands blancs* and the English intervention.

Toussaint Louverture's decision to join the French army greatly weakened the Spanish position. Within a few months the Spanish had lost all their conquered territory in the north of Saint-Domingue. Toussaint also occupied other Spanish territories in the center of the island, forcing the inhabitants of this region to seek refuge in the easternmost part of Santo Domingo. From then on, Toussaint and the French troops, commanded by the colony's governor, General Etienne Laveaux, were able to focus their energies on expelling the English from the colony.

Thus began an international war that would last five years and end with the retreat of the English forces following the loss of 12,000 men, mainly to yellow fever and malaria. The war was both a mirror of the European war and an additional episode in the long conflict between France and England to control the world sugar market. English documents of the period constantly refer to the importance of the occupation of Saint-Domingue in order to recover control of the European sugar trade.

Spain was dragged into the war due to family ties between the royal families of Spain and France. The danger posed by the French Revolution to the Spanish monarchy became evident when Louis XVI, cousin of the king of Spain, was beheaded in January 1793. Spain went to war to defend itself from French republicanism, which the Spanish nobility feared would sooner or later take root in the Iberian Peninsula. Eventually, Spain lost the war.

When the peace treaty was signed in the Swiss city of Basel on July 22, 1795, France agreed to return Navarre to Spain, in exchange for the Spanish colony of Santo Domingo.[2] To justify handing over Santo Domingo to the French, the Spanish prime minister, Manuel Godoy, declared that the island of Santo Domingo was "a cancer" that would sooner or later cause trouble to whomever owned it. He predicted that no one would be able to escape the social chaos produced by the slave rebellion. Spain, however, agreed to continue to govern Santo Domingo provisionally until it could be effectively occupied by France. The Spanish troops then retired from Saint-Domingue.

The loss of Santo Domingo to France worried the British government, which lodged a formal protest and refused to recognize the agreement, arguing that it violated old stipulations of the Treaty of Utrecht. To back up their protest, the British marched their troops in Saint-Domingue into Santo Domingo to prevent the French from occupying the Spanish colony, but they were unable to advance very far beyond the border, as Toussaint Louverture continued to harass their rear guard. The British troops nonetheless managed to occupy the strategic town of San Juan de la Maguana.

As he organized and expanded his army, Toussaint Louverture continued to grab new territory from the British. By September 1795 Toussaint had risen to the rank of brigadier general of the French army. The following year, after preventing proslavery mulattoes from overthrowing General Laveaux, Toussaint was named lieutenant general. At that moment his good fortune seemed unbounded.

A third French civil commission arrived in Santo Domingo in May 1796. Toussaint, General Laveaux, and the new civil commissioners began to work together on the reconstruction of the areas under their domain. They did so by forcing the freedmen to return to work on the plantations. In the northern part of the colony, Toussaint and the French army gradually worked to rebuild the plantations from the devastation of the war, although production never reached prewar levels. When Laveaux returned to France at the end of 1796, Toussaint was already the most powerful man in the colony.

In the south, the mulatto General André Rigaud, who fought for the French army and had been a decisive actor in the struggle against the English, also forced the black workers to go back to the plantations. The compulsory and harsh nature of the labor regime imposed by Toussaint and Rigaud upon the freedmen closely resembled slavery.

The English were finally defeated and left the island in September 1798, along with many *grands blancs*, who emigrated to Jamaica. Before their withdrawal, the British secretly negotiated an agreement with Toussaint: they would give up the military occupation of Saint-Domingue in exchange for some trading advantages. In the course of the negotiations, the British envoy, General Thomas Maitland, suggested to Toussaint that he declare his territory independent under the protection of England because his military power had made him the virtual owner of the colony. Toussaint rejected Maitland's propositions, preferring to continue to rule over Saint-Domingue in the name of France.

Toussaint Louverture's Rule

Toussaint reestablished the plantation system, returned land to its former owners, and tried to maintain harmony between the whites, blacks, and mulattoes. In order to discourage vagrancy, he forced those who had been freed to return to their former masters to work. He also established trade relations with the United States, exchanging colonial products for arms, food, and other merchandise and thereby increasing exports. While Toussaint was working on the reconstruction of the colony, however, General André Rigaud and his mulatto supporters rebelled in the south.

The *gens de couleur* did not accept being governed by an ex-slave who had been a coachman on a plantation in the north of Saint-Domingue. In February 1799 civil war erupted again, this time between blacks and mulattoes. After two years of hard-fought, bloody war, the superior numbers of the blacks, coupled with the brilliant military leadership of Toussaint, gave them victory in August 1800. Faced with defeat, Rigaud abandoned the island, and from then on Toussaint Louverture, governor and commander-in-chief of the French army in Saint-Domingue, led all factions while trying to reconstruct the colony's ruined economy.

Under Toussaint, the former slaves were forced to work as sharecroppers on the plantations. Toussaint refused to parcel out the land among the workers. His economic policy was based on the preservation of the plantation system, paying one-quarter of the profits to the workers, whose tasks were directly supervised by military commanders of the rural districts. One-quarter stayed in the hands of the owner, and half was paid to the colonial government. To compensate for imposing quasi-servitude on a free population, Toussaint took steps to ensure that the workers really received one-quarter of the harvests as promised. He outlined this system in an agricultural code dictated on October 12, 1800.

Toussaint's triumphant military campaign against both the British and the Spanish, combined with the widespread violence of the rebels against their former masters, unleashed an avalanche of accusations against Toussaint and the black revolutionaries throughout the West Indies, not to mention France and Great Britain. The planters charged Toussaint with every imaginable crime. The propaganda against him proliferated in all the Caribbean colonies, as well as in Brazil and the United Sates. But the decisive attack came directly from the French government, in whose name Toussaint governed the colony.

Napoleon Bonaparte had come to power in France as a result of the French bourgeoisie's profound desire for peace. Although the bourgeoisie was responsible for the French Revolution, it needed political stability in order for its businesses to thrive. Napoleon's famous coup d'etat of November 8, 1799, was financed by French bankers determined to eliminate unrest and instability in France, which still persisted under the government of the Directory. Napoleon was also supported by the peasants, who had acquired land during the French Revolution and who needed to defend their recently acquired rights against the claims of the former feudal landowners.

To preserve the changes that resulted from the Revolution, Napoleon saw the need to export French republicanism to the rest of Europe. These nations were run by monarchies and were, therefore, enemies of France. To conquer Europe, France needed the resources of its colonies, especially Saint-Domingue. Napoleon's grand scheme was to depose Toussaint Louverture, restore slavery, and then utilize the entire island as a center for colonial expansion. Louisiana would also be exploited in order to provide France with enhanced resources. According to these grandiose plans, the Spanish side of the island, ceded to France in 1795, would be converted into a great plantation colony, taking advantage of its fertile flat lands that had never been cultivated.

Though Napoleon hoped to prevent Toussaint from taking over the Spanish part of the island, the black leader was both well informed and very shrewd. When he heard about Napoleon's plans, Toussaint forced Commissioner Phillip Roume, the only remaining member of the third civil commission on the island, to enact a decree that would make Toussaint the successor of the governor of Santo Domingo. The Spanish colony at this point was still under Spanish rule; the French government had asked King Charles IV of Spain to continue governing Santo Domingo until France could send in an army to take over. After securing the commission's decree, Toussaint marched his troops toward the city of Santo Domingo. He arrived there on January 26, 1801, after crushing the resistance of a group of refugee French planters who confronted his troops.

Upon his arrival in Santo Domingo, Toussaint immediately proclaimed the abolition of slavery. Then he appointed civil and military officials, and entrusted them with the job of unifying the island under his government. He also dictated measures to replace cattle raising with plantation agriculture so as to develop exports. When he returned to the western side of the island, Toussaint continued to reorganize the colony and to work diplomatically to get Napoleon to respect the new colonial order in Saint-Domingue resulting from the French Revolution.

Napoleon, however, refused to change his plans. He was under constant pressure not only from French absentee planters living in Paris but also from the French seaport slave traders who wanted to regain control of the colony. As a first step in the execution of his plans, Napoleon convinced Spain secretly to cede Louisiana[3] to France in October 1800. Next, he sent a large fleet of more than eighty ships and 58,000 men to take the colony of Saint-Domingue out of the hands of the emancipated African slaves.

French Military Catastrophe and the Birth of Haiti

This fleet arrived at the island on January 29, 1802. Toussaint, who had gone to Samaná in the eastern part of the island to watch for the arrival of Napoleon's fleet, saw half of the ships arrive and immediately returned to the west to organize resistance. The other half of the fleet

arrived at Cap François on February 3. The French troops divided
themselves up in order to attack on all fronts. One group of soldiers
went to the city of Santo Domingo, which was taken with little difficulty; another group went to Montecristi; another remained in Samaná;
still another went to Port-au-Prince; and the largest group fought in the
city of Cap François under the command of General Charles Victor
Emmanuel Leclerc, Napoleon's brother-in-law and commander-in-chief
of the expedition.

This new war was to prove bloodier than all previous wars, particularly in terms of casualties among the emancipated slaves. Toussaint
himself was deceived by the French and captured on June 7, 1802.
Thinking they were now fighting for a lost cause, Toussaint's followers
began burning to the ground all properties belonging to their former
masters. Once again the towns and cities of Saint-Domingue were in
flames as the emancipated slaves fought to maintain their freedom.
Toussaint's deputy, Jean Jacques Dessalines, was soon elected to command the rebel army, seconded by Henri Christophe.

Dessalines and Christophe inspired their soldiers to fight to the last
man during the twenty-one months that the French tried to subdue
them. The French sent 58,000 men, some of whom, following their victories in Italy and Egypt, and were the most experienced troops in the
French armed forces. These troops were unable to achieve a military victory in the Caribbean because the emancipated slaves were aided by an
unexpected ally: yellow fever. According to French military records,
50,270 soldiers lost their lives, mostly to yellow fever, in a campaign that
ended with the surrender of the few survivors in December 1803. In
addition to 7,000 prisoners of war, only 1,000 French soldiers remained
alive in the garrison of Montecristi and 400 in the city of Santo
Domingo; 2,000 more survivors had escaped to other Caribbean islands.

Convinced that they could never come to an understanding with
proslavery France, Dessalines and the other black leaders decided to
abandon Toussaint's submissive diplomatic policies and on January 1,
1804, proclaimed Haiti to be an independent state. During and after the
war, Dessalines and Christophe expelled or killed all the white
Europeans in the colony, with the exception of some priests. The land
and plantations previously owned by the French colonists and mulatto
planters were confiscated and given to the generals of the new Haitian

army to be cultivated under the work regime established by Toussaint. Shortly thereafter, the black leaders wrote a new Haitian constitution that included laws prohibiting whites from ever owning land or buildings, thus officially ending the colonial regime in Saint-Domingue.

Revolution and Repression in the French Antilles

The Haitian Revolution was the largest of several rebellions in the Caribbean that resulted from the French Revolution. After 1789 all the French colonies were caught up in the revolutionary turmoil and the war against Great Britain, Spain, and Holland. In Cayenne, French Guiana, for example, which had experienced a five-year slave revolt starting in 1770, the French commissioners declared the abolition of slavery right after Commissioner Sonthonax did in Saint-Domingue. Napoleonic military forces reinstated slavery later, but the emancipated slaves preferred to run away into the jungle rather than going back to work on the plantations.

The revolutionary process in Martinique and Guadeloupe was also very complex and ran parallel to the Haitian Revolution. On these islands as well, the initial conflict between *grands blancs* and *petits blancs* for the establishment and control of colonial assemblies preceded the Revolution, as did the resentment against the metropolitan commercial monopoly.

By June 1787 the French colonists of Martinique and Guadeloupe had convinced the French government to recognize their right to organize their own colonial assemblies, and from then on these institutions became the seat of the colonists' struggle for political power. The assemblies served as an outlet for the planters to channel their aspirations of achieving political autonomy. Thus by 1789 political fervor and agitation had already become institutionalized in the French Antilles.

When the *grands blancs* who controlled the colonial assembly of Martinique learned of the revolution in France, they thought that their hope for autonomy had been affirmed. In January 1790 they limited the number of colonial ports open to free trade, organized a special police force, and refused to pay taxes to the colonial administrator and his agents. The following month, however, when the colonial assemblies were supposed to reconvene to elect their representatives to the revolutionary National Assembly in Paris, the *grands blancs* left out the *gens de couleur* and marginalized the *petits blancs*, who had become the most active defenders of the Revolution and continued to agitate for the recognition of their rights.

The *grands blancs* refused to accept the National Assembly's decree of March 8, 1790, which recognized the *gens de couleur*'s rights to vote and to be elected. Almost immediately there was a mulatto rebellion, which was forcibly repressed and served as a pretext for the colonial assembly to extend its mandate on July 1, 1790.

The *gens de couleur* responded to their rejection as citizens by organizing themselves into militias that stimulated slave rebellions on the plantations. The mulattoes also appealed to the French revolutionary government to punish the disobedience of the planters. After more than six months of conflict, the French National Assembly decided to suspend the colonial assemblies in Saint-Domingue and Martinique. In order to implement this decree and impose order, the French government created a commission of four officials. They arrived in Martinique in March 1791, on a war vessel with a large number of soldiers.

After the commission arrived, there was an uneasy peace. Although the colonial assembly and the planters accepted the validity of the decree of March 8, 1790, class struggles continued, exacerbated by the principles of equality espoused by the leaders of the Revolution. The tensions between rich and poor whites continued to build during the year, and by the summer of 1790 they were as explosive as the hostilities existing between whites and mulattoes.

The commission also found the authorities of Martinique divided: some were in favor of the French revolutionary government and opted to support the commissioners and their allies, the *gens de couleur* and *petits blancs*, while others, including the governor, favored the *grands blancs* and the monarchy. Until then, the *grands blancs* had been against the monarchy and had attacked royal despotism while defending their right to autonomy. But the revolutionary fervor of the *petits blancs* and the decrees of the National Assembly conceding political rights to the *gens de couleur* caused them to shift their political loyalties in support of the monarchy.

When the news of the slave rebellion in Saint-Domingue reached

Martinique and Guadeloupe in 1791, the *grands blancs* defied the French revolutionary government and sought the support of the British in an effort to become independent from France. After the overthrow of King Louis XVI on August 10, 1792, the Legislative Assembly decided not to tolerate the rebellion of the white planters in the Antilles. In October 1792 the French revolutionary government sent a new squadron of six warships to establish order in Martinique. After the squadron arrived in St. Pierre on December 1, its commanders removed the promonarchic colonial authorities from office, forcing the *grands blancs* and their rebellious colonial assembly to recognize the Republic.

At the beginning of February 1793, the new administrator, General Donatien Marie Joseph Rochambeau, arrived in Martinique on board another naval squadron.[4] Rochambeau immediately dissolved the colonial assembly and tried to integrate the *gens de couleur* into the colonial government. The mulatto militia supported the new French authorities in their effort to impose a republican regime. Within two months, however, the *grands blancs* rebelled again with a well-armed and organized militia, thus beginning a civil war in Martinique in April 1793. In this war, the *grands blancs* faced an alliance of *gens de couleur*, *petits blancs*, and the republican military authorities.

Since Great Britain and Holland had gone to war with France in February 1793, the British government intervened in support of the *grands blancs*. The first British troops landed in Martinique in mid-June 1793, but the conflict was not brought to an end until February 1794, when a fleet of thirty British warships arrived in Martinique and 6,000 soldiers disembarked at three different points on the island.

This important demonstration of force convinced the leaders of the *gens de couleur* that their cause was lost, and many abandoned the fight, shattering the unity of the revolutionary front. As militia groups quit the field, the French troops that had come to their aid were weakened, and on March 20, 1794, General Rochambeau surrendered to the British troops. Martinique became a British possession until July 1802, when it was handed over to France after the Treaty of Amiens was signed in March of that year.

The British occupation of Martinique gave the *grands blancs* exactly what they wanted: political autonomy from France and the preservation of slavery under a system that would guard against the catastrophe of

Saint-Domingue. In exchange, the island provided the British with an excellent naval base, Fort-Royal, which served them well during the war.

The islands of St. Lucia and Guadeloupe likewise fell into the hands of the British in 1794. The British maintained control of St. Lucia until 1802, but the French regained Guadeloupe almost immediately. Guadeloupe experienced the same tensions that existed in Martinique and Saint-Domingue between whites and mulattoes, planters and merchants, and *grands blancs* and *petits blancs.*

In Guadeloupe, there was more poverty than in Martinique, plots of land were smaller, and there were more white artisans and free mulattoes. The *petits blancs* and *gens de couleur* quickly aligned themselves with the Jacobins as soon as the French Revolution erupted, but they could not check the power of the *grands blancs* in the colonial assemblies.

Internal conflicts among the *grands blancs* in Guadeloupe could be traced to disputes over land and resources. The colony consisted of two large islands, Guadeloupe itself, with Basse-Terre as its capital, and Grand-Terre, whose capital and main port was Point-à-Pitre. These two towns were the centers of strong rivalries among the mercantile groups of both islands. Accustomed to free trade with foreigners, the *grands blancs* of both islands defended the practice. They hoped to take advantage of the changes occurring during the Revolution to expand their commercial contacts. Each group of *grands blancs* tried to gain privileges for its own ports at the expense of the others.

The unrest produced by public debates on individual and colonial rights and free trade soon reached the rest of the population, including the slaves. Before long, the first slave conspiracy was discovered, and its leaders were imprisoned and executed in April 1790.

In September 1791, when the slave revolt in Saint-Domingue occurred, the *grands blancs* still controlled Guadeloupe. They refused to give in to the popular demands of the *petits blancs* and *gens de couleur,* who sought to be recognized politically by the colonial assembly. The *grands blancs* of Guadeloupe were careful not to rebel against the French commissioners who had arrived in Martinique in March 1791. They accepted the hegemony of the National Assembly, allowing the revolutionary flag to fly on the island. But the commissioners could do very little to obligate the *grands blancs* to comply with all the decrees emanating from France because the commissioners themselves were divided on colonial issues.

Unrest continued during the following year. The *grands blancs* openly opposed the growing power of the *petits blancs*, who had taken control of the municipalities and organized revolutionary clubs. The situation deteriorated after the *grands blancs* rejected the French Legislative Assembly's decree of April 4, 1792, which gave the *gens de couleur* the same political rights as whites.

Travelers, soldiers, and sailors arriving from France and Saint-Domingue continuously rekindled the political upheaval. Fearful that a black revolt similar to the Haitian Revolution might occur in Guadeloupe, the *grands blancs* of Guadeloupe finally decided to turn against the Jacobin regime. In September 1792 they lowered the French revolutionary flag and allied themselves with the *grands blancs* of Martinique.

The timing of this counterrevolutionary reaction could not have been worse; it occurred at about the same time that Louis XVI was overthrown in France. The news of the fall of the monarchy quickly reached the islands, and in December 1792 Guadeloupe witnessed the expected uprising of *gens de couleur* and *petits blancs*. The rebellion was supported by a French frigate and its crew, whose commander, General Louis Lacrosse, supported the Revolution. Unable to defend themselves against the rebels, the promonarchic colonial authorities escaped to Trinidad. At the same time, the *grands blancs* requested British military protection.

On January 5, 1793, the *gens de couleur* and *petits blancs*, aided by General Lacrosse, declared that Guadeloupe was now governed by the Republic and installed a revolutionary government on the island. The local government followed the steps of the Jacobins in France, confiscating church property, dissolving old militias, and creating new ones. The colonial assembly was replaced by a Commission Général Extraordinaire, which represented the free citizenry, including the *gens de couleur* and *petits blancs*. The new government also decreed political equality between whites and mulattoes, thereby winning the support of the free mulattoes for the Republican cause.

Such was the political situation in Guadeloupe when General Georges Henri Victor Collot arrived in the Caribbean in February 1793, together with General Rochambeau. For one year Collot administered the island, assisted by the Commission Général Extraordinaire. In April

1794, however, the *grands blancs* called in the British troops, who landed just in time to rescue the large plantation owners from persecution by the Republicans. Collot saw that he had no option other than surrender. During the following months, the colony remained in the hands of British generals and 4,000 soldiers.

At the same time, the French government, unaware that Collot had capitulated, sent two new commissioners to Guadeloupe along with a fleet of nine ships and 1,100 soldiers. Commissioners Victor Hugues and Pierre Chrétien arrived in Guadeloupe in early June 1794, but found it occupied by the British. Hugues refused to accept the *fait accompli* and ordered his troops to land immediately. Although British reinforcements quickly arrived, they were unable to control the situation and had to surrender in Grand-Terre on October 7. The French troops had the support of the majority of the civilian population. Weakened by yellow fever, the British troops occupying Basse-Terre were also defeated, and their commanders abandoned the island on December 10 and 11, 1794. At that point, the French revolutionaries installed a Jacobin regime in Guadeloupe similar to the one Toussaint Louverture had created in Saint-Domingue.

Commissioner Hugues remained as the head of this revolutionary military government. He respected the decree of equal rights for the *gens de couleur* and ratified the abolition of slavery decreed in Paris on February 4, 1794. This permitted him to include in his "Army of the Antilles" close to 5,000 freedmen as "new citizens" (*nouveaux citoyens*). Many freedmen, however, remained trapped on the plantations in an obligatory work regime that was almost as harsh as slavery.

Now under a new revolutionary government, the ports were reopened to foreign trade in order to reactivate the economy, and privateers reappeared to wage war against British commerce in the West Indies. Despite the British naval presence in the Caribbean, Guadeloupe remained in the hands of the French Republic under the command of Hugues, who was given the title of Agent by the Directory in 1796.

Like Saint-Domingue, Guadeloupe was greatly affected by the political fluctuations in France and by France's war with Great Britain. Guadeloupe's economy suffered the effects of the war and political unrest. To defray their expenses, the authorities found themselves obliged to confiscate and sell colonial products. Many large plantation owners fled the island, leaving their properties in the hands of third parties, as many *petits blancs* had done earlier to escape persecution by the promonarchic authorities.

Hugues was removed from his position in June 1798, and for the next four years Guadeloupe was run by a rapid succession of governments, which kept the colony in a permanent state of turmoil. The commissioners sent to impose order, the military governors, and the local elite continued to be involved in a series of political and racial conflicts that discouraged investment and prevented the planters and merchants from taking immediate advantage of the new sugar market opened up by the revolution in Saint-Domingue.

Eventually, the consulate that had brought Napoleon Bonaparte to power rejected the abolition of slavery. This caused the Jacobins to begin discussing the need for Guadeloupe to declare its independence from France. Napoleon thought that Guadeloupe, like Saint-Domingue, should be brought back to order and that Jacobin influence should be eradicated from the Antilles. Thus, together with the great fleet sent to Saint-Dominque to depose Toussaint Louverture in 1802, a smaller fleet commanded by General Antoine Richepanse was dispatched to Guadeloupe. Its mission was to liquidate the Jacobin government of Guadeloupe and reestablish slavery.

Richepanse's troops began to disembark in Grand-Terre on March 2, 1802, and a few days later started operations in Basse-Terre. There was notable opposition, particularly from the Army of the Antilles, made up of Jacobin whites, mulattoes, and black "new citizens" who opposed slavery. Nevertheless, Richepanse's campaign was quick and bloody. More than 1,000 men died in combat, including the mulatto commander Louis Delgrès and 300 combatants who blew themselves up in a powder magazine rather than fall into the hands of Napoleon's troops. At the end of May 1802, the revolutionary government of Guadeloupe ceased to exist.

On July 16, 1802, the consuls of France decreed the reestablishment of slavery in Guadeloupe under the former colonial order. This decree recognized the political rights of the *gens de couleur*; however, only landowners were entitled to French citizenship. Slave owners also reacquired their former rights over their slaves. Although Napoleon managed to defeat the Jacobins in Guadeloupe, they remained victorious in

Saint-Domingue and succeeded in dismantling the colonial regime there. The black Jacobins prevailed over Napoleon in the tropics, a feat the white Jacobins were unable to achieve.

CHAPTER 12

New Peasantries in
Haiti and Santo Domingo

Haiti's Agrarian Policies

The Haitian Revolution brought about the destruction of the plantation system in Saint-Domingue. The first Haitian rulers were convinced
that it was necessary to preserve the plantation as a production model.
Nonetheless, in a relatively quick process most plantations disappeared
from the former French colony, which has been called Haiti since
January 1, 1804.

The foremost leader of the Revolution, Toussaint Louverture,
believed the plantation system to be the productive unit par excellence,
and he and his followers did all that they could to preserve the estates
confiscated from the French. To this end, in 1801 Toussaint enacted several laws intended to oblige the former slaves to work on plantations as
contracted laborers. Supervised by a rural police force, these workers
were to follow the orders of the new plantation owners and labored in
physical conditions that were not much better than those endured under
slavery.

Toussaint also dictated additional measures intended to boost the
production of agricultural products in Spanish Santo Domingo. Before
that policy could achieve results, however, the military expedition sent
by Napoleon Bonaparte occupied Santo Domingo. Thus in March 1802
the French reestablished slavery, while Saint-Domingue continued to
fight off the French in a brutal war that lasted nineteen months. When
the French troops were at last defeated, Haiti proclaimed its independence on January 1, 1804. The war left the majority of the sugar plantations in Haiti in ruins and removed all French colonial presence from
the land.

During the war, Toussaint Louverture was captured and deported to France, where he died in prison. General Jean Jacques Dessalines took Toussaint's place as Haiti's leader. Dessalines, like Toussaint, believed in the need to preserve the plantation system under state control and upheld the policies requiring workers to remain on the plantations. One of his first measures was to prohibit foreign ownership of property in Haiti.

In April 1804 Dessalines decreed the cancellation of all land transactions. With this measure, he tried to concentrate the majority of Haitian territory in the hands of the state. Both mulattoes and blacks resented this measure, and Dessalines became increasingly unpopular. He was assassinated in October 1806, but his confiscation of property was so effective that before his death, he managed to place more than two-thirds of Haitian territory under state control.

After Dessalines's death, the tensions between mulattoes and blacks resurfaced. As a result, in 1807 Haiti was divided into two independent countries with antagonistic governments. In the north, Henri Christophe, Dessalines's successor and a follower of Toussaint, became president of the State of Haiti, but his rule was not accepted by the mulatto elite. Therefore, in the south of Haiti, the mulattoes created an independent Republic of Haiti, headed by President General Alexander Petion. A bitter civil war erupted again. In 1811 Christophe converted the State of Haiti into a kingdom, and proclaimed himself king. Both countries remained separated until the death of Christophe in 1820.

Christophe maintained the policies of his predecessors and kept the plantations intact. The lands were distributed among his collaborators, who managed them on behalf of the state. These administrators were required to pay 25 percent of their production in taxes and another 25 percent in salaries to their workers, while the remaining 50 percent could be kept as profit. Plantation administrators were typically high-ranking military officers, on whom Henri Christophe conferred titles of nobility after declaring himself king. In this manner, Christophe assured the political support of the new black military elite emerging after the Revolution, while simultaneously maintaining production and exports.

In order to defend his republic from Christophe, President Petion sought the sympathy and loyalty of the black and mulatto population by giving land to all of his soldiers and officers. Because soldiers had been owed salaries for a long time and there was no money to pay them, Petion gave them parcels of land in lieu of cash. He also returned the large plantations confiscated by Dessalines to the former mulatto owners and in that manner consolidated the support of the class that had brought him to power.

Petion believed that it was easier to maintain peace when the majority of the people were landowners and free cultivators, rather than indentured servants and slaves. For this reason, when the workers from the old French plantations received parcels of land, the government let them cultivate whatever they wanted, without the intervention of the state farming inspectors created by Toussaint. Between 1806 and 1809, most of the cultivable land in the Republic of Haiti was privatized, and the economy of the region underwent a radical transformation. In addition to the large plantations under mulatto ownership, a new free peasantry emerged, consisting of former slaves who cultivated family plots on the lands previously owned by their French masters.

This policy of land redistribution resulted in a scarcity of manual labor, making it difficult to maintain a high level of production on the large plantations. Now that the former slaves were landowners themselves, the large planters had to find a new labor supply. Exports from the Republic of Haiti also declined because the new peasants preferred to grow subsistence crops to feed their families rather than cultivate sugarcane, cotton, or indigo for the European market.

The export crop most affected by land redistribution was sugar, because many of the old sugarcane plantations were converted into subsistence-crop family farms. In 1818, when Petion died, the Republic of Haiti only exported 1,168 tons of sugar, far fewer than the 30,000 tons the southern part of Saint-Domingue exported prior to the Haitian Revolution. Indigo, which also required large amounts of manual labor, was no longer grown at all, and cotton exports, which had risen to 2,500 tons before the Revolution, were reduced to fewer than 200 tons.

Only coffee remained as a significant commercial export crop, with 9,000 tons exported in 1818. That quantity, however, was less than one-third of the volume exported from southern Saint-Domingue in 1789. Cacao production did not decline as steeply as coffee production because peasants preferred this product as a food source, but exports in 1818 still came to a mere 163 tons, only a fraction of the amount formerly exported by Saint-Domingue. Consequently, agriculture in the Republic of Haiti underwent a profound transformation in only twelve years.

In the north, the decline of agricultural exports was slower due to the efforts of Henri Christophe, who tried to increase sugar exports after they reached a low point in 1805, when only 107 tons were exported from Cap Haitien, as Cap François was now known. In 1815 sugar exports reached their highest point since the Revolution, surpassing 3,100 tons. This quantity, however, was tiny compared to the output levels preceding the Haitian Revolution. In general, the average annual amount of sugar exported from northern Haiti between 1811 and 1820 was only 1,280 tons.

Christophe also made a great effort to increase coffee production, but exports never returned to pre-Revolution levels. In 1804 and 1809 the north of Haiti exported as much as 5,000 tons of coffee, but its annual average during that period was only 3,500 tons. The export of cotton experienced very pronounced fluctuations, but its general tendency was one of decline, eventually disappearing from the market. Before the Revolution, in 1789, the colony of Saint-Domingue exported 3,500 tons of cotton, but in 1820 cotton exports from the Kingdom of Haiti failed to reach 1 ton.

Only tobacco and cacao exports increased in the Kingdom of Haiti. Tobacco rose from only 1.5 tons in 1807 to 48 tons in 1820. Cacao exports increased from an average of 39 tons between 1803 and 1807 to 50 tons from 1817 to 1820. Rum and molasses practically disappeared as export products from both northern and southern Haiti.

When Alexandre Petion died in 1818, the presidency of the Republic of Haiti was taken over by his secretary and minister, Jean-Pierre Boyer. In 1820 King Christophe suffered a stroke while in church, and his sudden illness sparked among his own collaborators a conspiracy to overthrow him. Feeling betrayed and unable to defend himself, the sick king committed suicide by shooting himself in the chest. As word of his death spread, there was a general upheaval in the north of Haiti, where the people, tired of a rigid system of exploitation, clamored for freedom and land of their own. Boyer took advantage of the reigning confusion caused by the power vacuum and, with the support of a group of leaders in the north, marched with his army toward Cap Haitien, occupying the city at the end of October 1820, and thus beginning the reunification of Haiti as an independent republic.

Boyer found clear proof of the difference in economic performance between the northern and southern regimes when he discovered nine million gold francs at King Christophe's residence in Sans Souci and at the Castle of the Citadelle. The Republic of Haiti had never amassed even a third of that amount.

Many years before Boyer's unification of Haiti in 1820, a large number of workers had migrated from the north to the south, seeking land and liberty. Upon Petion's death, thousands of blacks and mulattoes had wept inconsolably at the loss of their *papá bon-ké* (good-hearted father) which contrasted greatly with Dessalines's and Christophe's ignominious deaths. Petion's successor, Boyer, who had worked closely with him, was warmly welcomed by the masses in the north as he offered to give them land and liberate them from quasi-slavery.

Boyer proceeded to redistribute the northern plantations among the military and civilians, giving officials and workers lots in proportion to their rank. These new peasant landowners and citizens of the Republic supported his government, but by 1823 the financial effects of this policy of land redistribution became visible. The gold found in Christophe's coffers had been spent, and exports showed an alarming decline. The peasants abandoned the cane fields for good, turning instead to the production of other crops and livestock for home consumption and for sale in local markets. They raised their crops and livestock on small family plots, which they controlled. The plantation system thus came to an end.

In 1823 sugar exports from Haiti were a mere 7 tons, ten thousand times less than in 1789, when they had reached 70,544 tons. Coffee exports fell to 16,901 tons, less than half the 38,417 tons that was exported on the eve of the Revolution. Exports of cotton were reduced to 166 tons, one-twentieth of the 3,502 tons exported in 1789. Cacao exports were only 177 tons in 1823, and indigo was no longer exported at all.

To compensate for the decline in plantation exports, many Haitians turned to logging and exported precious lumber and dyewood. The French had extensively exploited the mahogany forests of Saint-Domingue before the Revolution, but some uncut wood remained because Dessalines had prohibited logging. He believed that it was a drain on peasant labor and reduced agricultural production.

One of the most valuable trees for lumber was guaiacum (*lignum vitae*), which was highly prized. The trunks of guaiacum trees were preferred for naval and industrial uses, and its resin was used in the preparation of ointments and cough syrups. The other wood that became an important export article was *campeche* (brazilwood), which yielded a dye greatly in demand by both European and North American industries. Lumber production, however, never compensated for the ruin of commercial agriculture, and the Haitian rulers could not prevent the gradual impoverishment of the state.

Emigration and Decline in Santo Domingo

While the social and economic transformation in Haiti continued, Spanish Santo Domingo remained even more poverty-stricken, having suffered innumerable difficulties during and after the Haitian Revolution. Livestock, which had been the basis of its colonial economy, were confiscated and consumed by the French, Haitian, English, and Spanish armies during the wars and invasions between 1791 and 1809. Spain regained Santo Domingo in July 1809, after a nine-month local war against the French (known as the War of Reconquest), but the economy remained in ruins for many years later.

Inspired by the Haitian Revolution, slave rebels destroyed the eleven sugar mills built in Santo Domingo at the end of the eighteenth century. Exports from Santo Domingo were reduced to livestock traded to Haiti, tobacco sold to merchants in St. Thomas and Curaçao, and mahogany, guaiacum, and dyewoods sold to other foreign traders. Between 1809 and 1822, local taxes were not sufficient to pay the salaries of the small bureaucratic and military elite that governed Santo Domingo. Money to support the local government had to be sent from Havana.

More than two-thirds of the population of Santo Domingo, including the most educated families, abandoned the island in several waves between 1795 and 1809, leaving only 70,000 inhabitants in the colony in 1820. The first of these waves took place after Santo Domingo was ceded to France in 1795, when several thousand families opted to move to Cuba, Venezuela, or Puerto Rico. The second wave took place in 1801, following the invasion of Toussaint Louverture's forces. The third occurred after 1805, when Santo Domingo was invaded by Dessalines's Haitian troops.

In March 1805 the Haitian leaders tried in vain to expel the French garrison that had been stationed in Santo Domingo ever since Napoleon's invasion of 1802. As Dessalines's troops withdrew, they massacred hundreds of Creole and Spanish families in small towns on the island. Many survivors chose to emigrate, convinced that if the Haitians ruled the island, they would wipe out the Dominican population. Although the internal difficulties of the Haitian governments prevented any new invasions of Santo Domingo, the colony at this point received very few immigrants or new investors due to its dangerous proximity to Haiti.

With the Haitian economy in ruins, French bankers, merchants, and shipbuilders who had financed the original planters of Saint-Domingue pressured the French government to reconquer its old colony. In 1814 the French government encouraged two conspiracies by French colonial exiles to repossess its lost colony, but both failed.

The Haitian Invasion of Santo Domingo

In 1820, however, there was an attempt to reestablish the former colonial order based on slavery. French adventurers gathered in Martinique to join an expedition that would land on the Spanish side of the island and invade Haiti from the east. The Haitian authorities heard of this plot and became convinced that the Spanish side represented a weak link in their struggle to protect their independence. Spain and France had recently entered into an alliance, and the Haitians suspected that the Spanish government supported the French expedition.

The Haitian government prepared for the invasion by mobilizing its army and encouraging the people of Santo Domingo to rise up against the Spanish government and join the Republic of Haiti. President Boyer believed that it would be easier to defend the Republic from a French attack if he could unite the entire island, because one government could then control all the ports where the French might land. Starting in December 1820, Boyer sent his agents to neighboring Santo Domingo. They tried to convince the Spanish Creoles and free mulattoes that the political union of the island was to their advantage, promising that taxation of the important cattle trade would cease after the island was united.

Boyer worked intensely on this plan in 1821, ignorant of the fact that the colonial government officials of Santo Domingo were conspiring to declare their independence from Spain. For the most part, these functionaries, including the military and the Creole bureaucrats, were highly disenchanted with Spain. They plotted to expel the Spanish authorities in a coup d'etat and to proclaim an independent republic that would be part of Gran Colombia, the group of South American republics organized by Simón Bolívar.

On November 15, 1821, a pro-Haitian group of Creoles and free mulattoes from the border areas proclaimed the independence of the Spanish colony, and its leaders immediately circulated manifestos prepared by the Haitian government calling for Boyer's military support of their movement. When the conspirators in the city of Santo Domingo received this news, they reacted by carrying out their coup d'état, deposing the Spanish governor on December 1, 1821. They then proclaimed the creation of the "Independent State of Spanish Haiti."

The Haitian government quickly mobilized to prevent the French from taking advantage of the power vacuum created by the expulsion of the Spanish authorities from Santo Domingo. In early 1822, President Boyer obtained the Senate's authorization to organize an army of more than 12,000 soldiers, with whom he marched to the eastern part of the island, arriving in Santo Domingo on February 9, 1822.

Overwhelmed by the military might of the Haitian invasion, the Dominican separatists did not show any resistance and transferred power to Boyer. A few days later the French troops reached Samaná, in eastern Santo Domingo, by ship, but the Haitian army was lying in wait for them, prepared for war, and the French withdrew without even attempting to land.

The Abolition of Slavery and the Land Question

From then on the island remained politically unified under the absolute command of president-for-life Jean Pierre Boyer. His first public decision after taking possession of Santo Domingo was to abolish slavery and to promise farmland to all the freedmen. Although there were fewer than 4,000 slaves in Santo Domingo at the time, Boyer had to wait more than two years before he could give them their parcels of land. Because large amounts of land in Santo Domingo were owned communally, it was difficult for the Haitians to divide the land into smaller plots. With no place to go, most freedmen temporarily remained with their former masters and waited for land. Nevertheless, some who were more desirous of enjoying their immediate freedom joined the Haitian army and helped the new authorities maintain order.

The problem of determining which lands the state could redistribute among the former slaves of Santo Domingo created numerous political difficulties. In an effort to proceed quickly, Boyer formed a commission to study the situation and prepare a report. In October 1822 the commission determined that the state could claim as its own all property that had belonged to the Spanish government, the lands and buildings of the convents and religious orders that had been abandoned after 1795, all property of the Church, French land confiscated since 1809, and the property of collaborators with the French in their recently attempted invasion.

The Haitian authorities immediately began to confiscate these properties and redistribute them among the freedmen or sell them at a reduced rate to the military officials and Haitian functionaries who had also requested land and housing in Santo Domingo. These confiscations created a deep resentment among the Spanish and Creole population of Santo Domingo and had to be immediately suspended. Many of these properties had been in the possession of private citizens for over twenty years, and their ownership was legalized by prior usage. In January 1823 Boyer named a new commission to reexamine the matter of property titles. In February of that year he gave former residents and expatriates of Santo Domingo a four-month deadline to return to their land, with the penalty of confiscation if they failed to do so. When no one returned, the Haitian authorities tried to claim their land as state prop-

erty. This greatly irritated the occupants of the land in question, many
of whom were relatives of the absentee owners.

Plots against the government soon followed, encouraged by the archbishop of Santo Domingo, in response to the nationalization of Church
property and Boyer's decision of January 5, 1823, to eliminate the state-
funded salaries of the clergy. Later in 1823 the Haitian government
uncovered three more conspiracies and had to squelch a revolt against
Haitian troops. In mid-February 1824 a larger plot against the Haitian
government, led by a Catholic priest, was uncovered in Los Alcarrizos,
near Santo Domingo. Its participants were hunted down. Its leader and
five others managed to escape to Venezuela, but many were captured,
condemned to death, and executed on March 9, 1824. This repression
frightened large numbers of families, who recalled the 1805 massacres
of Dessalines and chose to immigrate to Puerto Rico, following the
example of those who had left for Venezuela in 1822.

Once peace had been achieved and Boyer had received the reports of
his commissioners, he promulgated a new law on July 8, 1824, defining
which areas could be claimed as state property on the eastern part of the
island. According to the law, these areas included land that did not
belong to private citizens before unification, as well as all property of
the Church, convents, hospitals, and other ecclesiastic organizations.
The property of individuals who were absent when unification occurred
and who did not return before the deadline established by the Haitian
government was also nationalized, as was the property of those who left
without pledging their allegiance to the Republic.

With this act, the Haitian government found a legal way to create a
new system of land ownership on the Spanish side of the island. This
system would give all citizens of the Republic the right to own land,
which would be protected by titles issued by the state. The system would
be regulated by a commission that would examine the old Spanish titles
to determine the validity of territorial rights and fix the limits of the
state's property.

The enforcement of this law required official examination of the
property titles held by Dominican landowners in order to determine
who owned land belonging to the state. Since these Dominicans continually refused to show their deeds to the Haitian authorities for assess-
ment, the massive redistribution of land among the former slaves, which

had occurred quickly in Haiti, took many years in Santo Domingo. Despite this problem, the Haitian government used the 1824 law to take possession of the newly declared state lands and gave them to the freedmen who wanted to use them for farming.

According to the law, first-time landowners could not own less than 12 acres of land, a new unit that the Dominicans, as time went by, referred to as a *boyerana*. These new landholdings were to produce fruit for export in addition to subsistence crops. If an owner was unable to keep his land under cultivation, he was obligated to sell it or give it to other producers.

Boyer also passed other resolutions to encourage Dominican landowners to devote themselves to commercial agriculture, but the Dominicans preferred to log the forests and raise livestock, because these products had a secure foreign market. Much of the lumber cut was on former communal lands, now considered state property. Boyer tried unsuccessfully to prevent this logging, claiming that it kept manual laborers from working in commercial agriculture, but his efforts were in vain.

The Haitian authorities attacked the sale of contraband lumber, claiming that it was the primary reason for the decline in exports. In fact, the bankruptcy of the plantations, and not the sale of lumber, had caused exports to drop. The land redistribution policy had been well received by the local population, including the mulatto elite, but over time it became evident that the national economy was suffering from diminishing exports.

Peasants' Resistance to the Rural Code

Gradually, the mulatto elite governing Haiti began to react to this situation and tried to promote the development of commercial agriculture in order to generate exports. On May 1, 1826, Boyer went before the Haitian Senate to present a set of laws intended to reorganize the Haitian economy. These laws, known as the Rural Code of Haiti, went into effect immediately and required peasants to work on plantations or be punished. Paradoxically, in 1826 only twenty-two sugar plantations of any importance remained in Haiti. Their joint production was less than eleven tons of sugar. Almost all of them were in the hands of commanding military officers and government functionaries.

The Rural Code was designed to help the Haitian economy reach its earlier production levels. Idleness was absolutely forbidden, and no one except government functionaries and recognized professionals could stop working the land or abandon his property without previous authorization from a justice of the peace or from the local military commander. The children of farmworkers could not abandon their parents' plots to go to school without the permission of these same authorities. Workers were not allowed to leave the countryside to go into business, nor were they allowed to spend more than eight days in a row away from the plantations. Once a farmer was employed on a plantation, he was obliged to serve a minimum of three years. If he left early, he would be fined, imprisoned, or subjected to forced labor. Women were required to work until their fourth month of pregnancy and resume work four months after delivery.

On both sides of the island, the army was in charge of enforcing the Rural Code. The plantations, supervised by the state, were expected to produce both export crops and food to feed their workers. Workers were assigned plots to cultivate and in return received 25 percent of their production in food or cash. The plantation owners were required to help their employees transport their crops to the market if the workers wanted to sell them.

In its day, the Rural Code was considered a masterpiece of Haitian legislation, but it was completely impracticable because the Haitian people simply ignored it, refusing to work on the plantations. In 1824 the population of the former French part of the island was 316,544 people, of whom 126,617 were landowners. The other 189,927 were women, children, and the elderly. At least one-third of the Haitian people worked someone else's land as well as their own. Many became sharecroppers, while others who remained landless worked on peasant farms as day laborers, usually paid in kind given the shortage of currency in Haiti. Whatever their status the Haitian peasants always preferred to pay more attention to their family plots than to the plantations.

On the Dominican side, the Rural Code did not work either, since the rural inhabitants of Santo Domingo had never experienced the type of forced labor Boyer now required of them. Tobacco farmers in the central regions of Santo Domingo resented and disobeyed the Rural Code. Tobacco was cultivated on small family plots, where manual labor was shared communally in times of planting and harvesting. It simply did not make sense for the Dominican tobacco farmers to obey the Code´s ordinances regarding obligatory labor or its other restrictive or punitive policies.

In the area near the city of Santo Domingo, where cattle raising had been the predominant economic activity for centuries, the policy of encouraging agricultural export production was also unpopular. In 1829 the government authorized farmers to kill any cattle that had damaged their crops. This law created a constant conflict between cattle ranchers and farmers in Santo Domingo and led to frequent acts of violence.

With the failure of the Rural Code, the Haitian government lost its last opportunity to reinstate the plantation system. Boyer and the governing Haitian elite could not prevent the Haitian peasantry from working for their own personal and family benefit. As the peasant economy thrived, the army had little motivation to enforce the Rural Code, especially after France recognized Haiti's independence in July 1825 in exchange for a compensation payment of 150 million francs.

The Haitian government was compelled to sign this agreement after King Charles X of France sent a war fleet to Port-au-Prince with instructions to bombard the city if Haiti did not agree to compensate the French planters, merchants, and bankers who had lost their plantations and businesses during the Haitian Revolution. Although humiliating to the Haitians, this agreement meant that France would no longer threaten Haiti. It also gave the Haitian army little incentive to maintain discipline or preparation for war. Instead, the soldiers and officers put their energies into caring for their families and little plots, neglecting their role as a country police force.

The Rural Code was also conceived as a way to increase export production to help Haiti pay its 150-million-franc debt to France. In 1824 the value of exports amounted to only 22.4 million francs, a mere 10 percent of the value in 1789. The price of independence from France was astronomical for the Haitian national economy. The Haitian government was able to make the first payment of its debt to France only by taking out a loan of 30 million francs from a French bank in 1825.

Financial Crisis and Economic Difficulties

To pay the second installment in 1826, the Haitian government declared its obligation to France's "national debt" and imposed an extraordinary tax of 300,000 *gourdes* on all of the island's inhabitants. This tax, which was to be paid annually over a ten-year period between 1827 and 1836, greatly displeased the Dominicans. The accord with France had clearly established that the inhabitants of the former French part of the island, and not the Dominicans, were to pay for Haiti's independence. Therefore the Dominicans refused to finance a debt that they believed was not theirs to bear. Many Haitians also refused to pay the tax, arguing that they had won their independence by force during the Revolution.

The situation became dire in 1827, when a campaign launched against the Haitian government by Boyer's adversaries in the Senate charged that the country was too poor to pay the debt to France. Boyer was compelled to reduce the annual tax to 200,000 *gourdes*, to be paid by the inhabitants of both sides of the island. As this sum was insufficient to pay down the debt, Boyer had to resort to issuing paper money. As a result, the Haitian *gourde* dropped in value by 250 percent in less than two years.

At the end of 1827, the Haitian government had to take out a new loan from another French bank in order to fulfill its obligations. The interest and commissions on this new loan were so onerous that Haiti became insolvent and could not continue to repay its debt to France. After twelve years of negotiations, France accepted the reduction of Haiti's debt to sixty million francs and granted Haiti a new term of thirty years to repay it. This new agreement was signed at the beginning of 1838, when Haitian exports were stagnating and the country was in an extreme economic crisis. At this point, it was of vital importance for Haiti to maintain control over the Dominican part of the island, because lumber and tobacco from former Santo Domingo had replaced sugar, indigo, and cacao as the main export products. The only product of similar importance from the western part of the island was coffee.

When Boyer took over Santo Domingo in 1822, Haiti was exporting only 55,000 cubic feet of mahogany annually, while Santo Domingo was exporting 2.5 million cubic feet. In the following twenty years, legal exportation of mahogany almost doubled, surpassing 4.0 million cubic feet in 1842. Exports of logwood and dyewood followed the same trend. In 1821 the Haitians were exporting 3.7 million cubic feet of brazil-wood, but by exploiting the uncut forests of Santo Domingo, they increased production eightfold, exceeding an annual average of 30 million cubic feet between 1839 and 1842.

Tobacco exports experienced similar growth. Before the unification of the island, Haiti exported only 38 tons of tobacco annually, while Santo Domingo was selling more than 256 tons. Two decades later, Haiti increased its tobacco exports until they surpassed 1,250 tons in 1842. This growth came as a result of incentives offered to tobacco planters in 1830 as Boyer arranged for the Haitian government to buy all the tobacco produced on the island at reasonable prices.

Coffee, which had become the preferred commercial crop of the Haitian people, did not even approach these growth rates. In 1825 Haiti exported 18,017 tons of coffee to France, England, and the United States. During the next fifteen years, Haitian coffee exports averaged 20,500 tons per year, but coffee prices dropped in the world market, with an especially steep decline in 1836 following four years of growth.

From then on, the Haitian economy faced serious difficulties. An economic depression that had begun in the United States quickly extended to Europe, causing a decline in the prices of coffee and tobacco in the world market over the following years. Although Haiti exported 23,500 tons of coffee in 1835, sales dropped to 18,500 tons in 1836. A drought that affected Haiti during the following year caused a further reduction in exports, to 15,400 tons in 1837, their lowest point in many years.

Haiti's economic difficulties caused extraordinary political dissent. The Haitian Congress, until then a docile instrument in Boyer's service, began to echo the protests of the mulatto opposition, who continually criticized Haiti's economic decline and the inability of the government to handle its crises. Boyer tried to justify the economic depression by saying that it came as a direct result of the commercial and financial crises in Europe and the United States. The propaganda of his enemies, however, reached the entire Republic, causing serious political tensions.

From 1837 on, Boyer attempted to resolve a series of political confrontations by dissolving Congress and imprisoning his critics. In response, a group of soldiers tried to assassinate Boyer in 1838. The plot failed, and Boyer continued to govern for five more years. His regime received a boost from the 1838 agreement that renegotiated Haiti's debt to France and from a sudden surge in export prices.

The Haitian and Dominican elites plotted to overthrow Boyer in order to put an end to his lifelong rule. There seemed to be no other way to change Haiti's political structure. In July 1828 the liberal Dominican leaders formed a secret society called La Trinitaria to fight his regime. Four years later, in September 1842, Haitian liberals similarly organized the Société pour les Droits de l'Homme et les Citoyens (Society for Human and Citizen Rights), with the intention of deposing Boyer.

The leaders of both societies met frequently, until they organized a military revolt that erupted on January 27, 1843. Boyer tried to fight back, but the conspiracy involved the highest strata of the military, and his regime fell on March 13, 1843. That day Boyer and his family fled to Jamaica. Boyer had governed Haiti for twenty-five years and presided over the creation of a peasant class and the consolidation of the Haitian and Dominican peasantry. The abolition of slavery, the destruction of the plantation system, and the creation of this peasant class were the longest-lasting legacies of the Haitian Revolution on the island of Española.

CHAPTER 13

Abolitionism and Crisis in the British West Indies

Early Abolitionist Activities

While Haiti was being transformed into a peasant economy, the British slavery system was undergoing a complex transformation. This process began before the Haitian Revolution, when Quaker groups in the United States and Great Britain initiated the first abolitionist campaigns. The struggle for the abolition of slavery was a long one, with many setbacks, but it eventually resulted in the transformation of the European conscience. The fundamental ideas of the movement were elaborated and spread by Quaker activists, liberal philosophers, evangelical theologians, poets, and writers in an outpouring of literature that helped mobilize British public opinion against the slave trade over a period of forty years.

In 1783 a group of Quakers petitioned the British Parliament to abolish the slave trade. That request was rejected, but the Quakers turned abolition into one of their fundamental missions and dedicated themselves to it for the next fifty years, helping mobilize British society. In 1787 the Quakers presented another formal motion to the British Parliament, which was again unsuccessful. Nevertheless, the leaders of the Quaker Society for the Abolition of Slavery did not give up and continued their campaign with renewed vigor.

In April 1791 the abolitionists presented several petitions to the British Parliament as well as a proposal for a law to abolish the slave trade. This proposal was also rejected, but the abolitionist literature and its arguments permeated so deeply that when an identical proposal was resubmitted to the House of Commons in 1792, the same members of

Parliament agreed to gradually abolish slavery in the British colonies starting on January 1, 1796.

This early triumph of the abolitionists was short-lived due to the Haitian Revolution and the tenacious opposition of the colonial representatives in Parliament. The latter argued that the colonies would fall into ruin if slavery were abolished, and that abolition would cause Great Britain to lose one of its main sources of income. The Haitian Revolution and the Anglo-French war caused prices of colonial products to inflate. At this point, the British sought to seize the opportunity to control the European sugar market once again by conquering the French colonies in the Caribbean. Faced with this new set of circumstances, the British Parliament indefinitely postponed the abolition of slavery.

The abolitionists, who believed the slave trade to be one of the worst crimes against humanity, were not discouraged and continued to present their legislative proposals to Parliament year after year. Despite their moral arguments, which were rarely questioned, the abolitionists' proposals to abolish the slave trade were always rejected by Parliament during the years of the Haitian Revolution. The financial, mercantile, and maritime groups of Great Britain supported the war, hoping to oust France from the Caribbean and take control of the European sugar market. In addition, radical abolitionist explanations justifying the slave revolt in Saint-Domingue made many members of Parliament fear a similar revolt in the British West Indies.

Caribbean Wars during the Haitian Revolution

When the war against France began in the Caribbean, the first French island conquered by the British was Tobago in April 1793. In mid-June of that year, English troops landed in Martinique at the request of the *grands blancs* there. As the first invasion of Martinique failed, the British then concentrated on invading Saint-Domingue, beginning their operations there on September 20, 1793. Later, in March 1794, British troops succeeded in taking over Martinique after only two weeks of intense fighting. The British also conquered St. Lucia in a quick two-day operation from April 2 to 4, 1794. The small islands of Les Saintes, adjacent to Guadeloupe, fell one week later, and Guadeloupe itself was taken on April 21, 1794.

In June 1794 the French recaptured Guadeloupe and St. Lucia after a quick campaign. These triumphs encouraged the French living on the islands of Grenada and Dominica to rebel against the English as well. There, French revolutionary emissaries offered to help fight against the English governors. In St. Vincent, the French emissaries encouraged a general uprising of the black Caribs, which was only quelled in June 1796 after the arrival of fresh British troops, who expelled 5,080 black Caribs, sending them into exile in Honduras. British casualties in this campaign, however, were very high due to yellow fever. In Grenada, many British lives were also lost in combat and to yellow fever. It is estimated that 25,000 British soldiers died in the Lesser Antilles in the course of these campaigns.

St. Lucia was retaken by the English in April 1796. They lost more than 500 soldiers in this operation because the French revolutionaries, with the help of black and mulatto rebels, carried on a guerrilla war from their mountain hideouts for an entire year. In November 1796 a French expedition from Guadeloupe attacked the island of St. Kitts. The French inflicted heavy damage, burning houses, plantations, and sugar mills, but could not occupy the island. In April 1796 the British encountered little resistance as they invaded the Dutch colonies of Demerara, Essequibo, and Berbice, in Guiana, but this invasion precipitated a war between Great Britain and Holland.

Spain reacted to the conquest of Guiana by declaring war on Great Britain on October 5, 1796. For some time, the Anglo-Spanish relationship had been deteriorating due to the British invasion of Saint-Domingue and several forays into Trinidad the previous year. At the beginning of 1797, the British government responded to Spain's declaration of war by sending a new expedition of sixty-eight ships to Trinidad and Puerto Rico.

In February 1797 the British took Trinidad without much struggle. When British ships reached Puerto Rico in April 1797, however, the Spanish authorities defended their position tenaciously. The British landed close to the city of San Juan with more than 6,000 soldiers, but after fifteen days of combat and more than 200 British casualties, the British commanders suspended the operation and abandoned the island.

For several months the British were busy with the military occupation of Saint-Domingue. When they abandoned it in 1798, they again began attacking other islands in the Caribbean. In August 1799 they occupied the Dutch colony of Surinam, followed by Curaçao in September 1800, the Danish islands of St. Croix, St. Thomas, and St. John and the Swedish island of St. Barthélemy in March 1801, and St. Martin, St. Eustatius, and Saba in March and April 1801.

By this time, however, the war was coming to an end. On October 1, 1801, France and Great Britain held preliminary peace talks that were formalized by the signing of the Treaty of Amiens on March 27, 1802. As on previous occasions, almost all the possessions taken during the war were returned to their former rulers, but the British permanently retained Trinidad, Demerara, Essequibo, and Berbice. Surinam was returned to Holland, although the British occupied it again in 1804 and did not return it to Holland until 1816.

Economic Impact of the Haitian Revolution

The economic performance of the West Indies during the Haitian Revolution was strongly influenced by the war between England and France. Martinique and St. Lucia, which had fallen to the British in 1793 and 1794, respectively, did not increase their exports before their return to France in 1802. Barbados, Grenada, and the Leeward Islands were also unable to take advantage of the ruination of the Saint-Domingue plantations. In Barbados, where the economy had been in decline for some time, exports continued to decrease during the years of the Haitian Revolution. Grenada's sugar production declined by one-third between 1791 and 1802 due to the conflicts between the French and English, in addition to confrontations with the black Caribs. Dominica and St. Kitts also remained stagnant.

Of the small British islands, only St. Vincent, Montserrat, and Antigua were able to increase their exports, but the added volume barely reached 4,000 tons. On the other hand, the planters of the Danish islands St. Croix, St. Thomas, and St. John doubled their sugar production, from 7,800 to 16,000 tons between 1791 and 1802, and captured part of the American molasses and rum market that had previously been controlled by the French. The production of cotton, on the other hand, decreased notably on the Danish islands.

Jamaica was not adversely affected by the military operations of those years, except for the quelling of a revolt of runaway slaves in 1795. On the contrary, Jamaica profited from the war. The colony had been expanding its sugar production prior to the revolution in Saint-Domingue. Its exports rose from 47,972 tons in 1783 to 60,000 tons in 1791. The Haitian Revolution gave Jamaica a greater share of the market, and Jamaican sugar exports continued to increase, reaching 92,300 tons in 1802. When the war ended, Jamaica was exporting 25 percent more sugar than prerevolutionary Saint-Domingue.

Coffee exports from Jamaica during this period multiplied almost eight times, rising from 1,150 tons in 1791 to 9,000 tons in 1802. In subsequent years, Jamaica would become one of the main producers of coffee in the Caribbean, with an output of 17,000 tons in 1813. Although this was a significant amount, it was still only half of what had been exported from Saint-Domingue in 1789. The importation of slaves also accelerated. The slave population of Jamaica grew from 226,000 in 1788 to almost 308,000 in 1802, even though Jamaica reexported slaves to other Caribbean islands, particularly to Cuba.

Jamaica's experienced planters were protected by the priority placed by the British government on control of the world sugar market. The British economy in those days had an unusual degree of liquidity, and the planters of Jamaica could count on easy access to credit from the capital accumulated during the first phase of the Industrial Revolution in England.

When the economy of Saint-Domingue collapsed, British West Indian production was unable to meet the demand of the European market, hence the importance of the new British conquests in the Caribbean. With additional sugar from Martinique, Tobago, Trinidad, Surinam, and Guiana during the last three years of the war, Great Britain managed to increase its sugar exports to Europe and control 69 percent of the market. For most of the eighteenth century, Great Britain had reexported only 18 percent of its imported sugar to the rest of Europe. During the Haitian Revolution, however, Britain's reexports rose to 48 percent of its colonial production.

As long as the continental ports remained open to British trade, it was possible to channel West Indian sugar production toward the European markets that Saint-Domingue had previously supplied. Since

there was always the risk that those ports could be blocked, glutting
Britain's market, British politicians tried to prevent this from happening
and defended the Treaty of Amiens's provisions for returning the
colonies that Britain had conquered from France and Holland.
Nevertheless, Trinidad was retained by Great Britain after 1802 and
became a new agricultural frontier which needed only capital and slaves
for its development.

Sugar was a new product in Trinidad. The first sugar mill was built
there in 1787, when the island still belonged to Spain. French and
English immigrants, attracted by generous land and tax concessions
from the Spanish government in 1784, helped jump-start this industry.
French capital quickly flowed in to support the creation of cotton and
sugar plantations. Between 1784 and 1791, cotton was Trinidad's main
export, but during the Haitian Revolution French colonists began to
plant sugarcane and build sugar mills. On the eve of the 1797 British
invasion, Trinidad had more than 150 sugar plantations and 130 sugar
mills, producing 7,800 tons per year. The number of slaves also grew,
from 2,462 in 1784 to 10,009 in 1797. The impressive rise of the sugar
industry was financed mainly with British capital, hence the British
Parliament's interest in retaining Trinidad after the war.

For the British slave traders, merchants, and bankers, the occupation
of Trinidad was a windfall. These groups exerted pressure on the British
Parliament to distribute vacant land quickly to interested new colonists
as had been done with the land confiscated from the black Caribs on St.
Vincent after the rebellion of 1796. However, the abolitionists thought
that an increase in sugar production in the conquered colonies would
stimulate the slave trade. Pressure from abolitionists and West Indian
planters prevented the land in Trinidad from being immediately distributed for the development of sugar plantations, causing the Trinidad
plantation economy to lag several years behind those of the other large
Caribbean islands. Yet Trinidad's black population kept growing
between 1797 and 1802; by 1802 there were 19,709 slaves and 5,276 "free
coloreds" on the island. In the same year the white population amounted to a mere 2,261 individuals.

The Napoleonic Wars in the Caribbean

In 1803 war erupted again in Europe. This time the conflict was caused by Napoleon's imperialist pretensions. France and Great Britain almost immediately transferred their naval operations to the Caribbean. Again, the British navy triumphed in the Antilles, capturing St. Lucia, Tobago, Demerara, Essequibo, and Berbice between June and September 1803. Surinam was taken in May 1804. Curaçao was captured in January 1807, while St. Thomas, St. John, and St. Croix fell under English control in December of that year. Deseada and Marie-Galante were conquered at the beginning of 1808, and Martinique fell in January 1809. Cayenne, in French Guiana, was taken in January 1809, followed by Guadeloupe, St. Martin, Saba, and St. Eustatius in January and February 1810.

With these conquests, Great Britain regained control of all the European colonies in the Caribbean, with the exception of the Spanish Greater Antilles. Even the city of Santo Domingo fell to the British for one month, in June 1809. At that point the French troops who had occupied it since 1802 surrendered to the British, who quickly returned the city to Spain. As Spain was Great Britain's ally against France, its colonies were spared from attack by the British navy.

Once Caribbean sugar production was again under British control, British capitalists invested large sums in new sugar mills, plantations, and slaves. At the beginning of the war in 1803, the British economy was highly liquid, and there was a large amount of available credit.

The Abolition of the Slave Trade

The British possession of the Guianas alarmed the abolitionists, who feared that more slaves would be introduced into these vast territories. After trying to halt the development of Trinidad, with no success, the abolitionists discovered that they could obstruct the expansion of the slave trade by allying themselves with the proslavery planters from the older West Indian colonies who did not want sugar production to increase in newly conquered colonies. These planters enjoyed the support of the king and the House of Lords, whose members were generally against abolition. The abolitionist campaign was thus revived in 1804 and became more active than ever before. Its new strategy was to convince the planters and merchants of the older colonies that in order to prevent the development of the newer colonies, they should choke off these colonies' labor supply by eliminating the slave trade.

In May 1804 the House of Commons approved the first version of a new law abolishing the slave trade. In January 1805 the House of Lords passed an ordinance prohibiting slaves from being introduced into the newer British colonies. With this ordinance, the planters and merchants of the old colonies prevented their competitors from supplying themselves with manual labor, while the abolitionists were temporarily appeased in the British Parliament.

Still, the abolitionists would be satisfied with nothing short of the complete elimination of the slave trade. Between 1804 and 1806, the abolitionists used anti-slave trade petitions signed by thousands of people to put pressure on the members of Parliament. The abolitionists shaped British public opinion with pamphlets, speeches, and sermons that highlighted not only the horrors of slavery but also the high cost British consumers were paying to protect pro-slave trade planters and sugar merchants.

Finally, after a dramatic parliamentary battle, on March 25, 1807, the British Parliament decreed that as of January 1, 1808, slave trading was "definitely abolished, prohibited and declared illegal" in British colonies and territories. According to this law, after March 1808, no more slaves could land in the British West Indies.

The great paradox of abolition was that it happened at a time of increased slave trade and sugar production. The Haitian Revolution had stimulated an increase in British participation in the world slave trade, which had risen from 43 percent of the total trade in 1791 to 61 percent in 1807, with an annual average of 40,000 slaves exported from Africa. The largest numbers of slaves exported occurred between 1791 and 1800, when the price of sugar had reached its highest level and the market was affected by the Haitian Revolution. Between 1800 and 1807, the yearly average was 36,000 slaves.

The abolition of the slave trade was facilitated by the temporary saturation of the British sugar market caused by Napoleon's blockade of continental European ports to British trade beginning in 1806. In 1807

British planters and merchants complained that their warehouses were full of sugar and that they were ruined. Some of the excess sugar that was shipped to Great Britain after abolition came not from the oldest colonies but rather from the recently conquered territories, such as Trinidad. In 1809 Trinidad alone produced 12,420 tons of sugar, up from 7,000 tons just seven years earlier.

In addition, sugar flowed into the British market from the former Dutch colonies of Demerara, Essequibo, Berbice, and Surinam, as well as from the Danish islands of St. Croix, St. Thomas, and St. John. In 1808 Great Britain controlled the production of 174,000 tons of Caribbean sugar. An additional 27,000 tons was added when Martinique and Guadeloupe were conquered again in 1809 and 1810, respectively.

These surpluses created an illusion of growth that for several years concealed the real impact of abolition on the economies of Jamaica, Barbados, and the Leeward Islands. With the signing of the Treaty of Versailles in 1814 to end the war, Great Britain had to return the majority of the colonies it had conquered, including Surinam in 1816, but it kept St. Lucia and Tobago as well as Demerara, Essequibo, and Berbice. These three former Dutch territories became unified under the name British Guiana.

Sugar Production: Growth and Decline

During the Napoleonic Wars (1804-1815), only Trinidad and British Guiana had sustained real growth, because the Jamaican economy, the most dynamic economy during the Haitian Revolution, had begun to slow down in 1806, after exports had reached their highest level ever a year earlier. In 1807, when the prohibition of the slave trade was enacted, Jamaica still exported 89,800 tons of sugar, but its annual average for the following thirteen years was only 73,700 tons. Beginning in 1821, sugar exports went into a decline that lasted the rest of the nineteenth century.

A similar trend occurred in the Leeward Islands and the British Virgin Islands, where there were many fluctuations before a general decline in sugar exports began in 1807. In St. Kitts, Nevis, and Montserrat, sugar exports declined slowly during the first half of the nineteenth century. Between 1807 and 1810, the Leeward Islands collectively produced about 20,000 tons of sugar annually, but between 1820 and 1838 the average dropped to about 16,000 tons and continued to fall over the following years.

Two factors help explain the decline in the sugar economy of almost all the British colonies in the Caribbean between 1807 and 1838. One was the abolition of the slave trade, which prevented the colonies from sustaining their labor supply. The other was Britain's reimposition of the Navigation Laws to revive its colonial monopoly in an era of free trade. This policy led to a long and devastating trade war between Great Britain and the United States, which lasted over two decades and resulted in the ruin of many planters and sugar merchants in the British West Indies.

The conflict began in 1805, when the British government ordered the capture and confiscation of American ships transporting colonial products produced in French territory. This measure was intended to prevent American merchants from supplying these products to the European market, which was then controlled almost entirely by the British.

The situation changed in 1806, when Napoleon imposed on British merchandise a general embargo, the so-called continental system, designed to exclude imports from Great Britain into Europe. From then on, British sugar exports to the Continent dropped quickly. Although the French blockaded British exports, they traded openly with American merchants who bought sugar in the West Indies and reexported it to Europe. So, while the British market was becoming saturated with unsold sugar, the Americans were taking advantage of Napoleon's policy—hence another motive for the British to block American trade in the Caribbean.

Impact of the British-American Trade War

In 1807 the British tried to exclude the Americans from the Caribbean trade entirely, under the supposition that the Canadian territories would supply the needs of their colonists in the West Indies. But the exports of smoked fish and lumber from Nova Scotia and Canada were insufficient to satisfy West Indian demand, and Great Britain itself was unable to supply its colonies with enough meat, grains, and flour. As a result, in 1808 a serious supply problem occurred in the West Indies, causing food shortages, high prices, hunger, and poverty. The colonists repeatedly petitioned the British government to permit the entry of American ships and products into their ports.

The Anglo-American war of 1812 further aggravated the situation, because it effectively interrupted what little remained of the legal trade between the British West Indies and the United States. During this war, exports of rum and molasses to the United States almost completely ceased, and the British West Indies, lacking food, lumber, and hardware supplies, suffered one of the most difficult periods in their history.

Famine became widespread in the Leeward Islands, while Jamaica, Grenada, St. Vincent, and Barbados likewise suffered severe price inflation and food shortages. The slaves, who received very little food and almost no clothing, suffered the most. Although many planters voluntarily increased their food crop production in order to be able to feed their slaves, in Jamaica the government had to offer monetary incentives to the planters to get them to do so.

In St. Lucia, the situation grew worse after 1813, when a fire entirely destroyed its capital, Castries. Four years later, the settlement was still unable to rebuild for lack of lumber. In 1817 the population of St. Lucia continued to suffer from hunger, and the British authorities finally agreed to allow American ships stocked with provisions to land. By the time the first shipments arrived, some slaves had already died of starvation. A hurricane in 1819 also battered St. Lucia, providing additional justification to the authorities to permit importation of American food and supplies.

Dominica experienced a similar situation at the time. Its white planters began to migrate to other colonies, taking their slaves with them. Many migrated to Trinidad and Guiana, which had become the new sugar frontiers of the British Empire. In 1818 the Dominican authorities discussed the possibility of abandoning the island and moving the entire population to Guiana. At that time, the planters did not make enough money to pay taxes, and the colonial government lacked the funds needed to pay its employees their salaries.

In 1812, the eruption of the volcano Mount Soufrière had caused great damage to the sugar plantations of St. Vincent, destroying most of the planted coffee and cacao. Between 1814 and 1822, cacao exports from St. Vincent were reduced to a mere two tons per year. Dominican cacao exports declined to a similar amount in the same years.

In addition to suffering from hurricanes and volcanic eruptions during this period, some islands, especially the Leeward Islands, were affected by drought. In Antigua and in St. Kitts, droughts caused the financial ruin of many planters. As in Dominica, the colonial government was unable to collect taxes and therefore had no money to pay its employees.

On almost all of the British islands, large quantities of molasses and rum, previously bought by Americans, remained unsold, because the Americans now got their supplies from Cuba, Puerto Rico, and the French islands, where they were received with open arms. Through their colonial assemblies, the frustrated planters began to pressure Great Britain to permit free trade with the Americans, but the British government did not give in to their demands.

The supply crisis in the West Indies lasted for almost twenty years. Even though the Anglo-American war had ended quickly and the prices of colonial products had risen again, reaching record levels in 1815, the trade war between England and the United States continued. British maritime interests forced the government to exclude American merchants from trade in the West Indies. In 1817 the U.S. government responded by imposing a tax of two dollars on each ton of cargo arriving on ships from countries that did not allow American ships to sell merchandise to them (in other words, British ships).

In 1820 these measures were broadened to prevent British colonists from supplying themselves with American products through Bermuda and Canada. As the Canadian territories were now prevented from supplying the British Antilles, shortages worsened and high prices, famine, and poverty continued. American exports to the West Indies of lumber, flour, fish, salted meat, iron articles, horses, clothes, and shoes ceased almost completely between 1817 and 1822. The scarcity of lumber became so severe that in St. Vincent old houses were torn down so that the lumber could be used to build boxes for sugar exports.

Shortages of food and supplies also affected the Leeward Islands after the hurricane of 1819. In Antigua, the lack of lumber forced the colonists to bury their dead in boxes and old trunks in 1820 and 1821. When the Canadian territories could not meet the demand for supplies, the planters of the Leeward Islands pressured the local authorities to allow American ships to land. Permission was occasionally granted in times of emergency, but these were very rare. The trade war between England and United States led to extreme shortages in almost all of the British West Indies, even though after 1818 the British colonists began to purchase American goods from the French and Spanish Antilles, where these products were in abundance.

The West Indian planters became discouraged. Unable to sell their products to the highest bidder, they stopped investing in the maintenance of their sugar plantations. Since they could no longer import slaves, production began to stagnate. Every year after 1816 they had to sell at lower and lower prices, which caused their income to decline. They fell behind in their tax payments and were unable to honor their debts either to European bankers or to local lenders. As a result, credit became more difficult to obtain, and money became scarce in the older British colonies. Many holdings were put up for sale by their owners, who were now ruined, but years went by and they remained unsold.

In 1822 the only British colonies in the Caribbean that showed signs of economic growth in the sugar sector were Barbados, Trinidad, and Guiana. Barbados was the only island that managed to improve sugar production consistently, from 8,046 tons in 1807 to a record 23,679 tons in 1838. After 1838, however, Barbados production began declining and only recovered in the second half of the century. In Jamaica, only the coffee planters did well.

Finally, the British authorities accepted the demands of the planters and sugar merchants and reinstituted free trade with the United States. In June 1822 the British government issued the first ordinances aimed at ending the Navigation Laws monopoly. One act authorized the British planters to export directly to any port in Europe and Africa as long as British ships were used. Another measure allowed the main West Indian ports to import cereals, lumber, food, cotton, wool, tobacco, iron articles, and livestock freely from North and South America, again provided that British ships were used. Foreign ships from countries that traded on equal terms with the British were subject to a 10-percent tax.

The impact of these measures was felt immediately. Rum exports from the British West Indies to the United States climbed from 54,000 gallons in 1821 to an annual average of 657,000 gallons between 1822 and 1826; molasses exports rose from 12,000 gallons in 1821 to more than 1.3 million gallons per year over the following four years; coffee exports increased from about 8 tons in 1821 to more than 650 tons per year over the following four years; cacao exports jumped from fewer than 3 tons to more than 96 tons annually in the same period; *muscovado* sugar exports grew from 28 tons to 1,428 tons during this time.

Despite these changes, the conflict continued as both sides manipulated custom duties. In August 1822 President James Monroe imposed a tariff on cargo brought to the United States on British ships in order to encourage the British colonists to export their products on American ships. In March 1825 the British government reacted to the American policy by opening the ports of Great Britain and the West Indies to ships from any country or colonial territory that likewise opened its ports to free trade with the British. This measure backfired when the United States government responded in March 1827 by prohibiting all American trade with the British West Indies.

Once again the colonists complained of shortages and famine. Plantations were abandoned; slaves died and could not be replaced; colonists emigrated, increasing the debts, which could not paid; and poverty permeated every aspect of life in the British West Indies.

The trade war between Great Britain and the United States proved to be the most important factor contributing to the decline of the British West Indian economy after 1815, and it was brought to an end in 1830 when the governments of both countries recognized it as a no-win situation. The U.S. government succumbed to pressure from merchants and ship owners who had previously engaged in trade with the West Indies by lifting the trade embargo against the British colonies. After intense negotiation, the two governments came to a reciprocal trade agreement that eliminated discriminatory customs duties and opened their ports and territories to each other's ships and traders. The British West Indies thus entered a new era of free trade with the United States.

The "Old" West Indies in Economic Decline

The reciprocal trade agreement of October 1830 arrived too late, however, to prevent the steep economic decline of the West Indies. After twenty years of privation, the British colonies could no longer compete with their rivals. Gone was the time when England and France ruled the sugar market. In the meantime, the large Cuban and Puerto Rican producers, together with those of Louisiana, had completely captured the American market.

The older British West Indies now faced competition from Trinidad and Guiana, whose planters sold their sugar more cheaply, as did the new and successful sugar colony of Mauritius in the Indian Ocean. Ironically, while the West Indian planters were struggling for free trade, their representatives in the British Parliament were fighting to exclude sugar produced in Mauritius from the British market by lobbying incessantly for the imposition of discriminatory tariffs, which would raise the cost of Mauritius sugar.

Despite these maneuvers, sugar from Mauritius continued to gain ground at the expense of sugar from the West Indies. Mauritius's sugar exports to Great Britain rose from 500 tons in 1812 to 38,000 tons in 1838, more than double Barbados's exports and more than half of Jamaica's. Mauritius's exports continued to grow until the island became one of the largest sugar producers in the world in the second half of the nineteenth century. By 1860 Mauritius was exporting 134,000 tons of sugar to Great Britain, while Jamaica's exports had plummeted to 26,000 tons and Barbados's, despite doubling in recent years, stood at just 32,000.

The decline of the British West Indies took place gradually between 1815 and 1834. Barbados, Guiana, and Trinidad were somewhat more successful at avoiding depression than the other British colonies. In their struggle to survive economically, the planters of Barbados sacrificed food production, and the island again reverted to a sugar monoculture. Between 1807 and 1834, the number of sugar mills in Barbados remained around 340, but they grew larger, the amount of land used for sugarcane increased, and the use of fertilizer became more widespread than ever.

Despite the British government's prohibition of the slave trade in

1807, the number of slaves in Barbados rose from 75,000 in 1807 to 83,150 in 1834. Barbados was the only island in the West Indies with a long history of British colonization where the slave population grew significantly after abolition. On the more recently acquired islands— Anguilla, Barbuda, and the Cayman Islands, where sugar was not produced—the number of slaves also grew over this period, from a combined total of 2,800 in 1807 to 3,980 in 1834.

The planters of British Guiana also managed to increase their sugar production during the Anglo-American trade war. They offered economic incentives to slave owners from other islands if they moved to British Guiana with their slaves. Between 1808 and 1825, the sugar-producing areas of Demerara and Essequibo boasted a net immigration of at least 7,500 slaves. Despite these additions, the combined slave population of Demerara and Essequibo decreased from 80,915 in 1807 to 70,745 in 1834. Even so, sugar production managed to rise from 12,000 tons in 1814 to 47,000 tons in 1834.

In Trinidad, the planters continued to import slaves after the prohibition of the trade. Between 1811 and 1813, they brought in at least 4,441 slaves, or 14 percent of the island's slave population. Over the next eleven years, an additional 4,000 slaves were introduced to Trinidad from other islands. Nonetheless, Trinidad's slave population decreased from 26,100 in 1807 to 20,655 in 1834. Despite this decrease in their labor force, the Trinidadian planters managed to raise their sugar production from 9,400 tons in 1807 to almost 17,000 tons in 1834.

The increase in sugar production in Guiana and Trinidad between 1800 and 1834 was partly attributable to the introduction of new varieties of sugarcane from Tahiti. Another factor was the expansion and modernization of some sugar mills, which began to use steam power, thereby reducing the need for slave labor. In Trinidad, the first steam-powered machine used in the sugar industry was put into operation in 1804. By 1810 there were 8 sugar mills powered by steam, 9 powered by water, and 226 powered by draft animals. Steam-powered machinery was used more frequently in subsequent years.

The abolition of the slave trade did not produce the immediate catastrophic economic effects that some historians have cited as the cause for the decline of the British West Indies. The Anglo-American trade war, the islands' numerous local supply shortages, and the constant decline in sugar prices after 1815 affected the competitiveness of the old British colonies more than the abolition of the slave trade.

Two other factors also hurt the British West Indies in the first half of the nineteenth century: Mauritius began to compete in the British sugar market, and the United States started to supply itself with sugar from Cuba, Puerto Rico, and new plantations in Louisiana. Despite the expansion of the world sugar market, sugar production in the West Indies lost its vitality. In 1840 production was less than 14 percent of the world market, which then totaled 820,318 tons.

Towards Amelioration and Emancipation

During these decades of crisis in the British West Indies, the abolitionist movement remained active. After the slave trade was abolished in 1807, the abolitionists and the West Indian planters began to lobby the British government to impose measures that would prevent the smuggling of slaves to the French and Spanish Antilles. In response, the British government adopted two courses of action. One was to establish a registry and periodic census of all slaves in the colonies. The second was to negotiate with the other European countries with colonies in the Caribbean to encourage them to abolish the slave trade.

In 1815 the British forced France to sign a treaty prohibiting the slave trade, and in 1817 Spain and Portugal signed a similar treaty with Great Britain. The success of these efforts was limited, however, and the slave trade continued illegally due to the extraordinary demand for slaves in Cuba, Puerto Rico, Brazil, and the United States. Although the U.S. government had also prohibited the slave trade in March 1807, Americans traders continued to send slave ships to Africa in order to smuggle slaves to Southern plantations, as well as to Cuba and Puerto Rico.

The British abolitionists attacked this problem with a new strategy. In 1823 they created an organization called the Society for the Gradual Abolition of Slavery, advocating a program of legal reforms to improve living conditions for slaves. This organization, also called the Anti-Slavery Society, was quickly accepted by the British population. Within a few months, its members established more than 200 branches in Great

Britain. In the following years, these branches sent more than 700 petitions with thousands of signatures to Parliament, requesting the abolition of slavery.

The planters' representatives in London, sensing the impending dismantling of the slave-based plantation system in a period of economic crisis in the West Indies, tried to buy time by proposing that Parliament adopt legal measures to reform slavery, thus echoing parts of the abolitionists' proposals. During the debates, a set of rules was adopted to ameliorate the condition of the slaves in the colonies. Among the most important of these was the prohibition of the use of whips to punish women and an obligatory waiting period of at least one day before whipping men. In addition, plantation owners were required to record in a book the occasions when slaves were punished with more than three lashes. This book had to be presented periodically to the authorities.

The planters were also required to avoid splitting up slave families and became responsible for their religious instruction, thereby allowing ministers and churches to operate without restriction in the Antilles. Furthermore, plantation owners were obligated to allow slaves to buy their freedom with their savings. Additionally, the slaves' workday was to be limited to no more than nine hours, and slaves were to be allowed a full day each week to rest. Slaves were also authorized to present evidence in courts of justice, provided they did so in the company of a clergyman.

This new policy for slavery reform failed completely because the British government did not have the means to enforce it in all of the colonies. In the three newer British possessions of Guiana, Trinidad, and St. Lucia, where there were no colonial assemblies, the British government was able to impose the amelioration policies through its governors. In the rest of the British colonies, however, the colonial assemblies protested and prevented the application of the new policy. Therefore, the slaves' living conditions changed very little.

The amelioration policy also failed because the British government was not sincerely committed to its success. Despite the political advances of the abolitionist movement after 1823, seven years later Parliament was still controlled by proslavery landowners supported by King George IV. After George IV's death in 1830, a new environment developed because his successor, William IV, supported the abolition of slavery.

In 1830 the political climate changed quickly: at the same time as the coronation of a new king, the conservative government was replaced by a liberal one representing broader social interests. In 1830 the Anti-Slavery Society launched a new campaign to mobilize public opinion and demanded that Parliament immediately and completely emancipate all slaves. Its members again circulated antislavery leaflets and obtained thousands of signatures in churches and on the streets in support of their petition.

In Jamaica, meanwhile, a Baptist slave preacher named Samuel Sharpe began a resistance movement that ended in open rebellion in the northern part of the island in December 1831. The planters reacted by burning and destroying sixteen Baptist churches, persecuting the missionaries and their followers, and engaging in other types of violence. The rebellion was repressed within a couple of months, and by February 1832 the area was calm again. The violent repression of the uprising was viewed with disgust in England in 1832. At this time, the British Parliament was being recomposed with new members from mercantile, industrial, and financial groups that had benefited from the Industrial Revolution. These new members of Parliament had little direct connection to the planters or to other proslavery interest groups.

As a result, the campaign against slavery intensified. British public opinion was mobilized by the abolitionists in the remotest corners of Great Britain, as more than a million signatures supporting the emancipation of the slaves were gathered and presented to Parliament. Politically cornered, the representatives of the West Indian planters could not defend themselves. In August 1833, after several months of debate, the British government decreed a "law to prohibit slavery in British colonies; to promote the emancipation of the slaves; and to compensate the persons who until then had received service from said slaves." This law opened a new era in the history of the West Indies.

CHAPTER 14

Sugar without Slaves in the British and French Antilles

The Apprenticeship Period

The Abolition Law declared slavery illegal in the British colonies starting August 1, 1834, and provided the following conditions: all children under six years old or born to slave mothers from that date on should be considered free; all other slaves would remain as apprentices under the care of their old masters for a period of six years, that is, until August 1, 1840. During this transitional period, the apprentices would work for their masters five days a week, or the equivalent of forty-and-a-half hours per week. They were free to work for their own benefit or hire themselves out as wage laborers on their two free days.

The masters were required to continue to feed, shelter, clothe, and care for the apprentices as they had in times of slavery. If the masters could not provide the apprentices with food, they were required to offer them land so they could raise their own food. The period of apprenticeship could be terminated or shortened if the slave were able to buy his or her freedom. If the master ended the apprenticeship, the law decreed that the master was responsible for caring for his former apprentices who were sick, disabled, or elderly for a period of six years.

To compensate the planters and other slave owners for the losses incurred due to emancipation, the British government created a fund of one million pounds sterling. An additional fund was created to pay the judges in charge of resolving the disputes that could result from the application of the law.

Just prior to the time that the Abolition Law turned the slaves into apprentices in 1834, there were 664,970 slaves in the British West Indies:

453,620 were farmworkers, and 79,215 were employed in other occupations.[1] The remaining slaves included children, the elderly, and the infirm.[2] In almost all the colonies, the gender distribution of the slaves was fairly balanced. There were generally slightly more women than men, with the exception of Trinidad and Guiana, where male manual laborers were needed to work on the new plantations that were created at the beginning of the century.

There were also significant numbers of free blacks, with free women slightly outnumbering free men in all of the colonies.[3] These "people without masters" worked at many occupations, both on and off the plantations. Many were peasants who raised food for the local market on marginal lands, while others were artisans, blacksmiths, vendors, casual laborers, domestic servants, muleteers, and longshoremen. There was also a minority of free black teachers, preachers, merchants, and professionals who worked in the towns that openly supported abolition. After 1834 some free blacks became judges in order to enforce the Abolition Law and protect the apprentices.

On almost all the islands, some slaves were available to be hired out. In certain cases, these slaves had belonged to owners with an excess of manual labor who were trying to supplement their income by hiring out laborers to other plantations. In other cases, the slaves belonged to small landowners who lived off the income produced by their hired-out slaves. When the slave population decreased in some colonies following the abolition of the slave trade, the hiring out of slaves became increasingly important. In Jamaica, there were as many as 19,558 slaves hired out in 1834, and many worked as gardeners, cooks, washerwomen, barbers, or servants. The total number of domestic slaves for that year was 31,966, equivalent to 19 percent of the slave population.

Regardless of whether they were owned or hired, domestic servants or manual laborers, the majority of the slaves aspired to obtain their freedom in order to be able to cultivate their own land with family labor. Many slaves were able to accomplish this goal on the plantations where they worked. A number of plantation owners allowed their slaves to cultivate marginal lands on Sundays. Fruits and root crops served to complement the family diet and in many cases generated some cash income through the sale of the surplus. Over time, many slaves used this cash to buy their freedom.

According to the Abolition Law, apprentices were required to work for their former masters without compensation from Monday morning to midday on Friday. On the weekends, the apprentices preferred to tend their own land and tried to avoid plantation work. During the so-called dead season, this practice had no serious consequences, and was a boon to the planters who saved on food expenses. During the sugarcane harvest, however, the lack of apprentices willing to work on weekends came as a blow to the planters, since harvesting required the continuous cutting, hauling, and grinding of sugarcane twenty-four hours a day, seven days a week.

The plantation owners cited the labor shortage at harvest time as one reason why the British government should compensate them for the emancipation of the slaves. Some colonial assemblies also demanded that the 4.5 percent export tax be abolished. When this petition was denied, the West Indian planters complained loudly. In Antigua, for instance, the planters refused to establish an apprenticeship system on the grounds that it was too expensive. They preferred, instead, to grant total emancipation to their slaves on August 1, 1834. Sir Bethel Codrington, the principal slave owner on the island of Barbuda, did the same.

The other colonial assemblies obeyed the Abolition Law and established the required apprenticeship system, but they maneuvered to maintain control of plantation workers on the weekends. The new apprentices of St. Kitts and Nevis responded with active resistance during the first three weeks of August 1834. The planters put down the revolt with soldiers sent from Antigua. In Jamaica that same year, there was grumbling among the apprentices, but they kept their peace. In Guiana, Trinidad, and the Windward Islands, the new two-tiered system, which combined apprentices with paid workers, made for a volatile situation. Nonetheless, in all the British colonies the apprentice period functioned for the most part as intended, as a period of preparation for the total emancipation of the slaves.

Still, the system led to constant conflict between the planters and their workers over salaries and the use of land for subsistence farming. During this period, the apprentices learned to negotiate. They knew that if they could accumulate enough savings, they could buy their freedom before the end of their apprenticeship. They could also purchase small lots of land where they could move with their families when they became free. Whereas the apprentices asked for higher salaries, the planters tried to impose contracts obliging them to relinquish some cash in favor of land to raise food crops.

The apprenticeship system evolved in a fairly uniform manner throughout the West Indies. The apprentices were forced to work for negotiated salaries, but they tried to work as little as possible and kept their families away from the plantations. The women refused to let their emancipated children work on the plantations. As a result, manual laborers became increasingly scarce, and the planters imposed more restrictions on the apprentices before they could attain their freedom.

For example, many planters forced the apprentices to accept new conditions that served to undermine their freedom. Some planters assigned their apprentices to distant properties to farm, so that they would have to spend part of each weekend walking to and from those properties. Other planters simply prohibited the apprentices from using plantation land to raise food crops or animals. Others refused to let the apprentices use plantation-owned farming tools on their own plots of land. Still others decreed a day's work to be nine hours instead of eight, so that the apprentices would have to stay on the plantation until late Friday afternoon.

The apprentices normally demanded the immediate payment of their wages, but sometimes the planters did not have sufficient cash and did not pay them their full salaries. Other planters tried to keep apprentices from cultivating their own land by selecting Saturdays to file accusations against their workers with the judges who oversaw the application of the Abolition Law. The apprentices greatly resented performing slave labor five days a week while being denied their freedom on Saturdays and Sundays.

Soon, apprentices, planters, and colonial authorities all chafed under the apprentice system. Planters thought that it would be cheaper to produce sugar with paid manual laborers than with apprentices whom they had to support even on days when the apprentices did not work. The planters began to discuss the possibility of shortening the apprenticeship period after observing that their counterparts in Antigua had experienced far fewer complications. In November 1837 the assembly of Montserrat decreed the complete emancipation of all Montserrat's apprentices after August 1, 1838. The assembly of Nevis followed suit in March 1838.

These events precipitated new legislation handed down by the British government. Since emancipation was a major goal of the Colonial Office of London, then dominated by the abolitionists, on April 11, 1838, the British government amended the Abolition Law and decreed that by August 1 of that year, all slaves in the West Indies would be freed. In May the assemblies of St. Kitts and Barbados declared their support for emancipation. In the following weeks the assemblies of Dominica, St. Lucia, St. Vincent, Grenada, and Tobago did the same, as did the Legislative Council of Trinidad, which decreed the emancipation of Trinidad's slaves in July. August 1, 1838, marked the date when slavery was officially terminated in the West Indies.

Exodus from the Plantations and Free Villages

The first consequence of the emancipation of the slaves was a massive exodus of apprentices from the plantations and their frantic search for land. The success or failure of freedom was linked to the availability of land on the various islands. In Jamaica, Trinidad, and Guiana, uncultivated arable land belonging to the British government was readily available. The freedmen here were more successful than in the Leeward Islands and Barbados. On these small islands, the sugarcane monoculture left little land available for the establishment of a free peasantry. In all the colonies, the planters conspired to keep their former slaves on the plantations by obstructing their access to land. In many cases, these planters refused to allow the measurement and registration of lands owned by the Crown.

In Jamaica, Trinidad, and Guiana, the abolition of slavery led to the establishment of many towns of emancipated slaves that quickly attracted other former slaves. These towns were built by associations of freedmen who combined their savings and bought land from the British government, sometimes at very high prices. If the colonial governments refused to sell Crown lands, or if the freedmen could not afford to buy a plot, many families that had left the plantations simply settled on vacant, unused land, building huts and growing crops there. In many cases, the freedmen managed to acquire land from former plantations that had been abandoned by their owners. Within a few years, more than half of the former slave populations of Jamaica, Trinidad, and Guiana had established themselves in these so-called free villages.

In 1838 in Jamaica, 2,014 freedmen owned plots smaller than forty acres. Two years later the number had grown to 7,840 freedmen, and by 1844, 19,000 freedmen had bought land, establishing sixty-eight free villages. In the Guianese region of Demerara in 1842, there were 2,493 plots belonging to 3,017 free black families (14,127 people), while in Berbice 1,223 free black families (4,646 people) had settled on 1,184 plots. In 1848 free blacks had built at least 10,541 dwellings to accommodate a population of 44,443.

In Trinidad, emancipation produced similar results. In 1846 approximately 5,400 freedmen abandoned the plantations to found free villages. Years later, in 1859, William Sewell, a journalist from the United States, calculated that more than 80 percent of the freedmen who had left the plantations had become owners of plots smaller than ten acres. Likewise, in St. Vincent, Grenada, St. Lucia, and Tobago, more than 10,000 freedmen had become peasant landowners by 1860. In that year, the resident population in the free villages had increased to about 20,000 people.

In almost all of the West Indies, the planters promulgated labor laws similar to the 1834 "Contracting Law" of Antigua, which mandated an automatic one-year contract to all freedmen who lived on the plantations and had worked for a planter for five consecutive years. This law established a one-month waiting period for each of the parties to suspend the contract, but if the worker broke the contract, he or she was obliged to abandon the plantation and vacate his or her living quarters and land without compensation. The law also established that in the case of negligence or insubordination, workers could be punished by expulsion, the loss of their salaries, and even one year in prison. Having nowhere to go if they were expelled from the plantations, many freedmen accepted the unfavorable contracts imposed by their employers. In the following years, other laws were added that were designed to suppress vagrancy, loitering, gambling, and the abandonment of children.

The enforcement of these labor laws in the larger colonies was not easy, because the freedmen were able to take refuge in the free villages.

But in the Leeward Islands and Barbados, where there was no open, arable land available for subsistence farming, the majority of the free blacks were obliged to work for hire. On these islands, the planters required the freedmen to pay rent for their dwellings and for the land that they cultivated on the plantations. In order to generate cash, the freedmen found themselves forced to work for wages on the plantations.

The lack of vacant land condemned the majority of freedmen in the Leeward Islands and Barbados to work as poorly paid wage laborers, while in Jamaica, Trinidad, and Guiana, freedmen were able to obtain their own plots. In Jamaica, for example, there were already more than 8,000 small landowners with less than ten acres in 1840, while Barbados had only 818.

Salaries on the plantations in Barbados and the Leeward Islands were therefore lower than in the other West Indian colonies, particularly Trinidad and Guiana. This was due to the relatively large number of workers without land on Barbados and the Leeward Islands. The larger colonies, on the other hand, suffered from a permanent shortage of manual labor. To recruit workers, the planters of Trinidad and Guiana sent agents to Barbados and the Leeward Islands offering better salaries, free transportation, and a small plot of farmland to freedmen who were willing to migrate. Many accepted these offers and went to live in Trinidad and Guiana, despite prohibitions from the colonial assemblies of Barbados and the Leeward Islands against emigration.

By 1841 some 2,000 freedmen had moved from Barbados to Guiana alone, and between 1839 and 1846, 5,993 left the Leeward Islands for Trinidad and Guiana. The majority of these migrants left Nevis and Montserrat, where the sugar economy was faltering and there were few other sources of employment. Although 203 freedmen from Antigua and 963 from St. Kitts emigrated between 1839 and 1846, emigration from these islands was slow because there was still some land available where the freedmen could take refuge and form free towns.

Since emancipation took place earlier in Antigua than elsewhere in the West Indies, and the planters there were more tolerant of the formation of free villages, in 1842 this island counted twenty-seven free villages with 1,037 dwellings and close to 3,600 inhabitants. By 1846 the population of the free villages had grown to 9,273. In St. Kitts, a similar exodus from the plantations took place despite the lack of available government-owned land and the reluctance of the planters to sell their unused land to the freedmen. By 1842 the population of the free villages of St. Kitts was 5,671. Montserrat had only 108 free villagers, while Nevis had none.

Eight years after abolition, the migration of freedmen from the plantations continued. Many free villages were founded close to the plantations so that the freedmen could work there and earn cash to pay rent for their land and homes. Although they practiced subsistence farming—growing rice, plantains, yuca, and yams and raising pigs, goats, and cattle for their own consumption—the freedmen had to purchase numerous articles with cash, and only by working on the plantations could they do so. For this reason, the plantations did not entirely lose their labor supply.

Labor Shortages and Imported Indentured Workers

Nonetheless, the labor shortage on the plantations grew increasingly severe, and the planters soon discovered that they needed alternative labor sources. One such source was Sierra Leone, where many people were eager to escape poverty and willing to work as contracted laborers on the West Indian plantations. Other sources were Ireland, Germany, and the United States. Between 1834 and 1842, Jamaican planters imported 2,685 workers from Ireland and Great Britain, 1,332 from Germany, 1,270 from Africa, and 778 from the United States, the Bahamas, and Canada.

The planters of Trinidad, on the other hand, brought in immigrants from the other Antilles, importing 10,278 freedmen between 1839 and 1849, as well as Africans, Europeans, and Chinese. Between 1841 and 1861, 3,338 workers from Sierra Leone and 3,198 from the South Atlantic island of Saint Helena came to Trinidad. In 1839 and 1840, 866 French and German peasants arrived in Trinidad, but the majority died soon thereafter. Of all the European workers imported during these years, the ones who best adapted to the working conditions in the tropics were the 1,298 Portuguese brought from the island of Madeira. Needing even more laborers, the planters of Trinidad also contracted 2,500 Chinese workers between 1853 and 1866. Even so, the labor shortage was not resolved.

Between 1839 and 1849, the planters of Guiana imported 10,278 West Indian freedmen, mostly from Barbados and the Leeward Islands. Between 1846 and 1868, Guiana received 2,800 Africans from Sierra Leone. Between 1856 and 1866, the planters imported 10,076 Portuguese recruited in Madeira, 11,282 Chinese, and 11,015 East Indians from Madras, Calcutta, and Bombay. Over the following two decades, the immigration of Portuguese and East Indians continued: between 1866 and 1884 close to 20,000 Portuguese and 86,510 East Indian workers entered Guiana. The total number of immigrants arriving in Guiana between 1855 and 1884 was 147,567.

In Jamaica and Trinidad, Portuguese and Chinese labor was insufficient, so East Indians were also imported. Between 1834 and 1865, 9,195 East Indians made the journey to Jamaica, and 28,772 arrived in Trinidad. Over the next twenty-seven years, Trinidadian planters managed to contract a total of 38,627 East Indians, while Jamaican planters imported 14,636.

The Leeward Islands planters also contracted some Portuguese and East Indian workers, as did the planters of Grenada, St. Lucia, and St. Vincent, but the small size of these latter islands permitted the importation of only a few dozen.

The mortality of the East Indian workers was very high, especially in Guiana, where malaria took many lives. In order to replace the constant casualties, the West Indian planters ended up importing 429,286 East Indians from 1835 until well into the twentieth century. In 1917 the government of India finally put an end to the contracting of laborers. While many died and others returned to India, a considerable Hindu population remained in the West Indies and contributed significantly to the social, cultural, and religious diversity of the islands.

Unlike in Haiti, where the plantation system collapsed with the abolition of slavery, in the British West Indies the sugarcane plantations did not disappear. When not enough workers could be imported, the planters replaced manual labor with machinery and technology, including plows, cultivators, weeding machines, and new types of hoes. Eight to sixteen workers could be replaced by a weeding machine or by a plow pulled by a horse led by a child. In addition, the planters on almost all the islands began to import guano to use as fertilizer, which, along with mechanization and the use of system engines, led to higher yields per acre.

Mechanization of Sugar Mills

In Trinidad, the mechanization of the sugar plantations began with the installation of the first steam engine in 1804 and continued for the next thirty years, due in part to the shortage of manual labor. When the price of sugar rose between 1840 and 1860, however, the plantation owners again began to receive credit from Great Britain to modernize and expand their enterprises and to finance the importation of contracted manual labor.

In Guiana, steam engines were also put into use early, but the abundance of slave labor delayed the widespread adoption of this technology. In addition to powering the sugar mills, steam engines were used to run water pumps that drained the floodplains of the Demerara and Essequibo rivers. Although very expensive, in the long run the water pumps proved profitable. By 1852 there were twenty-eight pumps operating on several plantations in Guiana. This number was too small to have a significant impact on the economy, but it points to a trend that continued for the rest of the century. In 1852 there were 208 steam engines functioning on 173 sugar plantations in Guiana.

In Jamaica, many planters also turned to mechanization and used guano and other fertilizers. The first steam sugar mills were established in Jamaica in 1808 and 1813, and this innovation spread slowly over the following decades. In 1852 there were 108 steam mills, almost a third of the mills on the island. There were also 125 mills run by animal power and an equal number using water power. In Antigua, St. Kitts, and Nevis, the planters installed steam engines as soon as income and credit status allowed. In 1878 there were thirty-five steam mills in operation in Antigua and seventy-four in St. Kitts.

In Barbados, the abundance of labor allowed the planters to preserve their traditional methods of production longer than in the other British colonies. Although the planters in Barbados in 1840 did not yet use the plow and had the most obsolete mills in all the Antilles, Barbados used more fertilizer than the other islands, which explains the high productivity of its plantations.

The other technological innovation that took several decades to become widespread was the vacuum sugar pan for boiling cane juice. In 1852 Guiana had only twenty-five sugar mills with vacuum sugar pans, and Barbados had only four. The Jamaican planters began to buy vacuum pans relatively late because they needed to produce at least 500 tons of sugar per year in order for their investment to be profitable. In 1854 Jamaica had only three sugar plantations capable of producing this amount. In Antigua, as late as 1878, vacuum pans were not generally used, as plantations there tended to be smaller.

The sugar industry in the French Antilles evolved in a similar manner to that of the British West Indies, but there were a few major differences. After the Haitian Revolution, the economies of Martinique and Guadeloupe continued to grow. When the Napoleonic Wars ended in 1815, the French government supported the planters of Martinique and Guadeloupe by giving them loans to develop new sugar plantations and promising them a monopoly on the French sugar market. This policy helped raise the number of sugar plantations in Guadeloupe from 389 in 1816 to 620 in 1835. As a consequence, Guadeloupe's production rose from 30,000 tons in 1822 to 42,000 tons in 1834. In Martinique, the number of sugar plantations increased from 371 in 1820 to 505 in 1837, and production grew from 26,000 tons in 1820 to 34,000 tons in 1836.

Although French colonial sugar was protected from foreign competition by the French government, sugar from Guadeloupe and Martinique could not compete in quality or price with beet sugar, which had been produced in France since 1812 and was also protected by the government. The planters of Martinique and Guadeloupe complained that there were no taxes on beet sugar, while colonial cane sugar was burdened with import tariffs. The French government agreed to reduce the taxes on colonial sugar and eventually taxed beet sugar as well to ease competition, but the French Antillean planters did not manage to improve the quality of their sugar and continued to lose part of their market share in France.

The French producers of beet sugar had the advantages of lower production and transportation costs, as well as much more advanced technologies for refining sugar than the Caribbean cane sugar producers. The beet sugar producers often used steam engines, centrifugal machinery, and vacuum pan evaporators in their mills. Beet sugar production increased from 5,000 tons in 1830 to 41,000 tons in 1847, thus meeting the increase in consumer demand for sugar in France during this period.

To compete successfully with French beet sugar producers, the French

Antillean planters had to adapt their industry to the modern technology used to produce beet sugar. Little by little they mechanized their sugar mills; imported new plows, weeders, and hoes; and, like their counterparts in the British West Indies, fertilized their land with guano imported from Peru.

The French planters experimented with steam engines and gradually installed horizontal iron mills. Martinique had nine steam-powered mills in 1826; twenty-one years later there were thirty-three. The first steam mill was installed in Guadeloupe in 1820, and in 1851 there were still no more than fifteen. Eleven years later, in 1862, however, the number had risen to seventy-two. This delay in adopting the steam engine can be explained by a lack of capital and the traditionalism of many planters, who did not see any reason to change their grinding methods.

The First French *Centrales*

The situation began to shift in 1841, when Paul Daubrée, a French industrialist, proposed to the colonists of Guadeloupe and Martinique that they follow the example of the beet sugar producers by separating farm work from industrial work. According to Daubrée, this could be accomplished by building totally mechanized "central factories" to process large quantities of sugarcane cultivated simultaneously on several plantations. These factories would be capable of producing more than 1,000 tons of sugar after processing the cane of six or eight colonists who would simply cultivate the sugarcane on their plantations, leaving the processing phase to the industrialized central factory.

The idea was discussed extensively in Guadeloupe and Martinique for two years, but no one was motivated to build factories until after the earthquake of February 8, 1843, which destroyed more than 400 sugar mills on Guadeloupe alone. In order to rebuild the devastated sugar industry, the colonial government authorized the creation of a steam-powered central factory capable of grinding the sugarcane of the ten or twelve planters who had lost their mills. This solution was very popular in Guadeloupe because many planters would have had to go into debt in order to rebuild their mills.

The cost of this first factory was very high, and the colonial government did not want to invest directly in the enterprise, but Daubrée took command of the project. After gathering more than one million francs in Paris, Daubrée began to construct two central factories in Grand-Terre within one year after the earthquake. Other French industrialists followed his example, and with eighteen million francs in start-up capital, they created a corporation in 1844 called La Société Royale des Antilles. By 1845 this company had already built four factories in Guadeloupe and Martinique: three in Grand-Terre and one in Marie-Galante. In subsequent years, other planters obtained credit in Paris and formed companies that built more central factories.

The revamping of the sugar industry, which began in the French Antilles, had revolutionary consequences throughout the Caribbean. Everywhere planters were willing to stop producing sugar and simply grow sugarcane. Thus the strategy of building factories equidistant from several plantations became a popular solution.

Central factories paid for their cane in processed sugar. Many early contracts required the planters to deliver a determined quantity of sugarcane to the central factories between January and June of each year. In exchange, the planters received 132 pounds of sugar per ton of sugarcane, or a percentage of the profits of the central factory, depending on the quantity of sugarcane delivered.

The first central factories built in the French Antilles between 1844 and 1848 differed from traditional sugar mills in several ways. They were completely mechanized and used steam engines built in France by the firm MM. Derosne et Cail. These engines ran the mills, evaporators, vacuum sugar pans, and centrifugal machinery. Some central factories used wagons on rails to move the raw materials inside the factory, but none made use of locomotives at that time. All used cane bagasse and coal as fuel.

The first central factories in the French Antilles utilized slave labor, but some had to contract salaried white workers to perform more specialized tasks. In order to subsidize the importation of white workers, the colonial government created a special fund in 1845, but the number of individuals contracted was always minimal. It was difficult to hire free mulattoes to work in these first central factories because they refused to work side by side with the slaves, even when the colonial government enacted a law in 1845 to increase their salaries.

End of Slavery in the French Colonies

After 1840, the abolitionists in France pressured the French government to create a commission to study the emancipation of the slaves. For this reason, the French planters were convinced that the days of slavery were numbered and that the French Antilles would follow the example of the British West Indies. Also, as a result of the abolitionists' campaign, the French government enacted a law on July 18, 1845, creating a fund of 300,000 francs to provide loans to slaves. Many French slaves took advantage of this fund to buy their freedom and small parcels of land.

The emancipation of the slaves in the French Antilles was slow but steady, as was evidenced by the increasing amount of productive land occupied by freedmen, who began raising food crops. Guadeloupe had only 13,417 acres dedicated to the cultivation of food crops on small plots in 1826, but by 1848 that amount had increased to 40,490 acres. This process of gradual emancipation took place while the slaves were displaying open resistance to slavery by going on strike or running away from the plantations. Numerous slaves escaped to the British islands of Antigua, St. Lucia, and Dominica, where they expected to find freedom in the free towns.

Slavery in the French Antilles finally met its downfall in April 1848, when the news arrived that a liberal revolution that had begun in France in February had brought the abolitionists to power. The slaves quickly mobilized and demanded their immediate release from bondage. Fearing a bloody slave insurrection, similar to that of the Haitian Revolution, the colonial authorities decreed the general abolition of slavery on April 22 in Guadeloupe and on April 26 in Martinique. These decrees coincided with the national proclamation of the abolition of slavery in Paris on April 27, 1848.

The French abolitionists, headed by Victor Schoelcher, who was then secretary of state of the colonies for the revolutionary government, refused to accept a transitional period similar to the apprenticeship period of the British West Indies. They preferred to give the French planters an indemnity of 126 million francs, 11 million of which would be earmarked for the creation of colonial banks to promote farming and industry. Following the abolition decrees, 87,719 slaves in

Guadeloupe and 72,859 in Martinique obtained their freedom.

The abolition of slavery in the French Antilles resulted in an exodus from the plantations very similar to that of the British colonies. The freedmen immediately went off in search of land where they could settle their families and practice subsistence agriculture. Those who had managed to save some money tried to buy land from their former masters, preferring to remain on the plantation lands that they were accustomed to farming. Many planters chose to sell or rent plots to their former slaves in order to keep them nearby, so as to be able to hire them as salaried workers. Other planters negotiated sharecroppers' contracts with the freedmen, which allowed the former slaves to continue subsistence farming but required that they continue to produce sugarcane for their former masters. In this manner, many planters managed to retain part of their manual labor supply.

The majority of the freedmen, however, preferred to become free farmers on their own land. In Martinique and Guadeloupe, there was still enough vacant land to accommodate them in the mountains or near the plantations of Grand-Terre. In Grand-Terre, even though sugarcane plantations dominated the terrain, the freedmen managed to find unused land. Once settled, they planted such crops as yuca, potatoes, yams, plantains, peanuts, and beans in rotation. Some purchased chickens, goats, and pigs and became breeders. By 1851 travelers were noting the proliferation of free villages in areas that the planters had abandoned or neglected.

The abolition of slavery in the French Antilles produced a serious labor crisis on the sugar plantations. Sugar production was gravely affected, falling from 31,337 tons in Martinique in 1847 to 15,068 tons in 1850. Guadeloupe experienced an even greater decrease, with exports falling from 37,894 tons in 1847 to 12,831 tons in 1850.

The French planters, through their colonial governments, immediately reacted by imposing an obligatory registration of freedmen to force them to work as salaried workers. Each freedman was required to carry with him, at all times, a workbook that stated his contracts, tasks, and workdays on the plantation. Those caught without the workbook were taken to court, condemned as idle, and forced to work without compensation for their former masters.

This "workbook system" had limited success for the planters.

Although the freedmen had to register, and many returned to the plantations as salaried workers, the majority managed to evade the controls and ended taking up refuge in the free villages. The authorities abandoned the system in 1870.

The French planters also resorted to importing contracted workers to solve the labor problem. After experimenting with several hundred French and Portuguese workers, they recruited 6,600 Africans to work in Guadeloupe and 10,521 in Martinique between 1857 and 1862. These workers were so mistreated that the French government prohibited the importation of Africans in 1861, following a petition by the British government.

As compensation, the French authorities authorized contracted workers from India to be brought to the French Antilles. Between 1854 and 1889, 25,509 East Indian workers arrived in Martinique, while Guadeloupe received 42,326 and French Guiana 9,200. Almost half of these immigrants died of malaria and other tropical illnesses. Nearly 12,000 died in Martinique, as well as 19,000 in Guadeloupe and almost 4,500 in French Guiana. Many of the survivors—9,460 in Guadeloupe and 11,077 in Martinique—returned to India at the end of their contracts.

By contracting foreign laborers and slowly mechanizing their sugar mills, the British and French planters managed to save their sugar industry despite the economic crisis caused by emancipation. The increase in sugar prices between 1854 and 1884 made it possible for the planters to obtain new loans to finance the mechanization of the industry during the transition from slavery to paid labor. Meanwhile, a new free peasantry emerged in the West Indies.

CHAPTER 15

The Sugar Revolution
in Cuba and Puerto Rico

Cuba's Ascent in the Sugar Market

The Haitian Revolution brought an end to the plantation system of Saint-Domingue. In less than ten years, sugar production was reduced by almost 90 percent and cotton production by over 80 percent. Until 1789 the French Antilles had supplied 43 percent of the European sugar market, but after the Haitian Revolution they could barely supply 10 percent. When shipments from Saint-Domingue were disrupted and Europe was deprived of its main source of sugar, prices shot up. The planters on the other Caribbean islands welcomed the opportunity to fill the vacuum.

Jamaica benefited the most from this crisis because it still had uncultivated lands that could be quickly put to cane sugar production. During the Haitian Revolution, Jamaican planters expanded their sugar exports from 60,000 tons in 1791 to more than 92,000 tons in 1802. Numerous French refugees from Saint-Domingue immigrated to Jamaica, and there they helped increase coffee exports from 2,300 tons in 1791 to almost 18,000 tons in 1802. Between 1791 and 1802, the slave population of Jamaica grew from 250,000 to 307,000.

Despite these advances, Jamaica was unable to expand production fast enough to meet the increasing demand. The only islands with sufficient land to replace the sugar production of Saint-Domingue were the Spanish Antilles, and of these just Cuba was poised to meet the new challenge. Santo Domingo had been dragged into the turmoil of the Haitian Revolution and had lost its few remaining sugar mills, while Puerto Rico continued to be controlled by the Spanish military and did not have a business elite that could quickly mobilize the capital necessary to increase sugar production.

The Cuban sugar industry had been steadily growing in the second half of the eighteenth century, and Havana already had a group of planters who supplied the Spanish market with more than 16,000 tons of sugar per year by the 1790s. With Spanish credit, the Cuban planters had managed to build an average of 8 sugar mills annually between 1759 and 1774, reaching a total of 478 mills by the latter year. These new mills were larger than the traditional ones but still did not utilize the Jamaican train and were built in an outdated style, with each boiler fired by a separate furnace, preventing an increase in productivity.

Although the Cuban plantations tripled their sugar exports between 1763 and 1792, this expansion was simply quantitative and could not be attributed to technological advances. The number of sugar mills, boiler houses, and imported African slaves, as well as the acreage farmed, increased during this time. Sugar plantations, which in 1763 had relied on an average of twenty slaves, averaged eighty slaves in 1792, while their average size expanded from 320 to 700 acres during the same period.

Plantations varied in size in the late 1700s. Many small plantations were located in the central and eastern parts of Cuba, while the largest could be found closer to Havana, with some planters owning 5,000 acres and over 350 slaves. The area around Havana became the main sugar-producing region, boasting as many as 227 sugar mills in 1792. Despite these numbers, the growth of the Cuban sugar industry before the Haitian Revolution lagged far behind that of Jamaica and Saint-Domingue.

The gradual expansion of the sugar industry had been initiated by the Real Compañía de Comercio de la Habana, but it accelerated with the British military occupation of 1762. Between August 1762 and July 1763, British traders legally introduced and sold more than 4,000 slaves. Because the British price for a slave was only 90 pesos, rather than the 200 pesos charged by the Real Compañía de Comercio de la Habana, the Cubans bought them up quickly. This doubled the slave population in Havana and allowed planters to expand production in the years that followed.

The Cuban colonists were also exposed to the benefits of free trade during the British occupation. Havana was visited by hundreds of

English and American merchants offering all kinds of merchandise, from fabrics, dresses, shoes, and soap to farming implements and equipment for the sugar mills. The English abolished taxes and offered their merchandise at lower prices than the Spanish. Havana, previously a lethargic port that had received an average of 15 merchant ships a year, became extraordinarily active during the eleven months of British occupation, receiving more than 700 merchant ships from London, Bristol, Liverpool, Boston, New York, Philadelphia, and Charleston.

At the end of the Seven Years War in 1763, Cuba was returned to Spain because the British planters on other islands feared that a permanent annexation would increase the sugar supply and cause prices to drop in the British market. The Spanish government immediately began a large-scale military construction program to defend the city from future invasion. In order to finance this program, the government had to transfer large sums of money from the Royal Treasury of Mexico. For the next fifteen years, some 500,000 pesos were spent annually on the construction of El Morro, Castillo del Príncipe, and two other castles in Havana. More than 4,000 slaves were imported to work on construction, make bricks, and cut and transport lumber and stone. It was also necessary to purchase additional materials and to pay the salaries of several thousand free workers.

Many colonists who owned slaves hired them out to the government to build the forts. Other colonists grew food crops for the market to feed the workers. In order to keep the city supplied with flour, meat, salted fish, construction tools, and other merchandise, the colonial government allowed free trade with the Americans. During these years, consumption increased considerably, and a minority of merchants, builders, and landowners accumulated large savings as a direct result of the military construction and the trade with the Americans. Much of this capital was later invested in the construction of new sugar mills by landowners and ranchers who wanted to become planters.

The gradual expansion of the Cuban sugar industry between 1763 and 1792 yielded a visible result: the destruction of tobacco farms and cattle ranches in the areas surrounding Havana. One by one, the cattle ranches on the fertile lands to the east and south of Havana fell into the hands of sugar planters. In 1763 there were 10,610 acres devoted to sugarcane in the area around Havana. By 1792 the land used for sugarcane had reached 150,670 acres.

The wealthiest landowners were firmly convinced of the convenience of entering the sugar industry, and many dismantled their cattle ranches or tobacco farms to convert them into sugar plantations. They were well connected to the court in Madrid and lobbied the Spanish authorities to promote these plantations by facilitating the importation of slaves. King Charles III accepted their petitions and in February 1789 issued a Real Cédula (Royal Decree) allowing the free importation of slaves regardless of their origin. It is estimated that between 1763 and 1792, Cuba legally and illegally imported between 60,000 and 70,000 slaves, an average of 2,000 per year.

These figures were still small compared to the importation of slaves into Saint-Domingue and Jamaica. Between 1783 and 1791, the French colony imported 30,000 slaves per year, while Jamaica imported 7,700 slaves per year between 1776 and 1791. The Spanish government's concession to the Cuban planters of unrestricted importation was originally designed to last two years, but in November 1791 it was extended for six more years to allow the planters to take advantage of the opportunity presented by the decline in sugar production in Saint-Domingue. According to Alexander von Humboldt, Cuban planters imported 77,189 slaves between 1791 and 1803, or almost 6,000 per year.

Impact of the Haitian Revolution

The Cuban planters responded to the growth in the market by enlarging their plantations, sugar mills, purge houses, and drying sheds and by planting more cane. They also introduced more slaves, carts, bulls, and mules; installed more kettles; and attracted more capital. There were 227 sugar mills in the vicinity of Havana in 1792; by 1808 there were 416. Not only did the number of sugar mills increase during this period, but the mills also increased in size. The average annual production per sugar mill in 1792 was 58 tons; by 1804 it was 127 tons.

New, expansive sugar mills began proliferating, some with over 300 slaves producing more than 300 tons of sugar annually. Although the largest of the old, traditional sugar mills was only capable of producing about 170 tons of sugar annually, many planters with large landholdings built multiple mills and boiler houses to maximize production.

The high price of sugar on the international market favored financial speculation. The traders and landowners of Havana borrowed money to buy slaves and install sugar mills. Metropolitan merchants lent money to sugar investors, while American traders established themselves in Cuba by offering capital or merchandise in exchange for sugar and molasses. Many Spanish colonists with connections to capitalists in Spain did the same. Furthermore, dozens of French planters from Saint-Domingue sought refuge in Cuba and shared their experience with the novice plantation owners.

The role of the French colonial émigrés in the expansion of the Cuban sugar industry was very important. They brought with them the secrets of the trade, including sugar mill administration techniques and experience in disciplining masses of slaves. The French were also responsible for the introduction of coffee cultivation to the eastern part of Cuba. Many established themselves in Santiago de Cuba, where they were able to take advantage of the favorable ecological conditions to start up numerous coffee plantations.

The Cuban sugar industry began to modernize. New varieties of sugarcane were imported, and the Jamaican train was introduced. Around 1790, new sugarcane was brought to Guadeloupe and Martinique from Ile de Bourbon (Reunion Island), in the Indian Ocean, as well as from Tahiti and Batavia, in the Pacific Ocean. These new varieties were then brought to Montserrat in 1793, from whence they were distributed throughout the Antilles.

Cuban planters brought the first seeds of these cane varieties from St. Croix. The new varieties from Tahiti and Ile de Bourbon soon proved to be more productive than the so-called Creole cane. Many Cuban planters began to use Tahitian cane along with Creole cane in order to have two separate harvests and extend the labor-intensive periods of cutting and grinding. By 1820 Tahitian cane had become the prevailing variety, and over time, it replaced Creole cane entirely.

Another change involved the replacement of old vertical wooden roller mills by iron mills. The most popular mill imported from Great Britain during the first years of the nineteenth century had horizontal rollers. In the beginning, its advantages were purely mechanical: the metal components resisted cane knots better and wore out more slowly than the wooden mills. But the energy needed to move the iron mills came, as before, from mules or bulls circling around the mill under the direction of one or two slaves.

The installation of iron mills in Cuba was one of the first innovations of the Industrial Revolution to reach the island. The use of the steam engine followed. In 1797 there were some early attempts to adapt the steam engine to the sugar industry, but it took until 1817 for an iron mill to be successfully powered by a steam engine. From then on, the Cuban planters began to experiment with the mechanization of their plantations. They began with small changes but soon worked their way up to full-scale mechanization.

The development of the Cuban sugar industry was stimulated by the Haitian Revolution but did not actually accelerate until after 1820. The sugar production of Cuba finally reached the pre-Revolution level of Saint-Dominque (about 70,500 tons) in 1826. The following year, however, Cuba produced 94,011 tons of sugar, almost equaling the production of Jamaica in 1805 and 1806. Cuba was slower than Jamaica to take advantage of the vacuum created by the collapse of Saint-Domingue, but when the Cuban planters finally began to mechanize their sugar mills by powering them with steam engines, they quickly surpassed Jamaica's production figures.

Another connection with the Industrial Revolution was the inauguration of the first railroad in 1837, which connected the sugar region of Güines with the port of Havana. Güines had been taken over by sugar plantations between 1800 and 1820. From that point on, the railroad allowed new plantations to be built in undeveloped areas of the island. Plantations were also established around Matanzas. Later the fertile plains of Cárdenas and Colón were developed. The latter town was not founded until 1837, but by 1857 the area surrounding it had become the most important sugar region in Cuba. In that year, the production of Matanzas, Cárdenas, and Colón combined provided 55 percent of the total Cuban sugar production. The development of these regions would not have been possible without the railroad.

As they moved toward the center of Cuba, the plantations and sugar mills took over the ports of Cienfuegos and Trinidad. Because of their geographical location, these ports, which had been among the most active in the illegal trade with Jamaica, now became two of the most important sugar centers. In 1827 Cienfuegos did not produce a single pound of sugar, but by 1846 its sugar mills were producing more than 12,000 tons a year. A similar phenomenon took place in the area around Trinidad, where by the 1840s forty-three sugar mills were exporting around 8,000 tons annually. The regions around Sancti Spiritus, Santa Clara, and Puerto Príncipe, in the central part of the island, did not escape the sugar fever. Sugar plantations in these regions, however, did not flourish as easily because of the competition for land from the cattle ranchers.

Sugarcane fields transformed the Cuban landscape during the first half of the nineteenth century. The only cities that did not grow quickly were Holguín and Santiago, in the eastern part of the island. The geography of these areas did not favor the development of large-scale plantations, and therefore their sugar mills were smaller and less advanced technologically. Nonetheless, the sugar mills in the east produced about 5,750 tons of sugar in 1820, which was the same quantity produced on the entire island sixty years earlier. Under the influence of the French émigrés, the eastern region specialized in coffee and tobacco production, a development that later had important political implications.

Between 1827 and 1846 in Cuba, many sugar mills were mechanized, the Jamaican train was adopted, and the first railroads were installed. Such changes led to significant increases in productivity, and Cuba's exports tripled. Prior to 1827, the increase in production had been due to an increase in the number of sugar mills, acreage cultivated in sugarcane, and the number of slaves. Between 1827 and 1846, the increases could be attributed to the modernization of the sugar mills. The average productivity per sugar mill rose from 94 tons in 1827 to 141 tons in 1846, when Cuba exported 203,906 tons of sugar.

Slave Labor and Chinese Indentured Workers

During the Haitian Revolution, the number of slaves imported to Cuba increased, but Cuba still could not bring in as many as Saint-Domingue or Jamaica. Between 1791 and 1808, Cuban planters imported 99,688 slaves, while the Jamaicans imported almost 170,000. If the slave importation figures are an indicator of the speed with which

Cuban and Jamaican planters adapted to replace the production lost by the French, then it can be concluded that Jamaica's economy was more elastic than Cuba's in its response to the demand for sugar created by the Haitian Revolution.

According to Alexander Humboldt, only 54,955 slaves arrived in Cuba between 1804 and 1815, while between 1816 and 1820, 95,821 were introduced. Modern calculations adjust the latter figure up to 111,014. In this period, the Cuban planters tried to maximize their slave supply, anticipating the prohibition of the slave trade that the British sought to impose on Spain. In subsequent years, imports continued to increase. Between 1827 and 1841, 155,000 additional slaves were introduced to Cuba, despite British efforts to end the slave trade.

The railroad facilitated the rapid colonization of the interior of Cuba. However, the railroad also demanded an increase in the production of sugarcane to fill the cars and supply the new semi-mechanized sugar mills installed throughout the island. Additional large quantities of sugarcane could not be cultivated without increasing the number of workers. Therefore the Cuban planters continued to import contraband slaves, despite a second prohibition of the slave trade in 1835. The census of 1841 shows a slave population of 436,495. Between 1836 and 1850, the Cuban planters imported 107,346 slaves, followed by 131,256 more between 1851 and 1860.

The slave trade was never sufficient to resolve the permanent shortage of manual labor. To compensate, Cuban planters resorted to importing contracted Chinese workers. The first contingent of 612 Chinese laborers reached Havana in 1848, after a long trip through the Indian and South Atlantic oceans. Numerous other shiploads of Chinese laborers arrived between 1853 and 1874. Over the years, at least 124,813 Chinese were imported, not counting the 16,576 who died during the voyage and over 5,000 who arrived illegally via California. This trade in contracted Chinese workers was initially directed by Creole and Spanish capitalists from Havana, who also controlled the African slave trade.

The traffic of Chinese, tolerated by the English under the pretext that it was being done with free men contracted voluntarily, became another chapter in the history of the slave trade. Chinese laborers were recruited by agents in Macao, who made them sign a contract committing them to work on the plantations for eight years. The contract established a salary of four pesos per month and a daily ration of eight ounces of meat and one-and-a-half pounds of plantains, manioc, potatoes, or yams. A Chinese worker also would receive a blanket, two changes of clothes, and one wool shirt every year.

Unlike the British planters, the Cubans did not give the Chinese rice or tea, and they made them work 84 hours per week rather than 45. During the sugarcane harvest, Chinese laborers worked up to 16 hours per day, seven days a week, totaling 112 hours weekly. They were also constantly whipped to force them to conform to plantation life. Furthermore, the Cuban planters did not allow their Chinese workers to use plantation lands to grow food crops, as they had done with the black slaves.

Most Chinese workers arrived in Cuba over the course of twenty years. Regulations were constantly changed to restrict their mobility and prevent them from gaining their freedom before their eight-year contract expired. Afterwards, if they survived the extreme working conditions, many planters used force to oblige them to renew their contracts. As a result of their poor treatment, the Chinese constantly tried to escape. Suicides were also more frequent among the Chinese than among any other group within the labor pool in Cuba: they took their lives fourteen times more often than black slaves, and a hundred times more often than white workers.

Suicide, death by overworking, illness, and escape diminished the Chinese working population. According to the census of 1872, more than 20 percent of the Chinese ran away, while the mortality rate was even higher, easily surpassing the replacement rate. Therefore, despite the large numbers imported, the shortage of workers for the Cuban sugar industry went unresolved. Nonetheless, the importation of Chinese laborers helped expand the sugar industry between 1855 and 1875 and prevented an even greater shortage of manual labor.

Cuba: The World's Largest Sugar Producer

By 1860 Cuba had 1,365 sugar mills, 949 of which were powered by steam, 7 by water, and the rest by animals. Almost all processed cane juice by using the Jamaican train, but 70 of the largest mills had modernized their boiler houses by incorporating the new mechanized trains built in England and France. By the mid-nineteenth century, the productivity of the main Cuban sugar mills surpassed that of all the other Caribbean islands. Cuba's large semi-mechanized mills produced between 500 and 630 tons of sugar per year, twice the level of 1792, while the Caribbean average per sugar mill was about 397 tons annually. By 1860 Cuba had become the world's leading sugar producer, surpassing both Jamaica and Brazil, with exports increasing that year to 541,695 tons.

Thus Cuba underwent a major transformation, similar to the evolution of the British and French West Indies in the seventeenth and eighteenth centuries. Cuba had been transformed from a cattle-ranching and tobacco-farming economy into a plantation economy. With the exception of tobacco-growing areas, which moved to Pinar del Río, in the west of the island, and the coffee-growing areas in the east, Cuba had become a colony devoted to a sugar monoculture. The ecological impact was notable: as the sugar mills multiplied, forests were cleared to open new fields for sugarcane and to supply wood for the sugar mill furnaces. Cuba became the first exporter of lumber to the United States, especially pinewood, which was used to build boxes for transporting sugar. Consequently, the central part of the island east of Havana was deforested.

Cuba stopped exporting salted meat and began to import meat and beef jerky from the United States, Argentina, and Uruguay to feed its enormous slave population. In 1841 Cuba imported more than thirty million pounds of beef jerky, indicating a decline in livestock after the growth of the sugar plantations. Cuba had previously imported flour, olive oil, dried fruits, wine, and other food, as well as clothes, from Spain, but now most of its flour came from the United States.

Not all food was imported, however. The prosperity created by the sugar revolution led to the development of commercial farming. Thousands of free farmers took advantage of the demand created by the new plantations and began to grow plantains, yuca, corn, rice, chickpeas, beans, potatoes, ginger, and cacao to supply the internal market. Many also produced cheese and cassava bread, flour, charcoal, honey, and wax on marginal lands close to the plantations.

From Peasant Agriculture to Plantations in Puerto Rico

Like Cuba, Puerto Rico also underwent a great economic transformation, but more slowly because the Puerto Rican colonists were too poor to take immediate advantage of the market opened up by the Haitian Revolution. At the end of the eighteenth century, most people in Puerto Rico worked the land with their own hands and with the help of a small number of slaves. They made a living in contraband livestock and foodstuffs sold to the Danish islands of St. Croix and St. Thomas. The city of San Juan was the administrative center, dominated by a military elite, along with a small group of merchants and landowners with limited resources.

In 1812 sugar exports from Puerto Rico were almost insignificant, only 838 tons. Coffee was the most important export crop, with exports that year totaling 3,905 tons. The Puerto Rican sugar plantations still used small "trapiche" mills powered by draft animals. In 1812 Puerto Rico was in a similar state of development to Cuba's a hundred years earlier. In the following twelve years, however, the Puerto Rican sugar economy took a leap forward, and in 1824 production rose to 8,972 tons, ten times higher than in 1812. Production continued to climb until it reached almost 40,000 tons in 1852.

Puerto Rico's impressive increase in sugar exports came as the result of several factors. First, sugar prices began to rise again between 1810 and 1815 as a consequence of the Napoleonic Wars, a factor that also stimulated Cuba's production during the same period. Second, several new groups of immigrants brought their capital, trade networks, and financial connections to Puerto Rico in order to develop new sugar mills. Some of these immigrants were former residents of St. Thomas who had left during the British occupation from 1807 to 1815. By moving, they were able to take advantage of the liberal policies then promoted by the Puerto Rican colonial government to attract investment.

The "Cedula de Gracias"

Unlike the Cuban sugar transformation, which had been directed by the Creole elite of Havana, Puerto Rico's sugar industry was driven by foreign investors attracted by the economic incentives of the famous Cédula de Gracias (Decree of Incentives) of August 10, 1815. This decree included a specific economic program to pull Puerto Rico out of stagnation by encouraging immigration, foreign investment, and the development of plantations.

The Cédula de Gracias established that any white Catholic foreigner from a nation on friendly terms with Spain could settle freely in Puerto Rico and could demand from the government up to six acres of land per family member and up to three acres per slave. These immigrants could also become Spanish citizens five years after acquiring title to their lands and could obtain additional lands. Furthermore, the foreigners who settled on the island could enjoy a tax exemption for a period of ten years.

The Cédula de Gracias eliminated the institutional barriers of the Spanish monopoly and liberalized foreign and domestic trade. With this decree, the Spanish Crown authorized Puerto Rico to trade with foreign countries for a period of fifteen years and totally freed trade between Spain and Puerto Rico as long as it was carried out on Spanish ships. Trade with the other Spanish colonies would be burdened with a tax of only 2 percent. When exports to foreign territories were transported on Spanish ships, they would be taxed 6 percent. If they were transported on foreign ships, however, the tariff rose to 15 percent.

Most import duties in Puerto Rico were reduced to a single tax of 15 percent if the merchandise arrived on foreign ships. The importation of food was taxed at 10 percent, while the importation of tools and farming and industrial machinery was taxed at only 3 percent. If these implements were imported from Spain, they entered Puerto Rico duty-free. In order to protect farming and stimulate sugar production, the Cédula de Gracias prohibited the importation of sugar, rum, molasses, and tobacco. In emergency cases, however, the local authorities were authorized to permit the entrance of products from the other Antilles.

Puerto Rico received thousands of immigrants during the first half of the nineteenth century. In 1815 Puerto Rico had a population of 202,276, but by 1828 the population had increased to 267,837 and continued to rise until it reached 317,018 in 1834. As in Cuba, however, the free population was rarely employed by the sugar industry during the first half of the nineteenth century because the planters preferred to import massive numbers of slaves. As a result, the slave population increased from 18,616 in 1815 to 31,874 in 1828 and 41,818 in 1843.

Many of the immigrants arriving in Puerto Rico during this period were Venezuelans who were escaping the wars of independence in their country. They brought their capital and slaves with them. There were also French immigrants from Saint-Domingue who established themselves on the west coast of the island and started coffee plantations. Some Catalans and privateers from the Mediterranean came to trade in the sugar-producing areas. Other immigrants included Germans from Hamburg, who had previously traded sugar through St. Thomas, and Americans, Dutch, English, and Danes.

Some immigrants quickly joined the local landowning elite in Ponce and Guayama, in the south of the island, as well as in Mayagüez and San Germán in the west. In 1827 four out of five planters in Ponce were immigrants. Other immigrants bought land in the floodplains of the north coast, in the vicinity of Arecibo, Toa Baja, Bayamón, Río Piedras, Trujillo, Loaiza, and Fajardo. In all of these regions, the foreigners usually acquired land suitable for sugar production; where it had previously been used for cattle ranching, land was now quickly converted into sugar plantations.

Importing Slaves for Puerto Rico's Plantations

Puerto Rican planters continued to import slaves after 1807, when Great Britain abolished the slave trade. British political leaders tried to impose worldwide restrictions on the slave trade in order to prevent other colonies from expanding their sugar production and exporting cheaper sugar at the expense of the British market share. In 1817 the British government was able to convince Spain to sign a treaty that would end Spanish slave trafficking on May 30, 1820. In exchange, the British government indemnified Spain with a cash payment of 400,000 pounds sterling.

Although the Spanish government, pressured by Great Britain, had signed the treaty, the Spanish colonial authorities received considerable income from the sugar industry and therefore continued to tolerate the illegal traffic of Africans. Contraband became the main supply source for the Cuban and Puerto Rican planters who continued to import slaves. The military governors assisted the planters by overlooking clandestine traffic in exchange for hefty commissions, which in fact constituted their main source of income in the mid-nineteenth century.

The British navy was placed in charge of guarding the African coasts and the Caribbean waters to prevent the shipment of slaves to Cuba, Puerto Rico, and the French Antilles. The navy intercepted many clandestine British shipments headed for Cuban and Puerto Rican plantations. That led Cuban and Puerto Rican planters to supply themselves directly with smuggled slaves. Companies of Spanish and Creole capitalists in Havana, San Juan, Ponce, and Mayagüez began sending expeditions to Africa, competing in the illegal slave trade with the Portuguese and American traders.

Established between 1809 and 1817, the Cuban companies were responsible for the importation of at least 60,368 slaves. In Puerto Rico, the slave-hunting expeditions began later because the planters had an ample supply source in the neighboring Danish and French islands. A significant number of the 26,400 slaves exported through St. Croix and St. Thomas between 1785 and 1807 were smuggled into Puerto Rico. Puerto Rico's slaves were predominantly supplied by Martinique and Guadeloupe, but by 1831 the number of slaves sold by the French in Puerto Rico began to decline, until the traffic completely stopped in 1833.

In 1835 Spain found itself obliged to sign a second treaty with Great Britain guaranteeing the end of the slave trade. To ensure compliance, the British navy had the right to search ships en route to Cuba and Puerto Rico. Consequently, the price of slaves increased steadily, making contraband trade even more attractive. The Puerto Rican planters, along with their Cuban counterparts, continued financing expeditions to bring slaves from Africa. As these expeditions were very risky, the direct acquisition of slaves from Africa began to lose popularity, and after 1840 Puerto Rico began to suffer economically from labor shortages.

The Labor Problem and the *Libreta* System

The Puerto Rican planters addressed this labor shortage problem in 1838 by convincing their government to require free peasants to register

in their municipalities and to work as salaried laborers on the plantations. If they did not, they would be declared idle and condemned to
forced labor in public works. The following year the Spanish government repealed this requirement, considering it overly repressive, but the
planters continued to demand regulations that would allow them to
forcibly contract poor peasants and the unemployed, who they claimed
totaled about 80,000 on the island. As a result of these efforts, the
planters and colonial authorities prepared a Reglamento de Jornaleros,
or Laborers Bylaw, which was approved and promulgated in June 1849.
From then on, peasants of both sexes with properties smaller than four
acres were required to register in their municipalities and work as day
laborers. Each peasant received a number and a *libreta* (workbook), in
which he or she was to record on which farms and plantations he or she
had worked, when and how long he or she was employed, and the tasks
he or she had performed. The authorities were in charge of examining
the *libretas* of all individuals suspected of being idle or without permanent employment. Those who were caught without a *libreta* were sentenced to at least eight days of public works.[1]

The purpose of the *libreta* was to create a population of laborers out
of the free peasantry and the sharecroppers. One of the poorest seg-
ments of society, the sharecroppers were generally people with no land
who offered to work for peasant families in exchange for lodging,
clothes, food, and protection. Many were the children of extremely poor
families who had been entrusted to certain families to be raised in
exchange for doing domestic work.

In June 1850 the colonial government prohibited the retention of
sharecroppers and required that they move from the rural areas to
towns, unless the landowners recognized them as their domestic servants or allowed them to rent at least four acres of land. By concentrat-
ing the sharecroppers in towns, the colonial authorities and the planters
sought to make them available for the plantation owners to contract as
needed.

Many Puerto Rican planters responded to these new requirements by
having their sharecroppers sign contracts to rent land. In a short time
the peasant population that rented land in the most populated areas of
Puerto Rico increased considerably. In the coffee-growing areas, there
were cases where more than 70 percent of the sharecroppers became

tenant farmers. But in the sugar-producing areas, the situation was different because there was no land available to rent, nor could the laborers easily free themselves from the planters, since they were bound to the land through debt servitude.

In both areas, the planters would keep their laborers' *libretas* until the workers had finished paying off their debts, while at the same time they would continue offering merchandise and food from the plantation stores on credit to workers, thereby increasing the workers' indebtedness. In this manner, the Puerto Rican planters managed to maintain control of their free labor in a period in which slave labor was becoming scarce. The *libreta* became one of the most unpopular instruments of the Spanish colonial regime in Puerto Rico, although it was not equally enforced throughout the island.

While the Cuban planters reacted to the deficit of manual labor by importing Chinese laborers and contraband slaves, the Puerto Ricans imposed the *libreta* system. These strategies helped sustain the plantation economy on both islands, but in the case of Puerto Rico, the *libreta* system did not allow for the continued expansion of the sugar industry. Between 1841 and 1860, Cuban planters imported 177,768 black slaves, but after 1850 Puerto Rican planters could no longer continue to import even contraband slaves.[2] From 1850 on, the manual labor crisis in Puerto Rico became even greater. Nonetheless, Puerto Rican plantation owners did not resort to contracting Chinese laborers, as did their Cuban peers.

Puerto Rico: The World's Second Largest Sugar Producer

After 1850 sugar production in Puerto Rico stagnated, while in Cuba it continued to grow until it reached 541,695 tons in 1860. Cuba became the largest sugar producer in the world, exporting ten times more than Puerto Rico. Nonetheless, in spite of its outdated sugar mills and small-to-average-sized plantations, Puerto Rico had become the second largest sugar producer in the Caribbean, exporting more than 50,000 tons in 1860. Jamaica lagged behind with only 26,040 tons.

In 1845 the majority of the Puerto Rican sugar mills were still powered by animals. In Ponce, for example, only six of the eighty-six sugar mills in the area were steam-powered. As a result, the Puerto Rican sugar mills were less efficient than their Cuban counterparts. The sugar mills in Ponce averaged only 122 tons each in 1845, while Cuban production in 1846 averaged 140 tons per sugar mill. In Cuba, the majority of the sugar mills were also powered by animals, but the proportion was lower than in Puerto Rico. In 1846 Cuba had 1,442 sugar mills, 286 of which, or nearly 20 percent, were powered by steam engines, as compared to only 7 percent in Puerto Rico.

These technological differences influenced production levels. In order to produce 50,000 tons of sugar in the mid-nineteenth century, Puerto Rican planters had to follow a strategy similar to that of the Cubans at the end of the eighteenth century: they increased the number of sugar mills, sugar pans, boiler houses, and workers, and enlarged their cane fields. Export figures suggest that in 1860, there were at least 409 mills operating on the island. This number was to diminish quickly, however, when the Caribbean sugar industry began to undergo new technological and economic changes that affected its structure and performance, producing the most dramatic economic revolution to date.

In Puerto Rico and Cuba, these changes took place in the midst of an atmosphere of political unrest caused by struggles for independence and the debates about the abolition of slavery.

CHAPTER 16

Abolitionism in the Spanish Antilles

Proindependence Political Movements

The abolition of slavery in the Spanish Antilles was closely connected to the struggle for political independence. It was a slow and complicated process influenced by the spread of abolitionist sentiment in Europe, the chronic tension between liberal and conservative groups in Spain, and the proximity of the proslavery regime of the United States. The Haitian rulers abolished slavery in Santo Domingo when they unified the island in 1822, but in Cuba and Puerto Rico, abolition was constantly obstructed by the conflicting interests of Spain, the United States, and Great Britain.

There are clear links between the abolition question and the early independence movements of Cuba and Puerto Rico. For example, in Cuba, a plot to create an "Independent Republic of Cuba" was uncovered in 1809. Its organizers wanted to guarantee the continuation of slavery in order to ensure the development of the sugar industry. Another scheme organized by a group of free blacks was discovered in 1812. Following the Haitian example, the rebels hoped to abolish slavery and destroy the plantation system.

In 1822 there was another conspiracy organized by Luis Du Coudray Holstein, a Swiss adventurer who planned to send an expedition from the United States to form a "Boricua Republic" in Puerto Rico. The leaders of the expedition tried to incite the slaves to rebel, although they never intended to end slavery. Some of the conspirators were captured and shot in October of that year.

Proindependence sentiment spread through Masonic lodges and

secret revolutionary societies via letters sent from Mexico, Venezuela, and Colombia. In Cuba, blacks, poor whites, and young intellectuals fighting for political independence established several such societies. One of the most important secret societies, known as Soles y Rayos de Bolívar, was exposed and repressed in 1823. Its leaders were either imprisoned or forced to emigrate.

New conspiracies were discovered in the following years, leading the colonial government to prohibit Masonic lodges in Cuba in 1824.[1] In 1826 two exiled politicians secretly landed in Cuba with arms from Colombia. The two men contacted several secret societies and groups of free blacks in an attempt to instigate an uprising. When this movement was exposed, its two leaders were sent to prison and subsequently shot.

Despite these failures, similar conspiracies continued to plague the Spanish Antilles. In 1827 the Puerto Rican authorities took extraordinary precautions after receiving news that Haitian agents were organizing a massive slave revolt in Cuba and Puerto Rico. In that same year, a secret society called the Gran Legión del Águila Negra was organized in Cuba, but it was exposed and repressed in 1830.

The independence movements lost momentum after 1830. By then it was evident that the conspirators could not overthrow the colonial governments. In 1825 Spain imposed a political system on Cuba and Puerto Rico that granted absolute power to the military governors while suspending all civilian legal rights. In this manner, Spain hoped to inhibit further development of the proindependence movements that had sprung up in Latin America and Haiti. Cuba and Puerto Rico were governed as military camps, and the governors in control were under no obligation to respect the law or the Spanish constitution. The ruling class in Madrid thought that this was the only way to keep Cuba and Puerto Rico under Spain's dominion.

The *Reformista* Movement

Yet, a new challenge to Spanish rule took place shortly after the death of King Ferdinand VII in 1833. The government of Madrid called for representatives to be elected to the Cortes (Spanish parliament) in an attempt to create a constitutional government. The deputies elected in

Cuba in 1836 were liberals who aspired to reform the Cuban political system. The governor of Cuba nullified the election results three times, but each time the voters elected José Antonio Saco, a young intellectual leader of the reform movement, as one of their representatives.

Initially, the Cuban *reformistas* did not seek independence, but simply the liberalization of the political system and the eventual abolition of the slave trade. Saco represented a group of landowners who were concerned about the growing demographic disparity created by the continuous importation of slaves. The Cuban *reformistas* feared that the black masses would incite a bloody revolution similar to the one that had occurred in Haiti.

The Spanish colonial authorities, closely allied with the planters and rich merchants, considered the *reformistas* to be radical and subversive. Several Spanish members of the Cortes believed that the influence of Hispanic American representatives in the Cortes in 1810 and 1812 had been the main cause of the independence movements in the colonies. For this reason, the Cuban deputies were prevented from participating in the Cortes debates of 1837.

This rejection of Cuban participation in the Cortes resulted in protests and a military rebellion in Cuba demanding the reestablishment of the 1812 liberal constitution. This rebellion was firmly repressed, and the most radical *reformistas* were persecuted. Faced with demands for reform in Cuba and Puerto Rico, the Spanish government responded in 1837 by decreeing that from then on, the constitution and laws of Spain would not be applicable in the Antilles, and the islands would be governed by "special laws." These "special laws" were never promulgated, and the military governor remained in control, aided by a military commission with the power to administer martial law.

Annexionism and the Slave Trade

Political repression weakened the *reformista* movement, and in its place a movement in favor of annexation to the United States began to grow. This movement had old roots. The U.S. government, under every presidency from Jefferson to Lincoln, seriously considered annexing Cuba, but postponed that decision numerous times to avoid the risk of war with England and Spain.[2] Instead, the American policy allowed Cuba to remain under Spanish domination until it could be incorporated into the United States. This position was adopted in order to dissuade England from intervening in Cuba. In addition, there was frequent lobbying in Washington by Cuban planters, who feared that a revolution would abolish slavery in their country.

By supporting Spanish rule over Cuba and Puerto Rico, the United States was trying to protect its own institution of slavery. Some American leaders believed that the abolition of slavery in Cuba would have a dangerous influence on the plantations of the Southern states. Others thought that preserving slavery in Cuba and Puerto Rico would guarantee the expansion of the sugar industry and of the related sugar, molasses, flour, and slave trade that benefited many American merchants. Almost two-thirds of the clandestine trade that supplied the Cuban plantations with slaves was carried out on American ships.

The abolition of slavery in the British Antilles in 1838 and the subsequent activism of British abolitionist agents in Cuba led Cuban planters and merchants to reconsider the idea of annexation to the United Sates. Between 1840 and 1843, David Turnbull, the British consul in Havana, and his vice consul openly and intensely pushed for the abolition of the clandestine slave trade, and they secretly met with groups of free blacks who were promoting a slave insurrection. These activities caused the Cuban planters and merchants to demand that the colonial government expel the British consuls from the island. After several diplomatic incidents, Turnbull was expelled from Cuba in 1842, but rumors of a slave uprising continued.

Antislavery Revolts and Conspiracies

In order to discourage new plots, in November 1842 the governor of Cuba promulgated a slave code that prescribed punishment for conspirators and rewards for informers. Despite these measures, on March 2, 1843, the slaves of several sugar plantations in Matanzas and Cárdenas rebelled en masse and abandoned the plantations. This rebellion was quickly put down. Later that month, another slave rebellion erupted in Toa Baja, Puerto Rico, but was quickly brought under control. There were two other upheavals on sugar plantations in Matanzas in November and December of that year which were also repressed. In all cases, the leaders were executed.

In January 1844 the governor of Cuba announced the discovery of a large plot to abolish slavery, declare Cuba's independence, and create a black republic, following the example of Haiti. The governor arrested 4,039 people; 3,000 were prosecuted in court. Among those captured were 2,166 free blacks, 972 slaves, and 74 whites, as well as 827 individuals whose category was not defined. Of those detained, 78 were sentenced to death, 1,292 were imprisoned, and 400 were banished from the island.

This conspiracy, known as La Escalera, produced great consternation among the white population of Cuba, particularly among planters and slave traders. When the government published the details of the event and showed the extensive participation of free blacks and slaves, many planters concluded that annexation to the United States would serve to preserve the institution of slavery in Cuba and avoid "another Haiti." At that time, the United States was involved in the annexation of Texas in 1845 and the war with Mexico between 1846 and 1848, and so the annexation of Cuba was postponed.

In 1848 the Cuban annexationists concluded that if Cuba were to change hands, it would be better if the United States bought the island. This idea was brought before the U.S. Senate but failed to garner immediate support. At the beginning of 1847, a group of rich Cubans from the so-called Club de La Habana suggested to President Polk that the United States purchase Cuba with the support of the large Cuban planters and merchants, who were ready to contribute $100 million to help fund the operation. Their only conditions were the continuation of slavery and the incorporation of Cuba as a state of the Union. From then on, the purchase of Cuba became an important American diplomatic goal. Nevertheless, the $100 million offer made to the Spanish government in 1848 was rejected after details of the negotiations were leaked to the press in Madrid.

Filibuster Expeditions

Almost simultaneously, a group of radical Cuban annexationists tried to speed up the process by collaborating with planters in the Southern states and veterans of the wars in Texas and Mexico. Some American planters believed that the union of Cuba and the United States would increase the political power of the Southern slave states. The Club de La Habana then offered up to $3 million to finance a military expedition that would be supported by an internal Cuban movement organized by Narciso López, a Creole officer born in Venezuela. The American government was informed of these military preparations and denounced the conspiracy to the Spanish government. López fled Cuba, while his companions were imprisoned and executed. The Washington decision makers did not want these operations to hinder the negotiations for the purchase of Cuba.

Despite this failure, the radical annexationists were not discouraged and put López in charge of a new expedition leaving from New Orleans. After numerous difficulties, López arrived in Cárdenas in May 1850, accompanied by 600 Americans and five Cubans. Attacked by Spanish troops, López and his men had to return to the United States, having recruited only two people to join the movement. After secretly preparing a new expedition, López invaded Cuba again in July 1851, but was quickly defeated by the Spanish forces and put in prison. López was executed on September 1, 1851, in Havana.

Lopez's death left the annexationists without a Creole leader to direct operations. The annexationist leadership remained in the hands of the governor of Mississippi, John A. Quitman, who was asked by the Cuban Junta of New York to organize a new invasion in 1853. The American government opposed this scheme because it preferred to acquire Cuba by purchasing it, not through a mercenary expedition. In September 1854 the United States increased its purchase proposal to Spain to $130 million, but Madrid likewise rejected that offer. The annexationists continued with their plans, and in November 1854 Quitman's expedition arrived in Cuba, where it was quickly defeated. In light of these numerous military failures, the Cuban annexationists began to weaken politically, giving way to a renewed reformist activity.

Santo Domingo's Struggle for Independence

These events in Cuba occurred at the same time that Spain was changing its policies toward Santo Domingo, which had been separated from Haiti and had become an independent state, the Dominican Republic, in February 1844. Trying to maintain control of the former Spanish territory, the Haitian government launched several Haitian military invasions against the Dominican Republic in the following years. In an effort to obtain diplomatic recognition of its independence, the Dominican Republic sent missions to the United States, Spain, France, and England. The United States appointed a trade agent to Santo Domingo in 1847 but did not formally recognize the new Dominican Republic. France and England, however, did recognize it and appointed consuls in 1849 with instructions to prevent Haiti from occupying Santo Domingo. Spain, on the other hand, made it known that it would not recognize the Dominican Republic and that it reserved its rights over Santo Domingo, which it had regained as a colony through the Treaty of Versailles in 1814.

In September 1854 the United States and the Dominican Republic negotiated the terms of a treaty for the American recognition of Dominican independence. In exchange, the United States would be permitted to rent the Samaná peninsula and the Bay of Samaná to establish a naval station for its ships operating in the Caribbean. When the Spanish government found out about these negotiations, it immediately appointed a trade agent to the Dominican Republic with instructions to paralyzc that project and revive the Dominican authorities' confidence in Spain.

The Spanish trade agent arrived in Santo Domingo in November 1854 and communicated to the Dominican authorities that his government was willing to recognize the Dominican Republic's independence. He immediately joined the French and English agents, who were also making great efforts to block the American negotiations. In their quest to obtain Spanish recognition, the Dominican leaders tried to modify the treaty with the United States, after promising the Europeans that they would not sell, rent, or lease any portion of Dominican territory to any foreign government. Consequently, the U.S. government abandoned the negotiations and did not recognize the Dominican Republic's independence.

Spain, intending to replace the United States quickly, recognized the independence of the Dominican Republic on February 18, 1855. In exchange, the Dominican government agreed to prevent its territory from being used as a base for expeditions against Cuba and Puerto Rico. Spain thus managed to achieve its objective of preventing the establishment of an American military base in the Dominican Republic at a time when Cuban and American annexationists intended to move their center of operations from New Orleans to Central America or the Caribbean.

The Dominican Republic faced new Haitian invasions in 1855 and 1856, followed by a coup d'état and a civil war in 1857. The country was suffering under great poverty and catastrophic financial disorder, while the Haitians prepared another invasion. This invasion did not occur because the Haitian government was overthrown at the beginning of 1859. The new Haitian leaders were ready to recognize Dominican independence and told the authorities in Santo Domingo that they need not fear a new invasion. The Dominican leaders did not believe that peace would last and approached Spain for political and military protection against the Haitians, asking Spain to help them with the fortification of Samaná, coveted by the Americans.

Initially, the Spanish government, headed by General Leopoldo O'Donnell, a former governor of Cuba, resisted making a military commitment to Santo Domingo, but in April 1860 negotiations improved. O'Donnell viewed the fortification of Santo Domingo as an opportunity to broaden Spain's power in the Caribbean and to rebuild its lost empire in America. Consequently, Spanish diplomats suggested that the Dominican Republic be annexed to Spain. The Dominican leaders immediately accepted the idea, as they were convinced that without Spanish protection, sooner or later the country would fall into Haitian or American hands. Their fears were validated in October 1860, when the Dominican navy had to oust some American adventurers who were attempting to reclaim an adjacent island[3] rich in guano deposits as a territory of the United States.

In late 1860 Santo Domingo began a process of reincorporation into Spain. In exchange for the annexation, Spain agreed to respect the end of slavery in Dominican territory, to consider Santo Domingo a Spanish province with the same rights and privileges as Cuba and Puerto Rico, to utilize the services of local officials in the country, and to recognize the acts of the Dominican government from 1844 to 1860 as valid. The United States was opposed to these negotiations but could not take action because the country was on the brink of a civil war. The Spanish authorities took advantage of these circumstances and began to send troops from Cuba and Puerto Rico to Santo Domingo in January 1861. Two months later, on March 18, 1861, the Dominican authorities officially proclaimed Santo Domingo to be a province of Spain.

On reaching Santo Domingo, Spanish officials and soldiers discovered that the people whom they were to govern were not as culturally and ethnically Spanish as they had been assured. Instead, the majority of the population was mulatto and black, with habits quite different from those of the Spanish after several centuries of isolation, twenty-two years of union with the Haitians, and seventeen years of independence. The differences between Dominicans and Spaniards immediately surfaced, leading to racial segregation. The Spanish government refused to accept the military ranks of the officers of the former republican army. Paper currency was not immediately redeemed, and Spanish troops behaved abusively toward local peasants.

The new Spanish archbishop offended the elite by persecuting the Masonic lodges. He alienated the local clergy by imposing new rules on their conduct. He also estranged the majority of the population by requiring church marriages. The Spanish sought to impose a judicial system alien to the Dominican legal tradition, which was based on the Napoleonic codes adopted under the Haitian rule. Spanish authorities tried to restrict the free trade of tobacco, the main Dominican export, in order to create a monopoly that would favor Spanish interests. Furthermore, local traders and merchants resisted the new import taxes that gave Spanish ships and merchandise a competitive advantage.

All these problems created a general feeling of unrest, which was evident at the end of 1862, when Spanish officials warned their superiors than an uprising was imminent. In February 1863 the rebellion erupted and quickly spread. To encourage the insurrection, the Haitian government supplied money, arms, and food to the Dominican nationalists. The rebels took Santiago, the main city of the interior, and installed a provisional government to lead the insurrection. With the exception of Santo Domingo and several neighboring villages, the entire country was at war.

This "War of Restoration" began as a peasant rebellion for Dominican independence but very quickly also became a racial war. Given the proximity of Cuba and Puerto Rico, black and mulatto Dominicans, who formed the majority, feared the return of slavery. Dominican strategists consciously promoted this fear and designed the conflict as a guerrilla war involving the entire population in a struggle for independence against the white, Spanish rulers. The conflict lasted almost two years and cost Spain more than 10,000 casualties and about thirty-three million pesos. The Dominicans likewise suffered thousands of casualties, and their economy was ruined. The Spanish troops were being reduced by 10 percent every month, a dilemma that sharpened Spanish opposition to the occupation of Santo Domingo. In mid-1864 Spain's minister of war ordered the suspension of military operations until the government came to a final decision on how to disentangle from Santo Domingo.

In Madrid, opposition to the war intensified a political crisis that toppled O'Donnell's government in 1864. The new Spanish government, headed by General Ramón María Narváez, brought the Santo Domingo issue before the Cortes. After a long and heated debate, members of the Cortes decided to abandon Santo Domingo. The Spanish troops were unable to conquer a territory that Spain did not really need, and almost all Dominicans supported the restoration of the republic. On March 3, 1865, the queen of Spain signed a decree annulling the annexation of Santo Domingo, and on the July 10 Spanish troops began to return to Cuba, Puerto Rico, and Spain. Fifteen days later there was not a single Spanish soldier in Santo Domingo.

Liberals and *Reformistas*

Political conditions in Spain, Cuba, and Puerto Rico changed during the Dominican War of Restoration. Negotiations for the annexation of Santo Domingo had coincided with the beginning of a liberal government in Spain, which was in power from June 1858 to March 1863 under the presidency of General O'Donnell, of the Liberal Union Party. O'Donnell had previously been the governor of Cuba and was known for repressing La Escalera, the antislavery conspiracy in 1844.

O'Donnell had been informed of the general frustration among the Cuban population that was provoked by their lack of political rights. He thought that the time had come to introduce reforms. To govern Cuba, O'Donnell selected General Francisco Serrano, a liberal officer married to a Cuban woman from a wealthy Creole family. Serrano was interested in collaborating with the *reformistas* and discontinuing the despotic policies of his predecessors. To coordinate operations in Santo Domingo, Serrano needed harmony and tranquility among the different political groups in Cuba.

Under Serrano, the Cuban reform movement was rejuvenated. The *reformistas* demanded that Cubans enjoy the same political rights as the Spanish and petitioned for judicial, administrative, and municipal systems identical to those of Spain. They insisted that the authority of the governors be limited to the execution of the law. They wanted to elect delegates who would represent them directly in the Spanish Cortes, as well as a colonial legislature whose members would be elected by the Cuban population. They also demanded freedom of the press in the Antilles, with the understanding that topics related to slavery would be omitted.

The leaders of the reform movement belonged to the wealthy classes, who feared a great slave rebellion. Chinese laborers were causing many problems on the plantations with their high suicide rate, inclination toward insubordination, and constant conflict with the black slaves. Many planters sought to solve the deficit of manual labor by importing white workers. In 1862 there were 41,661 free white salaried workers on Cuban sugar plantations, compared to 172,671 black slaves and 34,050 Chinese laborers. According to the *reformistas*, the best solution was to gradually replace Chinese and black labor with salaried white workers.

Acknowledging the demands of the *reformistas*, in 1865 the Spanish government created a Comité de Información de Ultramar (Foreign Information Committee), which was to study the proposed reforms and make recommendations to the Spanish government about the labor problem in the Antilles. This committee would be made up of twenty commissioners, sixteen from Cuba and four from Puerto Rico, who would be chosen in elections supervised by the government. The committee would then study the content of the "special laws" that were to be written in order to transform the Cuban and Puerto Rican political systems.

After a campaign that created great political agitation in Cuba and Puerto Rico, these elections took place in March 1866. Only plantation owners, industrialists, traders, and professionals were allowed to vote, and therefore the majority of the commissioners elected belonged to the *reformista* movement.

The Abolitionist Movement

Meanwhile, the Spanish Cortes passed a "law for the punishment and suppression of the slave trade" on July 9, 1866. This law was an important victory for the Spanish Abolitionist Society, which had mobilized public opinion in Madrid during the Cortes debates. The society had been founded in 1865 by Julio Vizcarrondo, a Puerto Rican who had arrived in Madrid in 1863 and had successfully obtained the support of the large liberal constituency in Spain.

When the Foreign Information Committee met in Madrid at the end of October 1866, the Puerto Rican delegates surprised everyone by declaring that the moment to abolish slavery in Puerto Rico had come and presenting a "Proposal for the Abolition of Slavery in Puerto Rico." This proposal insisted that emancipation be "immediate, radical, and definitive" and that the planters be compensated. Even without compensation for the slave owners, the Puerto Rican delegates said this act of justice should not be postponed.

The Puerto Rican proposal divided the Antillean commissioners. It stipulated that the compensation to the planters for the 41,000 slaves in Puerto Rico was to be financed by a government loan of almost 12 million pesos. The Cubans accepted the idea of financial compensation and calculated theirs to be almost 118 million pesos, but proposed a process of gradual abolition over the course of several years. According to the Cuban commissioners, incremental emancipation would begin with the liberation of the children and anyone born on the plantations, then continue with those who were not registered in the plantation books, and conclude with the rest of the slave population. The Cuban delegates also insisted on the need for political and economic reform, as well as lower tariffs and other taxes.

When the meetings of the Foreign Information Committee concluded at the end of April 1867, the *reformistas* assumed that their demands would be accepted. But the Spanish government, now dominated by conservatives, paid no attention to their recommendations. On the contrary, the government established new taxes that further burdened the sugar and coffee plantations. The reformers protested, causing the colonial authorities to unleash a wave of repression against all demonstrations advocating political reforms or the abolition of slavery. Many people were convinced that Cuba and Puerto Rico had only one way out: rebellion.

Rebellion for Independence

Spain's defeat in Santo Domingo had a profound psychological and political impact on Cuba and Puerto Rico. The fact that poorly trained and inadequately armed peasants could defeat the Spanish army gave Cubans and Puerto Ricans confidence to conspire once again and plan for a rebellion. The proindependence Cubans exiled in New York encouraged them, Masonic lodges supplied resources, and the free blacks, cognizant of the discussions of the Foreign Information Committee, reactivated their communication network with the slaves and began to prepare for war.

In Bayamo, in the east of Cuba, a revolutionary junta was formed in 1867. From that summer on, a subversive campaign began to develop in Cuba and Puerto Rico. In February 1868 another revolutionary junta was formed in the town of Lares, in Puerto Rico, where fighting erupted eight months later, on September 23.

In Lares, more than 600 armed revolutionaries arrested the local authorities and the town's Spanish merchants and proclaimed the independence of the Republic of Puerto Rico. The Spanish authorities mobilized quickly and within a few days put an end to the movement by jailing 551 people. Two weeks later, Spanish authorities tried to arrest the Cuban revolutionaries, but the rebels were warned in time and were able to flee.

On October 10, 1868, a group of Cubans rose up in arms on the sugar plantation of La Damajagua, in Yara, and published a manifesto proclaiming the creation of the Republic of Cuba, in which they objected to the tyranny of the Spanish government, the lack of freedom, the onerous taxes, the lack of political representation, and the obstacles that prevented Cubans from holding public positions. The manifesto also referred to the need to gradually abolish slavery and adequately compensate the owners. The leaders of this movement incorporated almost all the points of the reformers' 1866 proposal into their platform, despite the fact that the most prominent reformers opposed independence.

These events coincided with a liberal revolution in Spain, which overthrew the conservative regime and forced the queen into exile in France on September 16, 1868. The Cuban, Puerto Rican, and Spanish movements also shared a common element almost simultaneously: their leaders were liberal abolitionists. When it came to facing another colonial rebellion in Cuba, however, the Spanish liberals again resorted to military force. They were not ready to suffer another defeat in the Antilles or lose their colonial income.

The Ten Years War

The first war for Cuban independence lasted ten years.[4] In order to defeat the rebels, Spain used every resource available. The Spanish government recruited tens of thousands of men in Spain, mobilized its navy, bought modern armaments, and sent its best officers to the Caribbean. The revolutionaries, aided by the Cuban Junta in the United States, also received shipments of arms, munitions, and other military equipment. The revolutionary leaders—Máximo Gómez, Antonio Maceo, Ignacio Agramonte, and Calixto García—knew how to compensate for their insufficient weaponry and organized the struggle as a guerrilla war, following the example of the war in Santo Domingo, Gómez's homeland.

The revolutionaries elected Carlos Manuel de Céspedes, the owner of La Damajagua sugar plantation, as their supreme leader. He liberated his slaves on October 10, 1868, and used them as soldiers. Céspedes, however, opposed the immediate abolition of slavery as proposed by the mulatto leader Antonio Maceo and his black followers. Céspedes also resisted using runaway slaves in his revolutionary army. He did not want slaves to abandon the plantations to join the revolution unless their owners had granted them permission to leave.

When the revolutionaries met in Guáimaro in April 1869 to write the Republic of Cuba's first constitution, the abolitionist delegates proposed an article declaring that all inhabitants of Cuba were free. The planters and other conservative members of the rebel movement opposed such an article. Three weeks later the conservatives promulgated the Reglamento de Libertos (Freedmen Bylaws), which required emancipated slaves to continue working for their masters without salary or other compensation. The failure of Céspedes and his rich allies to stand up for the emancipated slaves limited the revolutionary army's recruiting capability and created intense resentment among the freeborn blacks and emancipated slaves who wanted to fight for independence.

The revolutionaries managed to control the eastern half of Cuba, but they did not succeed in penetrating the sugarcane heartland in the western part of the island. The Spanish army built a long fortified trench and established a line of defense between Júcaro and Morón, the narrowest part of the center of the island. This line separated the two antagonistic groups. On the eastern side, where the sugar industry was less developed, small landholdings prevailed, and there were many free black peasants. On the western side, where sugar plantations dominated the economy, slaves formed the majority of the rural population. Pinar del Río, also located in the west, had a large concentration of tobacco plantations worked by free peasants who used little slave labor. The people of Pinar del Río did not become involved in the war.

Apprenticeship under the Moret Law

The war in Cuba rekindled the abolitionist movement in Spain, where a number of leaders of the liberal government understood that some reforms, including the abolition of slavery, were necessary to resolve the colonial problem. The Spanish Abolitionist Society approached the Cortes at the beginning of the legislative session in February 1869 and urged members to pass a law that would at least grant freedom to children born to slaves after September 16, 1868, the date the Spanish liberal revolution began. The new liberal government decreed such a law—called the *ley de vientre libre* (law of the free womb—at the end of that month, but it was not enforced. In September 1869 the minister of foreign affairs created another commission to study the possibility of reform in the colonies, but the best its members could do was to reach a consensus that the abolition of slavery should be gradual.

Meanwhile, the U.S. government, under President Ulysses Grant, alarmed Spain by signing an annexation treaty with the Dominican Republic in November 1869. This step encouraged the struggle for independence in Cuba and Puerto Rico, and the Spanish feared that an American intervention in Cuba would follow. Furthermore, the American press and abolitionist groups in the United States sympathized with the Cuban rebels. In addition, the Cuban rebel leader, Carlos Manuel de Céspedes, was known to have openly favored the annexation of Cuba by the United States.

The Spanish foreign minister, Segismundo Moret, thought that if Spain did not make concessions with respect to slavery, the United States would use slavery as a pretext for a military intervention in Cuba. By then the United States had already abolished slavery after a bloody civil war, and its abolitionist activists, together with the annexationists, were paying close attention to the Cuban situation. After months of discussion, on May 28, 1870, Moret presented to the Cortes a bill for a "Preparatory Law for the Abolition of Slavery in the Spanish Antilles." With this law, the foreign minister sought to pacify the Antillean and Spanish abolitionists and ease the pressure exerted by abolitionists in the United States and Great Britain. Approved by the Spanish Cortes on July 4, 1870, after an intense debate, the "Moret Law" granted freedom to all slaves born after September 17, 1868; to those over the age of sixty; to those who aided Spanish troops during the war; to those belonging to the state; and to the so-called emancipated slaves. These were smuggled slaves who had been confiscated by the government and whom the Cuban authorities had illegally transferred to well-connected planters.

The Moret Law established that children would remain as apprentices, sponsored by their former masters or their mothers. The masters were obligated to support, dress, and educate them until they reached adulthood. In exchange, the freed youths were required to work for their masters without pay until they were eighteen years old. Then they were to receive half salary, depending on the type of work performed, until they were twenty-two years old, at which point they would be freed. Married apprentices were to be freed if they were over fourteen years old. Free parents were able to buy their children's freedom, and masters were forbidden to sell mothers and their children who were under fourteen years of age, nor could they separate slave couples united in marriage.

The Moret Law granted freedom to all slaves who were not registered in the general population census of Puerto Rico of December 31, 1869, as well as to those who were not registered in the census to be taken in Cuba on December 31, 1870. If the masters abused their apprentices and did not feed, dress, shelter, or educate them, the apprentices could appeal to the authorities. If the apprentices left their former masters' patronage, however, the masters had no obligations to them, and they had no right to claim protection. The law also prohibited punishment by whipping or beating in Puerto Rico and Cuba.

To supervise the application of the law, the Juntas for the Protection of Freedmen were created, but their function was obstructed by the Cuban planters, who prevented the publication of the Moret Law in Cuba until November 1870. The law did not begin to be executed fully until the publication of the regulations in 1872, after the Spanish Abolitionist Society and the governments of Great Britain and the United States had stepped up their pressure on the Spanish government.

The Moret Law did not deter the Puerto Rican delegates to the Cortes, who continued their campaign for the immediate abolition of slavery with compensation for the slave owners. Slavery in Puerto Rico had been quickly crumbling, as many owners had freed their slaves when they discovered that salaried workers were cheaper because they did not have to feed or support them. The number of slaves in Puerto Rico declined from 41,000 in 1869 to 31,041 in December 1872. For this latter number of slaves, the total compensation to be paid to the owners would be about thirty-five million pesetas, an amount that could be financed, if a guaranteed loan were granted, with income from the island's treasury. With this argument, the Puerto Rican delegates finally convinced the Cortes to approve the "Law for the Abolition of Slavery in Puerto Rico," liberating the last 29,335 slaves on the island on March 22, 1873.

In approving this law, the Cortes imposed two conditions: compensation to the slave owners was to occur within six months, and freedmen were to enter into contractual agreements with their former masters, the colonial government, or other property owners for a period of at least three years. If the freedmen did not do so, the local authorities would be allowed to punish them by forcing them into public service. "Commissions of protectors of freedmen" created by the government would supervise the contracts. In the months following emancipation, the majority of the freedmen entered into contracts with their former owners. Of 29,335 freed slaves, 27,038 were working under contract by the end of August 1873.

The abolition of slavery in Puerto Rico provoked a huge scandal and brought about widespread protest among the Cuban planters. After five years of war, the Cuban slavery system was also eroding. The Moret Law was not rigorously enforced due to the planters' resistance, but not all the Juntas for the Protection of Freedmen gave in to such maneuvering. Many Juntas managed to defend the emancipation of children, the elderly, and the previously emancipated, as well as those who claimed their freedom after escaping mistreatment by their masters.

Less than one year after the full promulgation of the Moret Law, the reduction of the slave population was notable. The number of slaves registered in Cuba declined from 363,288 in 1867 to 287,620 in 1871. This reduction was due mainly to the emancipation of children and the elderly, since the plantations managed to retain the majority of the adult population of working age. For the first time in the nineteenth century, Cuba's slave population was beginning to decline.

Sugar Production during the Ten Years War

Despite the war and the Moret Law, Cuba continued to produce more sugar every year, to the benefit of Spain and the United States. In 1867 Cuba produced 585,814 tons of sugar, and in the first seven years of the war (1868–1875), Cuba increased its annual sugar production by almost 200,000 tons, while prices also went up. This sugar bonanza turned many planters into stubborn opponents of the abolition of slavery. In October 1869 the nationalist revolutionary leaders convinced

Céspedes to order the destruction of all the plantations on the island, with the aim of bankrupting the Spanish. The war then acquired a marked economic character, because many revolutionary officers freed the slaves who were fighting in the ranks of the Republican army. Even so, the rebels were unable to win the war.

Internal quarrels within the nationalists' camp led to the overthrow of President Céspedes in October 1873. Together with the destruction of the plantations, this caused the independence movement to lose the support of the expatriate Cubans in the United States. As a result, the United States retreated from its former recognition of the Cuban Republic. Resources became scarce, and the rebel offensive came to a halt. To bring an end to the stagnation of the war, Máximo Gómez and Antonio Maceo planned an invasion of the western part of the island that would obliterate the Spanish plantations, thereby increasing the cost of the war so much that Spain would be forced to negotiate a peace.

The conservative faction of the rebel movement, however, was against extending the war to the west, and this opposition proved fatal for the insurgents. By having to operate in a limited territory that was rapidly becoming impoverished, and without recognition by the United States, the revolutionaries began to argue among themselves. Gómez and Maceo were finally authorized to carry out their scorched-earth operations in the west, but by then it was too late.

Divided and weakened, the revolutionaries were unable to resist the offensives launched by the new commander of the Spanish troops, General Arsenio Martínez Campos, in the spring of 1877. Martínez Campos invaded the eastern part of Cuba with 25,000 fresh troops and fought the rebels in their own territory. Before the end of the year, Spain had won the war, and the Republican leaders had to negotiate peace through the Zanjón Pact on February 11, 1878.

The Zanjón Pact granted freedom to all slaves and Chinese laborers who had fought as soldiers on either side. Although the Spanish government declared general political amnesty, the Zanjón Pact did not bring immediate peace. Antonio Maceo rejected the arrangement and continued to fight, arguing that the pact did not include the independence of Cuba or the complete abolition of slavery. Maceo had to end his fight and leave the island several months later. The following year, in the summer of 1879, several proindependence factions began what is known in

Cuba as the Guerra Chiquita ("the small war"), which lasted just over a year. They were defeated, too, in October 1880.

The Ten Years War left the eastern part of the island in ruins. Of the 100 sugar plantations in Santiago de Cuba in 1868, only 39 remained in operation in 1878. In Puerto Príncipe, the location of the majority of the guerrilla operations, hundreds of sugar plantations were devastated, and by 1878 only one sugar plantation remained there. The eastern region also suffered the destruction of 75 percent of its coffee plantations, 60 percent of its tobacco farms, 64 percent of its cattle ranches, and half of its other agricultural enterprises. The western area, on the other hand, remained intact, with 1,191 sugar plantations functioning to full capacity and producing an average of over 630,000 tons of sugar annually in the six years after the war (1878–1884).

Patronato and the End of Slavery

By emancipating children and the elderly, the Moret Law ended of the growth of the slave population in sugar-producing areas. The law was responsible for the emancipation of 50,046 slaves between 1870 and 1875. When the Zanjón Pact was signed in February 1878, there were only 199,094 slaves in Cuba, compared to 287,620 in 1871.

The reduction of the slave population during the war was more pronounced in the east than in the west. In the east, it was reduced by 85 percent in Puerto Príncipe between 1867 and 1877 and by 74 percent in Santiago de Cuba. In the west, it was reduced by 52 percent in the region of Havana, by 37 percent in Pinar del Río, by 28 percent in Matanzas, and by 42 percent in Santa Clara.

Despite the decrease in the slave population, the sugar areas managed to increase their production thanks to the modernization of the mills and the new procedures for the procurement of manual labor. The planters learned to replace slave labor with a variety of workers: Chinese laborers, free blacks and mulattoes, white Creoles, indentured workers, and immigrants from the Canary Islands. Even though Chinese immigration was legally prohibited in 1874, there were still 47,116 Chinese laborers working in the sugar industry in 1877. At the end of the war, many plantations used up to 40 percent salaried workers. Although the planters still preferred to work with slaves, they had to learn to combine them with salaried labor.

Abolition was only a matter of time. The main concern was the compensation to be paid to the slave owners, a topic that dominated the new debates in the Spanish Cortes after November 1879. The Cuban representatives to the Cortes had been elected in August of that year in the first free elections since 1837. With the proindependence movement defeated and dispersed, Cuban politics was controlled by the *reformistas* and the conservatives, organized into two parties allied with major Spanish political factions. These parties negotiated an intermediate solution based on the gradual abolition of slavery. This would create a patronage system in Cuba similar to the patronage system of Puerto Rico and the apprenticeship system imposed in the British West Indies in 1834.

This system was instituted by the Ley de Patronato (Patronage Law), which replaced the Moret Law on February 13, 1880. Consequently, the Cuban ex-slaves were to be apprentices (*patrocinados*) serving their former owners for eight years in exchange for a monthly stipend, food, clothes, shelter, and medical care. The stipend was between one and two pesos for apprentices between eighteen and twenty-two years of age and three pesos for those who were older. During the patronage period, the *patrocinados* were to be allowed to purchase their freedom at market value.

The Patronage Law established a schedule of gradual emancipation after 1885 for four age groups. The law envisioned that by 1888, there would be no more slaves. At the end of the patronage period, however, all freedmen were obligated to contract themselves for four years in a known trade. Those who did not contract themselves would be considered vagrants and forced to work in public service. At the end of their contracts, the freedmen would enjoy full political rights.

With the Patronage Law, the Spanish government and the Cuban planters tried to establish a transition mechanism to assure the continuity of slave labor for a minimum of five years and a maximum of twelve. In order to supervise the application of the law, the government created local, municipal, and provincial Patronage Committees. As with the Moret Law, the membership of these committees determined their function. If the planters were in the majority, decisions were generally in favor of the patrons; the reverse was true if abolitionists were in charge.

As in Puerto Rico, the majority of the freedmen in Cuba entered into contracts with their former owners. However, the patronage system in Cuba sped up the process of emancipation. Between 1880 and 1886, the slavery system in Cuba fell apart. During the first year of the patronage system, more than 6,000 apprentices acquired their freedom in various ways. During the second year, another 10,000 were emancipated, and during the third year, 17,000 were freed.

In order to minimize expenses and ensure their contracts, many patrons negotiated mutual agreements with their apprentices through the Patronage Committees, granting early emancipation to 32,102 apprentices. Another 18,826 apprentices acquired their freedom by simply renouncing the association with their owners who could not or did not want to support them. An additional 13,003 apprentices bought their freedom, while 7,423 were emancipated by the Patronage Committees as a punishment to patrons who had violated some provision of the law. An additional 14,224 apprentices were emancipated for unspecified reasons.

In 1885 the first 25,309 apprentices selected to comply with the schedule of gradual abolition were granted their freedom. By May 1886, 113,887 more had obtained their liberty, and almost all had become contracted workers. As a result of this accelerated process of emancipation, the apprentice population diminished rapidly, from 199,094 in 1877 to 53,381 in 1885.

In May 1886 there were only 25,381 apprentices left in Cuba. With these figures in view, in July 1886 the Spanish Cortes agreed to abolish the patronage system. After consulting with the Cuban planters about the mechanism by which salaries should be regulated, the Spanish government officially ended the patronage system on October 7, 1886. From then on, Cuba, like the other Antilles, would have to produce all of its sugar without slaves.

CHAPTER 17

Centrales and *Colonos*

Beet Sugar Competition

The abolition of slavery in the Spanish Antilles coincided with the greatest technological change in the history of the plantation system, namely the replacement of sugar mills based on the Jamaican train by steam-powered, highly mechanized central mills, called *centrales*. This transformation occurred at the same time that beet sugar was taking over the European market. The massive impact of beet sugar on the world market forever changed the course of the sugar industry in the Antilles.

For centuries, sugarcane had been the main source of sucrose, but during the nineteenth century, a new method for extracting sugar from beets was developed in Europe. From the time of the first experiments carried out in Austria in 1799, beet sugar was a protected industry. The strategic importance of beet sugar became evident during the British naval blockade of continental ports in 1806 which disrupted the sugar trade.

After that time, the governments of Russia, France, Germany, Austria, and Holland supported the construction of numerous beet sugar manufacturing plants. Initially, these plants could barely supply the local market, but production increased rapidly after the construction of new ones with modern steam engines. In 1826 France produced over 24,000 tons of beet sugar in more than 100 plants. By 1833 the amount had increased to 40,000 tons and the number of factories to 400. In 1837 French beet sugar production stood at 37,000 tons, while the country imported 45,000 tons of sugar.

Cane sugar continued to dominate the world market, but in 1840 it was surpassed by beet sugar in the French and German markets due to an effective policy of subsidies and incentives to the producers. Russia, Austria, and Hungary also had a significant beet sugar industry. By 1850 European beet sugar production had increased to 159,000 tons, 16 percent of the world's sugar production. European leaders quickly realized that the beet industry represented a lucrative market in the agricultural sector. Beet sugar reduced their dependency on imported sugar and, in the case of France and Germany, increased their exports. In addition to creating year-round employment, the cultivation of beets also contributed to the raising of livestock, as their leaves and molasses were used to feed cattle.

Increased productivity in the beet sugar plants, stimulated by official subsidies, led to lower production costs and, consequently, to a drop in the price of sugar. As a result, the consumption of sugar rose quickly, stimulating a whirlwind growth in production. World sugar production increased from 1.0 million tons in 1850 to 5.7 million tons in 1890 as the proportion of the world's sugar coming from beets grew from under 25 percent to 60 percent.

Never before had people consumed so much sugar. Per capita sugar consumption increased throughout the world, particularly in industrialized countries. In the United States, per capita consumption increased from thirteen pounds in 1839 to thirty-six pounds in 1879. In Great Britain, the increase was even more noticeable, rising from seventeen pounds in 1844 to eighty-four pounds in 1890. A rise in per capita income in industrialized countries led to increased consumption of tea and coffee, as well as many products containing sugar, such as chocolate, ice cream, marmalade, jelly, canned fruit, and pastries. The increase in demand led to the sudden establishment of new sugarcane plantations in several parts of the world, but by 1881 beet sugar dominated the market.

Beet sugar competition with cane sugar had important consequences for the Caribbean economies. It forced the planters to adopt the steam engine and to modernize their sugar mills. At first, these innovations spread slowly, but the installation of the first central mills in Martinique and Guadeloupe between 1843 and 1848 started an economic and technological revolution that spread throughout the rest of the region.

Central Factories in the French Antilles

The construction of central mills in the French Antilles was encouraged in 1851 by the creation of the Colonial Bank with funds contributed by the French government to pay for the abolition of slavery. This bank facilitated short-term loans for working capital. With these new financial resources, many planters were able to survive the economic crisis caused by abolition. Some acquired equipment and machinery to modernize their sugar mills, while others used their loans to import laborers from Asia.

These loans alone were insufficient to support the creation of new mills; therefore the main French banks agreed to form the Société de Crédit Colonial (Society for Colonial Credit) in 1860 to provide long-term credit to planters and investors interested in installing central mills. The society appropriated twelve million francs, to be loaned at an interest rate fluctuating between 8 and 10 percent for terms of twenty to thirty years. This credit society was renamed Crédit Foncier Colonial (Colonial Land Bank) in 1863.

With this infusion of capital, the planters of Guadeloupe financed the construction of twenty-three central mills between 1861 and 1869. These new mills were larger and more modern than the first industrial plants that had been installed almost twenty years earlier. The new plants were completely mechanized and equipped with modern evaporators, centrifugal machinery, and crystallizers from the French firm MM. Derosne et Cail, and they produced a lighter grade of granulated and dry sugar than the traditional sugar mills. Cane sugar from the plantations was now competitive with beet sugar, which had previously been preferred by the European refiners. These new plants were capable of producing up to 2,000 tons of sugar per year.

Due to the permanent scarcity of capital in Guadeloupe, the planters of the colony were particularly dependent on loans from the Crédit Foncier Colonial. As a result, new enterprises began their operations with large debts, which immediately affected their financial performance. When sugar prices began to decrease in France after 1860, the mill owners in Guadeloupe could not honor their commitments to the Crédit Foncier Colonial, and their mortgages began to be foreclosed, along with those of the cane farmers.

In Martinique, the planters and traders enjoyed a much more solid financial position and were capable of financing the installation of new central mills with local capital. Only one of the new mills built in Martinique in this period required loans from the Crédit Foncier Colonial. The new central mills of Martinique were built between 1868 and 1872. During these four years, the planters and traders of Martinique built seventeen central mills, which produced an average of 1,500 tons of sugar annually. As in Guadeloupe, the new mills of Martinique were installed in areas equidistant from several plantations. The owners of these plantations signed contracts pledging to supply sugarcane for the new plants and to close their traditional mills.

The impact of these new factories was similar in both colonies. Of the 498 traditional sugar mills that existed in Martinique in 1847, only 200 remained in 1880. In the latter year, the sixteen central mills of the island produced 23,000 tons of sugar, while the 200 traditional sugar mills combined to produce only 19,000 tons. Of the 490 traditional sugar mills in Guadeloupe in 1847, only 188 were left in 1882. The following year, the twenty-three central mills in Guadeloupe produced 41,782 tons, while the traditional ones produced only 11,820 tons.

Many planters who did not want to become cane farmers for the central mills partially modernized their traditional sugar mills with steam-powered machinery. Some had limited success operating medium-sized, semi-mechanized mills, called *bourbonières,* because of their similarity to those of Ile de Bourbon (Reunion Island) in the Indian Ocean. Nevertheless, with an average annual production of 242 tons, these mills were too small to operate on an economy of scale and thus could not compete with the central factories. When prices in France decreased by 40 percent between 1860 and 1863, due to the abundance of beet sugar, the *bourbonières* became insolvent and were liquidated by their owners. Of the twenty-five *bourbonières* in Guadeloupe in 1869, only two were functioning in 1880.

The older sugar mills on the French islands disappeared even faster after the great trade crisis of 1884, which resulted from the global overproduction of sugar. France's beet sugar production had increased to 535,800 tons by 1883, while its consumption of sugar was only 442,200 tons. If one adds the French colonial sugar produced that year, the surplus exceeded 154,000 tons. Consequently, French sugar prices dropped from eighty-three francs per ton in 1883 to twenty-five francs per ton in 1886.

This crisis reduced the colonial producers' incomes by more than half. Initially, the Guadeloupe planters tried to refinance their debts with new loans from the Crédit Foncier Colonial, which in 1885 created a special fund of two million francs to support the sugar industry. With prices continuing to decrease during the following years, however, the majority of the planters were ruined, and the Crédit Foncier Colonial foreclosed on their mortgages. By 1888 this bank owned six central mills and forty-six traditional sugar mills in Guadeloupe, Basse-Terre, and Marie-Galante, having also acquired numerous plantations.

Many of these assets were passed on at very low prices to traders and European investors, who consolidated the land into larger sugar plantations to supply their central mills. In Marie-Galante, for example, the two mills expropriated by the Crédit Foncier Colonial ended up controlling one-quarter of the island's arable land and all of the sugar production facilities. The few traditional sugar mills in Marie-Galante that survived at the end of the century were small, isolated units that had abandoned the production of granulated sugar and now specialized in manufacturing molasses and rum.

In Martinique, the local planters were less in debt and continued to control their mills; however, the liquidation of the traditional sugar mills continued. By the end of the century, the sugar industry in the French colonies consisted of a small number of central mills, with large tracts of land cultivated by contracted foreign workers and the descendants of slaves. Meanwhile, in the mountainous areas, a peasant society was developing, also made up of the descendants of slaves. Similar developments in the sugar industry took place throughout the rest of the Caribbean, with local variations.

In the British West Indies, the utility of building central mills to replace slaves after abolition was discussed early on, but only in Trinidad and St. Lucia were the planters able to gather sufficient capital to install one on each island. A company that owned sugar mills in Guiana constructed Trinidad's central mill in 1873. St. Lucia's was built by a French investor from Martinique with the support of British entrepreneurs. Both mills faced many difficulties in receiving sugarcane from local cane farmers and therefore needed to acquire their own plantations.

Mechanization of Mills in the British West Indies

The sugar industry of the British Antilles was only partially mechanized, and mechanization occurred at a very slow pace. The number of steam-powered sugar mills in Barbados, for instance, increased from 32 in 1862 to 90 in 1897; however, there were still 410 sugar mills utilizing wind or animal power. In 1894 Antigua had 74 sugar mills, 54 of which were powered by steam. In Montserrat, even as late as 1884, there were still no steam-powered mills. Partial mechanization of the mills proved ruinous for those whose sugar could compete neither in quality nor in price with beet sugar. When the less efficient planters disappeared, their lands were taken over by other producers. This caused an intense concentration of property into large landholdings consisting of several plantations owned by the same company.

During this period, the general tendency in the British West Indies was toward a decrease in the number of sugar mills. Land was consolidated even without installing central mills. Many semimechanized mills, such as those in British Guiana, increased in size and produced large quantities of sugar. They utilized hundreds of workers, and many were as big as the French central mills. As a result, in some areas, British sugar production continued to increase.

In Guiana, the concentration of land was significant. There were 404 sugar mills there in 1838. By 1870, however, there were only 128 sugar mills, decreasing further to 64 in 1897 and to 50 in 1900. Because sugar production in Guiana increased from 48,000 tons in 1838 to 95,000 tons in 1900, it is clear that the new mills were much larger and more productive than the previous ones.

A similar reduction occurred in Trinidad, where the number of mills decreased from 110 in 1856 to only 56 in 1897. On this island, sugarcane was concentrated on drier land in the west, between Port of Spain and San Fernando, while numerous peasant families transformed the lush lands of the east into extensive cacao and coconut plantations. The only central mill in Trinidad, St. Madeleine, continued to accumulate land, controlling approximately 4,000 acres by the turn of the century.

On the other British West Indian islands, traditional sugar plantations were also disappearing. Of the 2,200 sugar plantations in these islands in 1838, only 800 remained by 1900. In Grenada, for instance, where there had been 119 sugar plantations in 1838, none were left in 1900, and sugar for local consumption had to be imported. In Antigua, the number of sugar plantations decreased from 127 in 1841 to 107 in 1865 and 53 in 1900. In St. Kitts, the sugar mills were reduced from 137 in 1856 to 54 in 1901. In the Leeward Islands, many planters simply abandoned sugarcane cultivation, and their lands were transferred to more efficient producers.

In Jamaica, sugar planters also moved toward the drier, more productive land in the west, and many of the former plantations in the southeast became cattle ranches. In 1838 Jamaica boasted 600 sugar plantations. By 1865 almost half had been converted into cattle ranches, because their owners had been unable to recruit sufficient manual labor to run the plantations. In 1875 the number of sugar plantations had decreased to 244. By 1890 there were only 162 left, including 100 using steam engines and 19 powered by steam and water. Only 5 of the sugar plantations in Jamaica had installed vacuum vat pans by 1890; however, 73 were already using centrifugal machinery to produce a drier and more granular sugar. In that year, 64 sugar plantations continued to produce sugar with the Jamaican train technology.

Even this incomplete mechanization permitted a remarkable increase in productivity. From an annual average of 56 tons in 1852, sugar production per plantation in Jamaica increased to 104 tons in 1869 and 149 tons in 1890. Still, if this performance is compared with that of Cuban and French Antillean sugar plantations during the same period, the conclusion is clear: the sugar industry of Jamaica was, like that of Barbados, one of the least advanced in the region. The Jamaican sugar industry lagged even farther behind after the crisis of 1884, when some plantation owners who had acquired modern machinery abandoned the business and sold their machines to Cuban producers. In 1890 Jamaica was still producing the same quantity of sugar it had been in 1853, around 24,000 tons. The land area dedicated to cane cultivation declined from 48,246 acres in 1875 to 30,971 acres in 1895.

As Jamaican peasants acquired their own land, coffee became the primary export product. Subsequently, bananas became increasingly important as the wetter lands were converted to the cultivation of this crop in order to supply the growing market for bananas in the United States after 1869. By the end of the century, bananas competed with dyewood and rum as the third most important export. The new peasant farmers also produced ginger, cacao, pepper, and oranges for export. The number of peasant landholdings continued to increase rapidly. In 1895 there were 95,942 peasant parcels of less than five acres and 16,015 parcels between five and forty-nine acres. This indicates the degree of property division in Jamaica during the second half of the nineteenth century.

The increasing acquisition of land among the peasant population during the last thirty years of the nineteenth century was a common phenomenon in the West Indies, with the exception of Barbados.

In Barbados, peasant farms were minimal, and sugar plantations continued to be the norm. Of the 500 sugar plantations on the island in 1838, there were still 440 in 1897. In other colonies, such as Guiana and Trinidad, sugar was a speculative business controlled by anonymous companies. In Barbados, however, only 19 of the 440 sugar plantations belonged to commercial companies. Individuals, rather than corporate entities, owned the remaining 421 plantations. The sugar business in Barbados had always been in the hands of families who managed their plantations in a pure patriarchal fashion, holding on to the family land for generations and refusing to sell or to yield land to the freedmen. Unlike in the other British colonies where absenteeism was the norm, two-thirds of Barbadian planters resided on the island.

Sugar *Centrales* in Puerto Rico

In the Spanish Antilles, the abolition of slavery also stimulated the formation of large *centrales*. Shortages of manual labor and competition from beet sugar likewise contributed to the transition. The first central mill in Puerto Rico was installed in 1873, the same year that the slaves there were emancipated. This mill, Central San Vicente, built in Vega Baja in the north of the island, utilized the same technology as the French central mills, namely machinery and equipment manufactured by MM. Derosne et Cail. Some planters had partially mechanized their sugar mills in previous years, also utilizing machines built by that company.

The abolition crisis also led Puerto Rican planters to realize that only by modernizing their operations could they compete with beet sugar. Therefore, they requested and obtained permission to partner with French entrepreneurs to finance the conversion of their plants. The colonial government had previously ignored their requests, but once slavery was abolished, the members of the agricultural societies of Mayagüez, Ponce, and Guayama bought new steam mills, clarifiers, vacuum evaporators, crystallizers, and centrifugal machinery to modernize their sugar mills.

Between 1873 and 1876, Puerto Rican and French plantation owners installed six central sugar mills on the previously unexploited eastern and northern plains of the island. These mills were built according to the French model and were similar in size to the central mills of Guadeloupe. Most were capable of producing up to 2,000 tons of sugar per year, although some of the larger ones, such as Central San Vicente, were able to produce up to 4,500 tons if supplied with sufficient cane. Like their counterparts in the French Antilles, the Puerto Rican mill owners did not hesitate to go into debt to acquire as much land as possible by buying up neighboring plantations.

Within a few years, many planters who did not sell their properties to the *centrales* stopped producing sugar in their traditional mills and became *colonos*, that is, farmers who sold their cane to the *centrales*. Others turned their land into cattle ranches. Because of these rapid changes, which occurred during the abolition crisis, sugar production fluctuated greatly between 1870 and 1883, from as much as 105,000 tons in 1870 to as little as 57,000 tons in 1880, averaging 79,000 tons annually.

Foreign capital played a decisive role in the construction of Puerto Rican *centrales*. As very few individual planters could finance the modernization of their sugar mills on their own, they had to obtain fresh credit in France, England, and the United States. The manufacturers of sugar-processing machinery in Paris, Glasgow, and New York supplied some of this capital. Other credit came from local and foreign traders and sugar merchants. During this process, numerous companies were formed to finance the operations with complex credit plans. When these plans failed due to insufficient cane supply, the new *centrales* were sold to or liquidated by the foreign investors.

A good example of this phenomenon was Central Canóvanas,

created by the firm Latimer and Company of San Juan in 1879 through the merger of two sugar mills acquired in 1855. When this enterprise was unable to produce enough sugarcane, it began to incur enormous losses, and its owners were forced to sell it to the Colonial Company Limited of London in 1882. The new owners then created a subsidiary, the Canóvanas Sugar Factory Limited, and negotiated contracts with neighboring planters to be supplied with sugarcane. Central Canóvanas became the largest producer on the island when its production reached 5,000 tons annually.

As the expansion of the world sugar market continued, investors kept on building *centrales* in Puerto Rico, while some independent planters were still struggling to partially mechanize their plantations. In the six years following abolition in 1884, five large independent sugar plantations using Jamaican train technology mechanized their plantations with steam engines, while the central mills improved their facilities by building light railroads with wagons drawn by animal force. Between 1890 and 1897, ten new semimechanized mills were built in Puerto Rico, in addition to five new fully mechanized *centrales* capable of producing an annual average of 2,500 tons of sugar. All the investors in these projects were foreign merchants and businessmen.

In order to stimulate modernization of the sugar industry, in 1888 the colonial government of Puerto Rico contracted the French firm Crédit Mobilier to build a railroad connecting all the sugarcane districts around the island. This project was never completed, but by 1898 the main lines had been built. The longest line ran through the northern coastal plains from Arecibo to Carolina, west of San Juan. Another main line went from Mayagüez to Aguada, on the west coast, while a third crossed the sugarcane fields of Ponce, in the southwest. These railroads served eight of the eleven largest *centrales* in Puerto Rico and facilitated the transportation of cane to the mills and sugar to the ports.

The construction of *centrales* led to the dismantling of Jamaican train–based sugar mills in Puerto Rico and a rapid process of land consolidation. The abolition of slavery also profoundly affected the Puerto Rican sugar economy and caused production to decline from 98,000 tons in 1884 to 35,000 tons in 1899. The sugar industry suffered a shortage of manual labor because many freedmen and workers abandoned the sugarcane plantations and moved to the mountains, where they cultivated coffee for export.

The Coffee Alternative in Puerto Rico

Coffee was the preferred commercial crop among Puerto Rican peasants. After the colonial government granted the incentives of the Cédula de Gracias in 1815, coffee production increased dramatically. In the early nineteenth century, coffee dominated the economy of western Puerto Rico, and exports increased from 46,000 tons in 1817 to 130,000 tons in 1827. The towns of Yauco, Lares, Utuado, San Germán, and Añasco became important coffee cultivation centers. Immigrants from Cataluña, Mallorca, and Corsica settled in these towns and became coffee producers, exporting their produce to Europe via the Virgin Islands.

After 1830 sugar production eclipsed coffee production. Nonetheless, coffee continued to be the foundation of the Puerto Rican peasant economy, despite the fact that coffee production remained stagnant until 1860 due to a shortage of capital and manual labor. In the following decade, the arrival of immigrants gradually increased coffee production, until it reached 8,708 tons in 1870. After the abolition of slavery, many freedmen went to work in the coffee areas, and exports increased to 15,263 tons in 1879.

The price of coffee in the New York market increased from eight to sixteen cents per pound between 1882 and 1890 and remained high until the turn of the century. The combination of high prices and the ready availability of manual labor attracted European immigrants to Puerto Rico, many of whom had connections with the coffee merchants who traditionally financed the purchasing of coffee beans. The colony was quite prosperous in the last two decades of the nineteenth century, and coffee brought in more money than any other export crop after 1886, relegating sugar to second place. Coffee retained this position until 1899, when falling prices coincided with a powerful hurricane that destroyed numerous estates and reduced exports to 6,078 tons in 1900. This catastrophic event coincided with the U.S. military intervention, which had important effects on the plantation system of Puerto Rico.

Sugar *Centrales* in the Dominican Republic

In the meantime, the Dominican Republic was undergoing its own sugar revolution, also based on the construction of *centrales*. The Dominican Republic, unlike other areas of the Caribbean, did not export sugar throughout most of the nineteenth century and produced only *raspadura*, or dark pan sugar, for the local market. The only export product from the *trapiche* mills[1] was rum, produced both for local consumption and for the Haitian market. Peace with Haiti brought an increase in the rum trade, and after 1860 the number of *trapiche* mills increased in the southern region of the country. By 1871 there were more than 200 mills in Azua and Baní producing *raspadura* and rum, and 40 new mills were later built in San Cristóbal, near Santo Domingo. The Dominican economy at that time depended largely on tobacco and mahogany exports, combined with subsistence farming, but rum production became quite important as the Haitian market opened even more after Haiti and the Dominican Republic signed a peace treaty in 1874.

The first War of Independence (1868-1878) in Cuba influenced the development of the Dominican economy. During this period, the Dominican government welcomed almost 5,000 Cuban exiles, including some with experience in sugar production. These immigrants were attracted by the abundance of uninhabited and cheap land. Some established ranches, while others built sugar mills following the Cuban model.

For these investors, the Dominican Republic offered the attraction of fertile lands, which produced twice as much cane per acre as land in Cuba or Louisiana. In addition, salaries were lower: in Cuba, farmworkers earned 25 pesos per month on average, while in Santo Domingo they were paid only 13 pesos per month.

The first sugar mills built by these immigrants between 1874 and 1876 were located near the city of Santo Domingo. They were steam powered, as were others built soon afterwards near the cities of Puerto Plata in the north and Azua, San Cristóbal, and San Pedro de Macorís in the south. Cubans founded the first sugar mills, although in Puerto Plata some Dominicans invested in them as well. Later, American businessmen with connections to German, Italian, and French sugar-trading companies likewise invested in new sugar mills.

To encourage the development of new plantations, in 1876 the Dominican government granted free land to anyone willing to plant sugarcane, coffee, cacao, tobacco, cotton, or other export crops. Furthermore, in May 1879 the government reduced import taxes on equipment and machinery for the new estates. To stabilize the manual labor supply, workers were exempted from military service. In October 1880 the government created several agricultural committees, which recommended another tax reduction for the new planters.

The Dominican government was clearly interested in modernizing the sugar industry with central mills. A presidential decree in 1881 stated that in order for a sugar mill to be considered a *central*, and to receive benefits from the government, it had to be supplied by at least six *colonos* and produce a minimum of 400 tons of sugar or its equivalent in molasses. If it fulfilled these requirements, a central mill could import equipment and machinery without having to pay customs duties.

By 1882 the Dominican Republic had twenty-one modern steam-powered mills, but not all were equally mechanized, and only some had railroads. Four of these mills were large, producing an average of 1,700 tons per year. Eight were mid-size, producing 900 tons annually. The rest were very small, with an average production of 10 tons per year. The twelve main plantations produced 86 percent of the country's sugar and controlled 83 percent of the land used for sugarcane in 1882.

The construction of steamed-powered sugar mills continued in the following years. By 1885 there were already thirty-five modern mills on the southeast plains between Santo Domingo and San Pedro de Macorís. In 1882, 8,838 acres of sugarcane had been planted; this number increased to 19,595 in 1885 and 28,199 ten years later. By 1897 the new sugar mills were served by 164 miles of railroad.

Sugar quickly became the main industry of the Dominican Republic. Exports increased from 1,100 tons in 1877 to 20,263 tons in 1884. The world sugar crisis of 1884 did not stop this growth, although exports stagnated at an annual average of 21,000 tons over the next seven years. Exports increased to 31,640 tons in 1892 and continued to increase in the following years. In 1893 the Dominican sugar plantations exported 38,564 tons of sugar, mostly to the United States.

The impact of this sugar revolution was significant. Because the sugar-producing areas were sparsely populated, plantation owners found it necessary to pay higher salaries, which in turn encouraged the migration of laborers to the plantations. In 1885 the sugar industry employed 5,500 Dominican workers, in addition to some 200 technicians and machinists of other nationalities. The scarcity of local manual labor led planters to contract workers from the Leeward Islands. In 1885 there were 500 laborers on the new plantations from those islands.

As had occurred in the rest of the Caribbean decades earlier, the advance of the sugarcane fields led to the clearing of forests. Along with the forests, many peasant communities also disappeared. Some Dominican authors and journalists denounced the disappearance of the peasantry in the eastern part of the country under pressure from the sugar plantations. They were alarmed by the speed with which many livestock breeders sold their animals and converted their lands into cane fields in order to supply the *centrales*.

Centrales processed the cane produced on their own plantations as well as on the colonos' land. According to regulations established in 1884, the *centrales* were required to pay their *colonos* between $2.50 and $3.00 per ton of sugarcane. In many cases, compensation was given in sugar; the *colonos* received between seventy-five and eighty pounds of sugar for each ton of high-quality sugarcane. Many independent ranchers and landowners were convinced by sugar mill owners to become *colonos*. The mill owners offered them loans at rates between 8 and 16 percent, which could be paid in sugarcane. The contracts stipulated that the *colonos* were responsible for production costs and would sell their cane exclusively to the central mill that financed their operation.

The main limitation for the Dominican sugar industry was the shortage of manual labor. Only a small number of independent farmers went to work in the *centrales*, because living conditions on the plantations were harsh and food was scarce. As in Cuba, plantation owners and the government attempted to attract peasants from the Canary Islands by offering them arable land, cash advances, temporary lodging, building materials for their homes, and farming equipment. Very few Canary Islanders, however, chose to move to the Dominican Republic, instead preferring the more popular destination of Cuba.

The displacement of peasant communities ended food production in the plantation areas and produced a dramatic increase in food prices.

Even though salaries were high, workers could barely pay for the limited foodstuffs available in the plantation stores. This problem, described for the first time in 1882, gradually worsened. In 1894 plantains were sold in the sugarcane areas at prices nine times higher than in 1879. Rice cost twice as much, salted cod two-and-a-half times as much, lard four times as much, and beef three times as much.

In the Cibao valley, in the center of the island, prices did not increase to the same degree, despite the high population density. This region of the country had no roads, and it took almost a week to make the journey from Cibao to the plantations in San Pedro de Macorís, which made the peasants and farmers of Cibao reluctant to leave their land to go to work on the sugar plantations. Many peasants from the poorest regions in the southwest of the Dominican Republic traveled by schooner to the southeast region after being contracted by agents from the *centrales*. As these workers did not resolve the shortage of manual labor, the *centrales* continued to hire laborers from the Leeward Islands, which had experienced a severe economic depression since abolition.

As on the other Caribbean islands, landholdings were widely consolidated in the Dominican Republic after the economic crisis of 1884. This crisis led to the liquidation of fourteen sugar *centrales*, which fell into the hands of their creditors. By the end of the century, nine of these sugar mills and their plantations were owned by three companies, which turned them into larger sugar estates. In 1905 only fourteen of the twenty-six that existed in 1893 remained. The land concentration process continued without interruption. In 1907, 67 percent of the land devoted to sugar production was in the hands of seven *centrales* established in San Pedro de Macorís. The *centrales* surrounding the city of Santo Domingo controlled 16 percent of all sugarcane fields in the country, compared to 15 percent belonging to the three sugar plantations in Azua.

Sugar *Centrales* in Cuba

The construction of *centrales* and the formation of large sugar estates occurred throughout the Caribbean but was most dramatic in Cuba. During the Ten Years War production decreased in eastern Cuba due to the destruction of numerous sugar plantations, but in the western part, where the plantations were barely affected by the conflict, production increased to more than 600,000 tons a year. After the war, American businessmen began to buy sugar plantations and mills in the ravaged eastern area, where only thirty-nine sugar plantations remained.

These new investors gave cash advances to planters willing to cultivate cane under contract as *colonos*. Other plantation owners obtained American loans to purchase new machinery and to convert their mills into central mills. Many went deeply into debt, because loans had annual interest rates of between 18 and 30 percent. With these financial burdens, many could not pay their loans and lost their properties when their creditors foreclosed on their mortgages. Foreclosures became so common that in the area of Cienfuegos, for example, the majority of the sugar plantations changed ownership between 1873 and 1883.

After the 1884 crisis, and coinciding with the abolition of slavery in 1886, foreclosures accelerated when the most important banks of Havana went bankrupt. Many sugar brokers who had refinanced their loans with these banks were unable to sell the sugar that they had received as payment due to the glut on the market. The warehouses in Matanzas and Havana were filled with sugar without buyers while creditors had their lawyers foreclose on mortgages affecting insolvent mills and plantations. A large portion of these assets then went to American and Spanish companies that consolidated them into gigantic *centrales*.

Many plantation owners managed to survive the crisis without losing their land, but the era of independent sugarcane plantations was over, and the new *centrales* became the norm. During the crisis, several hundred smaller plantation owners closed their mills. When it was over, prices began to rise again. The owners of the central mills obtained American loans to enlarge their plantations and facilities in order to take advantage of the expansion of the market.

Once again, the Cuban sugar economy prospered, and production increased from 632,000 tons in 1890 to 976,000 tons in 1892 and reached a record of 1,000,000 tons in 1894. By 1895 there were several *centrales* that produced between 15,000 and 20,000 tons of sugar per year. The largest of these were owned by Americans. In 1895 American investment in the Cuban sugar industry exceeded $30 million.

The substantial American investment in Cuban sugar was due in part to the beneficial effects of a reciprocal trade agreement signed between the United States and Spain in 1891. This treaty reduced customs fees on Cuban sugar, most of which was sold to the United States. However, this agreement only lasted until 1894, when the United States increased customs taxes on Cuban and Spanish products, including sugar. Spain then responded by raising customs duties on American products.

Thus began a customs duty war, which harmed the Cuban economy just when Cuba was reaching its highest production levels. Many Cubans blamed Spain for the situation and demanded the elimination of the custom taxes that made American products more expensive. The Cuban economy was so dependent on the American market that any interruption in trade between the two countries spelled ruin for merchants, *centrales*, and *colonos* alike.

The customs duty dispute was not immediately resolved. At the beginning of 1895, a second War of Independence began and lasted four years. At the end of the war, many of Cuba's sugar plantations were destroyed, its livestock annihilated, its rural population impoverished, and its countryside devastated. There were almost no mules or bulls left to transport the sugarcane, so cattle, mules, and horses had to be imported from Venezuela, Mexico, and Central America. This new crisis bankrupted a number of plantations and mills, whose owners could not cover their mortgages.

The war also caused a sudden drop in sugar production. At this time, bands of guerrilla fighters roamed throughout Cuba, making frequent incursions against the sugar plantations, whose owners organized their own defense with the support of the Spanish army. In 1896 production decreased to 225,231 tons, and in 1897 it was reduced to 212,051 tons. According to the census taken in 1899, there were only 207 functioning sugar mills out of the 1,100 that had been in existence five years earlier.[2] The number of sugar mills continued to decrease until 1901, when there were only 168 plantations left that were still capable of producing sugar.

During the war, the sugar producers continually requested either annexation to the United States or the establishment of Cuba as an American protectorate. They reasoned that if Spain would yield control of the Cuban economy, sugar would enter the United States duty-free, and Cuba would be able to import American goods without paying taxes.

When the United States finally intervened in Cuba in 1898, it did not annex the island but rather imposed a military regime, which transformed Cuba into a political protectorate that made the proclamation of the Republic of Cuba a mere symbol of the long-lasting aspirations of the *independentistas.* Meanwhile, Cuba remained a neocolonial territory of the United States and during this transition most of the ownership of the Cuban sugar industry was transferred to American corporations.

CHAPTER 18

Plantations under American Control

Cuba's War of Independence

José Martí, the instigator of Cuba's second War of Independence, attributed the failure of the Ten Years War to a lack of coordination in the Republican movement. Martí held that the revolution could not triumph unless it were executed under a single command. In 1891, during his exile in the United States, Martí organized the Cuban Revolutionary Party and subsequently worked to unite the Cuban military leaders under the command of Máximo Gómez, who had excelled in the Ten Years War. After attempting to unify the nationalist movement from abroad, in 1895 Martí and Gómez met in the Dominican Republic and organized an expedition to Cuba. Other rebel leaders also went to Cuba from different points in the Caribbean and the United States.

Though Martí died shortly after landing in Cuba, the revolutionaries continued to fight. This time they followed Máximo Gómez's idea of invading the island from east to west. The Republican army marched 1,134 miles, from one end of the island to the other, in ninety days. In July 1895 Gómez ordered the suspension of all economic activities and the destruction of all the sugar mills, plantations, ranches, and cigar factories. The rebel strategy involved making war on the economic base. The guerrilla troops systematically burned all the property they found on their way and executed anyone who resisted.

The Spanish military leaders responded likewise. In the following three years, the Spanish government sent more than 300,000 soldiers to Cuba. The Spanish commander Valeriano Weyler responded to Máximo Gomez's rallying cry, *"tierra arrasada!"* (scorched earth!), by depopulating the rural areas. To reduce the support to the guerrillas, Weyler gathered the peasants into concentration camps. While the rebels were burning sugar mills and plantations, the Spanish soldiers razed entire towns and villages, killed livestock, destroyed crops, and imprisoned women and children. More than 300,000 Cubans were forced into the concentration camps, leaving the Cuban countryside entirely uninhabited. At least 23,000 people died in captivity. Nonetheless, the revolutionaries were still able to take the interior of the island, although the Spanish remained in control of the cities.

At this point, the war became a stalemate. The conservative and annexationist groups again repeatedly requested that the United States intervene and annex Cuba. Their petitions were accepted by President William McKinley, who requested authorization from Congress to intervene militarily in Cuba and put an end to the war. In early 1898 the revolutionaries broke the stalemate and quickly advanced on the Cuban cities, taking them one by one. To prevent them from taking over, the U.S. Congress agreed to intervene, on the condition that the United States would simply bring peace to the island and then leave the government in the hands of the Cuban people. This decision was greatly influenced by pressure from the Louisiana sugar producers, the northern beet sugar producers, and the East Coast sugar refiners, all of whom were opposed to the annexation of Cuba. The American producers feared that the entrance of Cuban sugar into the United States, duty-free, would mean a collapse in prices and unfair competition to the American sugar industry.

On April 20, 1898, McKinley sent Spain an ultimatum demanding the cessation of hostilities, which Spain rejected. The United States then declared war on Spain on April 25 and immediately invaded Cuba, Puerto Rico, and the Philippines, occupying them with little difficulty. In two months Spain was defeated. Peace negotiations took place from July to December 10, 1898. Spain yielded its sovereignty over Cuba, Puerto Rico, the Philippines, and Guam to the United States in exchange for twenty million pesos. The United States pledged to respect Cuba's independence.

Cuba under American Control

The revolutionaries could not prevent the Spanish from handing over the arsenals and fortifications to the American troops on January 1, 1899. Like Puerto Rico and the Philippines, Cuba was now under the military control of the United States. The revolutionary army was dissolved, although many of its soldiers and officers were eventually employed in a rural guard organized by the American military government. With the promise from the United States of a speedy withdrawal, the Cuban politicians quickly reorganized their political parties and prepared to hold elections.

The military government favored the American investors who had come to the island to acquire the plantations, sugar mills, and railroads destroyed by the war. In 1899, for example, the Cuban American Sugar Company bought about 80,000 acres of land to build the Central Chaparra in the northeast region of Cuba. That same year other landholdings of a similar size were sold to American companies in Camagüey, Las Villas, and Matanzas. In 1901 the United Fruit Company purchased more than 200,000 acres of land in the northeast region of Cuba from different owners. Between July 1898 and May 1902, many American companies acquired enormous tracts of land, ranging from 10,000 to 180,000 acres.

The list of acquisitions is impressive. The Nipe Company, a subsidiary of United Fruit, bought 40,000 acres. The Cuba Company acquired more than 50,000 acres as part of its concession to build new railroads in the east of the island. The Cuban Central Railway purchased more than 16,000 acres; the Taco Bay Commercial Land Company of Boston, more than 20,000 acres; the Illinois Cuban Land Company, 10,000 acres; the Herradura Land Company, 23,000 acres; the Carlson Investment Company of Los Angeles, 150,000 acres; the Cuba Colonial Company, 40,000 acres; the Canada Land and Fruit Company, 23,000 acres; the Cuban Land and Steamship Company of New Jersey, 55,000 acres; the Cuba Development Company of Detroit, 12,500 acres; the Cuba Agricultural and Development Company of Pittsburgh, more than 135,000 acres; and the Cuban Realty Company of New Jersey, 25,000 acres.

By 1905 more than 13,000 American individuals and corporations had bought land in Cuba and controlled more than 60 percent of the rural property. The Spanish managed to retain 15 percent of the rural farms, while the Cuban population barely held on to 25 percent. From then on, agrarian development in Cuba was dominated by the sugar *centrales*. American investors came to control other areas of the economy as well, including tobacco, mining, railroads, and power production. The opening of the economy to foreign capital also allowed some English, German, and French investors to acquire property in Cuba. Spanish capital, which had once dominated the economy, now barely controlled the banking sector.

Although independent from Spain, Cuba had essentially become a colony of the United States. Before handing over the government to the Cubans, the U.S. Congress established the conditions for Cuban political independence. These conditions, articulated by Senator Orville H. Platt, were converted by the United States into a law, which was to be imposed as an amendment to the Cuban constitution in 1901 before the election of the first Republican government.

The Platt Amendment mandated that the new government of Cuba recognize the right of the United States to intervene militarily in order to preserve Cuban independence or to maintain an adequate government for the protection of life, property, and individual freedom. According to the Platt Amendment, the Cuban government would lease or sell to the United Sates certain areas where naval bases or coal stations could be established. In addition, Cuba would refrain from entering into agreements with other countries for the purpose of carrying out the colonization or military occupation of any part of Cuban territory. Before assuming control of their government, the Cubans would ratify and validate all acts of the American military government and all rights acquired by third parties by virtue of those acts.

The Platt Amendment also imposed on Cuba the obligation to continue health programs that the military government had initiated to avoid epidemics and to protect populations in U.S. southern ports, which maintained active trade relations with the island. The Platt Amendment was tested for the first time in 1906, when the Cuban leaders unsuccessfully tried to remove President Tomás Estrada Palma from office, triggering a political crisis. The United States occupied the island once again and imposed a second military government. Under this new government, which lasted until 1909, American investments reached the eastern part of Cuba.

Cuba quickly regained its status as the major supplier of sugar to the United States. This was achieved despite competition from Hawaiian and Puerto Rican sugar, which had begun to enter duty-free to the United States. To protect American sugar producers in Cuba, in 1903 the U.S. government signed the Treaty of Commercial Reciprocity with the first Republican government. This treaty reduced the tariff on Cuban sugar by 20 percent, thus endowing Cuban sugar with a competitive advantage in the United States.

Between 1903 and 1910, almost all Cuban sugar exports went to the American market. In 1904 the production of the 170 sugar mills on the island once again surpassed 1,000,000 tons. During this period, investors favored the eastern area, accessible by railroad and dotted with forests that could be cleared and converted into sugar plantations. By 1913 Oriente, or the eastern part of Cuba, had thirty-one *centrales*, which used 206,600 acres of land and produced 611,000 tons of sugar.

The American Sugar Trust in Cuba

Cuban sugar production continued to increase under the control of a new industrial monopoly consisting of the main sugar refiners of the United States, directed by the American Sugar Refining Company. In the last twelve years of the nineteenth century, the president of this corporation, Henry O. Havemeyer, orchestrated a series of industrial consolidations and bought up the majority of the sugar refineries on the East Coast of the United States. With these consolidations and mergers, Havemeyer organized a powerful "Sugar Trust," which dominated 70 percent of the American sugar market.

The most important American refineries were horizontally integrated into the oligopoly of the American Sugar Refining Company, which became the sixth largest corporation in the United States. To defend itself from the antitrust legislation passed by Congress in 1891, the American Sugar Refining Company became a "holding company" with headquarters in New Jersey, because New Jersey legislation permitted corporations registered in the state to own stock in companies in other states. Havemeyer's power became so great that between 1893 and 1898, he alone established the price of sugar. After his announcement of the price every morning at ten o'clock from his office on Wall Street, the other refiners would receive the news by telegram and establish the same price, supposedly independently.[1]

The Spanish-American War gave the Sugar Trust the opportunity to dominate the market completely. Until then, the Caribbean sugar industry had been composed of numerous independent companies, which competed in the international market. By controlling the American refineries, the Sugar Trust set the price paid to the independent producers. Weakened by the war, Cuban planters and landowners could not resist the generous purchase offers made by American investors. During and after the war, Havemeyer used the extraordinary liquidity of the New York banks to integrate Cuban and Puerto Rican *centrales* vertically into his giant refinery complex. Other refiners followed his example and purchased sugar mills and plantations in the Caribbean.

Although it appeared that a large number of firms acquired property and built new *centrales* in Cuba, in fact many were linked to the American Sugar Refining Company. In 1906 one of Havemeyer's partners, James Howell Post, registered the Cuban-American Sugar Company as a holding company in New Jersey in order to consolidate sixteen *centrales* whose combined lands totaled more than 500,000 acres and produced almost 300,000 tons of sugar annually.

The National Sugar Refining Company, another conglomerate of the Sugar Trust, controlled sixteen additional *centrales* as assets of three companies whose administrative councils were all interrelated with the subsidiary companies of the Cuban-American Sugar Company. Many companies often had the same director. Furthermore, the primary stockholders were the directors of the National City Bank of New York, which financed most of the Caribbean operations of the Sugar Trust. By 1906 the Americans had invested approximately $200 million in Cuba.

Another American consortium organized to acquire property in Cuba was the Cuba Cane Sugar Company, a holding company supported by J. P. Morgan and the National City Bank of New York. This company was created at the end of 1915 by Manuel Rionda, the New York partner of the largest sugar brokerage house in the world, C. Czarnikov Ltd.[2] This company did not build new *centrales* but rather acquired existing ones, along with their plantations. Foreseeing a dramatic increase in the price of sugar due to the decline in beet production in Europe during World War I, Rionda traveled to Cuba in January 1916 and in several weeks bought twenty-two plantations and *centrales* for $44.6 million. Rionda's speculation brought immense profits to the Cuba Cane Sugar Company because prices increased to astronomical levels during the war. The banks had financed Rionda's speculations based on the price of 3.5 cents per pound, but by March 1916 prices had increased to 5.75 cents per pound.

To prevent prices from rising even further, the United States and England created an international committee intended to control the sale and distribution of sugar among allied nations. This committee had the power to set prices during the war. In January 1918 the committee reduced the price of sugar to 4.5 cents per pound, but at the end of the war the committee was dissolved, and prices rose again. In September 1918 a pound of sugar cost 9 cents. A year later, in November 1919, the price had increased to 17 cents, and in May 1920 it reached a record level of 22.5 cents.

This price spiral produced a new wave of sales of *centrales* and plantations. Some American companies that used large quantities of sugar, such as Coca-Cola and the Hershey Company, bought their own sugar plantations. More than fifty *centrales* changed hands between 1919 and 1920, and many *colonos* sold or rented their land at a large profit. Cuba entered into a frenzy of financial speculation known as the "*danza de los millones*" (dance of the millions).

The Cuban banks, owned by Spanish capitalists, actively participated in the sugar investment frenzy even before World War I by offering working capital to many Cuban and foreign companies. More than half of the capital invested came from within the Cuban economy, and the bank loans were actually reinvestments of the enormous profits made by the sugar industry. In the middle of this speculative fever, the bankers lent indiscriminately in expectation of even higher prices. But at the end of May 1920 prices began to fall, as the European beet sugar industry rebounded after the war.

In less than three months the *danza de los millones* came to an end. In September 1920 sugar was selling at 9 cents a pound. In December 1920 the price fell to 3.75 cents per pound, and many businesses went bankrupt. Cuban producers tried to lower sugar exports to slow the drop in prices, but they did not succeed. The Cuban banks quickly collapsed. In the summer of 1920 the eighteen main banks, with more than 140 branches, began to be liquidated because they were unable to collect on their loans. Many *centrales* and plantations were also liquidated. In this crisis, the only survivors were the American banks and four very small Cuban banks that had not overextended their assets.

Despite large financial losses, National City Bank, J. P. Morgan, Chase National Bank, and the Royal Bank of Canada quickly filled the vacuum left by the Cuban Spanish banks and took over the mortgages from their predecessors. In the summer of 1921 National City Bank appropriated ten sugar plantations in Cuba. The bank then created a corporation, the General Sugar Company, to administer these properties. The other American banks also created sugar corporations from their foreclosed property. These corporations increased their capital by selling stock on the New York Stock Exchange.

After the crisis of 1920, the Cuban economy came completely under the control of American banks. In 1913, for example, American investors owned thirty-eight *centrales* in Cuba and produced 40 percent of the sugar on the island; in 1924, there were seventy-four American *centrales* producing 60 percent of the Cuban sugar crop. That year the sugar crop reached a record figure of 4.2 million tons. In 1926 American corporations directly controlled seventy-five *centrales*, which produced 62.5 percent of the sugar in Cuba.[3] American investment in the sugar sector totaled $515 million in 1927, while the land under American control totaled 6.3 million acres, more than 22 percent of the island. Some scholars estimate that more than 75 percent of Cuban sugar production at the time was controlled by financial interests in the United States.

Puerto Rico under American Control

This history was to repeat itself with astonishing similarity in Puerto Rico, with one exception: Puerto Rico did not become a republic. The Puerto Rican parties that had supported the military intervention of the United States in 1898 were unable to prevent the island from being administered as a nonincorporated territory of the United States.

At the end of the nineteenth century, the Puerto Rican sugar industry was undergoing a series of crises. Due to the drop in the price of sugar over the previous years, many producers had stopped producing sugar and transformed their plantations into cattle ranches. With the arrival of the American troops, the economy lost momentum. The Puerto Rican currency dropped in value when the American authorities decreed an official exchange rate of 60 Spanish pesos per dollar. Many Spanish landowners opted to liquidate their businesses and leave the island. Thus the price of land plummeted due to the number of properties on the market.

Puerto Rico's small size facilitated its incorporation into the United States. Despite the objections of the sugar producers in the United States, Puerto Rican sugar began to enter the American market duty-free after 1899. Cuban sugar production was too great to be absorbed duty-free without creating conflict with the American producers. Puerto Rico's duty-free status turned it into an attractive investment opportunity, because the customs differential guaranteed a good income for the sugar plantation owners. American investors linked to the marketing and refining of sugar also went to Puerto Rico to purchase land and sugar plantations soon after the American troops disembarked there in 1898.

The first land transfers occurred in October 1898, when an American official, General Roy Stone, bought Hacienda Aguirre in Guayama at a public auction. Only twenty-three people owned all the land in this important sugar district, and two men controlled half of it. Twenty-seven mills existed in Guayama in 1898, but only ten produced sugar. During the first months of the American occupation, the transfer of land was frequent, as many of the Spanish and other foreign owners wanted to sell their holdings.

Taking advantage of the invasion, four Boston sugar refinery partners with important political and financial connections relocated to Puerto Rico and founded the De Ford and Company Bank. This bank was selected as a depository for the military government's funds. The rapid influx of capital to the bank permitted its owners to buy Hacienda Aguirre from General Stone in February 1899. In addition to Hacienda Aguirre's 2,000 acres, they also purchased three adjacent sugar farms totaling almost 2,500 acres. In July 1899 these businessmen formed the

Central Aguirre Syndicate, with a capital base of $525,000, and signed sugarcane production contracts with several landowners in Guayama to ensure that their new *central* had an adequate supply of sugarcane.

Central Aguirre, built with machinery from the United States, harvested its first crop in December 1900. Compared to other Puerto Rican sugar mills, this *central* was enormous. Its machinery was able to process between 7,000 and 10,000 tons of sugar annually. In its first year Central Aguirre produced 6,103 tons of sugar, but after the installation of additional machinery, its production increased to 22,272 tons in 1905.

To finance this expansion, the owners raised capital by issuing stock in the New York and Boston financial markets. By 1903 their capital base had increased to $2 million, but the original stockholders had been joined by other stockholders associated with the National Sugar Refining Company. In 1905, when the firm became a holding company incorporated in Massachusetts under the name of Central Aguirre Sugar Companies, three of its founders had already died. By 1911 the remaining surviving founder had lost control of the company to the National Sugar Refining Company and other financial interests in New York, which held the majority of the stock. From then on, Central Aguirre was part of the network of *centrales* vertically integrated into the Sugar Trust.

The Fajardo Sugar Company developed in a similar fashion. The company, which produced sugar in northeastern Puerto Rico under the vertical integration plan of the Sugar Trust, was organized in 1905 by Puerto Rican investors with the support of the National Sugar Refining Company and its associated banks in New York. Henry O. Havemeyer died in 1907, but his son Horace took over, represented by his partners B. H. Howell, Thomas A. Howell, and James Howell Post. These individuals occupied numerous interconnected positions on the boards of the largest sugar companies in Cuba, Puerto Rico, and the Dominican Republic, and were similarly connected to banks and refineries in New York and Philadelphia as well as several holding companies incorporated in New Jersey.

As in Cuba, the larger sugar companies in Puerto Rico fell into the hands of a small group of American entrepreneurs who sat on various boards, alongside representatives of the different banks and refining companies horizontally integrated into the Sugar Trust. The antitrust legislation of the United States forced them to diversify the management and stock holding of the companies, but the true bosses were still the members of the Havemeyer, Howell, and Post families, who controlled the American Sugar Refining Company and the National Sugar Refining Company. After the death of Henry O. Havemeyer, the American Sugar Refining Company distanced itself from the family of its founder, but the Howells and Posts were represented on numerous boards.

A third case of early American capital penetration into the Puerto Rican economy is the South Porto Rico Sugar Company, founded in 1900 and incorporated in New Jersey by a group of American investors and bankers who were descendants of Germans established in Puerto Rico and New York. Two of these businessmen, who handled the largest sugar export firm in Puerto Rico at the beginning of the twentieth century, were also treasury agents for the American government in Puerto Rico and took advantage of their extraordinary liquidity to make enormous investments in land and to build Central Guánica. This company was the largest on the island, with an initial annual production of 50,000 tons, and the second largest in the Caribbean, surpassed only by Central Chaparra in Cuba. By 1910, however, the South Porto Rico Sugar Company had become a subsidiary of the American Sugar Refining Company.

Aguirre, Fajardo, and Guánica were not the only *centrales* built at the beginning of the twentieth century in Puerto Rico. Central Mercedita and Central Fortuna were constructed by independent investors in Ponce, while in 1909 another group of investors founded the Florida Sugar Company, which was quickly acquired by Central Aguirre in 1910. Other *centrales* built in the early twentieth century were Providencia, in 1905, and the Santa Isabel Sugar Company, in 1908. The independent investors were not all American; some were French, Corsican, English, German, and Spanish.

The new totally mechanized *centrales*, which were heavily financed, sold their sugar to the protected American market. Puerto Rican sugar exports to the United States increased from 74,000 tons in 1900 to 125,000 tons in 1903, 251,000 tons in 1908, and 317,000 tons in 1910. The high price of sugar during World War I led to increased sugarcane planting. By 1920, Puerto Rico was producing 440,000 tons of sugar annually, and in 1930 its production was 786,000 tons. In 1934 it reached the record figure of 1,000,000 tons.

The new *centrales* planted sugarcane throughout the coastal plains, which until then had been used for grazing or simply left uncultivated. Between 1899 and 1929, the area planted with sugarcane increased threefold, from 70,000 acres to more than 230,000 acres. Sugarcane producers generally controlled more land than they cultivated. In 1935 more than 740,000 acres of the best land in Puerto Rico (38 percent of all arable land on the island) was in the hands of the sugar companies and their sugarcane farmers. Only 246,834 acres of this land was planted with sugarcane, however. As in Cuba, the large sugar companies expanded their land ownership both to prevent competition and to provide sufficient pasturelands for livestock.

As the sugar companies bought up more land, the number of sugar plantations decreased, from 446 in 1888 to 345 in 1899. Fully mechanized modern *centrales,* vertically integrated into the American refineries, accelerated the concentration process. In 1910, 41 *centrales* in Puerto Rico produced 97 percent of the island's sugar. The other 105 *centrales* and traditional mills were marginal units.

Most of the *hacendados* succumbed to pressure by the new *centrales* either to sell their land or to become *colonos* for the new corporations. The *hacendados* facilitated the American occupation by recruiting workers for the American sugar industry. In 1934 Puerto Rican cane farmers were producing 35 percent of the island's sugarcane and controlled almost 49 percent of the cane fields. In that year the *colonos* supplied almost 30 percent of the cane ground by the eleven American *centrales*.

In 1929 the four main American sugar corporations and their associated *colonos* controlled 165,000 acres of cane fields, or 72 percent of the area planted in cane. In 1934 the landholdings of these four companies surpassed 211,000 acres. More than half of the sugar production of Puerto Rico came from the eleven mills of the Central Aguirre, South Porto Rico Sugar Company, United Puerto Rico Sugar Company, and Central Fajardo Sugar Company. Just as in Cuba, large-scale production was the key to success. In 1927, for example, Guánica produced 93,000 tons of sugar, the five United Puerto Rico *centrales* over 86,000 tons, the two Fajardo *centrales* almost 68,000 tons, and Aguirre's three *centrales* more than 61,000 tons.

Unlike in Cuba and the Dominican Republic, where the local labor supply was insufficient, in Puerto Rico sugar production was sustained by local workers. During the early years of the American occupation, *central* owners could count on laborers from the coffee areas devastated by the famous San Ciriaco hurricane, which in August 1898 had destroyed more than half of the coffee plants. Furthermore, many Puerto Rican peasants had to find work in the sugarcane areas in order to pay the new taxes established by the American authorities. As the peasant population in the coffee areas continued to increase, the surplus of manual labor spilled over to the coastal plains. There the *centrales* offered better salaries than could be found in the depressed coffee regions. In 1919 the sugar industry employed 79,261 workers, the majority native to the island.

An American Protectorate in the Dominican Republic

In the Dominican Republic, however, the sugar industry required an external labor supply. The peasants of the Cibao region, where the majority of the Dominican population was concentrated, were fully employed farming tobacco and, later, cacao and coffee. After the introduction of these latter two commercial crops in 1880, even fewer local peasants chose to migrate toward the sugar areas. Cacao became such an important crop at the beginning of the twentieth century that in 1907 and 1908, exports of this product surpassed sugar exports in value.

During the first few years of the twentieth century, the Dominican sugar industry ran into serious difficulties with competition from sugar from Hawaii, the Philippines, and Puerto Rico. Sugar from these territories was entering the American market tax-free. Cuban sugar, which enjoyed reduced customs duties, was also a source of difficulty for the Dominican producers. The elimination of the subsidy system in the United Kingdom in 1903, however, opened the door to Dominican exports to Great Britain and Canada. Because the Clyde Steamship Company had a transportation monopoly in the Dominican Republic by virtue of a concession granted by the Dominican state, Dominican sugar was shipped to New York and then reshipped to Great Britain and Canada.

The Sugar Trust did not take control of the sugar industry in the Dominican Republic as early as it did in Cuba and Puerto Rico, even though Americans owned eleven of the fourteen *centrales* in 1905. The General Industrial Company, a firm registered in New Jersey, was owned by the Vicini family, who also controlled four sugar plantations: Angelina, Azuano, Italia, and Ocoa. The Bartram Brothers of New York owned three sugar plantations: Quisqueya, San Isidro, and Santa Fe, which they had bought from their former Cuban and British owners. Hugh Kelly, an American investor, owned the Santa Teresa, Ansonia, and Porvenir plantations. The largest estate in the country, Ingenio Consuelo, was also owned by an American. The Puerto Rico plantation was still owned by its founders, the Serrallés family.

These independent companies had been consolidated or had their assets acquired during the crisis at the turn of the century. Compared with Puerto Rican and Cuban plantations, Dominican plantations were small. In 1905 the largest, Ingenio Consuelo, only produced 9,600 tons of sugar. That year, the average production of the Dominican *centrales* was 4,800 tons. The increase in sugar consumption in Britain and Canada in the following years, however, stimulated their productivity, and by 1912 the average annual production per *central* had reached 9,500 tons.

Between 1905 and 1912, over half of the Dominican *centrales* doubled their production. With a secure market, their owners arranged for credit with American and Canadian banks and bought new American machinery. Almost all of the *centrales* installed new mills, evaporators, centrifugal machinery, purifiers, and water supply and power systems, while the largest *centrales* expanded their railroads. Central Consuelo, for instance, had only two miles of railroad track and one locomotive in 1893, but by 1911 its owners had built more than fifty miles of track and bought eight locomotives. Some *centrales* also expanded production by increasing the number of cane farmers they contracted.

This period of growth for the sugar industry coincided with the fiscal reorganization of the Dominican Republic, supervised by the U.S. government. After the death of the dictator Ulises Heureaux in 1899, the Dominican Republic fell into a serious financial crisis, caused by the large national debt that had been accrued imprudently over the preceding decades. This crisis brought about disputes with the governments of

Italy, France, Germany, Belgium, and Great Britain, whose citizens held Dominican government bonds. In 1901 these governments threatened to intervene militarily in Santo Domingo. The plan was to collect debts by taking over Dominican customs. These threats alarmed the U.S. government, intent on preventing any European nation from intervening in the Caribbean.

The United States managed to dissuade the Europeans from taking military action in the Dominican Republic by compelling the Dominicans to accept mediation in January 1903. This was only ten days after the U.S. government had forced Colombia to hand over the Isthmus of Panama. In February 1905, after two years of arduous negotiations with the bondholders, President Theodore Roosevelt managed to impose a settlement for debt repayment. According to this agreement, American government agents would administer Dominican customs and distribute the income equally among the foreign creditors and the Dominican government.

The U.S. Senate rejected this agreement because many senators argued that the United States was imposing the status of protectorate on the Dominican Republic. Despite this opposition, Roosevelt used his executive authority to uphold the agreement as a modus vivendi, appointing a general customs administrator in Santo Domingo. The European creditors began to receive their payments immediately, and customs revenue increased greatly due to the new efficient system of administration. Roosevelt was then able to convince the U.S Congress that American intervention in the Dominican Republic had been necessary to protect it from a European military intervention and to secure American hegemony in the Caribbean. This new policy became known as the "Roosevelt Corollary to the Monroe Doctrine."

The U.S. government persuaded the Dominican government to consolidate its entire debt with a single American bank. In 1906 the foreign debt was consolidated and reduced to $17 million. The American government arranged and guaranteed a loan of $20 million with Kuhn and Loeb Company of New York, to enable the Dominican Republic to pay its creditors. As collateral for this loan, Dominican customs remained under the administration of American officers appointed by the president of the United States. Fifty percent of the customs income was put aside to repay the loan; 45 percent was handed over to the Dominican

government; and the remaining 5 percent was earmarked for administrative costs.

This arrangement was formalized through the Dominican-American
Convention of 1907. The Dominican Republic agreed not to increase its
public debt or modify its affairs without the express consent of the president of the United States. At the same time, the United States reserved
the right to intervene in the Dominican Republic to protect the customs
collection, if necessary. Thus the Dominican Republic became a legal
protectorate of the United States, and the United States claimed the
power to intervene there, similar to the power granted by the Platt
Amendment in Cuba.

The Dominican-American Convention had the same effect as the previous modus vivendi. All customs offices, including the ones on the
Haitian border, were reorganized, contraband was outlawed, and the
system of accounting was perfected to reduce misappropriations of
funds. As a result, the Dominican government's income tripled, and for
the first time in many years the government had the resources with
which to pay its employees and ensure domestic peace. Political stability and an increase in cacao, coffee, tobacco, and sugar exports attracted new investors, who saw little difference between the Dominican
Republic, Cuba, and Puerto Rico.

The South Porto Rico Sugar Company made a particularly large
investment in 1910, when it bought 20,000 acres in La Romana to supply Central Guánica in Puerto Rico with cane. The advantages were
obvious: although the cane was grown abroad, the sugar produced in
Puerto Rico could be sold in America duty-free. The other *central* owners, who had to pay taxes on their sugar sold in the United States,
resented La Romana, the Sugar Trust's first investment in the
Dominican Republic. Dominican *central* owners thought that the Law
for Agricultural Franchises, promulgated in July 1911, was promoted by
agents of the Sugar Trust and Central Guánica to ensure their tax-free
export of sugarcane.

Another Dominican law promoted by the American sugar companies
was the "Law for the Partition of Communal Lands" of 1911, which
was designed to regulate the sale of agricultural land and end the traditional land tenure system. The communal land tenure system had previously obstructed the sugar companies' expansion, because the original

royal land grants of the colonial period could not be formally divided.[4]

In a sparsely populated and poor country such as the Dominican Republic, the communal land system allowed the land to be used without incurring partition and demarcation costs.[5] As foreign companies arrived and created plantations, however, the land became extraordinarily valuable, and the new foreign owners demanded a new system in which all properties would have titles, deeds, and clearly established boundaries. The participation of surveyors and notaries was necessary in order to divide the communal lands and distribute the land stock. The sugar companies often bribed surveyors and notaries to acquire rights based on false titles and arbitrary measures.

After 1911 the falsification of titles to the communal lands of the Dominican Republic was rampant. The best lands in the south and east were acquired either fraudulently or at ridiculously low prices by the American sugar corporations and became part of the huge sugar estates. South Porto Rico Sugar Company agents in La Romana actively participated in these operations and managed to increase the amount of land the company owned from 20,000 acres in 1911 to 144,000 acres in 1920.

With the extraordinary increase in sugar prices during World War I, the South Porto Rico Sugar Company decided to install a *central* in La Romana to expand its production. By 1918 Central Romana was producing about 40,000 tons of sugar per year, maintaining at the same time its shipments of sugarcane to Central Guánica in Puerto Rico. Because of the large amount of land under its control, Central Romana cultivated with sugarcane only about 24,000 acres of land, with the rest kept in reserve or used for grazing livestock.

There was widespread peasant resistance to the encroachment of lands by American sugar companies. As the American military occupation took hold of the country, peasant guerrillas fought the U.S. marines and the security forces of the *centrales* in the eastern plains of the Dominican Republic. This war lasted from 1917 to 1921, and it ended only when the military government decided to use the members of the Dominican National Guard, a constabulary organized by the U.S. Marine Corps, to persecute the *gavilleros*, as the guerrillas were called. The Dominican soldiers knew the territory as well as the *gavilleros* and were familiar with their fighting methods.

The guerrilla war did not disrupt the acquisition of land by the sugar companies. During World War I, the Barahona Company, registered in New York in 1916, acquired almost 50,000 acres of land in the western Dominican Republic and built the second largest *central* in the country. The Barahona Company was financed by the International Banking Corporation, a subsidiary of the National City Bank of New York, one of the main financiers of the Sugar Trust. In 1920, when the builders of Central Barahona were short of capital, the directors of the Sugar Trust organized the Cuban Dominican Sugar Development Syndicate to take over this *central*.

The Sugar Trust established this new company to expand its operations in the Dominican Republic. As part of this expansion, Cuban Dominican bought the *centrales* San Isidro and Consuelo in Santo Domingo, which were owned by the Bartram Brothers Company, as well as the Ansonia and Ocoa plantations in Azua and five other smaller *centrales*. In 1924 this firm also acquired the West India Sugar Finance Corporation and its six Cuban *centrales*, Altagracia, Santa Ana, Hatillo, Cupey, Alto Cedro, and Palma. By 1926 Cuban Dominican controlled ten of the nineteen Dominican *centrales* and was the largest sugar consortium in the country. The firm changed its name to the Cuban Dominican Company in 1924.

At this point, the American sugar companies controlled 438,182 acres of the best farmland in the Dominican Republic. As in Puerto Rico, much of this land was not cultivated. In 1925 only 146,903 acres were planted with sugarcane, while the rest was used for pasture or simply maintained in reserve to prevent the land from being acquired by other companies. In 1926 American investments in the Dominican sugar sector increased to $43 million. The declared value of the properties owned by the Cuban Dominican Company in the Dominican Republic increased to $25.5 million in 1926, while Central Romana and its plantations were appraised at $9.7 million. The smaller consortium of the Vicini family owned properties was valued at $4.1 million, while the five independent *centrales* were collectively worth $3.5 million.

In 1929 the American companies controlled 92 percent of the Dominican sugar production. The largest *centrales* were equal in size to the largest in Cuba and Puerto Rico. Central Romana, for example, produced 93,000 tons of sugar per year; Central Consuelo, 57,000 tons;

Central Barahona, 43,000 tons; Central Quisqueya, 30,000 tons; and Central Montellano, 12,000 tons. In 1929 overall production surpassed 420,000 tons, of which 309,400 tons, or 74 percent, was produced by the Cuban Dominican Company and the South Porto Rico Sugar Company.

As in Cuba and Puerto Rico, these *centrales* became independent enclaves that paid minimal taxes and had their own currency and internal social system. Sometimes *centrales* controlled entire towns, because the inhabitants depended exclusively on the employment they generated. As the American plantations grew, many rural communities that had previously farmed or raised cattle independently were swept away, and in their place grew cane fields worked by foreign laborers.

The Americanization of the sugar industry in the Dominican Republic increased during the U.S. military occupation of the country between 1916 and 1924. The military government actively protected American interests, proclaiming the Dominican Republic a safe haven where American investments were guaranteed. One of the companies invited to invest in the country was the National City Bank, which together with Canadian and British banks financed the sugar companies.

The Orme Mahogany Company, which was granted more than one million acres of forest for mahogany exploitation, was another of the American firms active in the Dominican Republic. Lumber companies such as the Enriquillo Company, the Habanero Lumber Company, and the Barahona Wood Products Company obtained similar concessions and rapidly logged uncut hardwood forests and precious timber. More American companies received concessions for cotton plantations, flour mills, and oil exploration in Azua, in the south of the island. Some established themselves in the Dominican Republic by displacing the German companies that had controlled much of the Dominican foreign market before World War I. American firms also opened new businesses which sold power plants, fuel, lubricants, automobiles, trucks, and industrial machinery.

To encourage the importation of American products, the military government enacted a customs tax law in 1919, which declared 254 specific articles manufactured in the United States to be duty-free. In addition, import taxes on over 700 other articles were greatly reduced. This simple measure caused an immediate flood of consumer goods into the Dominican Republic, thereby putting large numbers of local manufacturers and artisans out of business.

After 1919 about two-thirds of all imported goods were of American origin. Because the Dominican-American Convention of 1907, later modified in 1924, prohibited the Dominican government from altering the tariffs without the consent of the U.S. government, Dominican foreign trade remained subordinated to American commercial interests.

As in Cuba and Puerto Rico, the U.S. military occupation of the Dominican Republic left a very marked preference for American manufactured goods and entertainment. Dominicans, Puerto Ricans, and Cubans adopted American games such as baseball, which soon became the most popular sport in the Greater Antilles, gradually replacing pastimes of Spanish origin, such as cockfighting.

American Investments in Occupied Haiti

The Americans also penetrated into Haiti as this country collapsed under the weight of an unredeemable external debt, most of which was controlled by European banking interests, particularly German and French. A rapid succession of short-lived governments kept the debt growing. On several occasions between 1901 and 1914, the German government intervened militarily in Haiti by sending warships to impose diplomatic claims. The United States government felt increasingly uneasy with the meddling of European powers in Haiti, particularly after the construction of the Panamá Canal. As it had done in the Dominican Republic, the U.S. government pressed for the reorganization of Haiti's customs department under the direction of an American officer, but with no results. The U.S. government wanted Haiti to use most of its customs revenues to pay for the external debt.

As political violence exploded in 1914, following two years of relative calm, the U.S. government insisted that Haitians should allow Washington to establish a protectorate similar to the one in the Dominican Republic. The Haitians refused, further frustrating the Washington policy makers. Meanwhile, the First World War started in Europe, and Germany became the subject of American suspicion in Haiti, since the rumor was that the Germans wanted to establish a naval base in Môle St. Nicholas.

In addition to this rumor, revolutionary activity in the northern part of Haiti served as justification for the United States government to send a warship to Haiti on July 28, 1915, under the pretext of preventing anarchy, stopping political violence, and protecting the property of foreign owners. Most Haitians rejected the military intervention, but the United States decided to occupy the country and quickly found a puppet president to legalize the imposition of the customs receivership. Soon, the U.S. Marine Corps, in charge of Haiti's military affairs, arrested the guerrilla leaders, disarmed the population, and organized a national constabulary to fight the guerrillas and impose order.

In November 1917 the U.S. military rulers compelled the puppet government to pass a law imposing a system of forced labor that obliged male peasants to work without pay in the construction of roads and other public projects. Haitian and American soldiers were in charge of seeing that the peasants complied with their labor obligations. Peasant resistance to the military occupation was put down after November 1918, when the principal revolutionary leader, Charlemagne Péralte, was assassinated by two U.S. marines disguised as black peasants. From then on Haiti was gradually pacified.

The land in Haiti, unlike in the other Greater Antilles, was divided into numerous small properties occupied by peasants. Thus the creation of large plantations and *centrales* was more difficult. Nonetheless, during the American military occupation of Haiti between 1915 and 1934, several American firms obtained concessions to establish sugar, cotton, sisal, and banana and other fruit plantations. One of these American companies, the Haitian American Sugar Company (HASCO), established in Port-au-Prince in 1915, built a modern *central*, the first in Haiti, which was supplied by *colonos* with cane produced in the plains of Léogane and Cul-de-Sac.

The initial investment in HASCO was $7 million. The first sugarcane crop was harvested in 1918, just after the American military government had modified the Haitian constitution to permit foreign citizens and companies to own rural property in Haiti. The crisis of 1920 seriously affected the company, and HASCO was taken over by its creditors in 1921. During the following years, HASCO managed to recuperate financially and extended its network of *colonos* until it controlled 27,181 acres of cane fields, although only 9,884 acres were cultivated directly by the company. In 1930 the *central* employed about 1,000 workers who earned an average of twenty cents daily, the lowest salary in the Antilles.

Haiti, densely populated and with a virtually unlimited supply of unskilled labor, attracted the attention of foreign investors. After the elimination of legal barriers for the acquisition of land, American companies established cotton plantations. But the crops were infected with various pests, and the efforts had to be abandoned several years later. More successful was the Haitian Agricultural Corporation, which in 1926 established Plantation Dauphin in the north of Haiti to cultivate sisal around Fort Liberté.

CHAPTER 19

Migrants, Peasants, and Proletarians

Poverty and Emigration in the West Indies

While the best lands in the Greater Antilles came under the control of American companies and were converted into gigantic sugarcane plantations, the Lesser Antilles went through a long period of readjustment from the economic crisis of 1884. Unable to compete with European beet sugar, the British West Indian planters cut their production, fired large numbers of laborers, and reduced salaries. The situation of the British West Indies worsened in 1891, when American sugar interests, looking to protect the newly Americanized *centrales* in Cuba, Puerto Rico, the Dominican Republic, Hawaii, and the Philippines, closed the American market to sugar from the British West Indies.

Unable to find employment on their own islands, thousands of workers from the British West Indies emigrated in search of work. Many went to Panama, Trinidad, Guiana, Cuba, and the Dominican Republic to work on plantations. Others headed to Venezuela, and even as far as Brazil, to work in gold mines. These emigrations, however, did not resolve the problems of unemployment and poverty in the British West Indies.

Eventually, social tensions led to violence. One early revolt that foreshadowed later ones took place in 1865 in Morant Bay, Jamaica, where 588 rebels lost their lives and 1,000 homes were destroyed.[1] In Montserrat, there was a revolt in 1898; in British Guiana, there were several in 1893 and 1896; in Jamaica and Trinidad, there were more revolts in 1903.

In Barbados, in particular, population density created serious social problems. The population of Barbados increased substantially during the second half of the nineteenth century, reaching 182,000 in 1891. The planters of Barbados managed to keep their plantations intact and retain a large labor supply by preventing the formation of an independent peasant class. Plantation workers were paid very low daily wages of about eight cents. The universal poverty prevailing in rural areas triggered migrations to plantations in Trinidad and British Guiana, where salaries were slightly higher.

When work on the Panama Canal was resumed in 1904, new employment opportunities were created, and a wave of massive migration occurred. Between 1905 and 1914 as many as 45,000 workers left Barbados for Panama, despite the planters' efforts to prevent this shortage of manual labor. By 1911 the population of the island had decreased to 171,983. In the following decade, it dropped even more, falling to 156,312 in 1921. During this period, immigrants from Barbados also went to Cuban plantations, where they competed for jobs with Jamaicans and Haitians.

In 1898 and 1899 two hurricanes hit the Leeward Islands and ruined the already shattered economy. Many people were forced to migrate en masse to Bermuda, where a large shipyard was being built. By 1901 there were 1,600 workers from the Leeward Islands living in Bermuda. Between 1901 and 1904, 2,431 migrants, the majority of whom were men ready to work as loaders, carpenters, and masons, arrived in Bermuda from Nevis and St. Kitts. Only 10 to 20 percent of the immigrants were women. Most of these women earned a living by cooking for the workers, although many were employed as domestic servants. When the construction of the shipyard was completed in 1905, the majority of the recent immigrants had to leave Bermuda, and many went to Cuba and the Dominican Republic.

The Dominican plantations had been employing manual laborers from neighboring islands for some time. In 1890 alone the Dominican *centrales* imported more than 3,000 laborers from the Leeward Islands. In 1902, this figure rose to over 4,400. With the increase in population and the construction of new *centrales* after 1906, the demand for manual labor in the Dominican Republic grew considerably. In 1914 the number of contracted laborers in the Dominican Republic increased to 11,800. About 2,500 of these people came from the Leeward Islands.

The rest were from the Virgin Islands, the Turks Islands, Caicos, and Jamaica. Dominican plantation owners offered salaries of up to one dollar per day, a clear improvement over the thirty cents per day paid in the British West Indies.

During World War I, when Central Romana was being built in the Dominican Republic, the South Porto Rico Sugar Company transferred many Puerto Ricans workers and technicians there after they had been trained at Central Guánica. This was a "middle-class" migration when compared to that of the British West Indians, but many of these early Puerto Rican immigrants were still relatively poor people looking for better opportunities than could be found on their own island.

In Jamaica, poverty was widespread, but it was most extensive among rural villagers unable to find work on plantations. Though Jamaican workers preferred to migrate to nearby Cuba, many went to work in Panama during the first stage of the construction of the Panama Canal. The net emigration of Jamaican workers between 1881 and 1891 is estimated at 24,800 people, the majority of whom went to work temporarily in Panama. Several thousand returned to Panama when the construction of the canal was resumed in 1904. At this time, the salaries offered to construction workers on the canal fluctuated between eighty cents and one dollar per day. Even before the completion of the Panama Canal in 1914, many of these immigrants ended up working on banana plantations in Honduras and Costa Rica. Between 1891 and 1911, a total of 43,900 workers emigrated from Jamaica. Nonetheless, the population of Jamaica continued to increase, from 581,000 in 1881 to 831,000 in 1911.

Cuban plantations also attracted a large number of Jamaicans escaping the devastation of the hurricanes of 1903, 1912, 1915, 1916, and 1917, not to mention the earthquake of 1907, which destroyed the city of Kingston and left about 800 dead. In 1917, as many as 6,000 Jamaican workers entered Cuba, followed by 7,317 the next year. During the *danza de los millones,* salaries offered to Jamaican laborers in Cuba increased to two dollars per day. Cuban plantations drew more Jamaican immigrants than ever: 23,859 in 1919 and 24,461 in 1920. In 1921, when the *danza de los millones* ended, emigration decreased to 7,867 people; nonetheless, between 1922 and 1925 Cuba continued to receive an average of 5,200 Jamaican immigrants per year.

This ready supply of labor from neighboring islands was essential in facilitating the development of the sugar economies of Cuba and the Dominican Republic during the first thirty years of the twentieth century. Between 1902 and 1919, Cuba received 50,368 immigrants from Jamaica, 39,906 from Haiti, and 24,976 from the other islands of the West Indies. Cuba's economic growth also attracted more than 13,000 Puerto Ricans as well as some 8,000 workers from Panama and Central America.

During the *danza de los millones*, the need for manual labor on Cuban plantations forced Cuban *centrales* to import more than 1,300 Chinese laborers. There was also a massive wave of immigrants from rural Spain. Between 1902 and 1919, Cuba received 436,005 Spanish immigrants, almost half of whom became sugar plantation workers. This Spanish immigration helped to reduce immigration from neighboring islands. After the *danza de los millones*, however, thousands of Haitian laborers began to immigrate and soon outnumbered those from the British West Indies. Between 1921 and 1925, an average of 16,000 Haitian workers immigrated to Cuba each year, about twice the number of Jamaican immigrants.

Haitians also crossed over into the Dominican Republic in this period. A 1920 census indicates that 15,013 Haitian immigrants were living in sugar-producing areas there. The Dominican Republic also witnessed a seasonal immigration of workers from the Leeward Islands between 1914 and 1939. The Dominican sugar plantations offered wages that were more than double those paid on plantations in Nevis and St. Kitts. The *centrales* in La Romana and San Pedro de Macorís paid between $20 and $30 weekly for six consecutive days of work, while in the Leeward Islands the average salary was barely $12 per month. Unlike in Cuba, where laborers would often settle for years, in the Dominican Republic cane cutters from the Leeward Islands would frequently work for the six months of the harvest and then return to their homeland islands.

Year after year, between 2,500 and 4,000 laborers from St. Kitts and Nevis, as well as several hundred from Antigua, Montserrat, the Virgin Islands, Dominica, Anguilla, St. Vincent, and the Turks Islands, would sail to the Dominican Republic on ships rented by Dominican *centrales*, leaving the women, children, and elderly behind. This created a labor shortage on the Leeward Islands. Planters there were forced to employ women and the elderly to cut sugarcane and pick cotton. Migration statistics from Nevis and St. Kitts register more than 90,000 workers who went to the Dominican Republic between 1914 and 1939.

Many workers repeated the trip numerous times until they grew older or tired, or until they had saved enough to buy a plot of land or improve their homes on their islands. Others settled in the vicinity of Santo Domingo, San Pedro de Macorís, La Romana, or Puerto Plata. Dominicans nicknamed the laborers from the West Indies "*cocolos.*" The origin of this name is not clear, but it is widely accepted to be a corruption of "Tortolo," Spanish for an inhabitant of Tortola, one of the small British Virgin Islands that also sent laborers annually to the Dominican Republic. The 1935 Dominican population census registered 9,272 *cocolos.*

Due to emigration, the population of the Leeward Islands declined between the years 1901 and 1921. At least 2,000 Leeward Islanders settled in the Dominican Republic and other islands, and close to 1,000 moved to Bermuda. These numbers are small, however, when compared to the number of people who migrated to the United States in search of higher wages and better living conditions. Nevis and St. Kitts together lost about 12,000 inhabitants to the United States during the first twenty years of the century. Nearly 60,000 people from the rest of the British West Indies immigrated to the United States. Between 1901 and 1921, there were more than 80,000 West Indian immigrants registered in the United States. The majority of them relocated in New York City and other large cities in the eastern United States. Many others moved to Mexico and Canada.

Most of these migrants were peasants or proletarians who descended from the plantation slaves of the nineteenth century. Many of them had even been born into slavery. The British West Indian freedmen who had become peasants by occupying or buying Crown lands, or by squatting on plots outside of the plantations, were frequently unable to earn enough cash to sustain their families. Emancipation did not turn them automatically into peasants, and many became proletarians who were forced by economic necessity to return to the plantations as salaried workers. The lengthy economic crisis of the British West Indies in the second half of the nineteenth century created a sizable supply of laborers who were forced to leave their home islands to earn cash elsewhere.

Peasants and the Rural Economy in the Spanish Antilles

These people differed substantially from the older peasant communities that had developed on the Spanish Antilles from the early years of Spanish colonization. These peasants had seldom, if ever, worked on the plantations and had been independent smallholders planting cash crops like ginger and cacao in the sixteenth and seventeenth centuries, or tobacco and coffee in the eighteenth and nineteenth centuries.

Modern studies and contemporary sources show the parallel formation of these peasantries in the Spanish Antilles. The colonial economy of Santo Domingo, a nonplantation society, was based on cattle ranching, but most of the people were peasants who had become increasingly integrated into foreign markets by the middle of the eighteenth century, principally through the exportation of live cattle and hides, as well as tobacco produced in the densely inhabited central Cibao valley. By the third and fourth decades of the nineteenth century, Dominican peasants were collectively producing more than 5,000 tons of tobacco every year. This figure doubled by 1860.

By then, the Dominican economy had evolved into a more diversified rural economy based on a principal cash crop, tobacco, and on the production of rum and the exportation of mahogany and other woods. The tobacco industry required the existence of many other activities connected with the processing, packing, and transportation of tobacco. This can be seen in the proliferation of muleteers, peons, rope and bag manufacturers, packers, balers, cigar makers, merchants, financiers, and trade brokers who shared a peasant background.

Puerto Rico and Cuba also developed their own peasantries that were involved in the cultivation of coffee and tobacco for export and the production of foodstuffs to supply the plantations. On these two islands, the formation of Creole peasantries began as early as the seventeenth and eighteenth centuries. This trend intensified as sugar plantations multiplied on these islands in the nineteenth century, creating a growing slave population that required more food. Puerto Rican smallholders also took advantage of the growing demand for food and cattle in the Danish Antilles, particularly St. Croix and St. Thomas. The commodities purchased from this Spanish colony included cattle, plantains, yuca, yams, and even flour.

Even though a large number of independent peasants in Cuba were reluctant to work on the plantations, this did not deter them from selling their crops to the planters. Thus Cuban peasants supplied the island's internal market with much of the food needed on the plantations, including rice, although vast amounts of flour had to be imported from Spain and the United States. As the plantations expanded throughout the island, the Cuban peasants were restricted more and more to the eastern and western extremities of the island, where they continued to be a vigorous and dynamic class, particularly in the sectors of tobacco and coffee production. Both crops employed large numbers of people in the planting, harvesting, processing, marketing, and transportation phases. This helps explain why the Spanish islands were always short of labor and became net importers of workers in the nineteenth and early twentieth centuries.

The large number of people needed for work in tobacco and coffee production also explains why the poorest groups of the Spanish Antilles did not feel an urgent need to emigrate to find jobs elsewhere, as had happened in the British West Indies. Cuba, Puerto Rico, and Santo Domingo enjoyed a virtually unlimited supply of land for the size of the population, and the landscape on these islands presented numerous ecological niches suitable for a diversified agriculture. Though a similar landscape could be found in Jamaica, the planter class of this British colony had, from the beginning, taken steps to keep the best land out of the reach of the emancipated slaves, keeping many of them as full-time wage laborers or, in other instances, as marginal cultivators who had to go back to the plantation to earn enough cash to support themselves and their families.

In the Greater Antilles, Haiti was the exception to this favorable geographical endowment due to the serious ecological deterioration of the land there. After 200 years of deforestation, the Haitian environment was becoming increasingly incapable of sustaining a growing population, which had reached more than two million people by the beginning of the twentieth century. Occupying the driest part of Hispaniola,[2] and frequently hit by hurricanes and dense tropical rains that eroded the soil, the Haitian peasantry was forced to seek wage labor options when the big American corporations started taking over the sugar economy of the Greater Antilles. This special ecological drama of Haiti also helps explain the high level of Haitian seasonal migration, unusual in the Greater Antilles, to the plantations of Cuba and the Dominican Republic.

West Indian Peasants and Proletarians

British West Indian migrations had different causes. On the British islands, a peasantry evolved out of the plantations, but given the limited land resources available to the rural population there, family economies were usually precarious, even though many freedmen, turned peasants, cultivated coffee, tobacco, and, later, cocoa and bananas to supplement their income.

Rice cultivation became an important activity for the rural population of both British Guiana and Dutch Guiana. Bananas became the main staple of the peasants of Dominica, St. Lucia, and, later, St. Vincent. Nutmeg, introduced in 1843, was soon the cornerstone of the rural economy of Grenada, while coffee and bananas were the principal cash crops of the Jamaican peasants. People in Nevis and Monserrat experimented with cotton, but their efforts were unsuccessful, in part due to the small size of the islands. St. Kitts was more diversified, but the best available land was taken by the sugar planters, who were very reluctant to relinquish it to the peasants, a fact that also explains why emigration was such a popular option there. As we have already seen, Barbados was the most extreme case, because the peasants there had the least land at their disposal, and the planter class was more reluctant to transfer land to the peasants.

Thus, despite the existence of these pockets of independent peasantries, by 1930 the Caribbean was more reliant than ever on the plantation economy. Slavery had disappeared, but new proletariats of African and East Indian origins had emerged as the workforce of the plantations, coexisting with the new peasantries that had also come into being. By 1930 Spain, France, and Great Britain no longer reigned supreme. A stronger latecomer, the United States, occupied a prominent political and economic place in the region after displacing the older colonial powers from their traditional dominant positions.

This was an entirely new Caribbean. The region had evolved into an archipelago of colonies and republics. But despite very deep transformations, the region maintained its character as an organic plantation system that supplied the world with tropical products. Sugar was not the only export of the Caribbean islands. New plantations were also created for the large-scale cultivation of coffee, bananas, and cacao. Yet sugar was still by far the most important export. In terms of employment, other crops like cacao, coffee, tobacco, and bananas—together with arrowroot, yams, sweet potatoes, yuca, maize, and plantains—occupied more people and became the basis for the livelihoods of the local populations.

Immigration and the Emerging Middle Classes

Along with the sugar plantations, all the islands were dotted with numerous smallholder farms, whose peasant owners or tenants combined subsistence cultivation with production for markets. Caribbean peasants were inextricably linked to international markets or to the small island markets through local distribution chains. They were also the pool from which a new local middle class of people of color was emerging to join the ranks of another middle class composed of white European immigrants, along with an older middle class of people of color that had been forming out of a continuous process of emancipation on most of the islands since the beginning of the eighteenth century.

As time passed, these middle-class groups settled in towns and cities and became the intermediaries between the rural population and the foreign planters, merchants, bankers, and investors. They became a rich network of artisans, teachers, musicians, professionals, bureaucrats, politicians, military officers, merchants, clerks, masons, carpenters, longshoremen, street peddlers, and shopkeepers, who made up the social fabric of West Indian and Spanish Caribbean urban life.

By 1930 this urban social landscape had been enriched by new waves of immigrants from Europe and the Middle East, particularly in Cuba and the Dominican Republic. In these countries, eager for fresh labor, generous policies were enacted to favor the immigration of workers. More than 700,000 Spanish immigrants arrived in Cuba between 1901 and 1930. The numbers for the Dominican Republic are not yet available, but this country received numerous Spanish, Syrian, Lebanese, and Palestinian immigrants during the first three decades of the twentieth century, along with many Americans who went there to work for the sugar corporations.

Cuba received more American immigrants than the other Spanish Antilles. Haiti received some families from the Middle East, whereas Santo Domingo drew the bulk of the Lebanese, Syrian, and Palestinian immigrants, as well as many Catalans, together with a large group of Puerto Rican migrants who left their island after the devastating San Ciriaco hurricane in 1898. Out of these new populations and social groups, and under the shadow of political and economic domination of the United States, a new Caribbean was taking shape by 1930.

CHAPTER 20

Epilogue:
Why the Sugar Plantation?

This book has dealt mainly with the evolution of the sugar plantation as the dominant integrating force of Caribbean economic history.
I have chosen this focus because the functional unity of the region is
best viewed in the context of the plantation system as the underlying
economic structure that made the Caribbean economies very similar to
each other, despite ecological and political variations.

A different history of the Caribbean could, of course, have been written along other lines of analysis. But the major current that flowed
uninterruptedly and produced the historical unity of the region was the
evolution of the plantation system. It can be used to explain not only
many of the economic continuities of the colonies but also their demographic similarities. It also explains, more clearly than other structures
or phenomena, why the European powers became so involved in colonial wars in the Caribbean, and how their West Indian colonies became
integrated into the much broader Atlantic world.

The impact that Caribbean history exerted on other continents, like
Africa and North America, can best be understood and explained from
the perspective of the plantation system and its accompanying institution of slavery. The connections that linked the plantations in the
Caribbean with Africa, Europe, and North America, both before and
after the Industrial Revolution, are crucial to understanding the emergence of capitalism as a world economic system.

No other institution played the role that the plantation did in integrating the Caribbean into the world economy. Sugar was not the only
product coming out of the plantations, but it was the most important,
and the one that kept the islands in the eyes and grip of the metropoli-

tan powers. Together with the slave system, the sugar plantation dominated Caribbean economic history for almost 400 years.

The institution of the sugar plantation caused the Caribbean to function as a single economic unit within the capitalist world economic system, even though politically the colonies behaved as particular dependencies of distinct metropolitan powers. This dependency, together with
particular local events, eventually produced the social and cultural dif-
ferentiation of the West Indies that is so marked and visible today.

It has been said many times that the Caribbean is a fragmented
region, but this is only true from a sociopolitical perspective. From the
perspective of its production structures and its role within the Atlantic
economy, the Caribbean functioned as a homogeneous economic unit
more than as an internally diversified region. One has to recognize,
however, that beneath the unifying framework of the sugar plantation
system, distinct Creole societies were emerging, and new nationalities
were also taking shape. It is within this context that the fragmentation
of the Caribbean can be better understood and accepted in historical
analysis.

The formation of a fragmented Caribbean was a very long process,
but by 1930 there were clear signs of the increasing particularization
and pluralization of the Caribbean societies. Out of methodological
considerations, the period addressed in this book ends at 1930. There
are strong reasons for doing so. Beginning in 1930, the entire region was
dragged into the Great Depression, which affected the entire capitalist
world and wrought havoc in most colonial and neocolonial economies.
From that moment on, the Caribbean would never be the same.

The Caribbean was hit hard by the Depression. Each colony and
republic was forced to make profound local adjustments that ended up
transforming the region. Many external factors also contributed to this
transformation, like the impact of the Second World War and the
Korean War, or Europe's response to the demands for de-colonization
in Africa, Asia, and the Caribbean. Needless to say, as the region
became more integrated into the world economy, and as the influence of
the United States grew after the Second World War, the Americanization of the region increased as well.

Eventually, the sugar plantation system entered into a long and sustained crisis from which it never recuperated. The result was the eventu-

al abandonment of the sugar industry in Puerto Rico and some of the British Antilles, and its substantial weakening in Jamaica and the Dominican Republic. Only Cuba persisted in its dependency on the sugar plantation for many decades in the second half of the twentieth century, both under capitalist and socialist regimes. But eventually the revolutionary government that took over the island in 1959 and tried to convert it into a monocrop plantation economy had to modify that policy. The Cuban sugar economy is now shrinking, as has happened on the other islands.

Trade unionism, party politics, de-colonization, independence, nationalism, continuous emigration, the emergence of the middle classes, and massive immigration to the United States and Europe, among many other changes, mark the new Caribbean that emerged from the impact of the Great Depression and the Second World War. Industrialization by invitation or by import substitution, agrarian reform, regional integration, the promotion of tourism, and Americanization, among other important topics, eventually replaced sugar as new key words for the study of the development of the islands.

The sugar plantation system was one of the main components of what became a world economic system. It was at the core of the new Atlantic economy that emerged after the Europeans poured into the Americas in the sixteenth and seventeenth centuries. The development of capitalism cannot be fully understood without the sugar plantation system, nor can the independence of the United States be fully explained without the role played by the Caribbean sugar plantations.

The Caribbean functions today as a complex archipelago of nationalities and cultures with new diversified economies linked closely not only to the former European and North American rulers but also to South America and Asia. Globalization has dragged the Caribbean more deeply into the world market, but one should remember that it was in the Caribbean that the present process of globalization began more than 500 years ago. It was not until Columbus arrived on the islands that the Europeans started to recognize the unity of the planet and began acting accordingly. This is another reason why the history of the Caribbean is relevant to understanding today's modern world.

Not until mankind put a foot on the moon, almost five centuries later, had any other "discovery" had such momentous consequences as the European invasion of the Caribbean and the conversion of this region into a pivotal piece of the planetary economy. Making this process evident, and showing how it served to unify the region, has been the main purpose of this book.

NOTES TO THE CHAPTERS

Chapter 2

1. Santo Domingo was the center of operations for the exploration and conquest of the New World. From 1500 to 1520, there were extensive yuca plantations in Santo Domingo and Puerto Rico. Cassava was also grown to feed the Indians in the mines and to supply food for the sailors and conquering expeditions that went to the other islands and to South America. The development of the sugar industry enabled large *encomenderos* to transfer their fortunes to sugar production and thus maintain their grip on the colonial economy.

2. An *arroba* is a unit of weight in Spanish-speaking countries equal to twenty-five pounds.

3. The available statistics are interrupted in this year.

4. The sugar production of Madeira grew from 875 tons in 1508 to 2,500 tons in 1570, in spite of the fact that the number of plantations declined from eighty in 1490 to thirty-five in 1590. These numbers point clearly to the emphasis in Madeira on sugar production on larger and more efficient plantations.

5. The Madeira case is illustrative. In 1610 only eight plantations remained in operation on this island. They produced only 10 percent of the sugar produced in the mid-sixteenth century. The planters of Madeira made a serious effort to recuperate their sugar industry during the first half of the seventeenth century, but finally gave up in 1657 when they opted to convert their cane fields into vineyards.

Chapter 3

1. In 1589 Seville counted some 15,000 foreigners among its population of barely 90,000.

Chapter 4

1. The term adventurer was applied then to those who invested their money and effort in ventures.

Chapter 5

1. During the first half of the seventeenth century, Brazilian sugar was commonly shipped to Madeira or the Azores Islands and then reexported to Amsterdam or other parts of Europe as if it had been produced in the Atlantic islands.

2. Fifty-two sugar plantations were established in the north, thirty-four in the center, and thirty on the south Atlantic coast. A 1629 census of plantations shows 346 registered sugar mills in Brazil.

3. The Dutch population of New Holland in 1645 was close to 3,000 people. About half of them were Jews and New Christians.

4. In previous years, the Portuguese had also lost 220 ships to Dutch and English pirates when England was briefly at war with Portugal.

5. It is yet to be determined if this innovation passed into Peru and from there to Brazil, or if the Cuban planters copied the Peruvian model and claimed to have invented it.

Chapter 6

1. Poverty was so prevalent in Santo Domingo that when a ship with 400 African slaves arrived there in 1669, it could only sell 140 due to the colonists' lack of money. The slave population of the city barely reached 80 individuals the year before.

Chapter 8

1. Jamaican planters managed to raise their exports from 2,850 tons exported in 1702 to 6,300 tons by 1714. Barbados and the Leeward Islands, however, produced much more sugar. Barbados exported 10,150 tons in 1714, and the Leeward Islands exported 8,750 tons. In that same year, Saint-Domingue was already exporting 7,000 tons, while Martinique exported close to 5,000 tons and Guadeloupe around 4,000 tons. With an increased production of 16,000 tons in 1714, the French islands still lagged behind the English Antilles, which exported 25,000 tons that year. Brazil continued to be an important sugar supplier to the European market, exporting 21,800 tons in 1710. As Brazilian production stagnated, English sugar production overtook it, allowing England to briefly dominate the world sugar market, only until 1720. After that year, the French Antilles emerged as the largest sugar producer surpassing both Brazil

and the British West Indies. The Spanish Antilles exported almost no sugar; only Cuba continued to export some sugar to Spain, although far less than previously. In 1724 Cuba exported barely 600 tons of sugar.

2. From an average of twenty-seven shillings, six cents per hundredweight in 1689, the price of sugar rose to fifty-four shillings, nine cents per hundredweight in 1696. At this point, wildly fluctuating prices stimulated production for almost a quarter of a century, from 1689 until the end of the War of Spanish Succession in 1715.

3. Between 1700 and 1709 the average annual sugar consumption per capita in England was about four pounds. It doubled to around eight pounds during the decade from 1720 to 1729 and continued to increase until it reached twelve pounds between 1780 and 1789, even though prices were on the rise from 1734 on. Exports of sugar from the British Antilles to England grew consistently from 24,250 tons in 1700 to 97,000 tons in 1775.

4. Although there were 9,483 white people in the Leeward Islands in 1720, there were only 6,804 in 1775; over the same period, the slave population increased from 35,068 to 82,104 people.

5. Throughout the eighteenth century, France reexported between 60 and 70 percent of its Caribbean sugar. England reexported less than 20 percent; of this, 15 percent went to Ireland, leaving only 5 percent for the continental European market.

6. England was still reexporting two-thirds of the French volume in 1730, but by 1790 English exports had dropped to a mere 12 percent of the French output.

7. In 1768 Jamaica also had 110 cotton plantations, 8 indigo plantations, 30 ginger plantations, and 150 coffee plantations. In 1774 a census recorded 193,000 head of cattle.

8. The economy of Saint-Domingue was more diversified than that of Jamaica. In Saint-Domingue in 1768 there were 798 cotton plantations, 3,150 indigo plantations, 3,117 coffee plantations, 50 cacao plantations, 182 distilleries, 6 leather-tanning workshops, 36 brick factories, 29 pottery workshops, and approximately 240,000 head of cattle.

Chapter 9

1. This revolt is known as the *"revuelta de los capitanes"* (revolt of the captains) because its leadership was mainly composed of the Spanish captains serving in Santiago de los Caballeros.

Chapter 10

1. As the planters and merchants of the British West Indies complained of the French competition in North America, the British Parliament reacted to these complaints by enacting the famous Sugar Act of 1764, designed to regulate trade with the Antilles and enforce the collection of taxes for repaying the debt incurred by Great Britain during the Seven Years War. The Sugar Act raised duties on foreign sugar and molasses, prohibited the importation of foreign rum, and imposed a new tax on the importation of foreign wine, textiles, and coffee, as well as indigo in order to protect the indigo production of Georgia and South Carolina, which had recently begun.

The Sugar Act reduced the tax on molasses from the British West Indies from six pence to three pence per gallon, a measure that was supposed to protect the North American distilleries from the competition of foreign molasses. Yet, the rum industry went into an immediate decline, not because of the new taxes but rather because of the firm decision on the part of the British colonial authorities to collect them, which ended up obstructing North American trade with the French Antilles. The Georgian colonists protested the Sugar Act when they discovered that the lumber they exported to French Antilles would not be sold as before if the authorities insisted in collecting the duties on molasses and enforcing the other requirements of the act.

2. According to a report prepared by a Dutch rear admiral who lived in St. Eustatius for thirteen months between 1778 and 1779, during that period 3,182 ships loaded with merchandise sailed to North America and other parts of the West Indies. Another contemporary report prepared by a British observer stated that in 1779, the North Americans sent about 6,000 tons of tobacco and about 750 tons of indigo to St. Eustatius in exchange for European merchandise, especially spare parts for ships.

Chapter 11

1. The Code Noir was enacted by King Louis XIV in March 1685 with several intentions in mind. One was to expel all Jews from the French colonies within a period of three months. Another was to regulate the management of the slave population. By that time there was a growing free-colored population in the French Antilles (born free or manumitted), and the Code dictated, among many other things, that they should be considered French citizens with full rights. The Code denied the slaves most of those rights.

2. France had taken Navarre during the war and intended to annex it before the treaty was signed.

3. Louisiana was exchanged for the Duchy of Parma, in Italy.

4. Rochambeau had been appointed by the National Assembly before Louis XVI was decapitated, but arrived at Martinique more than six months later, together with General Georges Henri Victor Collot, his counterpart as administrator/governor of Guadeloupe.

Chapter 14

1. The slave population in the British West Indies decreased from 776,105 in 1807 to 664,970 in 1834. This was a 15 percent decline over the course of twenty-seven years.

2. Jamaica had the largest slave population with 311,070 individuals, followed by Guiana with 83,345 and Barbados with 83,150. Antigua, St. Vincent, Grenada, Trinidad, and St. Kitts had slave populations ranging from 17,000 to 28,000. The slave populations of Nevis, Montserrat, Dominica, St. Lucia, Tobago, and the Bahamas ranged from 6,400 to 14,000, and on the smaller islands of Anguilla, Barbuda, the Cayman Islands, and the British Virgin Islands, the number of slaves ranged from 505 to 5,000.

3. In 1834 the free black population in the British West Indies was 98,435, approximately 42,000 of whom lived in Jamaica, 16,000 in Trinidad, 7,000 in Guiana, 5,000 in Barbados, and 4,000 in Antigua. The other islands had smaller free black populations, ranging from 2,000 to 3,000 people. On the Leeward Islands in 1834, free blacks were more numerous than whites.

Chapter 15

1. A similar system was imposed in the French Antilles for the same purposes.

2. Low sugar prices, plus the rise in slave prices due to the obstacles imposed by the British navy, became too much for the Puerto Rican planters, who were also affected by a drought that lasted several years.

Chapter 16

1. In Ponce, Puerto Rico, the authorities discovered another conspiracy of slaves organized by Haitian agents in July 1825.

2. At that time, it was also important not to jeopardize the negotiations that allowed the United States to acquire Florida from Spain for $5 million.

3. Alta Vela.

4. This war is known by different names: Guerra de los Diez Años (Ten Years' War), Guerra Grande, and Guerra del 68.

Chapter 17

1. *Trapiches* were similar in size and performance to the old seventeenth-century mills which did not use the Jamaican train technology.

2. The province of Pinar del Río had only 7 sugar plantations, Havana 20, Matanzas 62, Santa Clara 73, Puerto Príncipe 3, and Santiago de Cuba 42.

Chapter 18

1. On the West Coast of the United States, the California Sugar Refining Company resisted being bought up by Havemeyer, despite the brutal price war he unleashed in an attempt to remove it from the market. After inquiring into the secrets of the California company, Havemeyer discovered that its owner, Claus Spreckels, was capable of resisting pressure because he had managed to vertically integrate his refinery with Hawaiian sugarcane producers. Spreckels had quickly built an efficient complex of *centrales*, railroads, and ships in Hawaii, which assured an uninterrupted flow of sugar from the plantations to the refineries. Spreckels and Havemeyer resolved their differences in 1891 and created a new consolidated company, dividing among themselves the West Coast market of the United States and buying up the plants of the refiners who had been driven out of business during the price war.

2. Rionda had previously owned several *centrales*, but had sold them during the second War of Independence to become the head of a subsidiary brokerage firm, Czarnikov-Rionda, where he spent most of his time buying and selling sugar.

3. In that year fourteen Cuban-American companies produced 8 percent, while ten Canadian companies produced 4 percent. The other 25.5 percent was produced by *centrales* owned by Cuban, Spanish, and English companies.

4. The most a buyer could obtain were the so-called *pesos de tierra* (land pesos) or *acciones de tierra* (land stocks). These were land-use rights purchased from the owners of the original deeds of the communal lands that authorized the buyer to exploit a certain amount of territory. Sales were registered on the back of the old titles, but no deeds were issued to the buyers. The foreign sugar companies did not feel comfortable with the communal land tenure system and therefore promoted its termination.

5. The total population of the Dominican Republic in 1908 was 638,000 people, living in a territory of 18,532 square miles.

Chapter 19

1. The Morant Bay rebellion is considered the most important post-slavery revolt in the British West Indies. It began when a local peasant was arrested after trespassing on an abandoned plantation. A group of angry peasants protested and broke into the prison where the man was held, liberating him. In a second demonstration, at the courthouse several days later, the militia shot at the protesters, killing seven of them. The population responded by rioting and attacking some white planters, killing eighteen people. The rebellion grew rapidly, eventually involving more than 2,000 peasants. When the governor of Jamaica sent troops to put down the riots, the soldiers behaved brutally. Four hundred and thirty-nine peasants were killed during the military operations, and more than 354 were arrested and later executed, in addition to several hundred more who received other punishments, including flogging and imprisonment. The brutality of the repression scandalized British public opinion and generated a movement towards the reformation of the colonial government in the British West Indies, leading to the conversion of Jamaica into a Crown Colony and thereby eliminating the political control exerted by the colonial assembly dominated by white planters.

2. Hispaniola is the official international cartographic name of the island since 1933, when the U.S. Board on Geographical Names and the American Geographical Society adopted it in order to standardize the island's name on international charts and maps. As early as 1913, the Board started receiving suggestions by map makers and cartographers to adopt Hispaniola as the island's name in order to avoid confusion. The Dominican Republic and Haiti still call the island by their official and traditional names: Dominicans call it Santo Domingo, while Haitians call it Haiti.

BIBLIOGRAPHICAL GUIDE

This is a list of essential books. For a comprehensive bibliography, including additional books and many of the most authoritative scholarly articles, the reader should consult the "Bibliographical Essay" in the hardbound edition of this book: Frank Moya Pons, *History of the Caribbean: Plantations, Trade, and War in the Atlantic World* (Princeton: Markus Wiener Publishers, 2007).

Chapter 1. The Spanish Occupation of the Antilles

Atkinson, Lesley-Gail. *The Earliest Inhabitants: The Dynamics of the Jamaican Taíno*. Jamaica: University of the West Indies Press, 2006.

Cárdenas Ruiz, Manuel. *Crónicas francesas de los indios caribes*. Río Piedras: Editorial de la Universidad de Puerto Rico, 1981.

Marrero, Leví. *Cuba: Economía y Sociedad. El siglo XVI*, vols. 1-2. Madrid: Editorial Playor, 1972.

Morales Padrón, Francisco. *Spanish Jamaica*. Kingston: Ian Randle Publishers, 2003.

Moreau, Jean-Pierre. *Les Petites Antilles de Christophe Colomb à Richelieu*. Paris: Karthala, 1992.

Moya Pons, Frank. *Después de Colón: Trabajo, sociedad y política en la economía del oro*. Madrid: Alianza Editorial, 1986.

Sauer, Carl Ortwin. *The Early Spanish Main*. Berkeley: University of California Press, 1966.

Sued Badillo, Jalil. *El dorado borincano: La economía de la conquista*. San Juan: Ediciones Puerto, 2001.

Veloz Maggiolo, Marcio. *Panorama histórico del Caribe Precolombino*. Santo Domingo: Banco Central de la República Dominicana, 1991.

Wilson, Samuel M. *Hispaniola: Caribbean Chiefdoms in the Age of Columbus*. Tuscaloosa: The University of Alabama Press, 1990.

Wilson, Samuel M., ed. *The Indigenous People of the Caribbean*. Gainesville: University Press of Florida, 1997.

Chapter 2. Sugar and Slaves in the Spanish Antilles

Marrero, Leví. *Cuba: Economía y Sociedad,* vol. 2. Madrid: Editorial Playor, 1974.

Moya Pons, Frank. *Historia Colonial de Santo Domingo.* Santiago de los Caballeros: Universidad Católica Madre y Maestra, 1973.

Río Moreno, Justo del. *Los Inicios de la Agricultura Europea en el Nuevo Mundo 1492-1542.* Sevilla: Gráficas del Guadalquivir, 1991.

Schwartz, Stuart B., ed. *Tropical Babylons: Sugar and the Making of the Atlantic World 1450-1650.* Chapel Hill: The University of North Carolina Press, 2004.

Sued Badillo, Jalil, and Angel López Cantos. *Puerto Rico Negro.* Río Piedras, P.R.: Editorial Cultural, 1986.

Chapter 3. Monopoly, Privateers, and Contraband

Andrews, Kenneth R. *English Privateering Voyages to the West Indies, 1588-1595.* Cambridge: Hakluyt Society, 1959.

Andrews, Kenneth R. *The Spanish Caribbean: Trade and Plunder, 1530-1630.* New Haven: Yale University Press, 1978.

Goslinga, Cornelis Ch. *The Dutch in the Caribbean and on the Wild Coast 1580-1680.* Gainesville: University Press of Florida, 1971.

Hoffman, Paul E. *The Spanish Crown and the Defense of the Caribbean, 1535-1585: Precedent, Patrimonialism, and Royal Parsimony.* Baton Rouge: Louisiana State University Press, 1980.

Marrero, Leví. *Cuba: Economía y Sociedad,* vol. 3. Madrid: Editorial Playor, 1974.

Newton, Arthur P. *The European Nations in the West Indies, 1493-1688.* London: A & C Black, 1933. Reprinted 1967, Barnes and Noble, New York.

Peña Batlle, Manuel Arturo. *Las Devastaciones de 1605 y 1606 (Contribución al Estudio de la Realidad Dominicana).* Ciudad Trujillo: Imprenta J. R. Vda. García, 1938.

Phillips, Carla Rahn. *Six Galleons for the King of Spain: Imperial Defense in the Early Seventeenth Century.* Baltimore: Johns Hopkins University Press, 1986.

Chapter 4. The Early Tobacco Colonies

Batie, Robert Carlyle. "A Comparative History of the Spanish, French, and English in the Caribbean Islands during the Seventeenth Century." Ph.D. diss., University of Washington, 1972.

Beckles, Hilary McD. *Black Rebellion in Barbados: The Struggle Against Slavery 1627-1838*. Bridgetown, Barbados: Antilles Publications, 1984.

Bridenbaugh, Carl, and J. Bridenbaugh. *No Peace Beyond the Line: The English in the Caribbean, 1624-1690*. London: Oxford University Press, 1972.

Dunn, Richard. *Sugar and Slaves: The Rise of the Planter Class in the English West Indies, 1624-1713*. Chapel Hill: University of North Carolina Press, 1972.

Goslinga, Cornelis Ch. *The Dutch in the Caribbean and on the Wild Coast 1580-1680*. Gainesville: University Press of Florida, 1971.

Gragg, Larry Dale. *Englishmen Transplanted: The English Colonization of Barbados, 1627-1660*. Oxford: Oxford University Press, 2003.

Moreau, Jean-Pierre. *Les Petites Antilles de Christophe Colomb à Richelieu*. Paris: Editions Karthala, 1992.

Paquette, Robert L., and Stanley L. Engerman, eds. *The Lesser Antilles in the Age of European Expansion* Gainesville: University Press of Florida, 1996.

Pluchon, Pierre, ed. *Histoire des Antilles et de la Guyane*. Toulouse: Edouard Privat, 1982.

Puckrein, Gary A. *Little England, Plantation Society and Anglo-Barbadian Politics, 1627-1700*. New York: New York University Press, 1984.

Chapter 5. The Sugar Revolution in the Lesser Antilles

Abenon, Lucien René. *La Guadeloupe de 1671 à 1759: étude politique, économique et sociale*. Paris: Editions L'Harmattan, 1987.

Baylin, Bernard. *Atlantic History*. Cambridge, Mass.: Harvard University Press, 2005.

Beckles, Hilary McD. *White Servitude and Black Slavery in Barbados, 1627-1715*. Nashville: University of Tennessee Press, 1989.

Bernardini, Paolo, and Norman Fiering. *The Jews and the Expansion of Europe to the West, 1450-1800*. New York: Berghahn Books, 2001.

Butel, Paul. *The Atlantic*. London: Routledge, 1999.

Coclanis, Peter A., ed. *The Atlantic Economy during the Seventeenth and Eighteenth Centuries: Organization, Operation, Practice, and Personnel*.

Columbia: University of South Carolina Press, 2005.

Chauleau, Liliana. *La société à la Martinique au XVIIe siècle.* Caen, 1966.

Davis, Ralph. *The Rise of the Atlantic Economies.* London: Weidenfeld and Nicolson, 1973.

Debien, Gabriel. *Les esclaves aux Antilles françaises (XVIIe-XVIIIe siècles).* Basse-Terre: Société d'Histoire de la Guadeloupe, 1974.

Deerr, Noel. *The History of Sugar.* London: Chapman and Hall Ltd., 1949-1950.

Dunn, Richard. *Sugar and Slaves: The Rise of the Planter Class in the English West Indies, 1624-1713.* Chapel Hill: University of North Carolina Press, 1972. Reprinted 2002.

Faber, Eli. *Jews, Slaves, and the Slave Trade: Setting the Record Straight.* New York: New York University Press, 1998.

Fortune, Stephen Alexander. *Merchants and Jews: The Struggle for British West Indian Commerce, 1650-1700.* Gainesville: University Press of Florida, 1984.

Galloway, John H. *The Sugar Cane Industry: An Historical Geography from Its Origins to 1914.* Cambridge: Cambridge University Press, 1989.

Greene, Jack P., and J. R. Pole. *Colonial British America: Essays in the New History of the Early Modern Era.* Baltimore: The Johns Hopkins University Press, 1984.

Goslinga, Cornelis Ch. *The Dutch in the Caribbean and in the Guianas 1680-1791.* Assen/Maastricht, The Netherlands: Van Gorcum, 1985.

Hamshere, Cyril. *The British in the Caribbean.* Cambridge, Mass.: Harvard University Press, 1972.

Higham, C. S. *The Development of the Leeward Islands under the Restoration, 1660-1688: A Study of the Foundations of the Old Colonial System.* Cambridge: Cambridge University Press, 1921.

McCusker, John J. *Essays in Economic History of the Atlantic World.* London: Routledge, 1997.

McCusker, John J., and Kenneth Morgan, eds. *The Early Modern Atlantic Economy.* Cambridge: Cambridge University Press, 2000.

Menard, Russell R. *Sweet Negotiations: Sugar, Slavery, and Plantation Agriculture in Early Barbados.* Charlottesville: University of Virginia Press, 2006.

Piffer Canabrava, Alice. *O Açucar nas Antilhas, 1697-1755.* São Paulo: Instituto de Pesquisas Econômicas, 1981.

Pluchon Pierre, ed. *Histoire des Antilles et de la Guyane.* Toulouse: Edouard Privat, 1982.

Sheridan, Richard B. *Sugar and Slavery: An Economic History of the British West Indies, 1623-1775.* Baltimore: Johns Hopkins University Press, 1974.

Solow, Barbara. *Slavery and the Rise of the Atlantic System.* Cambridge: Cambridge University Press, 1991.

Westergaard, Waldemar. *The Danish West Indies under Company Rule, 1671-1754.* New York, 1917.

Chapter 6. Poverty in the Spanish Antilles

Deive, Carlos Esteban. *La Mala Vida: Delincuencia y Picaresca en la Colonia Española de Santo Domingo.* Santo Domingo: Fundación Cultural Dominicana, 1989.

Gil-Bermejo García, Juana. *La Española: Anotaciones históricas, 1600-1650.* Sevilla: Escuela de Estudios Hispanoamericanos, 1983.

Gil-Bermejo García, Juana. *Panorama histórico de la agricultura en Puerto Rico.* Sevilla: Escuela de Estudios Hispanoamericanos, 1970.

Marrero, Leví. *Cuba: Economía y Sociedad. El siglo XVII*, vols. 3-4. Madrid: Playor, 1975-1976.

Morales Carrión, Arturo. *Albores Históricos del Capitalismo en Puerto Rico.* San Juan: Universidad de Puerto Rico, 1972.

Morales Carrión, Arturo. *Historia del pueblo de Puerto Rico, desde sus orígenes hasta el siglo XVIII.* San Juan, P.R.: Editorial del Departamento de Instrucción Pública, 1968.

Moscoso, Francisco. *Agricultura y sociedad en Puerto Rico, siglos 16 al 18: Un acercamiento desde la historia.* San Juan, P.R.: Instituto de Cultura Puertorriqueña, 1999.

Moya Pons, Frank. *Historia Colonial de Santo Domingo.* Santiago de los Caballeros: Universidad Católica Madre y Maestra, 1973.

Peña Batlle, Manuel Arturo. *La Isla de la Tortuga.* Madrid: Consejo Superior de Investigaciones Científicas, 1951.

Taylor, Stanley Arthur Goodwin. *The Western Design: An Account of Cromwell's Expedition to the Caribbean.* Kingston: The Institute of Jamaica and the Jamaica Historical Society, 1965.

Wright, Irene A., ed. *Spanish Narratives of the English Attack on Santo Domingo, 1655.* London: Royal Historical Society, 1926.

Chapter 7. The Emergence of Saint-Domingue

Charlevoix, Pierre François Xavier de. *Histoire de l'île Espagnole ou de S. Domingue.* Paris, 1731.

Debien, Gabriel. *Les femmes des premiers colonos aux Antilles, 1635-1680*. Le Havre: Notes de Histoire Coloniale, 1952.

Exquemelin, Alexander Oliver. *The Buccaneers of America*. Mineola, N.Y.: Dover Publications, 2000.

Haring, Clarence H. *The Buccaneers in the West Indies in the XVII Century*. New York: E. P. Dutton, 1910. Reprinted 1966, Archon Books, Hamden, Conn.

Mims, Stewart L. *Colbert's West India Policy*. New Haven: Yale University Press, 1912.

Moreau de Saint-Méry, Médéric-Louis-Elie. *Description topographique, physique, civile, politique et historique de la partie francaise de l'ile de Saint-Domingue*. Paris, 1797-1798.

Moya Pons, Frank. *Historia Colonial de Santo Domingo*. Santiago de los Caballeros: Universidad Católica Madre y Maesra, 1973.

Peña Batlle, Manuel Arturo. *La Isla de la Tortuga*. Madrid: Consejo Superior de Investigaciones Científicas, 1951.

Pluchon Pierre, ed. *Histoire des Antilles et de la Guyane*. Toulouse: Edouard Privat, 1982.

Price, Jacob M. *France and the Chesapeake: A History of the French Tobacco Monopoly, 1674-1791, and of Its Relationship to the British and American Tobacco Trades*. Ann Arbor: The University of Michigan Press, 1973.

Priestley, Herbert Ingram. *France Overseas Through the Old Regime: A Study of European Expansion*. New York and London: D. Appleton Century Company, 1939.

Chapter 8. Caribbean Sugar Economies in the Eighteenth Century

Beckles, Hilary McD. *Centering Women: Gender Discourses in Caribbean Slave Society*. Princeton: Markus Wiener Publishers, 1999.

Beckles, Hilary McD., and Verene A. Shepherd, eds. *Caribbean Slavery in the Atlantic World*. Princeton: Markus Wiener Publishers, 2000.

Bush, Barbara. *Slave Women in Caribbean Society, 1650-1838*. Bloomington and Indianapolis: Indiana University Press, 1990.

Campbell, Mavis C. *The Maroons of Jamaica, 1655-1796: A History of Resistance, Collaboration and Betrayal*. Granby, Mass., 1988.

Coughtry, Jay. *The Notorious Triangle: Rhode Island and the African Slave Trade, 1700-1807*. Philadelphia: Temple University Press, 1981.

Craton, Michael. *Testing the Chains: Resistance to Slavery in the British West*

Indies. Ithaca: Cornell University Press, 1982.

Curtin, Philip D. *The Atlantic Slave Trade: A Census*. Madison: The University of Wisconsin Press, 1969.

Deive, Carlos Esteban. *Los Guerrilleros Negros: Esclavos Fugitivos y Cimarrones en Santo Domingo*. Santo Domingo: Fundación Cultural Dominicana, 1989.

Dessens, Nathalie. *Myths of the Plantation Society: Slavery in the American South and the West Indies*. Gainesville: University Press of Florida, 2004.

Dunn, Richard. *Sugar and Slaves: The Rise of the Planter Class in the English West Indies, 1624-1713*. Chapel Hill: University of North Carolina Press, 1972.

Emmer, P. C. *The Dutch in the Atlantic Economy, 1580-1880: Trade, Slavery and Emancipation*. Aldershot: Ashgate, 1998.

Fouchard, Jean. *Les marrons de la liberté*. Paris: L'École, 1972.

Gaspar, David Barry. *Bondmen and Rebels: A Study of Master-Slave Relations in Antigua, with Implications for Colonial British America*. Baltimore: The Johns Hopkins University Press, 1985.

Goveia, Elsa V. *Slave Society in the British Leeward Islands at the End of the Eighteenth Century*. Westport, Conn.: Greenwood Press, 1965.

Kipple, Kenneth F. *The Caribbean Slave: A Biological History*. Cambridge: Cambridge University Press, 1984. Reprinted 2002.

Klein, Herbert S. *The Middle Passage: Comparative Studies in the Atlantic Slave Trade*. Princeton, N.J.: Princeton University Press, 1978.

Klein, Herbert S. *African Slavery in Latin America and the Caribbean*. New York: Oxford University Press, 1986.

Klein, Herbert S. *The Atlantic Slave Trade*. Cambridge: Cambridge University Press, 1999.

Mintz, Sidney W. *Sweetness and Power: The Place of Sugar in Modern History*. New York: Penguin Books, 1985.

Moitt, Bernard. *Women and Slavery in the French Antilles, 1635-1848*. Bloomington and Indianapolis: Indiana University Press, 2001.

Moore, Brian L., B. W. Higman, Carl Campbell, and Patrick Bryan, eds. *Slavery, Freedom and Gender: The Dynamics of Caribbean Society*. Barbados: University of the West Indies Press, 2001.

Morrisey, Marietta. *Slave Women in the New World: Gender Stratification in the Caribbean*. Lawrence: University of Kansas Press, 1989.

Palmer, Colin A. *Human Cargoes: The British Slave Trade to Spanish America, 1700-1739*. Urbana: University of Illinois Press, 1981.

Piffer Canabrava, Alice. *O Açucar nas Antilhas. 1697-1755*. São Paulo: Instituto de Pesquisas Econômicas, 1981.

Pitman, Frank W. *The Development of the British West Indies 1700-1763*. New Haven: Yale University Press, 1917.

Postma, Johannes M. *The Dutch in the Atlantic Slave Trade, 1600-1815*. Cambridge: Cambridge University Press, 1990.

Price, Richard. *Maroon Societies: Rebel Slave Communities in the Americas*. New York: Anchor Press, 1973.

Rawley, James. *The Transatlantic Slave Trade: A History*. New York: W. W. Norton & Company, 1981.

Sheridan, Richard B. *The Development of the Plantations to 1750: An Era of West Indian Prosperity 1750-1775*. Mona, Jamaica: Caribbean Universities Press, 1970.

Sheridan, Richard B. *Sugar and Slavery: An Economic History of the British West Indies, 1623-1775*. Baltimore: Johns Hopkins University Press, 1974.

Sheridan, Richard B. *Doctors and Slaves: A Medical and Demographic History of Slavery in the British West Indies, 1680-1834*. Cambridge: Cambridge University Press, 1985.

Stein, Robert Louis. *The French Slave Trade in the Eighteenth Century: An Old Regime Business*. Wisconsin: The University of Wisconsin Press, 1979.

Stein, Robert Louis. *The French Sugar Business in the Eighteenth Century*. Baton Rouge: Louisiana State University Press, 1988.

Thomas, Hugh. *The Slave Trade: The Story of the Atlantic Trade, 1440-1870*. New York: Simon & Schuster, 1997.

Watts, David. *The West Indies: Patterns of Development, Culture and Environment*. Cambridge: Cambridge University Press, 1987.

Chapter 9. Caribbean Trade Circuits in the Eighteenth Century

García-Baquero González, Antonio. *Cádiz y el Atlántico*. Sevilla: Escuela de Estudios Hispano-Americanos, 1976.

Gutiérrez Escudero, Antonio. *Población y Economía en Santo Domingo. 1700-1746*. Sevilla: Diputación Provincial, 1985.

Harman, Joyce Elizabeth. *Trade and Privateering in Spanish Florida 1732-1763*. Jacksonville: The St. Augustine Historical Society, 1969.

Harper, Lawrence. *The English Navigation Acts*. New York: Octagon Books, 1964.

Knight, Franklin W., and Peggy K.Liss, eds. *Atlantic Port Cities: Economy, Culture, and Society in the Atlantic World, 1650-1850*. Knoxville: The University of Tennessee Press, 1991.

Liss, Peggy K. *Atlantic Empires: The Network of Trade and Revolution, 1713-1826*. Baltimore: Johns Hopkins University Press, 1983.

Marrero, Leví. *Cuba: Economía y Sociedad. Del monopolio a la libertad comercial (1701-1763)*, vol. 7. Madrid: Editorial Playor, 1979.

McCusker, John James. "The Rum Trade and the Balance of Payments of the Thirteen Continental Colonies, 1660-1775." Ph.D diss., University of Pittsburgh, 1970.

McLachlan, Jean O. *Trade and Peace with Old Spain 1667-1750: A Study of the Influence of Commerce on Anglo-Spanish Diplomacy in the First half of the Eighteenth Century*. New York: Octagon Books, 1974.

McNeil, John Robert. *Atlantic Empires of France and Spain: Louisbourg and Havana 1700-1763*. Chapel Hill: University of North Carolina Press, 1985.

Morales Carrión, Arturo. *Puerto Rico and the Non Hispanic Caribbean: A Study in the Decline of Spanish Exclusivism*. Río Piedras: University of Puerto Rico, 1971.

Moreau de Saint-Méry, Médéric-Louis-Elie. *A Topographical and Political Description of the Spanish Part of Saint-Domingo*. Philadelphia: Printed and Sold by the Author, 1796.

Moreau de Saint-Méry, Médéric-Louis-Elie. *Description topographique, physique, civile, politique, et historique de la partie française de l'Ile Saint-Domingue*. Philadelphia: Chez l'auteur, 1797-1798. Reprinted 1984, Société Française d'Histoire d'Outre Mer, Paris.

Moya Pons, Frank. *Historia Colonial de Santo Domingo*. Santiago de los Caballeros: Universidad Católica Madre y Maestra, 1973.

Ojanguren, Montserrat Garate. *Comercio Ultramarino e Ilustración: La Real Compañía de La Habana*. San Sebastián: Real Sociedad Bascongada de los Amigos del País, 1993.

Ragatz, Lowell J. *The West Indian Approach to the Study of American Colonial History*. London: A. Thomas, 1934.

Sonesson, Birgit. *Puerto Rico's Commerce, 1765-1865: From Regional to Worldwide Market Relations*. Los Angeles: UCLA Latin American Center Publications, 2000.

Steele, Jan K. *The English Atlantic 1675-1740: An Exploration of Communication and Community*. Oxford: Oxford University Press, 1986.

Walker, Geoffrey J. *Spanish Politics and Imperial Trade, 1700-1789*. Bloomington: Indiana University Press, 1979.

Chapter 10. Trade and Wars

Andrews, Charles M. *The Colonial Background to the American Revolution.* New Haven: Yale University Press, 1958.

Burns, Alan. *History of the British West Indies.* London: Allen and Unwin, 1965.

Carrington, Selwyn H. H. *The British West Indies during the American Revolution.* Providence, R.I.: Foris Publications, 1988.

Gipson, Lawrence Henry. *The British Isles and the American Colonies: The Southern Plantations, 1748-1754.* New York: Alfred A. Knopf, 1967.

Gipson, Lawrence Henry. *The Triumphant Empire: New Responsibilities within the Enlarged Empire, 1763-1766.* New York: Alfred A. Knopf, 1968.

Gould, Eliga H. *Empire and Nation: The American Revolution in the Atlantic World.* Baltimore: The Johns Hopkins University Press, 2004.

Pares, Richard. *War and Trade in the West Indies, 1739-1763.* Oxford: Oxford University Press, 1936. Reprinted 1963, Frank Cass & Co., London.

Pares, Richard. *Yankees and Creoles.* Cambridge: Harvard University Press, 1956.

Ragatz, Lowell Joseph. *The Fall of the Planter Class in the British Caribbean 1763-1833.* New York: The Century, Co., 1928. Reprinted 1963, Octagon Books, New York.

Zapatero, Juan M. *La Guerra del Caribe en el siglo XVIII.* San Juan P.R.: Instituto de Cultura Puertorriqueña, 1964.

Chapter 11. The French Revolution in the Antilles

Abenon, Lucien, Jacques Cauna, and Liliane Chauleau. *Antilles 1789: La Révolution aux Caraïbes.* Condé-sur-Noireau: Éditions Nathan, 1989.

Bangou, Henri. *La Revolution et l'esclavage à la Guadeloupe 1789-1802: Epopée noire et genocide.* Messidor: Editions Sociales, 1989.

Brown, Gordon S. *Toussaint's Clause: The Founding Fathers and the Haitian Revolution.* Jackson: University Press of Mississippi, 2005.

Buckley, Roger Norman. *British Army in the West Indies: Society and the Military in the Revolutionary Age.* Gainesville: University Press of Florida, 1998.

Cooper, Ana Julia. *Slavery and the French Revolutionists (1788-1805).* Lewiston: The Edwin Mellen Press, 1988. Reprinted 2006, Rowman & Littlefield Publishers.

D'Auberteuil, Michael René Hilliard. *Considerations sur l'état present de la colonie française de Saint Domingue*. Paris: Grand-Imprimeur-Libraire, 1776.

De Vaissiere, Pierre. *Saint-Domingue: La société et la vie créoles, sous l'Ancien Regime, 1629-1789*. Paris: Librairie Academique Perrin et Cie, 1909.

Debien, Gabriel. *Les colons de Saint-Domingue et la Révolution: Essai sur le Club Massiac.* Paris: A. Colin, 1953.

Dubois, Laurent. *A Colony of Citizens: Revolution & Slave Emancipation in the French Caribbean, 1787-1804*. Chapel Hill: The University of North Carolina Press, 2004.

Dubois, Laurent. *Avengers of the New World: The Story of the Haitian Revolution*. Cambridge, Mass.: The Belknap Press of Harvard University Press, 2004.

Duffy, Michael. *Soldiers, Sugar, and Seapower: The British Expeditions to the West Indies and the War Against Revolutionary France*. Oxford: Clarendon Press, 1987.

Edwards, Bryan. *An Historical Survey of the French Colony in the Island of St. Domingo*. London: Printed for John Stockdale, Piccadilly, 1797.

Fick, Carolyn E. *The Making of Haiti: The Saint-Domingue Revolution from Below*. Knoxville: The University of Tennessee Press, 1990.

François, Pierre, and Regis Dessalles. *Historique des troubles survenus à la Martinique pendant la Révolution*. Fort-de-France: Henri de Fremont, 1982.

Frostin, Charles. *Les révoltes blanches à Saint-Domingue aux XVIIe et XVIIIe siècles*. Paris: L'École, 1975.

Garrigus, John D. *Before Haiti: Race and Citizenship in French Saint-Domingue*. New York: Palgrave Macmillan, 2006.

Gaspar, David Barry. *Turbulent Time: The French Revolution and the Greater Caribbean*. Bloomington: Indiana University Press, 2003.

Geggus, David Patrick. *Slavery, War, and Revolution: British Occupation in Saint-Domingue, 1793-1798*. Oxford: Clarendon Press, 1982.

Geggus, David Patrick, ed. *The Impact of the Haitian Revolution in the Atlantic World*. Columbia: University of South Carolina Press, 2001.

Geggus, David Patrick. *Haitian Revolutionary Studies*. Bloomington: Indiana University Press, 2002.

Girod, François. *La vie quotidienne de la société créole: Saint-Domingue au XVIIIe siècle*. Paris: Hachette, 1972.

Girod de Chantrans, Justin. *Voyage d'un suisse en differentes colonies*. Neuchâtel: Impr. de la Société Typographique, 1785.

Hall, Gwendolin Midlo. *Social Control in Slave Plantation Societies: A Comparison of St. Domingue and Cuba*. Baltimore: Johns Hopkins University Press, 1971.

James, C.L.R. *The Black Jacobins: Toussaint Louverture and the San Domingo Revolution*. New York: Vintage Books, 1963.

King, Stewart R. *Blue Coat or Powdered Wig: Free People of Color in Pre-Revolutionary Saint Domingue*. Athens: University of Georgia Press, 2001.

Moreau de Saint-Méry, Médéric-Louis-Elie. *Description topographique, physique, civile, politique, et historique de la partie française de l'Ile Saint-Domingue*. Philadelphia: Chez l'auteur, 1797-1798. Reprinted 1984, Société Française d'Histoire d'Outre Mer, Paris.

Ott, Thomas O. *The Haitian Revolution, 1789-1804*. Knoxville: The University of Tennessee Press, 1972.

Pérotin-Dumon, Anne. *Etre patriote sous les tropiques*. Basse-Terre: Société d'Histoire de la Guadeloupe, 1985.

Chapter 12. New Peasantries in Haiti and Santo Domingo

Ardouin, Beaubrun. *Etudes sur l'histoire d'Haiti, suivi de la vie du General Borgella*. Paris: Dézobry et E. Magdeleine, 1853-1860. Reprinted 1958, Francois Dalencour, Port-au-Prince.

Brown, Jonathan. *The History and Present Condition of St. Domingo*. Philadelphia: W. Marshall and Co., 1837. Reprinted 1972, Frank Cass and Co., London.

Candler, John. *Brief Notices of Hayti, with its Conditions, Resources, and Prospects*. London: T. Ward, 1842.

Franklin, James. *The Present State of Hayti. Santo Domingo with Remarks on Its Agriculture, Commerce, Laws, Religion, Finances, and Populations, etc., etc.* London: Murray, 1828. Reprinted 1971, Frank Cass and Co., London.

Leyburn, James. *The Haitian People*. New Haven: Yale University Press, 1941. Reprinted 1966.

MacKenzie, Charles. *Notes on Haiti, Made during a Residence in the Republic*. London: H. Colburn and R. Bently, 1830. Reprinted Frank Cass and Co., in London.

Madiou, Thomas. *Histoire d'Haiti*. Port-au-Prince: H. Deschamps, 1985-1991.

Manigat, Leslie F. *La politique agraire du government d'Alexandre Pétion, 1807-1818*. Port-au-Prince: Imp. La Phalange, 1962.

Moya Pons, Frank. *La Dominación Haitiana*. Santiago de los Caballeros: Universidad Católica Madre y Maestra, 1972.

Chapter 13. Abolitionism and Crisis in the British West Indies

Anstey, Roger T. *The Atlantic Slave Trade and British Abolition, 1760-1810*. London: Macmillan, 1975.

Carrington, Selwyn H. H. *Sugar Industry and the Abolition of the Slave Trade, 1775-1810. Gainesville:* University Press of Florida, 2002.

Clarkson, Thomas. *The History of the Rise, Progress and Abolition of the African Slave Trade by the British Parliament*. London: Brown & Merritt, 1808.

Craton, Michael. *Testing the Chains: Resistance to Slavery in the British West Indies*. Ithaca: Cornell University Press, 1982.

Dookhan, Isaac. *A Post-Emancipation History of the West Indies*. London: Collins, 1975.

Drescher, Seymour. *Capitalism and Antislavery: British Mobilization in Comparative Perspective*. New York, Oxford: Oxford University Press, 1987.

Drescher, Seymour. *Econocide: British Slavery in the Era of Abolition*. Pittsburgh: University of Pittsburgh Press, 1977.

Eltis, David. *Economic Growth and the Ending of the Transatlantic Slave Trade*. New York: Oxford University Press, 1987.

Eltis, David, and James Walvin, eds. *The Abolition of the Atlantic Slave Trade*. Madison: The University of Wisconsin Press, 1981.

Gemery, Henry A., and Jan S. Hogendon, eds. *The Uncommon Market: Essays in the Economic History of the Atlantic Slave Trade*. New York: Academic Press, 1979.

Handler, Jerome S. *The Unappropriated People: Freedmen in the Slave Society of Barbados*. Baltimore: Johns Hopkins University Press, 1974.

Inikori, Joseph E. *Africans and the Industrial Revolution in England: A Study in International Trade and Economic Development*. Cambridge: Cambridge University Press, 2002.

Solow, Barbara L., and Stanley L. Engerman, eds. *British Capitalism and Caribbean Slavery: The Legacy of Eric Williams*. Cambridge: Cambridge University Press, 1987.

Walvin, James. *Slavery and British Society 1776-1846*. Baton Rouge: Louisiana State University Press, 1982.

Ward, J. R. *British West Indian Slavery, 1750-1834: The Process of Amelioration*. Oxford: Oxford University Press, 1988.

Williams, Eric. *Capitalism and Slavery*. London: Andrew Deutsch, 1942.

Williams, Eric. *From Columbus to Castro: The History of the Caribbean, 1492-1969*. London: Deutsch Limited, 1970.

Chapter 14. Sugar without Slaves in the British and French Antilles

Adamson, Alan H. *Sugar without Slaves: The Political Economy of British Guiana, 1838-1904*. New Haven: Yale University Press, 1972.

Butler, Kathleen Mary. *The Economics of Emancipation: Jamaica and Barbados 1823-1843*. Chapel Hill: The University Of North Carolina Press, 1995.

Chaleau, Liliana. *Le régime de travail sur les habitations de la Martinique après l'abolition de l'esclavage 1848-1900*. Fort de France: Archives Departamentales, 1980.

Dhanda, Karen S. "Indentured Labor and the Integration of Trinidad into the World Economy." Ph.D. diss., Syracuse University, 2000.

Eisner, Gisela. *Jamaica, 1830-1930. A Study in Economic Growth*. Manchester: University of Manchester Press, 1961.

Green, William A. *British Slave Emancipation: The Sugar Colonies and the Great Experiment, 1830-1865*. Oxford: Clarendon Press, 1976. Reprinted 1991, Oxford University Press, Oxford.

Hall, Douglas. *Five of the Leewards, 1834-1870: The Major Problems of the Post-Emancipation Period in Antigua, Barbuda, Monserrat, Nevis, and St. Kitts*. St. Lawrence, Barbados: Caribbean University Press, 1971.

Hall, Douglas. *Free Jamaica 1838-1865: An Economic History*. London: Caribbean University Press, 1959.

Hoefte, Rosemarijn. *In Place of Slavery: A Social History of British Indian and Javanese Laborers in Suriname*. Gainesville: University Press of Florida, 1998.

Laurence, K. O. *Inmigration into the West Indies in the 19th Century*. London: Caribbean University Press, 1971.

Levy, Claude. *Emancipation, Sugar, and Federalism: Barbados and the West Indies, 1833-1876*. Gainesville: University Press of Florida, 1924.

Look Lai, Walton. *The Chinese in the West Indies, 1806-1995: A Documentary History*. Kingston: The Press, University of the West Indies, 1998.

Look Lai, Walton. *Indentured Labor, Caribbean Sugar: Chinese and Indian Migrants to the British West Indies, 1838-1918*. Baltimore: The Johns Hopkins University Press, 1993.

Mathews, Thomas. *Social Groups and Institutions in the History of the Caribbean*. Río Piedras, P.R.: Association of Caribbean Historians, 1975.

Mintz, Sidney. *Caribbean Transformations*. Baltimore: The Johns Hopkins University Press, 1974.

Mintz, Sidney. *From Plantation to Peasant in the Caribbean*. Washington, D.C.: Woodrow Wilson International Center for Scholars, 1984.

Saunders, Kay, ed. *Indentured Labour in the British Empire 1834-1920*. London: Croom Helm, 1984.

Schnakenbourg, Christian. *Histoire de la Industrie Sucrière en Guadeloupe, aux XIXe et XXe siècles: La crise du système esclavagiste, 1835-1847*. Paris: L'Harmattan, 1980.

Schuler, Monica. *"Alas, Alas, Kongo": A Social History of Indentured African Immigration into Jamaica, 1841-1865*. Baltimore: The Johns Hopkins University Press, 1980.

Sewell, William G. *The Ordeal of Free Labor in the British West Indies*. New York: Harper & Brothers, 1861. Reprinted 1968, Frank Cass and Co., London.

Singaravelou, *Les Indiens de la Caraibe*. Paris: Editions L'Harmattan, 1987.

Smeralda-Amon, Juliette. *La question de l'immigration indienne dans son environnement socio-économique martiniquais, 1848-1900*. Paris: L'Harmattan, 1996.

Thomas, Mary Elizabeth. *Jamaica and Voluntary Laborers from Africa, 1840-1865*. Gainesville: The University Press of Florida, 1974.

Tomich, Dale. *Slavery in the Circuit of Sugar: Martinique and the World Economy, 1830-1848*. Baltimore: The Johns Hopkins University Press, 1990.

Toumson, Roger. *Les Indes Antillaises: Présence et situation des communautés indiennes en milieu caribéen*. Paris: Editions L'Harmattan, 1994.

Turner, Mary. *Slaves and Missionaries: The Disintegration of Jamaican Slave Society, 1787-1834*. Kingston: University of the West Indies Press, 2000.

Ward, J. R. *British West Indian Slavery, 1750-1834: The Process of Amelioration*. Oxford: Oxford University Press, 1988.

Wilson, Andrew, ed. *The Chinese in the Caribbean*. Princeton, N.J.: Markus Wiener Publishers, 2004.

Wood, Donald. *Trinidad in Transition: The Years after Slavery*. London: Oxford University Press, 1968.

Chapter 15. The Sugar Revolution in Cuba and Puerto Rico

Baralt, Guillermo. *Esclavos rebeldes: Conspiraciones y sublevaciones de esclavos en Puerto Rico, 1795-1873*. Río Piedras, P.R.: Ediciones Huracán, 1982.

Bergad, Laird W. *Cuban Rural Society in the Nineteenth Century: The Social and Economic History of Monoculture in Matanzas*. Princeton, N.J.: Princeton University Press, 1990.

Ely, Roland T. *Cuando reinaba Su Magestad el azúcar*. Buenos Aires: Editorial Sudamericana, 1963.

Ely, Roland T. *La economía cubana entre los dos Isabeles, 1492-1832*. Bogotá: Aedita, 1962.

Goizueta-Mimó, Félix. *Bitter Cuban Sugar: Monoculture and Economic Dependence from 1825-1899*. New York: Garland, 1987.

Humboldt, Alexander von. *Essai politique de l'ile de Cuba*. Paris: J. Smith, 1926. Reprinted 2001 as *The Island of Cuba: A Political Essay*, Markus Wiener Publishers, Princeton, N.J.

Jiménez Pastrana, Juan. *Los chinos en la historia de Cuba*. La Habana: Editorial de Ciencias Sociales, 1983.

Kipple, Kenneth F. *Blacks in Colonial Cuba, 1774-1899*. Gainesville: University Press of Florida, 1976.

Klein, Herbert S. *Slavery in the Americas: A Comparative Study of Virginia and Cuba*. Chicago: Quadrangle Books, 1967.

Knight, Franklin. *Slave Society in Cuba During the Nineteenth Century*. Madison: University of Wisconsin Press, 1970.

Marrero, Leví. *Cuba: Economía y Sociedad. Azúcar, Ilustación y Conciencia (1763-1868)*, vols. 7-12. Madrid: Editorial Playor, 1983-1985.

Morales Carrión, Arturo. *Auge y decadencia de la trata negrera en Puerto Rico, 1820-1860*. San Juan: Centro de Estudios Avanzados de Puerto Rico y el Caribe, 1978.

Moreno Fraginals, Manuel. *El Ingenio: Complejo Económico-Social Cubano del Azúcar*. La Habana: Editorial de Ciencias Sociales, 1978.

Moreno Fraginals, Manuel. *The Sugarmill: The Socioeconomic Complex of Sugar in Cuba, 1760-1860*. New York: Monthly Review Press, 1976.

Nistal-Moret, Benjamín. *Esclavos prófugos y cimarrones: Puerto Rico, 1770-1870*. Río Piedras: Editorial de la Universidad de Puerto Rico, 1984.

Pérez de la Riva, Juan. *El barracón y otros ensayos*. La Habana: Editorial de Ciencias Sociales. Instituto Cubano del Libro, 1975.

Ramos Mattei, Andrés. *Azúcar y esclavitud*. San Juan: Universidad de Puerto Rico, 1982.

Ramos Mattei, Andrés. *La hacienda azucarera: Su crecimiento y crisis en Puerto Rico, siglo XIX*. San Juan: CEREP, 1981.

Scarano, Francisco. *Sugar and Slavery in Puerto Rico: The Plantation Economy of Ponce, 1800-1850*. Madison: University of Wisconsin Press, 1984.

Zanetti, Oscar, and Alejandro García Alvarez. *Sugar and Railroads: A Cuban History, 1837-1959*. Chapel Hill: University of North Carolina Press, 1998.

Chapter 16. Abolitionism in the Spanish Antilles

Chaffin, Tom. *Fatal Glory: Narciso Lopez and the First Clandestine U.S. War against Cuba*. Baton Rouge: Louisiana State University Press, 2003.

Corwin, Arthur F. *Spain and the Abolition of Slavery in Cuba*. Austin: University of Texas Press, 1967.

Crespo, Horacio, ed. *El azúcar en América Latina y el Caribe: Cambio tecnológico, trabajo, mercado mundial y economía azucarera: Perspectiva histórica y problemas actuales*. México: Senado de la República, 2006.

Díaz Soler, Luis M. *Historia de la Esclavitud Negra en Puerto Rico*. San Juan: Universidad de Puerto Rico, 1970.

Dorsey, Joseph C. *Slave Traffic in the Age of Abolition: Puerto Rico, West Africa, and the Non-Hispanic Caribbean, 1815-1859*. Gainesville: University Press of Florida, 2003.

El proceso abolicionista en Puerto Rico: Documentos para su estudio. San Juan: Centro de Investigaciones Históricas, Universidad de Puerto Rico, and Instituto de Cultura Puertorriqueña, 1974, 1978.

Figueroa, Luis A. *Sugar, Slavery, and Freedom in Nineteenth-Century Puerto Rico*. Chapel Hill: The University of North Carolina Press, 2005.

Foner, Philip. *A History of Cuba and Its Relations with the United States*. New York: International Publishers, 1962.

Franco, José Luciano. *Contrabando y la trata negra en el Caribe*. La Habana: Editorial de Ciencias Sociales, 1976.

Franco, José Luciano. *Comercio clandestino de esclavos*. La Habana: Editorial de las Ciencias Sociales, 1996.

García Menéndez, Alberto A. *La abolición de la esclavitud en las Antillas españolas. Cuba y Puerto Rico*. Hato Rey: Ediciones Antillas, 1975.

González-Ripoll, María Dolores, Consuelo Naranjo, Ada Ferrer, Gloria García, and Josef Opatrn?. *El rumor de Haití en Cuba: Temor, raza y rebeldía, 1789-1844*. Madrid: Consejo Superior de Investigaciones Científicas, 2004.

Guerra y Sánchez, Ramiro. *Manual de la Historia de Cuba*. La Habana: Cultural S. A., 1938.

Hauch, Charles C. *La República Dominicana y sus Relaciones Exteriores, 1844-1882*. Santo Domingo: Sociedad Dominicana de Bibliófilos, 1996.

Hendrickson, Kenneth E. *The Spanish-American War*. Westport, Conn.: Greenwood Press, 2003.

Hunt, Alfred N. *Haiti's Influence on Antebellum America: Slumbering Volcano in the Caribbean*. Baton Rouge: Louisiana State University Press, 1988. Reprinted 2006.

Jensen, Larry R. *Children of Colonial Despotism: Press, Politics, and Culture in Cuba, 1790-1840*. Tampa: University Press of Florida, 1988.

Jiménez Wagenheim, Olga. *Puerto Rico's Revolt for Independence: El Grito de Lares*. Princeton: Markus Wiener Publishers, 1993.

Marrero, Leví. *Cuba Economía y Sociedad, Azúcar, Ilustración y Conciencia*, vols. 13-15. Madrid: Editorial Playor, 1987-1992.

Martínez Fernández, Luis. *Torn Between Empires: Economy, Society, and Patterns of Political Thought in the Hispanic Caribbean, 1840-1878*. Athens: University of Georgia Press, 1994.

Moreno Fraginals, Manuel. *Cuba/España, España/Cuba*. Barcelona: Crítica, 1975.

Nelson, William Javier. *Almost a Territory: America's Attempt to Annex the Dominican Republic*. Newark, Del.: University of Delaware Press, 1990.

Paquette, Robert L. *Sugar Is Made with Blood: The Conspiracy of La Escalera and the Conflict between Empires over Slavery in Cuba*. Middletown, Conn.: Wesleyan University Press, 1988.

Piqueras, José A., ed. *Azúcar y esclavitud en el final del trabajo forzado: Homenaje a M. Moreno Fraginals*. México: Fondo de Cultura Económica, 2002.

Schmidt-Nowara, C. *Empire and Antislavery: Spain, Cuba and Puerto Rico, 1833-1874*. Pittsburgh: University of Pittsburgh Press, 1999.

Scott, Rebecca. *Slave Emancipation in Cuba: The Transition to Free Labor 1860-1899*. Princeton, N.J.: Princeton University Press, 1985.

Tansill, Charles Callan. *The United States and Santo Domingo, 1798-1873: A Chapter in Caribbean Diplomacy*. Gloucester, Mass: P. Smith, 1967.

Tone, John Lawrence. *War and Genocide in Cuba 1895-1898*. Chapel Hill: The University of North Carolina Press, 2006.

Turnbull, David. *Travels in the West: Cuba, with Notices of Porto Rico and the Slave Trade*. London, 1840.

Welles, Sumner. *Naboth's Vineyard: The Dominican Republic, 1844-1924*. New York: Payson & Clarke Ltd., 1928. Reprinted 1966, Paul P. Appel, Mamaroneck, N.Y., and 1972, Arno Press, N.Y.

Chapter 17. *Centrales* and *Colonos*

Albert Bill, and Adrian Graves, eds. *Crisis and Change in the International Sugar Economy 1860-1914*. Norwich and Edinburgh: ISC Press, 1984.

Beachey, R. W. *The British West Indies Sugar Industry in the Late Nineteenth Century*. Oxford: Basil Blackwell, 1957.

Deerr, Noel. *The History of Sugar*. London: Chapman and Hall, 1949-1950.

Galloway, J. H. *The Sugar Cane Industry: An Historical Geography from Its Origins to 1914*. Cambridge: Cambridge University Press, 1989.

Guerra Sánchez, Ramiro. *Sugar and Society in the Caribbean: An Economic History of Cuban Agriculture*. New Haven: Yale University Press, 1964.

Hoetink, Harry. *The Dominican People, 1850-1900: Notes for A Historical Sociology*. Baltimore: The Johns Hopkins University Press, 1982.

Iglesias, Fe. *Del Ingenio al Central*. San Juan: Editorial de la Universidad de Puerto Rico, 1998.

Marte, Roberto. *Cuba y la República Dominicana: Transición económica en el Caribe del siglo XIX*. Santo Domingo: Universidad Apec, 1989.

Martínez Vergne, Teresita. *Capitalism in Colonial Puerto Rico: Central San Vicente in the Late Nineteenth Century*. Gainesville: University Press of Florida, 1992.

Moreno Fraginals, Manuel, Frank Moya Pons, and Stanley L. Engerman. *Between Slavery and Free Labor: The Spanish-Speaking Caribbean in the Nineteenth Century*. Baltimore: The Johns Hopkins University Press, 1985.

Ortiz Tilles, Helen. "The Era of Lilis: Political Stability and Economic Change in the Dominican Republic." Ph.D. diss., Georgetown University, 1975.

Pérez Jr., Luis A. *Cuba Between Empires, 1878-1902*. Pittsburgh: University of Pittsburgh Press, 1987.

Ramos Mattei, Andrés. *La hacienda azucarera: Su crecimiento y crisis en Puerto Rico, siglo XIX*. San Juan: CEREP, 1981.

Ramos Mattei, Andrés. *La sociedad del azúcar en Puerto Rico, 1870-1910*. Río Piedras, P.R.: Universidad de Puerto Rico, 1988.

Sánchez, Juan José. *La Caña en Santo Domingo*. Santo Domingo: Imprenta García Hermanos, 1893.

Schnakenbourg, Christian. *Histoire de la industrie sucrière en Guadeloupe aux XIXe et XXe siècles: La crise du système esclavagiste, 1835-1847*. Paris: L'Harmattan, 1980.

Scott, Rebecca J. *Slave Emancipation in Cuba: The Transition to Free Labor 1860-1899*. Princeton: Princeton University Press, 1985.

Chapter 18. Plantations under American Control

Alvarez, J., et al. *A Study on Cuba*. Coral Gables: Miami University Press, 1963.

Ayala, César J. *American Sugar Kingdom: The Plantation Economy of the Spanish Caribbean*. Chapel Hill: University of North Carolina Press, 1999.

Benjamin, Jules R. *The United States and Cuba: Hegemony and Dependent Development, 1880-1934*. Pittsburgh: University of Pittsburgh Press, 1977.

Caban, Pedro A. *Constructing a Colonial People: Puerto Rico and the United States, 1898-1932*. Boulder, Co.: Westview Press, 2001.

Calder, Bruce J. *The Impact of Intervention: The Dominican Republic during the U.S. Occupation of 1916-1924*. Austin: University of Texas Press, 1984.

Collins, Richard H. *Theodore Roosevelt's Caribbean: The Panama Canal, the Monroe Doctrine, and the Latin American Context*. Baton Rouge: Louisiana State University Press, 1990.

Dye, Alan. *Cuban Sugar in the Age of Mass Production: Technology and the Economics of Cuban Sugar Central*. Stanford: Stanford University Press, 1998.

Franks, Julie Chery. "Transforming Property: Landholding and Political Rights in the Dominican Sugar Region, 1880-1930." Ph.D. diss., State University of New York at Stony Brook, 1997.

García-Muñiz, Humberto R. "The South Porto Rico Sugar Company: The History of a United States Multinational Corporation in Puerto Rico and the Dominican Republic, 1900—1921." Ph.D. diss., Columbia University, 1997.

Guerra, Ramiro. *Sugar and Society in the Caribbean: An Economic History of Cuban Agriculture*. New Haven: Yale University Press, 1964.

Healy, David. *Drive to Hegemony: The United States in the Caribbean, 1898-1917*. Madison: University of Wisconsin Press, 1988.

Healy, David F. *The United States and Cuba, 1898-1902*. Madison: University of Wisconsin Press, 1963.

Jencks, Leland. *Our Cuban Colony: A Study on Sugar*. New York: Vanguard Press, 1928.

Knight, Melvin. *The Americans in Santo Domingo. Studies in American Imperialism*. New York: Vanguard Press, 1928.

Langley, Lester D. *The Banana Wars: United States Intervention in the Caribbean, 1898-1934*. Lexington: University Press of Kentucky, 1985.

Mayes, April Janice. "Sugar's Metropolis: The Politics and Culture of Progress in San Pedro de Macoris, Dominican Republic, 1870—1930." Ph.D. diss., University of Michigan, 2003.

McAvoy, Muriel. *Sugar Baron: Manuel Rionda and the Fortunes of Pre-Castro Cuba*. Gainesville: University Press of Florida, 2005.

Munro, Dana Gardner. *Intervention and Dollar Diplomacy in the Caribbean, 1900-1921*. Princeton, N.J: Princeton University Press, 1964.

Munro, Dana Gardner. *The United States and the Caribbean Republics, 1921-1933*. Princeton, N.J.: Princeton University Press, 1974.

Nelson, L. *Rural Cuba*. Minneapolis: University of Minnesota Press, 1951.

Pérez Jr., Luis A. *Cuba under the Platt Amendment*. Pittsburgh: University of Pittsburgh Press, 1993.

Pérez Jr., Luis A. *Intervention, Revolution and Politics in Cuba, 1913-1921*. Pittsburgh: University of Pittsburgh Press, 1987.

Plummer, Brenda Gayle. *Haiti and the Great Powers, 1902-1915*. Baton Rouge: Louisiana State University Press, 1988.

Santamaría García, Antonio. *Sin azúcar no hay país: La industria azucarera y la economía cubana, 1919-1939*. Sevilla: Universidad de Sevilla, 2001.

Schmidt, Hans. *United States Occupation of Haiti, 1915-1934*. New Brunswick, NJ.: Rutgers University Press, 1995.

Veeser, Cyrus. *A World Safe for Capitalism: Dollar Diplomacy and America's Rise to Global Power*. New York: Columbia University Press, 2002.

Yerxa, Donald A. *Admirals and Empire: The United States Navy and the Caribbean, 1898-1945*. Columbia: University of South Carolina Press, 1991.

Chapter 19. Migrants, Peasants, and Proletarians

Baldrich, Juan José. *Sembraron la no siembra: Los cosecheros de tabaco puertorriqueños frente a las corporaciones tabacaleras, 1920-1934*. Río Piedras, P.R.: Ediciones Huracán, 1988.

Baud, Michiel. *Peasants and Tobacco in the Dominican Republic, 1870-1930*. Knoxville: University of Tennessee Press, 1995.

Bergad, Laird W. *Coffee and the Growth of Agrarian Capitalism in Nineteenth-Century Puerto Rico*. Princeton, N.J.: Princeton University Press, 1983.

Colomban Rosario, José. *The Development of the Puerto Rican Jíbaro and His Present Attitude towards Society*. San Juan: The University of Puerto Rico, 1935. Reprinted 1975, Arno Press, New York.

Del Castillo, José. *La Immigración de Braceros Azucareros en la República Dominicana 1880-1930*. Santo Domingo: Universidad Autónoma de Santo Domingo, 1978.

Dietz, James L. *Economic History of Puerto Rico: Institutional Change and Capitalist Development*. Princeton, N.J.: Princeton University Press, 1986.

Hoetink, Harry. *The Dominican People 1850-1900*. Baltimore: The Johns Hopkins University Press, 1982.

Inoa, Orlando. *Azúcar: Arabes, cocolos y haitianos*. Santo Domingo: Editora Cole, 1999.

Knight, Franklin W., and Colin A. Palmer. *The Modern Caribbean*. Chapel Hill: The University of North Carolina Press, 1989.

Lafleur, Gérard. *Les Libanais et les Syriens en Guadeloupe*. Paris: Karthala, 1999.

Lewis, Lancelot. *The West Indian in Panama: Black Labor in Panama, 1850-1914*. Washington, D.C.: University Press of America, 1980.

Lundahl, Matts. *Peasants and Poverty: A Study on Haiti*. London: Croon Helm, 1979.

Millet, Kethly. *Les paysans haitiens et l'occupation américaine d'Haiti, 1915-1930*. La Salle, Quebec: Collective Paroles, 1978.

Picó, Fernando. *Amargo café: Los pequeños y medianos caficultores de Utuado en la segunda mitad del siglo XIX*. Río Piedras, P.R.: Ediciones Huracán, 1979.

Richardson, Bonham C. *Caribbean Migrants: Environment and Human Survival on St. Kitts and Nevis*. Knoxville: The University of Tennessee Press, 1983.

Richardson, Bonham C. *Panama Money in Barbados, 1900-1920*. Knoxville: The University of Tennessee Press, 1985.

San Miguel, Pedro. Luis *Los campesinos del Cibao: Economía de mercado y transformación agraria en la República Dominicana, 1880-1960*. San Juan: Universidad de Puerto Rico, 1997.

Seda Prado, Jorge. *El campesinado en Puerto Rico a fines del siglo XIX y principios del XX: El caso de Toa Alta, 1894-1910*. Río Piedras, P.R.: Ediciones Huracán, 1996.

Stubbs, Jean. *Tobacco on the Periphery: A Case Study in Cuban Labour History, 1860-1958*. Cambridge: Cambridge University Press, 1985.

Turits, Richard Lee. *Foundations of Despotism: Peasants, the Trujillo Regime, and Modernity in Dominican History*. Stanford: Stanford University Press, 2003.

Chapter 20. Epilogue: Why the Sugar Plantation?

Beckford, George L. *Economy: Dependence and Backwardness*. Mona, Jamaica: Institute of Social Research, University of the West Indies, 1975.

Beckford, George L. *Persistent Poverty: Underdevelopment in Plantation Economies of the Third World*. New York: Oxford University Press, 1972.

Benítez Rojo, Antonio. *The Repeating Island: The Caribbean and the Postmodern Perspective*. Durham: Duke University Press, 1992. Reprinted 1996.

Comitas, Lambros. *The Complete Caribbeana, 1900-1975: A Bibliographic Guide to the Scholarly Literature*. Millwood, N.Y.: KTO Press, 1977.

Curtin, Philip D. *The Rise and Fall of the Plantation Complex: Essays in Atlantic History*. Cambridge, U.K., and New York: Cambridge University Press, 1988. Reprinted 1990.

Land, Aubrey C. *Bases of the Plantation Society*. New York: Harper and Row Publishers, 1969.

Pan American Union. *Plantation Systems of the New World*. Washington, D.C.:

Pan American Union, 1959. Published in Spanish as *Sistemas de Plantaciones en el Nuevo Mundo*. Washington, D.C.: Unión Panamericana, 1964.

Thomas, Clive Y. *Plantations, Peasants and State: A Study of the Mode of Production in Guyana*. Los Angeles: Center for Afro-American Studies, University of California, 1984.

Thompson, Edgar T. *The Plantation: An International Bibliography*. Boston: G.K. Hall, 1983.

General Histories of the Caribbean

Arciniegas, Germán. *Biografía del Caribe*. Buenos Aires: Editorial Sudamericana, 1945. Translated into English and published as *Caribbean: Sea of the New World*. Princeton: Markus Wiener Publishers, 2003.

Augier, F. R., Douglass Hall, Shirley Gordon, and M. Reckord. *The Making of the West Indies*. London: Longmans, 1960. Reprinted 1999.

Benn, Denis M. *The Caribbean: An Intellectual History, 1774-2003*. Kingston, Jamaica: Ian Randle Publishers, 2004.

Bosch, Juan. *De Cristóbal Colón a Fidel Castro: El Caribe: Frontera imperial*. Madrid: Ediciones Alfaguara, 1970.

Burns, Alan. *History of the British West Indies*. London: Allen & Unwin, 1965.

Carrera Damas, Germán, ed. *General History of the Caribbean*, 6 vols. London: Unesco Publishing and Macmillan Education, 1997-2003.

Dookhan, Isaac. *A Post-Emancipation History of the West Indies*. London: Collins, 1975.

Ferguson, James. *The Story of the Caribbean People*. Kingston, Jamaica: Ian Randle Publishers, 1999.

Ferguson, James. *Traveller's History of the Caribbean*. New York: Interlink Publishing Group, 2007.

Knight, Franklin W. *The Caribbean: The Genesis of A Fragmented Nationalism*. New York: Oxford University Press, 1990.

Lewis, Gordon K. *Main Currents in Caribbean Thought: The Historical Evolution of Caribbean Society in Its Ideological Aspects, 1492-1900*. Baltimore: The Johns Hopkins University Press, 1983. Reprinted 2004, University of Nebraska Press.

Parry J. H., Philip M. Sherlock, and Anthony P. Maingot. *A Short History of the West Indies*. New York: St. Martin's Press, 1987. Update of the 1956 edition by Macmillan, London.

Posada Carbó, Eduardo. *The Colombian Caribbean: A Regional History, 1870-1950*. Oxford and New York: Clarendon Press, 1996.

Randall, Stephen J. *The Caribbean Basin: An International History*. London: Routledge, 1998.

Rogozinski, Jan. *A Brief History of the Caribbean: From the Arawak and the Carib to the Present*. New York: Facts on File, 1999.

Torres-Saillant, Silvio. *An Intellectual History of the Caribbean*. Basingstoke, England: Palgrave Macmillan, 2006.

Watts, David. *The West Indies: Patterns of Development, Culture and Environment*. Cambridge: Cambridge University Press, 1987.

Williams, Eric E. *From Columbus to Castro: The History of the Caribbean, 1492-1969*. London: Deutsch, 1970. Reprinted 1984, Vintage Books, New York.

Country Histories

Abénon, Lucien-René. *Petite histoire de la Guadeloupe*. Paris: L'Harmattan, 1992.

Alamkan, Myriam. *Histoire maritime des petites Antilles, XVIIe et XVIIIe siècles: De l'arrivée des colons à la guerre contre les Etats-Unis de l'Amérique*. Guadeloupe: Ibis Rouge, 2002.

Bangou, Henri. *La Guadeloupe, 1492-1848, ou l'histoire de la colonisation de l'île liée à l'esclavage noir de ses débuts à sa disparition*. Paris: Éditions l'Harmattan, 1987.

Bangou, Henri. *La Guadeloupe, 1848-1939, ou les aspects de la colonisation après l'abolition de l'esclavage*. Paris: Éditions l'Harmattan, 1987.

Beckles, Hilary McD. *A History of Barbados: From Amerindian Settlement to Nation-State*. Cambridge and New York: Cambridge University Press, 1990.

Bellegarde-Smith, Patrick. *Haiti: The Breached Citadel*. Boulder: Westview Press, 1990.

Black, Clinton V. *History of Jamaica*. London: Collins Clear-Type Press, 1958.

Blerald, Alain-Philippe. *Histoire économique de la Guadeloupe et de la Martinique: Du XVIIe siècle à nos jours*. Paris: Éditions Karthala, 1986.

Borde, Gustave-Louis. *The History of Trinidad under the Spanish Government*. Port-of-Spain: Paria Publishing Co., 1982.

Boromé, Joseph Alfred. *Aspects of Dominican History*. Dominica, W.I.: Government Printing Division, 1972.

Bouyer, Christian. *Au temps des isles: Les Antilles françaises de Louis XII á Napoleón III*. Paris: Tallandier, 2005.

Brereton, Bridget. *A History of Modern Trinidad, 1783-1962*. Kingston, Jamaica: Heinemann, 1981.

Butel, Paul. *Histoire des Antilles françaises: XVIIe-XXe siècle.* Paris: Perrin, 2002.

Cambeira, Alan. *Quisqueya la Bella: The Dominican Republic in Historical and Cultural Perspective.* Armonk, N.Y.: M. E. Sharpe, 1997.

Carmichael, Gertrude. *The History of the West Indian Islands of Trinidad and Tobago, 1498-1900.* London: A. Redman, 1961.

Craton, Michael. *A History of the Bahamas.* London: Collins, 1962. Reprinted 1968 by the same publisher, and 1986 by San Salvador Press, Waterloo, Ontario, Canada.

Craton, Michael, and Gail Saunders. *Islanders in the Stream: A History of the Bahamian People.* Athens: University of Georgia Press, 1998.

Devas, Joseph. *A History of the Island of Grenada, 1498-1796, with Some Notes and Comments on Carriacou and Events of Later Years*, 2nd ed. St. George, Grenada: Carenage Press, 1974.

Dietz, James L. *Economic History of Puerto Rico: Institutional Change and Capitalist Development.* Princeton: Princeton University Press, 1986.

Dookhan, Isaac. *A History of the British Virgin Islands, 1672-1970.* Essex, England, 1975. Reprinted 1994, Canoe Press, Kingston, Jamaica.

Eisner, Gisela. *Jamaica, 1830-1930. A Study in Economic Growth.* Manchester: University of Manchester Press, 1961.

Fernández Méndez, Eugenio. *Historia cultural de Puerto Rico, 1493-1968.* Río Piedras: Editorial Universitaria, Universidad de Puerto Rico, 1975.

Figueroa, Loida. *Breve historia de Puerto Rico: Desde sus comienzos hasta 1800.* Río Piedras, P.R.: Editorial Edil, 1970.

Fortuné, Felix-Hilaire. *Les îles françaises d'Amerique: De la vision géopolitque de Richelieu à l'Union Européen.* Paris: L'Harmattan, 2000.

García Leduc, José M. *Apuntes para una historia breve de Puerto Rico: Desde la prehistoria hasta 1898.* San Juan, P.R.: Isla Negra, 2003.

Gardner, William James. *A History of Jamaica from Its Discovery by Christopher Columbus to the Present Time.* London: E. Stock, 1873. Reprinted 1909 as *A History of Jamaica from Its Discovery by Christopher Columbus to the Year 1872,* T. F. Unwin, New York and London.

Gott, Richard. *Cuba: A New History.* New Haven: Yale University Press, 2004.

Guerra, Ramiro. *Manual de historia de Cuba: Desde su descubrimiento hasta 1868.* Madrid: Ediciones R, 1975.

Hall, Douglas. *Free Jamaica, 1838-1865: An Economic History.* New Haven: Yale University Press, 1959.

Hartog, J. *Curaçao: Short History.* Aruba: DeWitt, 1967. Reprinted 1979.

Hartog, J. *History of the Netherlands Antilles.* Aruba: DeWitt, 1979.

Heinl, Robert Debs, and Nancy Gordon. *Written in Blood: The Story of the*

Haitian People, 1492-1971. Boston: Houghton Mifflin, 1978. Reprinted 2005, University Press of America, Lanham, Md.

Holt, Thomas C. *The Problem of Freedom: Race, Labor, and Politics in Jamaica and Britain, 1832-1938.* Baltimore: The Johns Hopkins University Press, 1992.

Honychurch, Lennox. *The Dominica Story: A History of the Island.* Roseau, Dominica: Honychurch, 1975. Reprinted 1984, Dominica Institute, Roseau.

Hoyos, F. A. *Barbados, A History from the Amerindians to Independence.* London: Macmillan, 1978.

Hubbard, Vincent K. *A History of St. Kitts: The Sweet Trade.* Malaysia: Macmillan Caribbean, 2002.

Jiménez de Wagenheim, Olga. *Puerto Rico: An Interpretive History from Pre-Columbian Times to 1900.* Princeton, N.J.: Markus Wiener Publishers, 1998.

Johnson, Howard. *The Bahamas from Slavery to Servitude, 1783-1933.* Gainesville: University Press of Florida, 1996.

Le Riverend, Julio. *Historia económica de Cuba.* La Habana: Editorial Nacional de Cuba, 1965. Translated and published as *Economic History of Cuba.* Havana: Ensayo Book Institute, 1967.

Léger, Nicolas. *Haiti, Her History and Her Detractors.* New York, Washington: The Neale Publishing Co., 1907.

Léo, Elisabeth. *La société martiniquaise aux XVIIe et XVIIIe siècles, 1664-1789.* Paris: Éditions Karthala, 2003.

Lewisohn, Florence. *St. Croix under Seven Flags.* Hollywood, Fla: Dukane Press, 1970.

Lobdell, Richard A. *Economic Structure and Demographic Performance in Jamaica, 1891-1935.* New York: Garland, 1987.

Logan, Rayford W. *Haiti and the Dominican Republic.* London and New York: Oxford University Press for the Royal Institute of International Affairs, 1968.

Marrero, Leví. *Cuba: Economía y Sociedad.* 15 vols. Madrid: Editorial Playor, 1972-1992.

Morales Carrión, Arturo. *Puerto Rico, A Political and Cultural History.* New York: W. W. Norton, 1983.

Moya Pons, Frank. *The Dominican Republic: A National History.* Princeton, N.J.: Markus Wiener Publishers, 1998.

Nicholls, David. *From Dessalines to Duvalier: Race, Colour, and National Independence in Haiti.* Cambridge: Cambridge University Press, 1979.

Pérez Jr., Luis A. *Cuba: Between Reform and Revolution.* New York and Oxford: Oxford University Press, 1995. Reprinted 2005.

Picó, Fernando. *A General History of Puerto Rico.* Princeton: Markus Wiener Publishers, 2005.

Pluchon, Pierre. *Histoire des Antilles et de la Guyane*. Toulouse: Edouard Privat, 1982.

Price-Mars, Jean. *La République d'Haïti et la République dominicaine: Les aspects divers d'un probleme d'histoire, de géographie et d'ethnologie. Depuis les origines du peuplement de l'île antilléenne en 1492, jusqu'à l'évolution des deux États qui en partagent la souveraineté en 1953*. Port-au-Prince: n.p., 1953.

Ribes Tovar, Federico. *A Chronological History of Puerto Rico*. New York: Plus Ultra Educational Publishers, 1973.

Rodney, Walter. *A History of the Guyanese Working People 1818-1905*. Baltimore: The Johns Hopkins University Press, 1981.

Saunders, Gail. *Bahamian Society Since Emancipation*. Princeton: Markus Wiener Publishers, 2003.

Scarano, Francisco A. *Puerto Rico: Cinco siglos de historia*. San Juan: McGraw-Hill, 1993.

Sherlock, Philip. *Story of the Jamaican People*. Princeton: Markus Wiener Publishers, 1998.

Silvestrini, Blanca G., and María Dolores Luque de Sánchez. *Historia de Puerto Rico: Trayectoria de un pueblo*. San Juan, P.R.: Ediciones Cultural Panamericana, 1991.

Staten, Clifford L. *The History of Cuba*. Westport, Conn.: Greenwood Press, 2003.

Suchlicki, Jaime. *Cuba: From Columbus to Castro*. New York: Scribner, 1974.

Théodat, Jean-Marie. *Haiti-République Dominicaine: Une ile pour deux, 1804-1916*. Paris: Éditions Karthala, 2003.

Thomas, Hugh. *Cuba: The Pursuit of Freedom*. London: Eyre & Spottiswoode, 1971. Reprinted 1998, Da Capo Press, New York.

Thompson, Anthony A. *An Economic History of the Bahamas*. Nassau, Bahamas: Commonwealth Publications, 1979.

Tree, Ronald. *A History of Barbados*. London: Hart-Davis, 1972. Reprinted 1977, Granada, London and New York.

Watson, Karl S. *The Civilised Island, Barbados: A Social History, 1750-1816*. Barbados: K. Watson, 1979.

Welles, Sumner. *Naboth's Vineyard: The Dominican Republic, 1844-1924*. New York: Payson & Clarke Ltd., 1928. Reprinted 1996, P. P. Appel, Mamaroneck, New York.

Williams, Eric E. *History of the People of Trinidad and Tobago*. Port-of-Spain, Trinidad: PNM Publishing Co., 1962. Reprinted 2002, A&B Publishing Group, Brooklyn, N.Y.

INDEX

abolition 150, 155, 159, 161, 166-167, 177, 184-186, 191-194, 200-202, 204-208, 211-212, 217-218, 236-237, 239-240, 248-255, 257-259, 261, 263, 266-269, 273-274
Abolition Law 155, 204-208, 252-253
abolitionist campaigns 185, 192
abolitionist movement 201-202, 248, 251
abolitionist societies 149
abolitionists 149, 153, 185-186, 190-192, 201-203, 208, 217, 250, 252, 258
abortions 7, 107
absentee landowners 100
absentee planters 104, 106, 113-114, 148, 159
absenteeism 266
acciones de tierra 318
accumulation of capital 106
adventurer 52, 86, 237, 313
Africa ix, xi, 1, 4, 18, 26, 35, 44, 62, 68-69, 103-107, 112, 118, 126, 146, 192, 197, 201, 211, 233, 309-310
African coasts 69, 104-105, 147, 233
African slaves 11, 13-14, 16, 18-19, 24, 32, 47, 58, 66, 68-69, 96, 105-107, 111, 134, 136, 147, 159, 221, 314
Africans ix, 3, 13, 17-18, 20, 66, 80, 91, 107, 211-212, 219, 232
Agramonte, Ignacio 250
agrarian reform 311
agricultural code 158
agricultural colonies 27, 95
agricultural development 137, 279
agricultural revolution 127
agricultural societies 267
agriculture 7, 57, 59, 121, 159, 172, 174, 179, 218, 230, 305
Aguada 268
Aguilón 12
Alicante 132
Alta Vela 318
Altagracia 294
Alto Cedro 294
Amazon 47, 49-50
Amazonian forests 3
amelioration policies 202
American adventurers 244
American authorities 129, 197, 285, 289
American banks 284, 290
American *centrales* 280, 284, 288
American companies 274, 279, 283, 292-295, 297-299

American corporations x, 276, 279, 284, 288, 293, 305
American entrepreneurs 286
American Geographical Society 319
American government 196, 242, 279-281, 287, 291, 295, 297
American interests 295-296, 299
American investments 281, 294-296
American investors 224, 279-280, 282, 284-285, 287
American loans 274
American machinery 290
American market 199, 275, 281, 285, 287, 289, 299
American merchants 128, 133, 140, 194, 196, 222, 240
American military base 244
American military government 279-280, 297
American occupation 285, 288-289, 293, 297
American planters 242
American ports 133, 144
American producers 278, 281, 285
American products 120, 128, 132-133, 140, 195-196, 198, 275, 295
American protectorate 275, 289
American refineries 281-282, 288
American Revolution 126, 136-137, 139, 142-143, 147-148
American ships 117, 128-129, 141, 145, 194-198, 240
American sugar companies 292-294
American sugar industry 278, 288
American sugar market 281, 299
American Sugar Refining Company 281-282, 287
American trade 119, 129, 132, 194, 196, 198, 316
American troops 279, 285
American warships 140
Americanization 295, 310-311
Americans 111, 113-114, 117, 133, 137, 140-144, 147, 194, 196, 201, 222, 232, 242, 244, 274, 282, 290, 296, 308, 316
Americas 26, 311
Amsterdam 28, 45-46, 60, 63, 103, 126, 314
anarchy 297
Añasco 13, 40, 269
ancien régime 152
Andalucía 6, 48
Angelina 290

Anglican 55
Anglo-American trade war 200
Anglo-American war 195-196, 200
Anglo-French war 186
Anguilla 144, 200, 302, 317
annexation 222, 239-241, 244, 246, 252, 275, 278
annexationists 241-242, 244, 252
Ansonia 290, 294
Antigua 55, 66, 70, 96, 99, 104, 113, 142-144, 188, 196, 206-207, 209-210, 213-214, 217, 264-265, 302, 317
Antilles x, 1, 3, 5, 7-9, 11-17, 19, 21, 23, 25, 27-29, 32-33, 35-37, 46-47, 50, 52-53, 57-58, 60-61, 63, 65-81, 83-85, 89, 94-98, 101, 104-115, 118-120, 122, 127-128, 130-131, 133-134, 137, 140-141, 143-151, 153, 155, 157, 159, 161, 163, 165-167, 187, 191, 196-197, 201-202, 204, 211, 213-214, 216-220, 224, 231, 233, 237-241, 243, 245, 247, 249-253, 255, 257-259, 261, 264, 266-267, 296-299, 304-306, 308, 311, 314-317
antislavery leaflets 203
Anti-Slavery Society 201, 203
antitrust legislation 281
Antwerp 23, 28, 60
apprentices 204-208, 252-253, 257-258
apprenticeship 204, 206-207, 217, 251, 257
arable land 66, 208, 210, 263, 272, 288
Arabs 4
Aragonese 9
Arawak ix, 3
Araya Peninsula 39-40
archbishop of Santo Domingo 41, 178
Arecibo 232, 268
Argentina 229
Army of the Antilles 166-167
arsenals 279
artisans 151, 164, 205, 296, 307
Aruba 46
Asia 1-2, 44-45, 62, 109, 261, 310-311
Asian fabrics 105
asiento 69
asylum 151
Atlantic ix, 2, 16, 23, 25-26, 30, 36, 45, 47, 49, 107, 110-111, 130, 139, 211, 227, 309-311, 314
Atlantic economy ix-x, 110-111, 310-311
Atlantic islands 2, 16, 23, 25, 314
Austria 60, 154, 259-260
Austrian throne 116
automobiles 295
auxiliaries 155
Azores 24, 26, 314
Azua 30, 40, 270, 273, 294-295
Azuano 290
azúcar prieta 71

bag manufacturers 304
bagasse 72, 216
Bahamas 3, 8, 142-143, 211, 317
Bahía 24, 45-46, 61-62
balers 304
Baltimore 140-141
banana plantations 301
bananas 265, 306-307
Baní 270
bank loans 261, 283
bankruptcy 15, 179
banks 5, 217, 261, 274, 282-284, 286, 290, 295
Baoruco 19-20
Baptist churches 203
Baracoa 31, 40, 115
Barahona Company 294-295
Barahona Wood Products Company 295
Barbadian planters 266
Barbados 55-60, 63-64, 66-67, 69-70, 72, 76, 96, 98, 100-101, 103-104, 109, 112-114, 126, 136-137, 141, 143-144, 188, 193, 195, 197, 199-200, 208, 210, 212-214, 264-266, 299-300, 306, 314, 317
barbers 205
Barbuda 200, 206, 317
Barcelona 132
Barinas 48
Barlovento Armada 51
Bartram Brothers 290, 294
baseball 296
Basse-Terre 119, 137, 164, 166-167, 263
Batavia 224
Bay of Havana 30
Bay of Matanzas 45
Bay of Pernambuco 60
Bay of Samaná 243
Bay of San Juan 30, 38
Bay of Santiago de Cuba 30-31
Bayaguana 42
Bayajá 40, 42
Bayamo 40, 75, 80, 249
Bayamón 232
beans 120, 218, 229, 269
beds 33
beef 16, 40, 81, 94, 229, 273
beer 97, 118
beet sugar 214-215, 259-262, 264, 266-267, 278, 283, 299
Belgium 291
Benzoni, Girolamo 19
Berbice 187-188, 191, 193, 209
Bermuda 196, 300, 303
Biassou, Georges 153
biological clash ix
birth rates 107
black Caribs 134-136, 187-188, 190
black families 209
black Jacobins 168

black peasants 251, 297
black population 17, 67, 100, 107, 170, 190, 317
black rebels 19, 154, 187
black republic 241
black revolutionaries 158
black slaves 1, 11, 13-19, 33, 48, 51-52, 59, 66-69, 81, 89, 91, 99, 124, 146, 153, 228, 235, 247
blacksmiths 205
boiler houses 71, 221, 223, 229, 236
boilers 15, 17, 24, 72, 75, 109
Bolívar, Simón 176
Bombay 212
Bonaire 46
Bonaparte, Napoleon 158, 167, 169
bondholders 291
books x-xi, 27, 33, 248
Bordeaux 102, 105, 146-147
Boricua Republic 237
boucans 54
bounty hunters 19-20
bourbonières 262
bourgeoisie 149-150, 158
Boyer, Jean-Pierre 172
boyerana 179
brandy 106, 112, 147
Braudel, Fernand xi
Brazil 24, 45-46, 57-65, 76, 158, 201, 229, 299, 314
Brazilian Creoles 62
Brazilian ginger 79, 95
Brazilian guerrillas 62
Brazilian mills 61
Brazilian planters 25
Brazilian producers 25, 61
Brazilian sugar industry 23, 25, 60-63, 101, 314
brazilwood 35, 174, 183
bread 7, 81, 118, 229
bricks 222
Bridgetown 144
Bristol 102, 104, 144, 222
British abolitionists 149, 153, 192, 201
British Antilles 106-107, 112, 114, 196, 204, 240, 264, 311, 315
British banks 295
British capitalists 191
British casualties 187
British colonies 104, 110, 138, 153, 186, 192, 194, 197-199, 201-204, 206, 213, 218, 266
British Commonwealth 58
British consumers 100, 192
British economy 114, 143, 185, 189, 191, 198
British government 73, 104, 113, 128-129, 133, 135-136, 139, 141, 144, 153, 156, 163, 187, 189, 194-199, 201-204, 206, 208, 219, 232, 240, 319

British Guiana 193, 200, 202, 264, 299-300, 306
British market 130, 189-190, 192-194, 199, 201, 222, 232
British navy 117-118, 129-130, 191, 233, 317
British Parliament 100, 104, 108, 113-114, 116, 131, 185-186, 190, 192, 199, 203, 316
British planters 99, 131, 193, 197, 200, 219, 222, 228, 299
British public 113, 116, 185, 192, 203, 319
British public opinion 116, 185, 192, 203, 319
British squadron 130, 140
British traders 115, 190, 198, 221
British troops 131, 156, 163, 166, 186-187
British Virgin Islands 193, 303, 317
British West Indies 95, 98-99, 107, 112-114, 118, 124, 133, 135, 137-138, 140, 143-144, 147, 150, 185-187, 189, 191-195, 197-201, 203-204, 212, 214-215, 217, 257, 263-264, 299, 301-303, 305, 315-317, 319
Brower, Peeter 63
buccaneers 53-54, 86-87, 89-90
buildings 37, 42, 106, 161, 177
bullion 28
bulls 94, 121, 223, 225, 275
bureaucracy 33, 78-79
bureaucrats 176, 307
business elite 221
butter 120, 147

C. Czarnikov Ltd. 282
cabildos 20, 75-76, 78
cacao ix, 79-80, 84, 89-90, 95-96, 119-120, 134-137, 146, 171-173, 182, 196, 198, 229, 264, 266, 271, 289, 292, 304, 307, 315
cacao exports 136, 172-173, 196, 198
cacao plantations ix, 79-80, 134, 146, 264, 315
cacao production 171
Cádiz 27, 123-124, 132
Caicos 301
Calcutta 212
California 227, 318
California Sugar Refining Company 318
Calvinist 54
Camagüey 279
Campeche 116, 134, 174
Canada 130-131, 194, 196, 211, 279, 284, 289-290, 303
Canada Land and Fruit Company 279
Canadian banks 290, 295
Canadian companies 318
Canadian territories 194, 196-197
Canary Islands 12, 14, 16, 29, 35, 82, 120, 256, 272
cane farmers 60, 63, 67, 95, 99-100, 261-263, 288, 290
cane fields 75, 94, 173, 236, 272, 288, 295,

298, 313
cane juice 71, 75, 109, 213
cane knots 224
cane sugar 71, 75, 214, 216, 220, 228, 259-261, 282-283
cane supply 64, 267
Canela, Luis xiii
cannibalism 3, 8
cannons 37, 40, 51
Canóvanas Sugar Factory Limited 268
Cap François 89, 92-93, 119, 129, 141, 145, 160, 172
Cap Haitien 172
Cape Breton 130
Cape Verde 23, 26
capitalism 106, 309, 311
Caracas 134
Cárdenas 225, 240, 242
Carenage 133, 144
cargo ships 30, 196
Carib 3, 8, 50, 52, 58, 67-68, 118, 134
Carib Indians 8, 50, 52, 67, 118, 134
Carib population 68
Caribbean 2-4, 6-8, 10-11, 14, 16-18, 20-24, 27-40, 42-50, 52, 54-58, 60, 62, 64, 66, 68-74, 76-80, 82, 84-85, 88, 90, 92, 94-130, 132, 134-144, 148, 150, 152, 154, 156, 158, 160-162, 164-166, 168, 170, 172, 174, 176, 178, 180, 182, 184, 186, 188-194, 196-198, 200-202, 206, 208, 210, 212, 214, 216, 218, 220, 222, 224, 226, 228-230, 232-236, 238, 240, 242-244, 246, 248, 250, 252, 254, 256, 258, 260, 262-264, 266, 268, 270, 272-274, 276-278, 280, 282, 284, 286-288, 290-292, 294, 296, 298, 300, 302, 304, 306-312, 314-316, 318, 320-321
Caribbean islands ix, 39, 57, 74, 95, 106, 110-111, 124, 127-128, 137-138, 142-143, 160, 188-190, 220, 229, 273, 307
Caribbean molasses 111-112, 114
Caribbean planters xi, 16, 35, 68, 103, 106, 216
Caribbean sugar industry 21, 102, 236, 282
Caribs 3, 8, 67-68, 134-136, 187-188, 190
Carlson Investment Company 279
Carolinas 96, 112
carpenters 17, 300, 307
Cartagena 29, 37-38, 45, 47, 51, 78-79, 93, 116, 120, 132
carts 22, 64, 71-72, 223
Casa Centuriona 13
Casa de Contratación 26-27
cash crop 304
cassava 7, 81-82, 120, 123, 229, 313
cassia fistula 15, 21, 37, 39-40
Castilians 4
Castillo del Príncipe 222
Castries 195

Catalans 232, 308
Cataluña 269
Cateau-Cambrésis Treaty 31, 35
cathedral 39
Catholic adventurers 54
Catholicism 54
Catholics 41, 65
cattle 8-9, 11, 16, 19, 22, 32-35, 40, 51, 54, 56, 75, 83-84, 87, 90, 94, 119-122, 159, 176, 181, 211, 222-223, 226, 232, 256, 260, 265, 267, 275, 285, 295, 304, 315
cavalry 33
Cayena 66
Cayenne 161, 191
Cayman Islands 200, 317
Ceded Islands 131, 134-136
Cédula de Gracias 230-231, 269
census 8, 11, 17, 23, 78, 89, 99, 124, 136, 201, 227-228, 253, 275, 302-303, 314-315
Central Aguirre 286-288
Central Aguirre Sugar Companies 286
Central Aguirre Syndicate 286
Central America xi, 54-55, 131, 244, 275, 302
Central Barahona 294-295
Central Canóvanas 267-268
Central Chaparra 279, 287
Central Consuelo 290, 294
central factories 215-216, 261-262
Central Fajardo Sugar Company 288
Central Fortuna 287
Central Guánica 287, 292-293, 301
Central Mercedita 287
central mills 124, 259-264, 266-268, 271, 274, 286, 288
Central Montellano 295
Central Quisqueya 295
Central Romana 292-294, 301
Central San Vicente 266-267
centrales x, 215, 259, 261, 263, 265-275, 280-284, 286-290, 293-295, 297, 299-300, 302, 318
centrifugal machinery 214, 216, 261, 265, 267, 290
cereal 32, 49
cereals 118, 133, 197
charcoal 229
Charles I 29, 55, 58
Charles II 69
Charles III 132, 223
Charles IV 159
Charles V 13-15, 29-30, 32
Charles IX 64
Charles Leigh 47
Charles X 181
Charleston 222
Chase National Bank 284
Chavannes, Jean Baptiste 151
Chesapeake Bay 140

chickens 218
chickpeas 229
children 7, 41, 89, 180, 204-205, 207, 209, 234, 248, 251-254, 256, 278, 302
Chinese x, 211-212, 226-228, 235, 247, 255-256, 302
chocolate 97, 260
Chrétien, Pierre 166
Christians 6, 61, 64, 68, 314
Christophe, Henri 160, 170, 172
Church 15, 82, 165, 172, 177-178, 245
church marriages 245
Church property 165, 177-178
churches 15, 37, 39, 82, 202-203
Cibao 273, 289, 304
Cienfuegos 225, 274
cigar factories 277
cigar makers 304
Citadelle 173
citizens 149, 162, 166-167, 173, 177-178, 231, 291, 297, 316
citrus fruits 81
civil war 152-153, 157, 163, 170, 244-245, 252
clandestine trade 114, 119, 129, 240
class struggles 162
Claus Spreckels 318
clay molds 16, 71
clergy 78-79, 178, 245
clerks 307
Clifford, George 38
clothes 54, 58, 66, 81-82, 84, 88, 105, 196, 228-229, 234, 257
Club de La Habana 241-242
Club Massiac 148, 150
Clyde Steamship Company 289
coal stations 280
coastal towns 39, 92
Coca-Cola 283
cockfighting 296
Cocolos 303
coconut plantations 264
coconuts 81
Code Noir 70, 149, 316
Codrington, Bethel 206
coffee ix, 97, 119, 122, 133-134, 136-138, 146, 171-173, 182-183, 189, 196-198, 220, 224, 226, 230, 232, 249, 256, 260, 265, 268-269, 271, 289, 292, 304-307, 315-316
coffee cultivation 224, 269, 304, 307
coffee exports 136, 172-173, 183, 189, 198, 220, 269
coffee production 138, 171-172, 226, 269, 305
Colbert, Jean Baptiste 73, 88
Collot, Georges Henri Victor 165, 317
Colombia ix, 29, 176, 238, 291
Colón 225
colonial assemblies 70, 113, 114, 129, 148, 150-152, 161-165, 164, 196, 202, 206, 210,

319
colonial authorities 10, 19, 30, 37, 56, 80, 99, 113, 124, 129, 140, 149, 151, 153, 163, 165, 207, 217, 232, 234, 239, 249, 316
Colonial Bank 261
colonial commerce 103
Colonial Company Limited 268
colonial development 106
colonial elite 9, 13
Colonial Land Bank 261
colonial life 106
colonial market 101
colonial monopolies 133
Colonial Office 163, 208
colonial ports 134, 161
colonial profits 103
colonists 6-14, 18, 20, 22-24, 27-28, 30-34, 36, 41-42, 46-52, 55-58, 62-64, 74-84, 87-88, 90-93, 111-116, 118-124, 127-128, 132, 134-138, 140, 144-149, 151-152, 160-161, 190, 194-198, 215, 221-222, 224, 230, 316
colonos 259, 261, 263, 265, 267, 269, 271-275, 283, 288, 297-298
Columbus, Bartolomé 5
Columbus, Christopher 2, 12
Columbus, Diego 9, 18
Comitas, Lambros xii-xiii
Comité de Información de Ultramar 247
commercial capital 102
commercial credit 103
commission agents 27, 103
Commission Général Extraordinaire 165
communal lands 179, 292-293, 318-319
Compagnie de la Guinée 104
Compagnie des Indes Occidentales 104
Compagnie des Isles des Ameriques 52-54, 64
Compagnie du Sénégal 69, 104
concentration camps 278
Congo 24
conspiracies 70, 175, 178, 238, 240
conspirators 176, 237-238, 240
constabulary 293, 297
Consuelo 290, 294
Consulado 28, 41
consulate 167
consuls of France 167
consumers 97-98, 100-101, 106, 131, 192
continental system 194
contraband 22, 26-27, 29, 31-33, 35, 37, 39-41, 43, 48, 74, 76, 82-84, 113, 117, 119-120, 128-129, 132, 134, 145, 179, 227, 230, 232-233, 235, 292
contracted laborers 66, 169, 211, 300
contracted workers 63, 88, 219, 227, 258, 263
Contracting Law 209
contracts 66, 88, 96, 207, 209, 216, 218-219, 228, 234, 254, 257-258, 262, 268, 272, 286
convents 42, 177-178

cooks 17, 205
copper 15-16, 24, 75, 105
copper mines 75
corn 23, 82, 90, 120, 229
Coro 120
Corsica 269
Corsican 287
Cortázar, José Domingo 115
Cortes 238-239, 246-248, 251-254, 257-258
Costa Rica 301
cotton ix, 34, 52, 55, 57-58, 82, 89-91, 95,
    110-111, 127, 134-138, 146-147, 171-173,
    188, 190, 197, 220, 271, 295, 297-298, 303,
    306, 315
cotton exports 138, 171-173
cotton plantations 91, 127, 146, 190, 295,
    298, 315
cough syrups 174
Council of the Indies 75
Count of Cumberland 38
Count of Nassau 61-62
coup d'etat 158, 176, 244
credit 17, 28, 62, 78, 91, 102-104, 106, 108,
    125, 139, 147, 189, 191, 197, 213, 216, 221,
    235, 261-263, 267-268, 290
Credit Act of 1732 108
Crédit Foncier Colonial 261-263
Crédit Mobilier 268
creditors 103, 273-274, 291, 297
Creole bureaucrats 176
Creole capitalists 227, 233
Creole elite 230
Creole peasantries 304
Creole societies 310
crisis of 1884 262, 265, 271, 273, 299
Cromwell, Oliver 55, 86
crossbows 33
Crown Colony 319
Crown lands 208, 303
crushers 17
crystallizers 261, 267
Cuba x, 3, 5, 8-11, 14-15, 19-20, 22, 30-32,
    34-35, 40-43, 45, 48, 56-57, 74-79, 82, 84,
    89, 91, 115-117, 119-124, 130, 132, 139,
    175, 189, 196, 201, 220-231, 233, 235-258,
    270, 272-273, 275-284, 286-290, 292, 294-
    296, 299-302, 304-308, 311, 315, 318
Cuba Agricultural and Development
    Company 279
Cuba Cane Sugar Company 282-283
Cuba Colonial Company 279
Cuba Development Company 279
Cuban-American Sugar Company 279, 282
Cuban annexationists 241-242, 244
Cuban banks 282-284
Cuban Central Railway 279
Cuban colonists 22, 74-75, 84, 123, 221
Cuban commissioners 248

Cuban constitution 280
Cuban Dominican Company 294-295
Cuban Dominican Sugar Development
    Syndicate 294
Cuban economy 124, 274-275, 283-284, 311
Cuban independence 250, 280
Cuban Junta 242, 250
Cuban Land and Steamship Company 279
Cuban military leaders 277
Cuban mills 124, 229, 270
Cuban people 278
Cuban plantations 76, 121, 123, 221, 224,
    233, 240, 247, 290, 300-302
Cuban planters 75-76, 122-123, 221, 223-228,
    235, 240-241, 253-254, 257-258, 282, 305,
    314
Cuban politicians 279
Cuban politics 257
Cuban population 122, 247-248, 280
Cuban Realty Company 279
Cuban rebels 252
Cuban reformistas 239
Cuban Republic 255
Cuban revolutionaries 249
Cuban Revolutionary Party 277
Cuban sugar 76, 123-124, 221-222, 224-225,
    228-230, 236, 247, 274-276, 278-279, 281,
    284-285, 289, 294, 311
Cuban sugar economy 274-275, 311
Cuban sugar industry 76, 124, 221-222, 224-
    225, 228, 274, 276, 281, 284-285
Cul-de-Sac 87-89, 297
cultivation methods 109
cultivators 79, 96, 171, 212, 305
cultural zones ix
Cumaná 39, 48, 120
Cupey 294
Curaçao 46, 57, 63, 88, 112, 115, 118, 122,
    128, 174, 188, 191
customs collection 292
customs duties 73, 123-124, 132, 198, 271,
    275, 289
customs tax law 295
Czarnikov-Rionda 318

d'Esnambuc, Pierre Belain 51-52
d'Ogeron, Bertrand 87
da Costa, Benjamin 64
Dakar 130
dance of the millions 283, 301-302
Danes 232
Danish Antilles 304
Danish colonies 118, 143
Danish islands 128, 133, 188, 193, 230, 233
Danish market 132
Danish ships 119, 132
Danish sugar plantations 122
Daubrée, Paul 215

de Arana, María 34
de Ballester, Miguel 12
de Bastidas, Rodrigo 34
de Bobadilla, Francisco 6
de Castellón, Tomás 13, 15
de Castro, Alvaro 19
de Castro, Hernando 14
de Castro, Melchor 17-18
de Cerrato, Alonso 19
de Céspedes, Carlos Manuel 250, 252
de Chávez, Antonio 14
de Cussy, Tarin 91-92
de Esquivel, Juan 9
de Fontenay, Timoleón Hotman 54
De Ford and Company Bank 285
de Garay, Francisco 9
de Grasse, François 142
de Guzmán, Diego 19
de Guzmán, Gonzalo 14
de la Torre, Pedro 115
de Narváez, Pánfilo 9
de Ovando, Nicolás 6, 9, 18
de Poincy, Phillipe de Lonvilliers 53, 64
de Pouancey, Jacques 88-91
de Segura Sandoval y Castilla, Francisco 90
de Sores, Jacques 31
de Sousa, Martim Afonso 24
de Toledo, Fradique 51
de Vellosa, Gonzalo 13
debts 7, 78, 103, 108, 147, 197-198, 235, 261,
    263, 291
Declaration of the Rights of Man and of the
    Citizen 150
decline of the West Indies 199
de-colonization 310-311
deeds 178, 293, 318-319
Deere, Carmen Diana xiii
deficiency laws 100
deforestation 305
del Campo, Diego 19-20
Delgrès, Louis 167
demand for slaves 25, 104, 201
Demerara 126, 142, 187-188, 191, 193, 200,
    209, 213
demographic decline 80
demographic history xi
demographic imbalance 18, 69
demographic stagnation 122
Denmark 60, 119, 127
Deschamps, Jérémie 86
Deseada 191
Dessalines, Jean Jacques 160, 170
devastation 11, 43, 85, 156, 301
Directory 158, 166
diseases 8, 17, 95
distillers 112
domestic servants 7, 107, 205, 234, 300
domestic service 23

Dominica 67-68, 118, 130-131, 133-136, 139,
    142, 144, 187-188, 195-196, 208, 217, 302,
    306, 317
Dominican centrales 270, 290, 294, 300, 302
Dominican customs 291
Dominican economy 270, 304
Dominican elites 184
Dominican foreign trade 296
Dominican friars 10, 34
Dominican independence 243-244, 246
Dominican landowners 178-179
Dominican legal tradition 245
Dominican nationalists 245
Dominican peasantry 184
Dominican population 175, 289, 303, 319
Dominican Republic xiii, 243-244, 252, 270-
    273, 277, 286, 289-296, 299-303, 306-307,
    311, 319
Dominican separatists 176
Dominican sugar plantations 271, 302
Dominican tobacco 181, 245
Dominican-American Convention 292, 296
Dominicans 115, 178-179, 182, 245-246, 270,
    291, 296, 303, 319
doors 33
draft animals 16, 64, 72, 98, 121-122, 200, 230
Drake, Francis 36
Drax, James 63
dried fruit 32, 120
droughts 83, 125, 144, 183, 196, 317
druggists 149
drumstick fruit 15, 95, 120
dry beans 120
Du Coudray Holstein, Luis 237
du Parquet, Jacques Dyel 53
Ducasse, Jean 92, 146
Dutch Antilles 47, 60, 63, 65, 113-114, 140
Dutch Brazil 45-46, 57, 59, 61-63, 314
Dutch economy 39
Dutch fleets 39
Dutch garrisons 141
Dutch Guiana 65-66, 306
Dutch immigrants 64
Dutch investors 46, 62
Dutch islands 46, 57, 63, 84, 122, 128
Dutch market 60
Dutch merchants 23, 58, 62-63, 102, 113
Dutch plantations 62
Dutch privateers 47, 140
Dutch ships 39-40, 42, 44, 58, 65, 88, 119, 314
Dutch smugglers 41, 48, 113
Dutch trade 45, 60, 88, 112
Dutch war of independence 39
Dutch West India Company 45-46, 51-52, 61-
    62
dyewood 15, 21, 110, 173-174, 183, 266

Earl of Albemarle 130

earthquake 215-216, 301
East Coast 278, 281
East India Company 45
East Indians x, 212
East Indies 44
ecological niches 47, 305
economic crisis 182, 202, 219, 261, 273, 299, 303
economic decline 77, 183, 199
economic depression 183, 273
eggs 81
Egypt 160
El Ferrol 134
El Morro 38, 45, 139, 222
El Seibo 79
elderly 180, 204-205, 254, 256, 302-303
Elizabeth I 36
Elmina 62
emancipation 201, 203-204, 206-210, 217, 219, 248, 254, 256-258, 303, 307
emigration 10, 14, 174, 210, 299, 301, 303, 306, 311
enclaves 295
encomenderos 8, 10-13, 313
encomienda 6-7, 10-11, 19
England 36-38, 44, 47, 49-50, 55-58, 60, 62, 72-74, 83, 89, 91, 97, 100-101, 103, 105, 108, 110, 112-117, 127-128, 131, 136, 138, 147, 151, 154-155, 157, 183, 188-189, 196-197, 199, 203, 229, 240, 243, 267, 283, 314-315
English adventurers 43, 47
English Antilles 58, 69-70, 74-75, 96, 98, 108, 110-113, 130, 314
English cannons 51
English Channel 130
English colonial authorities 113
English colonies 49-50, 58, 69, 84, 92, 101, 104, 110, 153
English colonists 36, 41, 49, 56, 63, 74, 83-84, 92, 112-113, 115, 118, 134
English commanders 56
English Crown 38, 49, 65
English distillers 112
English flotilla 93
English industrial cities 138
English investors 96
English Parliament 73
English planters 58, 67-68, 108
English ports 111
English privateers 30, 38, 44, 47
English refiners 111
English ships 36, 38-39, 58, 65, 73, 97, 110
English traders 35, 41, 104
English troops 51, 56, 186
Enlightenment 133
Enriquillo 18-19, 295
Enriquillo Company 295

enumerated articles 110
epidemic 4, 11, 21, 80-81
epidemics 80-81, 122, 280
Española 3-15, 17-23, 25, 29-30, 33-36, 38, 40-44, 48, 51-54, 56-57, 60, 69, 74, 76-82, 84-88, 90, 93, 120, 184
Essequibo 66, 126, 142, 187-188, 191, 193, 200, 213
Estrada Palma, Tomás 280
Europe ix, 2, 7, 12, 14-15, 26-29, 33, 39-40, 46-49, 57-58, 60-61, 72, 74, 90, 92, 97-98, 101, 103, 105-106, 109-111, 117, 119, 126-127, 141-142, 154, 158, 183, 189, 191, 194, 197, 220, 237, 259, 269, 283, 296, 307, 309-311, 314
European banking interests 296
European conscience 185
European consumers 106
European creditors 291
European economy 28, 33, 110
European investors x, 108, 263
European leaders 260
European market 23-25, 62, 66, 101, 103, 171, 186, 189, 194, 220, 259, 314-315
European merchandise 15, 21, 35, 47-48, 51, 57, 82-83, 90, 119, 132, 141, 316
European powers ix, 28, 57, 296, 309
European workers 211
evaporators 214, 216, 261, 267, 290
excise tax 19-20, 34
exodus from the plantations 208, 210, 218
export taxes 64, 102
Extremadura 6

fabric 23, 32, 34, 143, 147, 149, 307
factoría 4-6
factories 33, 147, 215-216, 259, 261-262, 277, 315
Fajardo 232, 286-288
Fajardo Sugar Company 286, 288
falsification of titles 293
families x-xi, 29, 72, 79, 81, 99, 155, 171, 174-175, 178, 181, 202, 207-209, 218, 234, 264, 266, 287, 303, 305, 308
Family Pact 130
family plots 171, 173, 180-181
famine 195-196, 198
farmers 3, 29, 56-57, 60, 62-63, 66-68, 80, 89, 91, 95, 99-100, 151, 180-181, 218, 229, 235, 261-263, 266-267, 272-273, 288, 290
farming inspectors 171
farmland 177, 210, 294
farmworkers 180, 205, 270
female slaves 17, 89, 107
feral livestock 51, 54, 87, 90
Ferdinand VII 238
Fernández de Oviedo, Gonzalo 34
fertilizers 213

feudal landowners 158
Filibusters 53, 88-89
financial markets 286
financial speculation 224, 283
financiers 2, 28, 62, 65, 108, 294, 304
First Anglo-Dutch War 73
fiscal policy 102
fish 3, 81, 111-112, 114, 118, 120-121, 143,
     194, 196, 222
fleets 30-31, 37-40, 44-47, 49, 55, 76, 117, 123,
     140
Flemish 23-24, 64
Fleury, Jean 29
French privateers 29-32, 35, 47, 50, 92
Flood, Roger 52-53
Florida ix, xii-xiii, 37, 87-88, 131, 143, 287,
     318
Florida Sugar Company 287
flotilla 30, 36, 38, 93
flour 32, 81, 84, 97, 111-112, 118, 120, 140,
     143, 147, 195-196, 222, 229, 240, 295, 304-
     305
food 4-5, 7, 54, 58, 66, 72, 84, 88, 90, 92, 98,
     120, 122-123, 125, 132, 143, 147, 157, 171,
     180, 195-197, 199, 204-207, 217, 222, 228-
     229, 231, 234-235, 245, 257, 272, 304-305,
     313
food crises 125
food crops 180, 207, 217, 222, 228
food prices 195, 272
food production 98, 180, 195, 199, 272
food shortages 195-196
food supply 90, 123, 143, 313
forced labor 7, 180, 234, 297
foreclosures 274
Foreign Information Committee 247-249
foreign trade 32, 110, 148, 166, 231, 296
foreign traders 174, 267
forestland 16, 24
forests ix, 3, 56, 66, 93, 173, 179, 183, 229,
     272, 281, 295
Fort Dauphin 129
Fort Niagara 130

Fort-de-France 119
fortifications 30, 38, 45, 54-55, 79, 86, 139,
     279
fortified cities 55, 116
fortified settlements 89
Fort-Royal 141, 164,
France 29, 32, 38, 44, 47, 52-53, 57, 60, 63-64,
     72-74, 87-92, 99, 101-106, 112-113, 116-
     117, 125-127, 130-131, 135, 139-140, 142-
     145, 147-149, 151-161, 163-167, 170, 175,
     181-184, 186, 188, 190-191, 199, 201, 214,
     216-217, 229, 243, 250, 259-262, 267, 291,
     306, 315-316
Francis I 29

François, Jean 154
free blacks 122, 152, 205, 209-210, 237-238,
     240-241, 249, 256, 317
free citizenry 165
free coloreds 190
free cultivators 171
free farmers 89, 218, 229
free mulattoes 81, 148, 152, 164-165, 176,
     216, 256
free peasantry x, 171, 208, 219, 234
free people x, 10, 151, 154
free ports 132-134, 161, 198
free towns 210, 217
free trade 62, 73, 111, 125, 132-134, 143, 145,
     161, 164, 194, 196-199, 221-222, 245
free villages 208-211, 218-219
freebooters 53-54, 97
free-born blacks 251
freedmen x, 156-157, 166, 177, 179, 208-212,
     217-219, 251, 253-254, 257-258, 266, 268-
     269, 303, 306
Freedmen Bylaws 251
freedom of the press 247
French abolitionists 149, 217
French adventurers 175
French Antilles 52-53, 58, 65, 69, 72, 74-75,
     104, 106-107, 112-114, 118, 127-128, 130,
     137, 140, 143-145, 147-148, 150-151, 153,
     161, 197, 201, 204, 214, 216-220, 233, 261,
     267, 314, 316-317
French bank 181-182
French bankers 158, 175
French bourgeoisie 150, 158
French citizenship 167
French civil commission 156
French colonial émigrés 224
French colonial exiles 175
French colonies 70, 73, 84, 101, 110, 117-118,
     143, 147, 161, 186, 217, 263, 316
French colonists 52, 74, 84, 87-88, 90-91, 118,
     120, 123, 140, 145-146, 148, 160-161, 190
French colonization 85
French commissioners 161, 164
French Company of the West Indies 87-88
French corsairs 44
French Crown 88
French émigrés 224, 226
French entrepreneurs 267
French establishments 86
French fleet 141
French garrison 175
French Guiana 161, 191, 219
French immigrants 190, 232
French islands 64-66, 69-72, 84, 112, 129,
     131, 133, 138, 150, 196, 233, 262, 314
French maritime bourgeoisie 150
French market 73, 89, 104-105, 214
French merchandise 133

French military 139, 159-160
French National Assembly 149-150, 154, 162
French navy 73, 139, 233
French nobility 149
French peasants 52, 211
French production 52, 64, 102, 147, 153, 188, 259
French republicanism 155, 158
French Revolution 146-147, 149-153, 155, 157-159, 161, 163-165, 167, 190
French settlements 50, 87-88, 92-93
French ships 65, 91, 105, 117, 133, 148
French smugglers 69, 113
French soldiers 139-140, 152-153, 160
French squadrons 142
French sugar 65, 68, 71-73, 76, 101-102, 111, 113-114, 117-120, 123, 128, 130, 140, 214, 259, 262, 265
French sugar industry 68, 73, 101, 111, 120
French train 109
fruit plantations 297
fruits 37, 81, 205, 229
fuel 24, 216, 295
fur pelts 114
furnaces 16, 72, 109, 229
furniture 33

Gage, Thomas 55
galleon fleets 37-38, 44, 55, 76, 117
galleys 31
gambling 209
Gandía, Margarita xiii
García, Calixto 250
García Muñiz, Humberto xii
gardeners 205
garlic 120
garrisons 56, 78, 141, 154
gavilleros 293
Geggus, David Patrick xii
General Industrial Company 290
General Sugar Company 284
Geneva 28
Genoese 1-2, 4, 13-14, 17, 23, 28
Genoese merchants 13-14, 17
gens de couleur 148, 152-155, 157, 162-167
George IV 202
German capital 24
German companies 295
German government 296
German peasants 211
Germans 232, 287, 297
Germany 29, 60, 211, 259-260, 291, 296
germs 17
Gibraltar 115, 118, 140
Gijón 132
ginger 21-23, 25, 38-40, 55, 77, 79-80, 82-84, 95, 110, 119-120, 133, 135, 137, 229, 266, 304, 315

ginger farms 23
Girondist bourgeois government 154
Glasgow 138, 267
glass 106
Globalization 311
goats 90, 211, 218
Godoy, Manuel 156
gold 1-2, 6-11, 14-15, 17, 27-28, 31, 34, 37, 173, 299
gold mines 8, 10-11, 17, 299
gold mining 11, 14, 34
Gómez, Máximo 250, 255, 277
Gorée 130-131
gourdes 182
government bonds 291
gradual abolition 201, 248, 257-258
grain 23, 32, 70, 111
Gran Colombia 176
Gran Legión del Águila Negra 238
Grand-Terre 164, 166-167, 216, 218
grands blancs 148, 150-155, 157, 161-166, 186
Grant, Ulysses 252
granulated sugar 261, 263
Great Britain 96, 99, 101, 103, 106, 113, 116-119, 124-125, 131-133, 136, 139-142, 144, 158, 161, 163, 166, 185-191, 193-196, 198-199, 201, 203, 211, 213, 224, 232-233, 237, 252-253, 260, 289, 291, 306, 316
Great Depression xi, 310-311
Greater Antilles 191, 296-297, 299, 305-306
Grenada 50, 67-68, 134-136, 139, 142, 144, 187-188, 195, 208-209, 212, 264, 306, 317
Groningen 45
Guadeloupe 52, 63-64, 67-70, 72, 88-89, 104, 113, 117, 119, 128-133, 137, 139, 142, 144-145, 147, 150-151, 161, 163-167, 186-187, 191, 193, 214-219, 224, 233, 260-263, 267, 314, 317
guaiacum 21, 122, 174
Guáimaro 251
Guam 278
Guamá 19
Guánica 287-288, 292-293, 301
guano 212-213, 215, 244
Guantanamo Bay 116
guardacostas 115-116
Guarico 92
Guayama 232, 267, 285-286
Guerra Chiquita 256
Guerra de los Diez Años 318
Guerra del 68 318
Guerra Grande 318
guerrilla 56, 62, 187, 246, 250, 256, 275, 277, 294, 297
guerrilla fighters 275
guerrilla war 56, 62, 187, 246, 250, 294
Guiana 47, 65-66, 161, 187, 189, 191, 193, 195, 197, 199-200, 202, 205-206, 208-210,

212-213, 219, 263-264, 266, 299-300, 306,
    317
Guianas ix, 49, 58, 191
Guinea 1, 24, 35, 62
Güines 225
Guipuzcoana 134
Gulf of Guinea 24
Gulf of Mexico 31
Gulf Stream 37
gunpowder 54, 105, 141

Habanero Lumber Company 295
hacendados 288
Hacienda Aguirre 285
haciendas 15, 20, 31, 33, 36, 120
Haiti 159-160, 169-177, 179-185, 212, 238-
    239, 241, 243, 270, 296-298, 302, 305, 308,
    319
Haiti's customs 296
Haiti's debt 182, 184
Haiti's independence 181-182
Haitian agents 238, 318
Haitian Agricultural Corporation 298
Haitian American Sugar Company (*see*
    HASCO)
Haitian army 176-177, 181
Haitian authorities xii, 175, 177-179, 245
Haitian border 292
Haitian Congress 183
Haitian constitution 161, 297
Haitian environment 305
Haitian gourde 182
Haitian government 175-176, 178-179, 181-
    183, 243-245
Haitian immigrants 302
Haitian laborers 302
Haitian legislation 180
Haitian market 220, 270
Haitian peasantry 180-181, 184, 305
Haitian people 180, 183
Haitian Revolution xii, 126, 160-161, 165,
    169, 171-172, 174, 181, 184-186, 188-190,
    192-193, 214, 217, 220-221, 223, 225-227,
    230
Haitian rulers 169, 174, 237
Haitian territory 170, 243
Haitians 173, 175, 177, 181-183, 244-245,
    296-297, 300, 302, 319
ham 120
Hamburg 232
Hampton, Thomas 36
Harcourt, Robert 47
hardware supplies 195
hardwood forests 295
harnesses 33
HASCO 297
Hatillo 294
Havana 20, 30-32, 34, 37-38, 40-41, 45-47, 75-

76, 78-79, 83, 115, 117, 119, 122-124, 130-
    131, 139-141, 174, 221-225, 227, 229-230,
    233, 240, 242, 256, 274, 318
Havana landowners 124, 224
Havemeyer, Henry O. 281, 286-287
Havemeyer, Horace 286
Hawaii 289, 299, 318
Hawaiian sugarcane 318
Hawkins, John 35, 38
health programs 280
Hector, Charles 131
Henríquez, Miguel 115
heretics 41, 64
Herradura Land Company 279
herring 39, 144
Hershey Company 283
Heureaux, Ulises 290
hides 15, 21, 25, 30, 32-40, 48, 51, 54, 56, 78,
    81-84, 90, 94, 111, 119-121, 304
Hieronymite friars 10-12
high prices 49, 82, 103, 195-196, 208, 269
Higüey 7, 20, 79
Hispanic Caribbean 33
Hispaniola 3, 305, 319
hoes 212, 215
holding company 281-282, 286
Holdip, James 63
Holguín 226
Holland 61-63, 74, 89, 91, 119, 135, 140-141,
    154, 161, 163, 187-188, 190, 259, 314
Holy Brotherhood 2
Holy Roman Empire 29
Holy Week 78
Honduras 15, 18, 55, 116, 187, 301
honey 23, 229
Honfleur 105
horizontal wooden rollers 16, 224
horses 83, 90, 94, 111-112, 114, 118, 120-122,
    132-133, 143, 196, 275
hospitals 106, 178
Houel, Charles 64
House of Commons 185, 192
House of Lords 191-192
House of Trade 26
Howell, B. H. 286
Howell, Thomas A. 286
Hugues, Victor 166
Humacao 80
Humboldt, Alexander von 223
Hungary 260
hunger 143, 195
hunters 3, 8, 19-20, 35, 51
hurricanes 76, 80, 83, 125, 143-144, 195-196,
    269, 289, 300-301, 305, 308

Ibarra, Carlos 47, 52
Iberian middlemen 39
Iberian Peninsula 18, 155

ice cream 260
Ile de Bourbon 224, 262
Ile-à-Vache 91
Ilheus 24
illegal exports 121
illegal trade 32, 83, 121, 225, 233
illegal traffic 33, 232
illicit trade 40
Illinois Cuban Land Company 279
illness 5, 107, 172, 228
immigrants 27, 47, 49, 52, 57-58, 61, 64-65,
    96, 128, 135, 175, 190, 211-212, 219, 230-
    232, 256, 269-270, 300-303, 307-308
immigration xi, 127, 135-136, 200, 212, 231,
    256, 302, 307, 311
import substitution 311
import taxes 15, 101, 114, 245, 271, 295
importation of slaves 13, 17-18, 24, 69, 123,
    135, 189, 223, 239
indentured labor 66, 226
indentured servants 58, 66-67, 68, 91, 96, 171
indentured workers 63, 66, 68, 88-89, 91, 96,
    146, 211, 226, 256
independence movements 237-239
Independent Republic of Cuba 237
Independent State of Spanish Haiti 176
independent traders 105
independentistas 276
India 1-2, 45-46, 51-52, 61-62, 212, 219, 294
Indian labor 24, 47
Indian Ocean 45, 199, 224, 262
Indian slaves 5, 7, 9-10, 106
Indian women 6-7
Indians x, 2-3, 5-11, 13, 17, 19-20, 24, 46, 48,
    50, 52, 58, 67, 89, 112, 118, 134, 212, 301,
    313
indigenous population 11
indigo ix, 55, 89-91, 110, 134, 136-137, 146,
    171, 173, 182, 315-316
industrial machinery 231, 295
industrial plants 261
Industrial Revolution 138, 189, 203, 225, 309
industrialists 106, 216, 248
industrialization 311
infirm 205
Ingenio Consuelo 290
insolvent mills 274
intellectuals 238
intercolonial trade 111, 113-114, 119-120
interest payments 107
interest rates 62, 65, 108, 139, 274
International Banking Corporation 294
Ireland 49, 58, 111-112, 128, 143, 211, 315
Irish colonists 112
Irish ships 128
iron 24, 32, 105, 111, 118, 147, 196-197, 215,
    224-225
iron mills 215, 224-225

iron products 111, 118
ironworkers 17
Italia 290
Italian merchants 2
Italy 14, 60, 160, 291, 317
Itamaraca 61

J. P. Morgan 282, 284
Jacobin regime 165-166
Jacobin revolutionary party 153
Jacobins 154, 164-165, 167-168
Jamaica 5, 8-9, 38, 50, 56-57, 65, 67, 69-70,
    80, 83, 92-93, 96-97, 99-100, 104, 108-109,
    112-115, 124, 126, 129, 132-133, 136, 138,
    141-144, 152-154, 157, 184, 189, 193, 195,
    197, 199, 203, 205-206, 208-210, 212-214,
    220-221, 223, 225-227, 229, 235, 265-266,
    299, 301-302, 305, 311, 315, 317, 319
Jamaican assembly 70
Jamaican authorities 92
Jamaican colonists 113
Jamaican economy 97, 193
Jamaican immigrants 301-302
Jamaican landowners 96, 100, 143
Jamaican merchants 113
Jamaican planters 96, 100, 144, 211-212, 214,
    220, 227, 314
Jamaican train 108-109, 221, 224, 226, 229,
    259, 265, 268, 318
Jamaican workers 301
jams 97
Jefferson, Thomas 239
jelly 260
Jenkins, Robert 116
jewelry 37, 118
jewels 31
Jewish bankers 2
Jewish credit 28
Jewish refugees 65
Jewish settlers 65
Jews 2, 47, 61, 63-65, 314, 316
Jiménez de Cisneros, Cardinal Francisco 10
João IV 62
journalists 272
Júcaro 251
Judaism 61
judges 9, 204-205, 207
Juntas for the Protection of Freedmen 253-
    254

kegs 33
Kelly, Hugh 290
Keppel, George 130
King Dom Sebastião 24
King Ferdinand 2, 4, 9-10, 26, 238
King of Portugal 24, 62
Kingdom of Haiti 172
Kingston 133, 301

Klein, Herbert S. xii
knives 32, 105
Korean War 310
Kuhn and Loeb Company 291

L'Exclusif 73, 88, 102
La Concepción 12, 19-20
La Coruña 132
La Damajagua 249-250
La Escalera 241, 246
La Fuerza 139
La Grande Anse 89
La Guaira Maracaibo 120
La Rochelle 105, 146
La Romana 292-293, 302-303
La Trinitaria 184
La Yaguana 14, 32, 35, 40, 42, 87
labor laws 209
labor supply 24, 62, 67, 104-105, 171, 192,
   194, 211, 218, 271, 289, 298, 300, 302
Laborers Bylaw 234
Lacrosse, Louis 165
Lancaster 104
land ix, 4-7, 15-16, 25, 37, 39, 42-43, 50-51,
   58, 64, 66, 68, 75, 80, 86, 88, 90-91, 93-94,
   96, 98-100, 106, 108, 115, 120-121, 124,
   126-127, 135-138, 143-144, 146, 148, 157-
   158, 160-161, 164, 166, 169-173, 175-180,
   190, 192, 195, 197, 199, 204-211, 215, 217-
   218, 220, 222, 226, 230-232, 234-235, 261,
   263-268, 270-274, 279-281, 283-285, 287-
   288, 292-294, 297-298, 303, 305-306, 318-
   319
land concentration 98-99, 264, 273
land redistribution 171, 173, 178-179
land tenure system 292, 319
land transactions 170
landholdings 179, 223, 251, 264, 266, 273,
   279, 288
Lando, Francisco 17
landowners 34, 58, 66, 95-96, 100, 124, 143,
   158, 167, 171, 173, 178-180, 202, 205, 209-
   210, 222-224, 230, 234, 239, 272, 282, 285-
   286
landowning elite 98-99, 232
lard 54, 82, 273
Lares 249, 269
large plantations 17, 22, 25, 96, 171, 268, 274,
   297
Las Villas 279
Latimer and Company 268
laundry women 17
Laveaux, Etienne 155
Law for Agricultural Franchises 292
Law for the Abolition of Slavery in Puerto
   Rico 253
Law for the Partition of Communal Lands
   292

law of the free womb 252
laws of navigation and trade 110
Le Clerc, Francis 31
Le Havre 28, 72, 102, 105, 147
Le Rouchelot 89
Lebanese 308
Leclerc, Charles Victor Emmanuel 160
Leeward Islands 67, 69-70, 72, 96, 98-100,
   112-113, 115, 119, 126, 136-137, 142, 144,
   188, 193-197, 208, 210, 212, 265, 272-273,
   300, 302-303, 314-315, 317
Legislative Assembly 163, 165
Legislative Council of Trinidad 208
Leigh, Charles 47
Lemba 20
Lenten ship 78, 81
Léogane 87, 89, 93, 119, 297
Les Cayes 145, 151
Les Saintes 142, 186
Lesser Antilles 3, 8, 46, 50, 52, 57-58, 60-61,
   63, 65-69, 71, 73-76, 83, 94, 118, 128, 187,
   299
Letters Patent 101, 105
Levasseur, Jean 53
Ley de Patronato 257
ley de vientre libre 252
liberal constitution 239
liberal government 246, 251-252
liberal philosophers 133, 185
liberal revolution 217, 250, 252
Liberal Union Party 246
libreta system 233, 234, 235
life expectancy 106
Lincoln, Abraham 239
liquor 112
Lisbon 23
Liverpool 102, 104, 138, 144, 222
livestock 1, 22, 29-30, 33-35, 40, 42-43, 46,
   51, 54, 57, 76-77, 81, 83, 87, 89-91, 94,
   120-123, 133-134, 142, 173-174, 179, 197,
   229-230, 260, 272, 275, 278, 288, 293
Loaiza 232
loans 12-14, 63, 65, 68, 74-76, 108, 124, 139,
   144, 147-148, 214, 217, 219, 261-263, 272,
   274, 283-284
local manufacturers 296
local markets 173, 307
logwood 122, 183
loitering 209
London 28, 38, 44, 50, 55-56, 72, 98, 100,
   102-104, 113-114, 118, 130, 135, 138, 143-
   144, 153, 202, 208, 222, 268
longshoremen 205, 307
López de Castro, Baltasar 42
López, Bartolomé 115
López, Narciso 242
Lorient 105
Los Alcarrizos 178

Los Angeles 279
Losch, Paul xiii
Louis Lacrosse 165
Louis XIV 70, 86-87, 89, 104, 316
Louis XV 105
Louis XVI 155, 163, 165, 317
Louisbourg 130
Louisiana 131, 134, 158, 199, 201, 270, 278, 317
Louisiana sugar producers 278
Louverture 155-158, 166-167, 169-170, 175
lubricants 295
Lucayas 8
lumber 98, 111-112, 114, 116, 118, 132-133, 143-144, 173-174, 179, 182, 194-197, 222, 229, 295, 316
Luquillo 80
Luther, Martin 41

Macao 227
Maceo, Antonio 250, 255
machinery 15, 24, 106, 200, 212, 214, 216, 231, 261-262, 265-267, 271, 274, 286, 290, 295
machinists 272
Madeira 16, 23-26, 211-212, 313-314
Madras 212
Madrid 116, 223, 238, 241-242, 246, 248
mahogany 173-174, 182-183, 270, 295, 304
Maitland, Thomas 157
Maize 3, 307
Málaga 132
malaria 68, 155, 212, 219
Mallorca 134, 269
Manchester 104, 138
Manhattan 63
manioc 228
manual labor 4, 8, 17-18, 21, 49, 58, 62, 67-68, 105, 107, 137, 146, 171, 181, 192, 205, 210, 212-213, 218, 227-228, 235, 247, 256, 265-266, 268-269, 271-273, 289, 300, 302
manual workers 16, 271
manufactured goods 28, 32-33, 39, 105-106, 118-119, 133-134, 143, 147-148, 296
manufacturing sugar 22, 71, 109, 259
Margarita xiii, 48, 82, 120, 132
marginal lands 205, 229
Marie-Galante 137, 191, 216, 263
maritime war 39
marmalade 97, 260
maroons 19-20, 70
marronage 16, 18
Marseille 102, 105, 146
Martí, José 277
Martínez Campos, Arsenio 255
Martinique 52-53, 63-64, 67-70, 72, 87-89, 102, 104, 113, 117, 119, 128, 130-133, 137, 139, 141, 144-145, 147, 150-151, 161-165,

175, 186, 188-189, 191, 193, 214-219, 224, 233, 260, 262-263, 314, 317
Maryland 58
Masonic lodges 237-238, 245, 249
masons 300, 307
masters 14, 16-17, 20, 68, 71, 149, 157-158, 160, 171, 177, 204-206, 218, 251-254
Matanzas 45-46, 225, 240-241, 256, 274, 279, 318
Mauritius 199, 201
Maurits, John 61
Maxada Blanca 33
Mayagüez 232-233, 267-268
McAvoy, Muriel xii
McKinley, William 278
meat 1, 19-20, 31, 34, 40, 54, 81, 83-84, 90, 94, 120-121, 123, 143-144, 147, 195-196, 222, 228-229
meat shortage 40
mechanization 212-213, 219, 225, 264-265
mechanized centrales 268, 287-288
medicine 4, 21, 32, 48, 92, 97, 118
Mediterranean 13, 23-24, 111, 232
members of Parliament 116, 186, 192, 203
mercantilism 72-73
mercantilist principles 73, 110
mercantilist system 133
mercenary troops 56
merchandise 7, 15, 21, 27, 32-33, 35-36, 47-48, 51, 57, 73, 82-83, 90, 113, 115, 117-119, 121, 129, 132-133, 140-141, 157, 194, 196, 222, 224, 231, 235, 245, 316
merchant ships 31, 77-78, 117, 141, 145, 222
merchants xi, 2, 13-14, 17, 21, 23, 27-28, 30, 34, 41, 45, 50, 55, 58, 62-63, 65, 69, 74, 78, 81, 100-108, 112-113, 115-119, 128-130, 133, 140, 144, 146-147, 150, 164, 167, 174-175, 181, 190, 192-194, 196-198, 205, 222, 224, 230, 239-241, 245, 249, 267-269, 275, 304, 307, 316
Mermoz, William 31
Mesa, Rosa xiii
mestizos 89
Mexico 14-15, 21, 28, 30-31, 33, 36, 45, 79, 82, 222, 238, 241-242, 275, 303
Middelburg 45
middle classes 301, 307, 311
migrations 300, 301, 306
military class 78
military construction 78, 222
military elite 78, 170, 174, 230
military expenses 29
military government 153, 166, 180, 279-280, 285, 293, 295, 297
military intervention 152, 252, 269, 284, 291, 297
military invasions 243
military officers 121, 170, 180, 307

Military Order of Calatrava 6
military patrols 19, 86
military service 271
militia 36, 56, 92, 149, 154, 163, 319
mill operators 17
mines 7-8, 10-11, 17, 20, 33, 75, 299, 313
mining center 12, 19
missionaries 203
Mississippi Valley 131, 242
MM Derosne et Cail 216, 261, 266
modernization of the sugar industry 268
Modyford, Thomas 96
molasses 16, 71-72, 109-114, 117, 124, 128-
    130, 132-133, 137, 140-141, 145, 147, 172,
    188, 195-196, 198, 224, 231, 240, 260, 263,
    271, 316
Molasses Law 114, 129
Môle St. Nicholas 133, 141, 297
Mona Island 29, 40, 115
monarchies 158
moneylenders 102, 147-148
monoculture 98-99, 122, 199, 208, 229
monopoly 26-29, 31, 33, 35, 37, 39, 41, 43,
    45, 49, 52, 55, 64, 69, 73-74, 82-83, 88,
    101, 103-105, 110, 125, 133, 145, 147-148,
    161, 194, 197, 214, 231, 245, 281, 289
Monroe Doctrine 291
Monrovia 60
Monte Plata 42
Montecristi 40, 42, 128-129, 160
Montego Bay 133
Montreal 130
Montserrat 55, 96, 99, 142-144, 188, 207, 210-
    211, 224, 264, 299, 302, 317
Moorish servants 4
Morant Bay 299, 319
Moret Law 251-254, 256-257
Moret, Segismundo 252
Morón 251
mortality rate 17, 107-108, 228
mortgages 261, 263, 274-275, 284
Mount Soufrière 195
mountainous areas 263
mulatto elite 170, 179
mulatto militia 163
mulattoes 81, 89, 148-153, 156-157, 162, 164-
    165, 167, 170, 173, 176, 216, 256
mules 111-112, 120-122, 143, 223, 225, 275
muleteers 205, 304
munitions 27, 54, 105, 141, 149, 153, 250
muscovado sugar 71, 101-102, 110, 124, 198
musicians 307

nails 32
Nantes 102-103, 105, 146-147
Napoleon 158-160, 167-169, 175, 191-192,
    194
Napoleonic codes 245

Napoleonic Wars 191, 193, 214, 230
Narváez, Ramón María 246
National Assembly 149-150, 152-154, 162,
    164, 317
National City Bank 282, 284, 294-295
national debt 182, 290
National Guard 293
National Sugar Refining Company 282, 286-
    287
nationalism 311
nationalist movement 277
native population ix, 5, 7-8, 11, 50, 67
nautical supplies 111, 118
naval bases 280
Navarre 156, 316
Navigation Laws 73, 102, 110-111, 113, 194,
    197
neocolonial territory 276
Netherlands 25, 39-40, 44, 46, 54, 57, 60-61,
    73
neutral islands 118-119, 125, 131
neutral ports 118, 128-129
Nevis 55, 66-67, 96, 99, 128, 142-144, 193,
    206, 208, 210-211, 213, 300, 302-303, 306,
    317
New Amsterdam 63
New Andalucía 48
New Christians 61, 64, 314
new citizens 166-167
New Holland 61-62, 314
New Jersey 112, 279, 281-282, 286-287, 290
"New Laws" 20
New Orleans 140, 242, 244
New Providence 142
New World ix, xii, 1, 4, 27-29, 47, 59, 104,
    313
New York xii-xiii, 112-113, 115-116, 119, 128-
    129, 222, 242, 249, 267, 269, 282, 284, 286-
    287, 289-291, 294, 303
New York Stock Exchange 284
Newport 115
Nipe Company 279
Nippe 89
Nombre de Dios 29-30
nonplantation society 304
North America ix, 32, 49, 63, 73, 96, 110,
    112-114, 119, 122, 125-126, 129-131, 133,
    135, 140-143, 197, 309, 316
North American colonies 58, 110-113, 126,
    128-129, 132, 139-140, 147
North American colonists 111, 113-116, 119
North American Indians 112
North American merchandise 113, 118, 129,
    133
North, Roger 47, 50
northern Haiti 172, 297
notaries 293
nouveaux citoyens 166

nutmeg 135, 306

O'Donnell, Leopoldo 244
obsolete mills 213
Ocoa 30, 290, 294
Ogé, Vincent 151
oil 120, 229, 295
ointments 174
oligopoly 281
Olinda 46, 61
onions 120
orchard keepers 17
Oriente 281
Orinoco River ix, 3
ornaments 106
Ozama River 5

Pacific Islands 109
packers 304
Palestinian 308
Palma,Tomás Estrada 280
Palma de Mallorca 134
pamphlets 192
Panama 15, 29-30, 291, 296, 299-302
Panama Canal 296, 300-301
paper currency 48, 182, 245
Paraíba 24, 61
Paris 104, 118, 131, 148-150, 153, 159, 162,
    166, 216-217, 267
Parliament 73, 100, 104, 108, 113-114, 116,
    131, 153, 185-186, 190, 192, 199, 202-203,
    238, 316
party politics 311
pastimes 296
pastries 260
pasturelands 288
Pata de Palo 31
patrocinados 257
patrol vessels 31
patronage 253, 257-258
Patronage Committees 257-258
Patronage Law 257
patronato 15, 256-257
Peace of Westphalia 55
peanuts 3, 218
peasant class 184, 300
peasant communities 272, 304
peasant economy 84, 181, 185, 269
peasant farms 180, 266, 307
peasant guerrillas 293
peasant labor 174, 297
peasant landowners 173, 209
peasant parcels 266
peasant resistance 293, 297
peasant society 263
peasantry x, 171, 181, 184, 208, 219, 234, 272,
    305-306
peasants 52, 84, 158, 171, 173, 179-180, 205,

    211, 233-234, 245, 249, 251, 265, 269, 272-
    273, 278, 289, 297, 299, 301, 303-307, 319
Pennsylvania 112, 116, 129
peons 304
people of color x, 307
people without masters 205
pepper 2, 48, 266
peppers 3
Péralte, Charlemagne 297
perfume 32
Pernambuco 24, 46, 57-58, 60-63, 73
Pérotin-Dumon, Anne xii
Peru 14-15, 18, 33, 61, 215, 314
pesos de tierra 318
pests 298
Petion, Alexander 170
Petit Goave 89, 93
petits blancs 150-153, 161-165, 167
pharmacists 48, 149
Philip II 35-36, 41
Philip III 42, 44, 48-49, 74, 84
Philip IV 44, 46, 75
Philip V 123-124
Philippines 278-279, 289, 299
Phillips, Richard xiii0
physicians 149
pigs 81, 211, 218
Pinar del Río 229, 251, 256, 318
pineapples 3, 81
pinewood 229
pipes 49, 106
pirate attacks 60
pirate expeditions 117
pirates 29, 42, 53-54, 57, 75, 89, 93, 97, 314
Pitt, William 130
plantains 16, 31, 81, 211, 218, 228-229, 273,
    304, 307
plantation agriculture 159
plantation gardens 72
plantation owners 15, 18, 21-25, 34, 61-62,
    66, 70, 72-73, 75, 78, 94, 96-97, 99, 106,
    144-145, 148, 166, 169, 180, 202, 205-206,
    213, 224, 234-235, 248, 265, 267, 272, 274,
    285, 301
plantation system x-xi, 134, 136-137, 157-158,
    169-170, 173, 181, 184, 202, 212, 220, 237,
    259, 269, 307, 309-311
plantation work 18, 109, 206
plantations x, xii, 11-19, 21-25, 30, 33-34, 36,
    42, 48, 50, 59, 61-62, 65-68, 70, 72-73, 74-
    77, 79-80, 91-94, 96-100, 102-103, 106-110,
    112, 120-128, 134-137, 139, 144-146, 148,
    152, 156-159, 160-162, 166, 169-171, 173,
    179-181, 184, 187-188, 190-191, 196-198,
    201, 202, 205-219, 220, 221, 223-226, 228-
    235, 237, 240-241, 247-250, 251, 254-256,
    259, 260-269, 271-275, 277-279, 281-285,
    287-291, 293-295, 297-307, 309-311, 313-

315, 318, 319
planter class 84, 305-306
planters 0, 13, 16, 21, 23-25, 35, 51, 58-59, 61-62, 65-68, 70, 72, 75-76, 80, 84, 90-91, 96-100, 102-108, 113-114, 122-124, 126-127, 131, 135-136, 139, 144, 147-149, 158-164, 167, 171, 175, 181, 183, 188-197, 199-204, 206-228, 231-236, 239-242, 247-248, 251-254, 256-258, 260-268, 271-272, 274, 282, 299-300, 303, 305-307, 313-314, 316-317, 319
Platt Amendment 280, 292
Platt, Orville H. 280
plows 212, 215
poets 185
Point-à-Pitre 144, 164
Poland 60
police force 161, 169, 181
political fervor 161
political reforms 249
politicians 190, 238, 279, 307
Ponce 8, 232-233, 236, 267-268, 287, 317
Ponce de León, Juan 8
poor families 234
poor whites 152, 162, 238
population of Jamaica 67, 100, 189, 220, 301
Port de Paix 89, 92-93
Port of Spain 264
Port Royal 97
Porto Seguro 24
Portobelo 38, 45, 47, 82, 116-117, 120
Portugal 14, 24, 26, 46, 60, 62-63, 76, 78, 201, 314
Portuguese 1, 4, 15-17, 23-26, 35, 39, 44-45, 57, 60-64, 78, 105, 211-212, 219, 233, 314
Portuguese Brazil 24, 61-62, 64
Portuguese colonies 44
Portuguese Crown 60
Portuguese planters 24, 61
Portuguese smugglers 35
Portuguese workers 219
Porvenir 290
Post, James Howell 282, 286
potatoes 3, 143, 218, 228-229, 307
poverty 77, 79, 81-85, 88, 91, 121, 164, 195-196, 198, 211, 244, 299-301, 314
Powell, John 57
power plants 295
preachers 205
Prevatt, Patricia xiii
price inflation 195
price of coffee 269
price of slaves 68, 103-104, 107, 233
price of sugar 97-98, 117, 124, 130, 143, 192, 213, 224, 260, 282-283, 285, 287, 315
prices 12, 27-28, 32, 41, 49, 58, 76, 79, 82, 89, 91, 97-98, 100-101, 103, 117-118, 123, 128, 131, 137-138, 143-144, 153, 183-184, 186,

195-197, 201, 208, 219-220, 222, 230, 254, 261-263, 269, 272-274, 278, 283-284, 293, 315, 317
priests 12, 15, 41, 83, 160
primogeniture 15
Prince Charles 10
Prince Rupert's Bay 133
privateering 29, 115-117, 121
privateers 26-27, 29-33, 35, 37-39, 41, 43-44, 47, 50, 75, 92-93, 115-117, 140, 143, 166, 232
production costs 137-138, 214, 260, 272
professionals 151, 180, 205, 248, 307
profitability of the slave trade 107
proindependence movement 257
proletarians 299, 301, 303, 305-307
proletariat, rural x
promonarchic authorities 163, 165, 167
property titles 177-178
protectorate 275-276, 289, 291-292, 296
protectors of freedmen 254
Protestant princes 29
Protestants 41
Providence 55, 115
Providence Company 51-52
Prussia 154
public buildings 106
public works 7, 15, 106, 234
Puerto Plata 14, 32, 35-36, 40, 42, 270, 303
Puerto Príncipe 40, 226, 256, 318
Puerto Rican delegates 248, 253
Puerto Rican immigrants 301
Puerto Rican investors 286
Puerto Rican peasants 269, 289
Puerto Rican privateers 115
Puerto Rican producers 199
Puerto Rican sugar 230, 235-236, 268, 281, 285-287
Puerto Ricans 235, 249, 296, 301-302
Puerto Rico x, xii, 3, 5, 8-15, 17, 21-23, 25, 29-31, 34, 38, 40-43, 45-46, 48, 56-57, 60, 74, 76-82, 84, 88-89, 115, 119-122, 132, 139, 175, 178, 187, 196, 201, 220-221, 223, 225, 227, 229-240, 244-249, 252-254, 257-258, 266, 268-269, 278-279, 284-290, 292-296, 299, 304-305, 311, 313, 317
pumps 213
Punta de Araya 47
purifiers 17, 290
Puritans 49

Quakers 185
quasi-slavery 173
Quebec 130
Queen Isabella 2, 4, 10, 26
Quisqueya 290, 295
Quitman, John A. 242

racial imbalance 67
railroads 225-227, 268, 271, 279-281, 290, 318
Raleigh, Walter 47
Ramírez de Fuenleal, Sebastián 15
ranchers 33, 35, 42, 56, 84, 94, 121, 123, 181,
    222, 226, 272
ranches 40, 75, 121, 222-223, 256, 265, 267,
    270, 277, 285
raspadura 270
raw sugar 71
Real Audiencia 9, 15, 32, 41
Real Compañía de Comercio de la Habana
    124, 221
Real Fábrica de Tabacos of Seville 124
rebel Indians 20, 48
rebel leaders 153, 277
rebellion in Cuba 239, 250
rebellions 18, 21, 70, 87-88, 135, 161-162
Recife 46, 61
refined sugar 101, 111-112
refineries 102, 111, 147, 281-282, 286, 288,
    318
Reformation 29, 319
reformista movement 238-239, 248
reformistas 239, 246-247, 249, 257
regional integration 311
registered ships 82
Reglamento de Jornaleros 234
Reglamento de Libertos 251
religious intolerance 49
religious orders 177
religious wars 25
Republic of Cuba 237, 249, 251, 276
Republic of Haiti 170-173, 175
Republic of Puerto Rico 249
Republican army 245, 255, 277
republican regime 163
reunification of Haiti 173
Reunion Island 224, 262
revolts 20, 70, 88, 99, 104, 145, 240, 299
revolutionaries 150, 158, 166, 187, 249-251,
    255, 277-279
revolutionary activity 297
revolutionary army 250-251, 279
revolutionary clubs 165
revolutionary propaganda 152
revolutionary societies 238
Rhode Island 112-113, 116, 119, 128-129
rice 81, 111, 211, 228-229, 273, 305-306
Richelieu, Cardinal 52
Richepanse, Antoine 167
Rigaud, André 156-157
right of conquest 90
Rio de Janeiro 24
Río de la Hacha 134
Río Piedras 232
Rionda, Manuel xii, 282
roads 32, 106, 273, 297

Rochambeau, Donatien Marie Joseph 163
Rodney, George 130
Roldán, Francisco 5
Roosevelt, Theodore 291
Rotterdam 45
Rouen 104-105
Roume, Phillip 159
Rouseau 133
Royal Adventurers into Africa 103
Royal African Company 69, 73, 103-104
Royal Bank of Canada 284
royal despotism 162
royal licenses 18, 69
royal officials 9-10, 27, 78
Royal Treasury 26-28, 79, 222
Royal Treasury of Mexico 79, 222
rum 54, 106, 110-114, 128-130, 132-133, 140-
    141, 144-145, 147, 172, 188, 195-197, 231,
    263, 266, 270, 304, 316
runaway black slaves 18-20, 35, 48, 70, 97,
    151, 189, 250
Rural Code 179-181
rural guard 279
rural police force 169, 181
Russia 60, 259-260

Saba 46, 57, 63, 122, 141-142, 188, 191
Saccharum officinarum 109
Saco, José Antonio 239
saddles 33
Safa, Helen xii
sailors 3, 46, 48, 56, 91, 115, 165, 313
Saint Helena 211
Saint-Domingue 69-70, 86-89, 91-94, 98, 100,
    102, 104-105, 108-109, 113-115, 117, 119,
    121, 123, 126, 128, 132-133, 138, 141, 145-
    148, 150-162, 164-169, 171-173, 175, 186-
    189, 220-221, 223-226, 232, 314-315
salaried workers 4, 216, 218-219, 247, 253,
    303
salaries 5, 16-17, 78, 170-171, 174, 178, 195,
    206-207, 209-210, 216, 222, 258, 270, 272-
    273, 289, 299-301
Salem 115
salt 1, 39-40, 44, 46-47, 84, 111, 120, 131, 144
salt pits 46-47
salted cod 273
salted fish 111-112, 118, 120-121, 143, 196,
    222
salted meat 83, 90, 120-121, 123, 143, 147,
    196, 222, 229
Samaná 89, 159-160, 176, 243-244
Samaná peninsula 243
San Ciriaco hurricane 289, 308
San Cristóbal 45, 139, 270
San Fernando 264
San Germán 14, 29-30, 32, 40, 80, 115, 232,
    269

San Isidro 290, 294
San Juan 5, 8, 14-15, 19-20, 30-32, 34, 36, 38, 41-42, 45, 77-78, 80-83, 115, 119, 139, 156, 187, 230, 233, 268
San Juan de la Maguana 19, 156
San Juan de Ulúa 36, 45
San Pedro de Macorís 270-271, 273, 302-303
Sánchez-Albornoz, Nicolás xii
Sancti Spiritus 226
Sanlúcar 27
Sans Souci 173
Santa Ana 294
Santa Clara 226, 256, 318
Santa Cruz de Tenerife 134
Santa Fe 290
Santa Isabel Sugar Company 287
Santa Lucia 133
Santa Marta 120, 134
Santa Teresa 290
Santander 132
Santángel, Luis 2
Santiago 30-32, 35, 40, 42, 75, 78, 83, 87, 92, 115-117, 121, 224, 226, 245, 256, 315, 318
Santiago de Cuba 30-32, 35, 42, 115-117, 224, 256, 318
Santiago de los Caballeros 87, 92, 121, 315
Santo Domingo x, 5, 8, 10, 12-15, 19, 22, 29-32, 34, 36-38, 40-42, 45, 51, 56, 59, 77-84, 86-87, 89, 91, 93, 115, 117-123, 128, 132, 142, 151, 154-156, 159-160, 169, 171, 173-183, 191, 220, 237, 243-247, 249-250, 270-271, 273, 291, 294, 303-305, 308, 313-314, 319
São Tomé 23-24
São Vicente 24
Saona Island 115
Sardinia 154
sarsaparilla 95
Savannah la Mar 133
savannas 34, 42, 54, 56, 87, 95
sawyers 17
Scarborough 144
Schoelcher, Victor 217
schools 106
schooners 119-120, 122, 128
scorched earth 277
Scotland 49, 111
Scottish trade 111
second civil commission 154-155
Second World War 310-311
secret societies 184, 238
security forces 293
semimechanized mills 264, 268
semirefined sugar 101-102
Senegal 18, 69, 104, 130
Sephardic Jews 47, 61
Sergipe 24
sermons 192

Serrallés family 290
Serrano, Francisco 247
servants 4-7, 17, 58, 66-67, 89, 91, 96, 107, 171, 205, 234, 300
Seven Years War 126-129, 132, 134, 136-137, 222, 316
Seville 13-14, 17, 23, 26-30, 32-34, 37-38, 41, 48, 55, 79, 84, 124, 132, 313
Sevillian economy 28
Sevillian merchants 27-28, 69
Sevillian monopoly 28, 41
Sewell, William 209
sharecroppers' 157, 180, 218, 234
Sharpe, Samuel 203
sheep 90
shipbuilders 28, 65, 105, 108, 175
ships 4, 21, 27-32, 35-36, 38-42, 44-47, 54, 56, 58, 61, 65, 73, 77-79, 82-84, 88, 91, 97, 105, 107, 110-112, 115-119, 123, 128-129, 131-133, 140-141, 145-146, 148, 159, 166, 187, 194-198, 201, 222, 231, 233, 240, 243, 245, 302, 314, 316, 318
shoes 32-33, 82, 84, 118, 147, 196, 222
shopkeepers 151, 307
shops 82
short-term loans 261
Sicilian model 16
Sierra Leone 211-212
silver 15, 27-28, 31, 33, 37, 45-47, 51, 113
silver fleet 47, 51
silver mines 33
sisal 297-298
situado 78-79, 81-82
slave ix-xi, 18, 20-22, 56, 62, 65, 67-70, 73, 99, 103-109, 112, 122, 127, 130, 133, 143-150, 152-153, 156, 159, 161-162, 164, 167, 174, 185-186, 189-194, 199-207, 209, 213, 216-217, 220-221, 226-227, 229, 231-233, 235, 238-242, 247-248, 251, 253-254, 256-257, 304, 310, 314-317
slave cargoes 105
slave families 202
slave funds 20
slave laws 70
slave market 62, 69, 73, 104-105
slave population 18, 21, 56, 67, 99, 107, 127, 143, 189, 200, 205, 220-221, 227, 229, 231, 248, 254, 256, 304, 314-317
slave rebellions 18, 162
slave revolts 99
slave ships 105, 201
slave trade xi, 18, 65, 69, 103-108, 112, 122, 146-150, 185-186, 190-194, 199-201, 205, 227, 232-233, 239-240, 248
slave traders 104-105, 159, 190-192, 241
slaves ix-xi, 1, 5-21, 23-25, 30-36, 39, 42, 47-48, 51-52, 56-59, 62-77, 80-81, 84, 89, 91-93, 96-97, 99, 103-108, 111-112, 114, 118,

121-127, 130, 133-139, 143-144, 146-148,
150-154, 157, 159-161, 164, 167, 169, 171,
177-178, 189-192, 195, 197-198, 200-209,
211, 213, 215-219, 221-228, 230-233, 235,
237, 239-241, 247-258, 263, 266, 303, 305,
314, 316-318
slave-trading companies 103
sloops 119-120
small landowners 205, 210
Small War 256
smallpox 11, 21, 80-81
smoked fish 194
smoked herring 144
smoked meat 54, 123
smoking 49
smugglers 32, 35, 41-42, 48, 69, 83, 104, 113-
114, 140
smuggling 39-40, 43-44, 69, 113-114, 118-119,
121-123, 128, 201
soap 32, 118, 222
Société de Crédit Colonial (Society for
Colonial Credit) 261
Société des Amis des Noirs (Society of
Friends of the Blacks) 149-150
Société des Colons Americains (Society of
American Colonists) 149, 151
Société pour les Droits de l'Homme et les
Citoyens (Society for Human and Citizen
Rights) 184
Societé Royale des Antilles 216
Society for the Abolition of Slavery 185
Society for the Gradual Abolition of Slavery
201
soldiers 5, 42, 46, 56, 78, 121, 130, 139-140,
151-154, 160, 162-163, 165-166, 170, 176,
181, 183, 187, 206, 245, 250, 255, 277-279,
293, 297, 319
Soles y Rayos de Bolívar 238
Sonthonax, Léger Félicité 155
South America ix, 3, 39-40, 197, 311, 313
South Atlantic 1, 211, 227, 314
South Porto Rico Sugar Company 287-288,
292-293, 295, 301
South Sea Company 122
Southern Haiti 172
Southern plantations 201, 240
Spain ix, 2, 5-6, 9-10, 13, 18, 22, 26-32, 34-44,
46, 48-49, 54-57, 60-62, 69, 74, 76-79, 81-
83, 89-91, 115-121, 123-125, 127, 130-132,
134-135, 139-140, 142-143, 153-156, 159,
161, 174-176, 187, 190-191, 201, 222, 224,
227, 229, 231-233, 237-240, 242-252, 254-
255, 264, 275, 278, 280, 302, 305-306, 315,
318
Spaniards 4-6, 10, 17, 45, 56, 92-93, 245
Spanish Abolitionist Society 248, 251, 253
Spanish ambassador to London 56
Spanish America 18, 20, 28, 134, 244

Spanish Armada 38, 42
Spanish army 249, 251, 275
Spanish authorities 29, 36, 42, 48, 51, 56, 83,
86, 90, 92, 115, 120-121, 128, 154, 176,
187, 223, 232, 239, 245, 249
Spanish capitalists 227, 233, 283
Spanish Cortes 238, 247-248, 252, 257-258
Spanish credit 221
Spanish Creoles 176
Spanish Crown 4, 6, 15, 22, 27-28, 32, 41-42,
48-49, 60, 231
Spanish Empire 15, 37, 43, 45
Spanish farmers 56
Spanish flotillas 47
Spanish government 36, 38, 69, 75-76, 80,
116, 123-124, 130, 132, 134, 139, 175, 177,
190, 222-223, 232, 234, 239, 241-247, 249-
250, 253, 255, 257-258, 277
Spanish immigrants 302, 307
Spanish immigration 302
Spanish liberals 250
Spanish Main 55, 70, 85, 116
Spanish market 22, 25, 132, 221-222
Spanish merchants 41, 119, 128, 249
Spanish military leaders 277
Spanish militia 56
Spanish monarchs 2, 5, 26, 36
Spanish monopoly 26-27, 33, 45, 49, 73, 231
Spanish nobility 15, 155
Spanish parliament 238
Spanish pesos 285
Spanish political factions 257
Spanish privateers 30-31, 38, 115, 117
Spanish ships 27, 29-30, 36, 39, 46-47, 54,
117, 231, 245
Spanish silver coins 113
Spanish tobacco 47, 49, 51, 55
Spanish troops 20, 51, 92-93, 156, 242, 245-
246, 252, 255
Spanish-American War 282
special laws 239, 247
speeches 192
spice trade 1
St. Augustine 37-38
St. Barthélemy 141-142, 188
St. Croix 118-119, 122, 126-128, 132, 188,
191, 193, 224, 230, 233, 304
St. Eustatius 46, 53, 57, 63, 118-119, 122,
128-129, 140-142, 188, 191, 316
St. John 127-128, 188, 191, 193
St. Kitts 46, 50-53, 55, 57, 66-67, 96, 98-99,
128, 140, 142-144, 187-188, 193, 196, 206,
208, 210-211, 213, 265, 300, 302-303, 306,
317
St. Lucia 50, 67-68, 118, 130-131, 133, 137,
139, 142, 144, 164, 186-188, 191, 193, 195,
202, 208-209, 212, 217, 263, 306, 317
St. Maarten 142

St. Malo 105
St. Martin 46, 51, 53, 57, 63, 118-119, 122, 140-141, 188, 191
St. Pierre 141, 144, 163
St. Thomas 112, 115, 118-119, 122, 127-128, 132, 174, 188, 191, 193, 230, 232-233, 304
St. Vincent 68, 118, 130-131, 134-136, 139, 142, 144, 187-188, 190, 195-196, 208-209, 212, 302, 306, 317
state lands 177, 179
State of Haiti 170, 176
state property 178-179
steam engines 213-216, 225, 236, 259, 260, 265, 268
steam mills 200, 213, 267
steam-powered machinery 200, 262
steam-powered mills 215, 262, 264, 271
steel 32
Stone, Roy 285
street peddlers 307
subsidies 74, 77-79, 260, 289
subsistence crops 30, 171, 179
subsistence farming 77, 81, 206, 210-211, 218, 270
sucre brut 71
sucrose ix, 16, 24, 70-71, 109, 259
sugar xi, 12-17, 19, 21-25, 29-30, 33, 35-39, 46, 48-49, 56, 58-79, 82-85, 91-114, 117-120, 122-143, 146-147, 153, 155, 167, 169, 171-174, 179-180, 182, 186-201, 204-205, 207, 209-211, 213-233, 235-237, 240-241, 247, 249-251, 254, 256, 258-290, 292-295, 297, 299, 301-302, 304-311, 313-319
sugar business 60-61, 65, 74, 101, 124, 266
sugar *central* 24, 33, 229, 267, 271, 286, 288, 292, 294
sugar companies 94, 282, 286, 288, 292-295, 319
sugar consumption 97-98, 260, 262, 265, 290, 315
sugar economy 65, 93, 96, 99, 127, 194, 210, 230, 268, 274-275, 305, 309, 311
sugar exports 21, 75, 99, 101, 124, 127, 136, 172-173, 189, 193-194, 196, 198-199, 220-221, 230, 281, 284, 287, 289, 292, 315
sugar industry 14-15, 17, 21, 23-25, 56, 60, 62-65, 67-69, 73-79, 101-102, 105, 111, 120, 123-124, 127, 130, 136, 190, 200, 214-216, 219, 221-225, 228, 230-232, 235-237, 240, 251, 256, 259-260, 263-265, 268, 271-272, 274, 276, 278, 282-283, 285, 288-290, 295, 311, 313
sugar loaf 16, 71
sugar market ix-xi, 21, 24, 60, 73, 76, 96, 101, 110, 118, 124, 155, 167, 186, 189, 192, 199, 201, 214, 220, 260, 268, 281, 287, 289, 299, 314
sugar masters 14, 17, 71

sugar mills xi, 12-14, 15-17, 19, 21-22, 24, 61, 63-64, 70-73, 75, 92, 94, 98-99, 108-109, 120, 124, 135, 142-143, 146, 174, 187, 190-191, 199-200, 213-216, 219-230, 235-236, 259-268, 270-271, 273-275, 277-279, 281-282, 286, 314
sugar plantation 13-16, 70, 73, 75-76, 94, 96-97, 108, 249-250, 256, 265, 285, 302, 309-311
sugar prices 12, 76, 98, 100-101, 117-118, 123, 131, 201, 219-220, 230, 261-263, 283, 293, 317
sugar production 12, 16, 21-22, 24-25, 58-62, 64-66, 70-71, 74, 76-77, 96-102, 111, 118, 123-124, 127, 130, 135-137, 153, 188-193, 197, 200-201, 214, 218, 220-221, 223, 225, 231-232, 235, 254, 259-260, 262-265, 267, 269-270, 273, 275, 281, 284-285, 288-289, 294, 313-314
sugar refiners 101, 106, 112, 131, 153, 278, 281
sugar revolution 59-61, 63, 65, 67, 69, 71, 73-75, 94, 100, 112, 188, 220-221, 223, 225, 227, 229, 231, 233, 235, 270-271
sugar traders 106, 153, 267
sugar transportation 105
Sugar Trust 281-282, 286, 290, 292, 294
sugarcane 10-12, 16, 21-22, 24, 42, 58, 61-67, 70-72, 89, 94-96, 98-99, 104, 109, 122, 127, 134-135, 138, 144, 171, 190, 199-200, 206, 208, 212, 215-216, 218, 222, 224, 226-229, 251, 259-260, 262-265, 268, 271-275, 286-289, 292-294, 297, 299, 303, 318
sugar-trading companies 270
suicide 7, 172, 228, 247
Surinam 65, 188-189, 191, 193
surveyors 126, 293
Sweden 60
Swedish island 188
Swiss adventurer 237
Syrian 308
syrups 97, 174

Taco Bay Commercial Land Company 279
Tahiti 109, 200, 224
Taínos 3
tariff on Cuban sugar 281
taverns 48, 54
taxes 1, 12, 15, 24, 26-27, 30, 35-36, 64, 87, 101-102, 114, 121, 123-124, 132-133, 161, 170, 174, 195-196, 214, 222, 245, 248-250, 271, 275, 289, 292, 295, 316
taxpayers 54, 150
tea 97, 228, 260
teachers 205, 307
technological innovation 108, 213
technological revolution 260
technology 61, 64, 71-72, 95, 109, 135, 212-

213, 215, 265-266, 268, 318
Ten Years War 250, 254, 256, 273, 277, 318
Texas 241-242
textiles 105, 118, 316
theologians 185
Thirty Years War 46-47, 49, 54, 57, 62, 75, 78, 83
tierra arrasada 277
tierra grande 54
titles of nobility 170
Toa Baja 232, 240
tobacco ix, 3, 22, 39, 44-45, 47-55, 57-59, 65-66, 68, 73, 76-77, 82-91, 95-96, 99, 106, 110-111, 120, 122-124, 133, 136-137, 141, 146, 172, 174, 180-183, 197, 222-223, 226, 231, 245, 251, 256, 270-271, 280, 289, 292, 304-307, 316
tobacco cultivation 47, 49, 51, 54, 57, 84, 89
tobacco cultivators 96
tobacco export 84, 304
tobacco farmers 57, 66, 89, 95, 180-181
tobacco farming 77, 99, 289
tobacco fields 51, 58, 95, 123
tobacco growers 86, 88-89
tobacco industry 304
tobacco market 49, 57
tobacco planters 51, 84, 183
tobacco trade 52, 83, 124, 245
Tobago 46, 67, 118, 130-131, 134-136, 142-144, 186, 189, 191, 193, 208-209, 317
tools 15, 106, 118, 207, 222, 231
Torres-Saillant, Silvio xii-xiii
Tortola 128, 303
Tortolo 303
Tortuga 51-54, 84, 86-89
torture 54
tourism 311
Toussaint Louverture, François-Dominique 155
town councils 15, 34, 121
towns 10-11, 34, 39, 79, 81, 89, 92, 115, 129, 160, 164, 175, 205, 208, 210, 217, 234, 269, 278, 295, 307
toys 106
trade xi, 1, 13, 18, 26-28, 32-37, 39-41, 45-46, 49-50, 52, 55, 57, 60, 62, 65, 69, 72-73, 81-84, 88, 90-91, 94, 101, 103-108, 110-135, 137, 139-141, 143-150, 155, 157, 161, 164, 166, 176, 185-186, 189-201, 205, 221-222, 224-225, 227, 230-233, 239-240, 243, 245, 248, 257, 259, 262, 270, 275, 280, 296, 304, 311, 316
trade agent 243
trade brokers 304
trade circuits 110-111, 113, 115, 117, 119, 121, 123, 125
trade monopoly 101, 133, 145
trade networks 230

trade routes 1, 35, 50
trade unionism 311
trade war 194, 196-198, 200
trade with North America 119, 143
traders 13, 34-36, 41, 48, 65, 101, 104-106, 115-116, 140, 151, 153, 159, 174, 190, 198, 201, 221, 224, 233, 241, 245, 248, 262-263, 267
trading networks 23
traditional mills 216, 223, 261-263, 267, 288
transportation networks 65
transportation systems 109
trapiche mills 230, 270
travelers 106, 165, 218
Treaty of Aix-la-Chapelle 118
Treaty of Amiens 163, 188, 190
Treaty of Commercial Reciprocity 281
Treaty of London 44
Treaty of Paris 131
Treaty of Ryswick 93
Treaty of Tordesillas 26
Treaty of Utrecht 99, 156
Treaty of Versailles 142, 193, 243
Treaty of Vervins 38, 44
Tretzel, Daniel 64
triangular trading 105
Trinidad 3, 40, 67, 82, 115, 132, 165, 187-191, 193, 195, 197, 199-200, 202, 205-206, 208-213, 225-226, 263-264, 266, 299-300, 317
Trinidadian planters 200, 212
troops 20, 37, 45, 51, 56, 86, 92-93, 131, 135, 139-141, 153-156, 159-160, 163, 166-167, 169, 175-176, 178, 186-187, 191, 242, 245-246, 252, 255, 277, 279, 285, 319
tropical climate 6
tropical lands 12
tropical products 57, 111, 135, 307
tropical vegetation 33
trucks 295
Trujillo 232
Turks Islands 131, 142, 301-302
Turnbull, David 240

U.S. Board on Geographical Names 319
U.S. Congress 278, 280, 291
U.S. government 196, 198, 201, 239, 243, 252, 281, 290-291, 296
U.S. Marine Corps 293, 297
U.S. military rulers 297
U.S. Senate 241, 291
Ulises Heureaux 290
Ulysses Grant 252
uncultivated land 100, 208
unemployment 49, 299
United Fruit Company 279
United Kingdom 289
United Provinces 25, 39
United Puerto Rico Sugar Company 288

United States x, 139-140, 142-144, 147-148, 151, 157, 183, 185, 194-198, 201, 209, 211, 229, 237, 239-245, 250, 252-255, 260, 265, 267, 271, 275-281, 283-287, 291-292, 295-297, 303, 305-306, 308, 310-311, 318
unskilled labor 298
unsold sugar 194
urban life 307
Uruguay 229
useless islands 8
utensils 106
Utuado 269

vacant land 190, 208, 210, 218
vacuum pans 213-214, 216, 265
vagrancy 157, 209
Valadón, Bartolomé 115
vecinos 10
Vega Baja 266
Velázquez, Diego 8, 11
vendors 205
Venetians 1, 23
Venezuela ix, 3, 34, 39-40, 44, 47-48, 57, 80, 82, 134, 175, 178, 238, 242, 275, 299
Venezuelan tobacco 49
Venezuelans 232
venture capitalists 62
Veracruz 30, 38, 45, 47, 78, 82, 120
Vicini family 290, 294
Vigo 37
vinegar 120
vineyards 313
Virgin Gorda 128
Virgin Islands 127, 193, 269, 301-303, 317
Virginia xii, 49, 58, 116
Vizcarrondo, Julio 248
volcanic eruptions 196

wagons 216, 268
Wall Street 282
war fleet 46, 117, 130, 141, 181
War of Independence 25, 39, 141, 270, 275, 277, 318
War of Jenkins's Ear 118, 127
War of Reconquest 174
War of Restoration 246
War of Spanish Succession 97-98, 101, 112, 115, 315
War of the League of Augsburg 74, 92-93, 97
warehouses 37, 39, 118, 193, 274
Warner, Thomas 50, 57
warships 46, 117, 140, 163, 296
Washington 240, 242, 296
Washington policy makers 296
water-powered mills 135
wax 229
weeding machines 212
West Coast 1, 29, 40, 232, 268, 318

West India Sugar Finance Corporation 294
West Indiamen 105
West Indian Committee 136
West Indian immigrants 303
West Indian migrations 306
West Indian planters 103-104, 107-108, 131, 135, 190, 197, 199, 201, 203, 206, 212, 299
West Indian sugar 101-102, 106, 108, 111, 114, 189
West Indies xi, 9, 27, 35, 45, 55, 60, 71, 74, 87-88, 95, 98-99, 101-107, 109, 111-114, 118, 122, 124, 126-127, 131, 133, 135, 137-138, 140, 143-144, 147, 150, 158, 166, 185-189, 191-204, 207-210, 212, 214-215, 217, 219, 229, 257, 263-264, 266, 299, 301-303, 305, 310, 315-317, 319
Western Design 55-56
Weyler, Valeriano 277
white colonists 84, 134-135, 148-149, 151-152
white indentured laborers 58, 66
white indentured servants 66-67, 91, 96
white Jacobins 168
white population 67, 80, 96, 99-100, 136, 146, 190, 241
white revolts 88, 145
white workers 63, 66, 68, 88, 91, 96, 100, 146, 216, 228, 247, 256
whites 17, 67, 69, 81, 100, 150, 152-153, 157, 161-162, 164-165, 167, 238, 241, 317
wild cattle 51, 90
William IV 202
windmills 72, 135
Windward Islands 206
wine 23, 32, 34, 81, 106, 111-112, 118, 120, 147, 229, 316
Wolof 18
women xi, 5-7, 17, 51, 89, 107, 149, 180, 202, 205, 207, 278, 300, 302-303
wood 16, 22, 71-72, 116, 173-174, 229, 295
woodcutters 17
woodlands 34
wool 23, 197, 228
work for hire 210
work for wages 210
workbook system 218
working capital 261, 283
world economy 110, 309-310
world market x-xi, 76, 101, 110, 137, 155, 183, 189, 201, 259, 268, 295, 311, 314
world sugar market 101, 110, 155, 189, 201, 268, 314
World sugar production 260
World War I 283, 287, 293-295, 301

Xaraguá 7

yams 143, 211, 218, 228, 304, 307
Yáñez Pinzón, Martín 2

Yara 249
Yauco 269
yellow fever 68, 155, 160, 166, 187
yuca 3, 7, 16, 23, 29, 31, 80, 143, 211, 218,
     229, 304, 307, 313
Yucatán 8, 11, 116, 131, 134

Zanjón Pact 255-256